THE UNITED NATIONS UNIVERSITY/ THIRD WORLD FORUM

STUDIES IN AFRICAN POLITICAL ECONOMY

# Popular Struggles for Democracy in Africa

# THE UNITED NATIONS UNIVERSITY/THIRD WORLD FORUM

## STUDIES IN AFRICAN POLITICAL ECONOMY
### General Editor: Samir Amin

The United Nations University's Project on Transnationalization or Nation-Building in Africa (1982–1986) was undertaken by a network of African scholars under the co-ordination of Samir Amin. The purpose of the Project was to study the possibilities of and constraints on national autocentric development of African countries in the context of the world-system into which they have been integrated. Since the 1970s the world-system has been in a crisis of a severity and complexity unprecedented since the end of the Second World War; the Project examines the impact of this contemporary crisis on the political, economic and cultural situation of Africa today. Focusing on the complex relationship between transnationalization (namely, the dynamics of the world-system) and nation-building, which is seen as a precondition for national development, the Project explores a wide range of problems besetting Africa today and outlines possible alternatives to the prevailing development models which have proved to be inadequate.

## TITLES IN THIS SERIES

M. L. Gakou
**The Crisis in African Agriculture**
1987

Peter Anyang' Nyong'o (editor)
**Popular Struggles for Democracy in Africa**
1987

Samir Amin, Derrick Chitala, Ibbo Mandaza (editors)
**SADCC: Prospects for Disengagement and Development in Southern Africa**
1987

Faysal Yachir
**The World Steel Industry: Dynamics of Decline**
1987

Other titles in preparation.

# Popular Struggles for Democracy in Africa

edited by
Peter Anyang' Nyong'o

**The United Nations University**
**Zed Books Ltd.**
London and New Jersey

*Popular Struggles for Democracy in Africa* was first published in 1987 by:
Zed Books Ltd., 57 Caledonian Road, London N1 9BU, UK, and
171 First Avenue, Atlantic Highlands, New Jersey 07716, USA
and:
The United Nations University, Toho Semei Building,
15-1 Shibuya 2-chome, Shibuya-ku, Tokyo 150, Japan
in co-operation with
The Third World Forum, B.P. 3501, Dakar, Senegal.

Copyright © The United Nations University, 1987.

Cover designed by Andrew Corbett.
Typeset by EMS Photosetters, Rochford, Essex.
Printed and bound in the United Kingdom
by Biddles Ltd., Guildford and Kings Lynn.

**British Library Cataloguing in Publication Data**

Popular struggles for democracy in Africa.——
(Studies in African political economy).
1. Democracy   2. Africa——Politics and
government——1960-
I. Nyong'o, Peter Anyang'   II. United Nations.
*University*   III. Series
321.8'096        JQ1872

ISBN 0-86232-736-9
ISBN 0-86232-737-7 Pbk

**Library of Congress Cataloging-in-Publication Data**

Popular struggles for democracy in Africa.

(United Nations University studies in African
political economy)
1. Political participation—Africa.   2. Africa—
Politics and government—1960-     3. Africa—
Economic conditions—1960-     I. Nyong'o, Peter
Anyang', 1945–     II. Series.
JQ1879.A15P67  1987      320.9'67      87-13286
ISBN 0-86232-736-9
ISBN 0-86232-737-7 (pbk.)

# Contents

**Tables**

# Acknowledgements

This book was produced in the framework of the United Nations University (UNU) African Regional Perspectives programme, conducted by the African Bureau of the Third World Forum (TWF) and the network of African researchers associated with it. We would like here to thank the UNU, which met a large part of the financing of this programme, and the Swedish agency, SAREC, which gives generous and constant support to the African Bureau of the Third World Forum. But, of course, in the hallowed formula, the opinions expressed here are those of their authors only and in no way commit the institutions mentioned.

**Peter Anyang' Nyong'o**

# List of Contributors

**Peter Anyang' Nyong'o** is currently Research Consultant at the Eastern and Southern Africa Management Institute (ESAMI) in Arusha, Tanzania. He was previously Associate Professor of Political Science and International Relations at Addis Ababa University, Ethiopia; Associate Research Professor at El Colegio de Mexico, Mexico City; and Senior Lecturer in Political Science at the University of Nairobi. His publications have been mainly in the area of states and social processes in Africa.

**Horace Campbell** is a Senior Lecturer in the Department of Political Science, University of Dar es Salaam. Dr Campbell has also lectured previously at Makerere University, Kampala. A Jamaican of African origin, Dr Campbell has published several essays on popular movements in both the Caribbean islands and the continent of Africa. He is co-author of *Imperialism and Militarism in Africa* (forthcoming).

**Michael Chege** is at present Director of the Diplomacy Training Programme, and Senior Lecturer in the Department of Government, at the University of Nairobi. His publications have been chiefly in the areas of social movements, African bureaucracies and Africa's international relations.

**Abdelali Doumou** is a Moroccan political economist who has done extensive research and writing in the problematic of the state in the Arab world.

**Harry Goulbourne** is currently a Senior Research Fellow in the Centre for Research in Ethnic Relations at Warwick University, UK. Dr Goulbourne lectured in politics at the University of Dar es Salaam, Tanzania; the University of the West Indies (Mona) where he was also Vice-Dean of the Faculty of Social Sciences (1982–84); and as the Leverhulme Fellow in the Centre for Caribbean Studies, University of Warwick. He is the author of *Politics and State in the Third World* (London: Macmillan, 1980). Dr Goulbourne is a Jamaican of African origin.

**Emmanuel Hansen** is currently a tutor at the Open University and a Visiting Fellow at the Institute of Commonwealth Studies, University of London, UK. He has taught and researched at the University of Ghana, the University of Dar es Salaam (Tanzania), the University of Indiana (USA), and at the universities of Sussex and Durham (UK). His major publications include *Frantz Fanon: Social and Political Thought* and *The Food Crisis in Ghana*. He was, until his resignation in 1983, Secretary of the Provisional National Defence Council in Ghana.

**Mahmood Mamdani** is currently Associate Professor of Political Science at Makerere University, Kampala, Uganda, where he was until recently Dean of the Faculty of Arts and Social Sciences. Dr Mamdani is the author of *The Myth of Population Control* (New York: Monthly Review Press, 1974), *Politics and Class Formation in Uganda* (London: Heinemann, 1976) and *Imperialism and Fascism in Uganda* (London: Heinemann, 1983).

**Joshua Mugyenyi** is currently a Ph.D. student in African politics at Dalhousie University, Canada. Mugyenyi previously lectured in Political Science and Public Administration at the University of Swaziland, at Makerere University and at the Institute for Public Administration in Kampala, Uganda.

**Nzongola-Ntalaja** is currently Associate Professor of Political Economy at Howard University, Washington DC, USA. He has written extensively on African and Zairean politics. He is the author of *Class Struggles and National Liberation in Africa* (Roxbury: Amenana, 1982).

**Wamba dia Wamba** is Associate Professor of History, University of Dar es Salaam, Tanzania. Dr Wamba lectured in History in his own country, Zaire, before moving to Tanzania. He has published several essays on problems of methodology and epistemology in social science research in Africa, including problems of historical evidence.

# List of Abbreviations

| | |
|---|---|
| **ABAKO** | *Alliance des Bakongo* |
| **ACP** | Action Congress Party of Ghana |
| **AFRC** | Armed Forces Revolutionary Council of Ghana |
| **AFL–CIO** | American Federation of Labour – Congress of International Organisations |
| **ANC** | African National Congress of South Africa |
| *ANC* | *Armée Nationale Congolaise* |
| **APL** | *Armée Populaire de Libération (Congo)* |
| **ARMSCOR** | Armaments Development Production Corporation |
| **AYC** | African Youth Command (Ghana) |
| **AZAPO** | Azanian People's Organisation (South Africa) |
| **BCM** | Black Consciousness Movement (South Africa) |
| **CDC** | Commonwealth Development Corporation |
| **CEREA** | *Centre de Régroupement Africain* |
| **CGAT** | African General Confederation of Labour (Congo) |
| **CMP** | Military Committee of Congolese Party |
| **CNL** | *Conseil National de Libération* (Congo) |
| **CNR** | *Conseil National de la Révolution* |
| **CONAKAT** | *Confédération des Associations Tribales du Katanga* |
| **COSAS** | Congress of South African Students |
| **COTU** | Central Organisation of Trade Unions (South Africa) |
| **ECOWAS** | Economic Community of West African States |
| **EEC** | European Economic Community |
| **EJCSK** | *Eglise de Jésus-Christ sur la terre parte prophète Simon Kimbangu* |
| **ERP** | Economic Rehabilitation Plan (Ghana) |
| **FDR** | Democratic Revolutionary Front (El Salvador) |
| **FLNC** | *Front de Libération Nationale du Congo* |
| **FMLN** | Farabundo Martí National Liberation Front (El Salvador) |
| **GIHOC** | Ghana Industrial Holding Corporation |
| **HCP** | *Huileries du Congo Belge* |
| **ICFTU** | International Confederation of Free Trade Unions |
| **ISI** | Import Substitution Industrialisation |

| | |
|---|---|
| **IMF** | International Monetary Fund |
| **INM** | Imbokodvo National Movement (Swaziland) |
| **JFM** | June 4th Movement |
| **JMNR** | National Revolutionary Youth Movement (Congo) |
| **KANU** | Kenya African National Union |
| **KAWC** | Kenya African Workers Congress |
| **KFL** | Kenya Federation of Labour |
| **KNRG** | Kwame Nkrumah Revolutionary Guard |
| **KUSPW** | Kenya Union of Sugar Plant Workers |
| **LAP** | Liberian Action Party |
| **LPA** | Lagos Plan of Action |
| **LUP** | Liberian Unification Party |
| **MNC/K** | *Mouvement National Congolais – Kalonji* |
| **MNC/L** | *Mouvement National Congolais – Lumumba* |
| **MNR** | National Revolutionary Movement (Congo) |
| **MOAC** | Ministry of Agriculture and Co-operatives |
| **MOJA** | Movement for Justice in Africa |
| **NATO** | North Atlantic Treaty Organisation |
| **NDC** | National Defence Committee (Ghana) |
| **NDM** | New Democratic Movement (Ghana) |
| **NDPL** | National Democratic Party of Liberia |
| **NIC** | National Investigation Committee (Ghana) |
| **NNLC** | Ngwame National Liberatory Congress (Swaziland) |
| **NRC** | National Redemption Council (Liberia) |
| **NUGS** | National Union of Ghana Students |
| **NUM** | National Union of Mineworkers of South Africa |
| **OAU** | Organisation of African Unity |
| **PAC** | Pan–Africanist Congress of Azania |
| **PANYMO** | Pan African Youth Movement |
| **PDC** | People's Defence Committee (Ghana) |
| **PEBCO** | Port Elizabeth Black Civic Organisation |
| **PFP** | Popular Front Party (Ghana) |
| **PME** | Promotion of Small and Medium Enterprises |
| **PNP** | *Parti National du Progrès (Congo)* |
| **PNDC** | Provisional National Defence Council (Ghana) |
| **PPP** | Progressive People's Party (Liberia) |
| **PRLG** | People's Revolutionary League of Ghana |
| **PRP** | *Parti de la Révolution Populaire (Zaire)* |
| **PSA** | *Parti Solidaire Africain (Congo)* |
| **RDA/P** | Rural Development Area/Programme |
| **SADCC** | Southern African Development Co-ordination Conference |
| **SADF** | South African Defence Force |
| **SASOL** | South African Coal, Oil and Gas Corporation |
| **SECOM** | Special Election Commission (Liberia) |

| | |
|---|---|
| **SEDCO** | Small Enterprises Development Corporation (Swaziland) |
| **SNL** | Swazi Nation Land |
| **SOWETO** | South Western Townships (South Africa) |
| **TANU** | Tanganyikan African National Union |
| **TWP** | True Whig Party (Liberia) |
| **UDC** | Uganda Development Corporation |
| **UDDIA** | Union for the Defence of African Interests |
| **UDF** | United Democratic Front of South Africa |
| **UDPL** | United Democratic Party of Liberia |
| **UGEC** | *Union Générale des Etudiants Congolaise* |
| **UJC** | Union of Congolese Youth |
| **UNC** | *Union Nationale Congolaise* |
| **UNLF** | Uganda National Liberation Front |
| **UNOC** | United Nations Congo Mission |
| **UP** | United Party (Liberia) |
| **UPP** | United People's Party (Liberia) |
| **USA** | United Swaziland Association |
| **WDC** | Workers' Defence Committees |
| **WIGMO** | Western International Ground Maintenance Organisation |
| **ZANU** | Zimbabwe African National Union |
| **ZAPU** | Zimbabwe African People's Union |

# Preface:
# The State and the
# Question of 'Development'

## by Samir Amin

This book that ZED is publishing in our 'Studies in African Political Economy' series is the fruit of a collective endeavour directed by our Kenyan colleague Peter Anyang' Nyong'o with his well-known verve. The dozen case studies of the nature of the African state give a detailed and subtle idea of the variety of histories and situations as well as of the problematic that they share. In the general introduction to the book, Peter Anyang' Nyong'o brings out what seems to him — as indeed it does to me — to be the essential lesson of what we are indeed obliged to call the failure of the 'development' of independent Africa: the impossibility of achieving anything significant economically in the absence of a popular national state, that is one that is both strong (to resist the negative pressures coming from the world system and their internal ramifications) and democratic. The experience of independent Africa demonstrates the narrow limits of attempts at a national bourgeois development; the crisis of this form of development has demonstrated how vulnerable it is to pressures whose purpose is to subordinate its development to the demands of the redeployment of globalised capital, by means of so-called adjustment policies advocated by the West (and particularly by its collective instruments for intervening, the International Monetary Fund (IMF) and the World Bank).

This is not the place to deal at length with this failure of 'development'. In brief it can be said that Africa as a whole has not even begun the essential agricultural revolution, which is the prerequisite to any other development, of whatever form: and that, concomitantly, it has not yet entered the industrial era. We have analysed this African tragedy elsewhere; responsibility for it undoubtedly goes back to the brutal and primitive forms of colonial pillage, which was satisfied to have Africa produce and then cream off an agricultural surplus without technological and social transformations that would make it possible to move from extensive to intensive forms of farming the land. Independent Africa's responsibility lies in having pursued this policy; it is true that it did so with the blessing and on the urgent advice of all those who, today, from the World Bank to the agencies of Western states, deplore its wretched results, foreseeable though these results were.[1]

Overcoming this wretched heritage poses all sorts of problems, some apparently technical, others more directly political. There are at least two sets of questions: (i) can the agricultural revolution be accomplished without industrialisation, and (ii) is there any hope of being able to resolve the inheritance of underdevelopment

1

without systematic intervention by the state, and by what sort of state?

On the first set of questions, we have also given our views elsewhere, arguing against the demagogic proposals of the World Bank which dares to criticise Africa for an alleged preference for industrialisation to the detriment of agriculture.[2] Poor Africa! It is hard to see how it could have committed this additional crime, given that up until now it has not even begun to embark on any industrial development! Contrary to these arguments, we demonstrated that the agricultural revolution was impossible without industrialisation, on condition, of course, that this industrialisation be of neither the import substitution nor the export-oriented industry type (the only two models known to the World Bank), but an industry articulated on giving absolute priority to the agricultural revolution (and that is precisely the form of industrialisation that the World Bank knows absolutely nothing about).

The papers collected in this volume concern the second set of questions, and it is about them that we would like to add a few additional general remarks.

Conventional economic theory was built on the deliberate exclusion of the question of the state, which was ignored in the analysis of 'economic mechanisms'. This omission is, of course, ideological. For *laissez-faire* or *laissez-aller* has never actually happened in reality, and itself presupposes the state and its intervention (to outlaw trade unions for example). As a result, even the best economic theory has only a limited scope. At best it makes it possible to grasp the rationality of the conjunctural behaviour of economic actors and to foresee its short-term consequences. It makes it possible, therefore, to rationalise the eventual collective strategies of these agents and the state. But it is powerless to account for the profound evolution of societies, structural changes, and it is powerless to account for unequal development in world capitalist expansion (the problem of 'development' and 'underdevelopment').

The (limited) validity of economic theory lies in two factors, specific to capitalism, two factors that are indeed closely linked to one another: economistic alienation which defines the dominant ideology appropriate to capitalism on the one hand and the specificity of capitalist civil society on the other.[3]

The capitalist mode of production is in fact the only mode of production that is directly governed by economic laws; these laws result from the generalisation of the commodity form of social relations (in turn, this is the product of the generalisation of the commodity form to every product of social labour and to the labour force itself). The obscuring of social relations by the market for goods and labour power, which is specific to capitalism, gives the economic laws their objective status specific to this mode of production. Commodity alienation, its expression in the ideological domain, gives the functioning of these laws the appearance of being laws of nature. In contrast, in all precapitalist modes, the determination in the last instance by the material base operates only indirectly. It is so because the transparency of relations of exploitation and production involves the direct active intervention of political–ideological relations.

As a result, the very concept of civil society is peculiar to capitalism, precisely in that the very existence of civil society implies an autonomy of economic relations *vis-à-vis* the political. Bourgeois democracy — with all the historical limitations that it involves — is based on this separation of civil society and the state. This separation, which is of course only relative, is portrayed in bourgeois ideology as absolute; this makes it possible to eliminate the very existence of the state from economic theory — which it would be better, for this very reason, to call, more accurately, economistic ideology.

Comparative analysis of the state/economic life (civil society) relationship in the central ('developed') forms of capitalism and in its peripheral ('underdeveloped') ones throws a most instructive light on the nature of this relationship.

In the central capitalist societies, the state is of course present, and its intervention is even decisive. We shall describe this presence below: it defines capitalism in its completed form, that is mastery of accumulation by the bourgeois national state. But this presence is not directly experienced; it is even eliminated from the ideological self-image that the system produces, in order to play up civil society and economic life, as if these existed and functioned without the state. Conversely, in the societies of peripheral capitalism, precisely because that capitalism is not completed capitalism, civil society is feeble or even non-existent. Economic life is sickly and seems little more than an appendage to the exercise of state functions, which directly and visibly occupies the front of the stage. But that is only an illusion since the state here is in reality weak (in contrast to the true strong state, the state of the developed centre). At the same time, economic life is reduced to being a process of adjustment to the demands of accumulation at the centre (it is its appendage).

In a fine study of the relations between the African state and the peasant world, Mahmood Mamdani has brought out this subordination of the economic to the political, which is peculiar to peripheral systems.[4] The absence of any economic life autonomous in relation to state power, and the concomitant absence of any autonomy of expression on the part of social forces in relation to this power, renders any talk of democracy meaningless, for democracy is truly impossible in these conditions. This subordination is also the expression of the narrow limits of 'development'; it is simply the means by which it reproduces itself. In the final analysis, the subordination expresses the specificity of capitalist expansion in the periphery — the 'adjustment' of the latter to the demands of global accumulation. This domain (of relations between state and peasantry) is certainly not the only one in which this characteristic of 'underdevelopment' is found. It is well known, for example, that governments in Africa are not at all tolerant of national 'private enterprise'. They see in enrichment outside their control a threat to their own stability. Such an attitude is proof of the real weakness of the states in question. The infatuation with the public sector, even in countries which officially profess 'liberalism', and proclaim their membership of 'the Western camp', is the expression of this fear of civil society on the part of a state that is weak because it is peripheral.

Why is this so? Is it possible to 'go beyond this stage' by imitating the institutions of the developed West, i.e. by throwing open some areas of economic life to 'private initiative'? We shall explain below why that is not possible, precisely because this specificity is an essential condition of the reproduction of inequality in capitalist expansion (the polarisation between centres and peripheries), and because this inequality is itself immanent in capitalist expansion. In other words, it is a

3

contradiction which cannot be overcome within capitalism.

And yet this is indeed what the West 'recommends' to the countries of the Third World. This is the essential content of the dominant language of 'liberalisation': the one the World Bank uses in its systematic endeavour directed at dismantling this state, which it claims is too strong (whereas in reality it is too weak!), in favour of privatisation. Today, the swing to the right in the West and the triumph of Reaganomics (and its European imitators — Thatcherism and others), use this language like an incantation, a true 'theology of the market'. As if it was enough to proclaim the will to 'accept the laws of the market' for (by a miracle belied by four centuries of history) 'underdevelopment' to be rapidly overcome by a prodigious growth, its dormant potential liberated by the market — which only this wicked and stupid state is keeping locked up. As if, moreover, the present crisis demanded only 'readjustments' guided by the rationality of the market, i.e. as if this crisis was not a profound structural crisis. Rarely has bourgeois ideology dared go to its logical limits with such arrogance; as if moved by a religious conviction. In this sense, we have written that President Reagan and the Ayatollah Khomeini were engaged in the same 'fundamentalist' behaviour.[5]

There is no dispute about the fact that the world expansion of capitalism was and is unequal. Our thesis goes further since it argues that every region that has been integrated into the world capitalist system as a periphery has remained so down to the present day. It should be noted that on this thesis New England, Canada, Australia and New Zealand have never been peripheral formations; conversely, Latin America, the West Indies, Africa and Asia — except Japan — were and have remained so. The thesis also distinguishes zones integrated as peripheries of non-peripheralised backward countries which later crystallised into centres, although later than others (Germany and Eastern Europe, Southern Europe, Japan).[6] But we are told that today some Third World countries 'are acceding' to full centre-type capitalist development. That remains to be proved; exactly similar things, with the same arguments, were said a century ago, even two centuries ago, but subsequent events failed to confirm the optimism of the homogenising vision of capitalist expansion.[7]

This key fact needs then to be explained, and this is one of the main aims of all our efforts to spell out the thesis of unequal development. But, in our view, this analysis cannot be carried on simply at the level of what is called the 'economics' of the system. This is no more than the immediate expression of realities whose roots go deep into the level of social and political relations which, in the last analysis, govern the nature of economic evolution. The centrality of the question of the state here stands out starkly.

The decisive qualitative criterion that makes it possible to classify the societies of the world capitalist system into centres and peripheries is in the last analysis that of the nature of their state. We have spelled out elsewhere this qualitative difference. The societies of central capitalism are marked by the crystallisation of a bourgeois nation state, whose essential function (beyond the simple maintenance of the domination of capital) is precisely to control the conditions of accumulation through the national control that it exercises over the reproduction of the labour force, the market, the centralisation of the surplus, natural resources and technology. The state here fulfils the conditions that make possible what I have suggested calling 'autocentred accumulation', that is the subordination of external relations (usually aggressive) to the logic of that accumulation. Conversely, the peripheral state (which fulfils like any state the function of maintaining internal class domination) no longer controls local accumulation. It is then — objectively — the instrument of the 'adjustment' of the local society to the demands of globalised accumulation, and which direction that takes is determined by the direction taken by the central powers. This difference makes it possible to understand why the central state is a strong state (and when it becomes 'democratic', in the bourgeois sense of the word, that is simply one more expression of that strength), while the peripheral state is a weak state (and that is why, among other things, access to true bourgeois democratisation is practically closed to it, and why the existence of civil society there is necessarily limited).[8]

Why was the national bourgeois state able to crystallise in the centre and not in the periphery? That raises three sets of questions.

The first set of questions: how, in this differentiation, are the internal factors and the external factors articulated? Which are the decisive ones? For us, there can be no doubt that it is always the internal conditions that constitute the decisive factor. But that is simply a platitude: and it is dangerous and naïve to stop with the analysis of these internal conditions alone. To do so is to assume — implicitly and sometimes explicitly — that the external conditions (i.e. those that flow from integration into the world system) are in themselves 'favourable', i.e. that they offer the possibility of a capitalist development, *tout court*, and that whether this will be 'central' or 'peripheral' — used as synonyms for 'completed' or 'incomplete' ('backward', 'underdeveloped', etc.) — will depend wholly on internal conditions.

This assumption seems to us to be absolutely false; for in fact the external conditions are unfavourable, in the sense that they constitute an obstacle, not of course to capitalist development in general, but to the acquisition by it of the characteristics of central capitalist development. In other words: the crystallisation of the bourgeois national state among some is a block to its crystallisation among others. Or again: the 'underdevelopment' of some is the product of the 'development' of others. And it must be said clearly here that this proposition is not systematic and reversible; for we have not said that its converse ('the development of some is the product of the underdevelopment of others') was true. This observation, which is too often passed over without comment, and the confusion that is then made between our proposition and its converse, are the source of serious misunderstandings and sterile polemics.[9] For the exploitation of the periphery, in its successive and varied historical forms (pillage, 'unequal exchange', etc.), which is not, in our opinion, in itself deniable (it remains of course to define it precisely and grasp its movement), does not explain the 'wealth' of the centre; it does not even constitute the main reason for 'high wages' for example. On the other hand, it is essential, in our analysis, to understand clearly that the destruction wreaked on the periphery by that exploitation is massive and decisive. And this destruction goes far beyond the economic domain alone, and affects the whole political and cultural domains; it kills local creativity, i.e. precisely the possibility of taking up the historic challenge.[10]

5

The second set of questions: why did this crystallisation of the bourgeois national state appear in the centre early (in Western Europe, then in Central and Eastern Europe, New England, Japan) and not elsewhere? This is a new set of questions, distinct from the previous ones. The thesis that we have suggested in this area is that of unequal development in the birth of capitalism. In our view, it is because precapitalist Europe (and, in the same way, Japan) was 'backward' in relation to the more advanced East, that it made this move more easily. The greater flexibility of the backward regions of a system (in this case the precapitalist system) made possible a quicker shift to a qualitatively more advanced system (capitalism). Nevertheless, the same contradictions operated too in the more advanced precapitalist East. The solution to them called for capitalist development here too, and there is a great deal of scattered evidence to indicate that it was maturing. The European headstart and then its expansion, far from favouring the acceleration of this maturation, broke its inner dynamism and distorted subsequent development in the direction of the peripheral impasse.[11]

The third set of questions: are there not, between the central situations and the peripheral ones, intermediate cases, which could be described as 'semi-peripheries'? Their existence would be evidence that peripheralisation is not 'inevitable' and that, when it occurs, it is indeed for reasons that have to do mainly with internal factors. Simultaneously, it would be possible — despite the external obstacle — if one exists — to set oneself up as a new centre. There is no doubt that, in society as in life, there always exist intermediate cases, or cases that are apparently so. The fact in itself would be difficult to dispute. But that is not the real question. Our thesis is that the world capitalist system is moved by a strong tendency to polarisation. Just as in the capitalist mode of production, there is a tendency towards a polarisation between the two fundamental classes (bourgeoisie and proletariat). The crystallisation of the centres at one extreme and peripheralisation at the other, more and more marked despite appearances, do not exclude, at any point, the emergence of 'semi-peripheries', analogous to the middle classes engendered by the concrete dynamic of capitalist accumulation. To rule out the repeated emergence of such features would imply an absurd static view, as if the polarisation between centres and peripheries had magically appeared in its fullness from the very beginning, whereas it is precisely the result of the concrete movement of the world system.[12] At the same time, no doubt, the emergence of these 'semi-peripheries' reveals the true nature of the dialectic which governs this movement, that is, the convergence, or the conflict, between the internal factors (favourable and unfavourable) and the external factor (unfavourable). History, in any case, shows that the 'semi-peripheries' are not 'centres in the process of formation'. How many 'semi-peripheries' located in the history of the last four centuries have become centres? To our knowledge, not one. That fact alone would be enough to demonstrate how far the external conditions are unfavourable, indeed strongly so, since even when the internal conditions are relatively favourable, the external ones thwart attempts by 'semi-peripheries' to raise themselves to the rank of 'centres'. More than that, our thesis is that the crystallisation of new centres is increasingly difficult; that means that the obstacle represented by the external factor is increasingly difficult to overcome. This is so even when we consider the historical formation of new centres that were formed from 'backward', but not peripheralised, situations (Germany and Japan, for example), *a fortiori* when we examine the fate of societies described as 'semi-peripheries'. For example, it is obvious that, despite its lateness, Germany was able to catch up and overtake England in a few decades in the 19th Century. How long will it take Brazil to catch up and overtake the US? Is such a prospect even conceivable in the foreseeable future? The concept of a break represented by the formation, at the end of the 19th Century, of the imperialist system — in the sense that Lenin gave the term — seems to us, from this viewpoint, perfectly justified. We have set out the meaning of it in the following manner: before this break there was no contradiction between the crystallisation of a new centre (starting from a backward but not already peripheralised situation and if the internal conditions were favourable to such a crystallisation of course) and its integration into the world system; since then, this contradiction has become glaring (and, for that reason, there no longer exist any 'backward' societies that are not peripheralised). In other words, the imperialist break marks a qualitative change in the constitution of the world system.[13]

Faced with this series of theses concerning the formation of the bourgeois national state, the outline of a counter-thesis has been appearing over the last few years. The key element in it consists in claiming that all that belongs to the past and that the polarisation between 'centres' and 'peripheries' as the dominant form of the bourgeois national state, is disappearing, and giving way to a new form of globalised capitalism.

The arguments advanced are a very mixed bunch. The most common — and, no doubt, most widespread — is basing its argument on the capacity of capitalism to adapt, claims that 'the North's interest lies in the South becoming more developed': all the partners in capitalism would gain from such development, because this is not a zero-sum game, in which one's gain is necessarily another's loss. This reasoning is ideological and lacks any scientific basis; it is the dominant political discourse of states. ('We are all in the same boat and share a common long-term interest', etc.) The proposal for a New International Economic Order, put forward in 1975 by the countries of the Third World, was, from this point of view, indicative, as we have demonstrated elsewhere. For this proposal in no way conflicted with the long-term abstract logic of capitalism, in that the proposed new order would have been the basis of a stronger expansion in the North as well as in the South. Yet this proposal was rejected by the North.[14] Why? Quite simply because capitalism is not moved by the quest for the strongest growth of all in the long term, but by the maximum profit of the strongest in the short term. The argument based on the ideology of possible universal harmony overlooks — or pretends to overlook — this reality. That does not mean that capitalism is not effectively sufficiently flexible to be able, not only to adapt, but eventually to profit from the structural transformations imposed on it by the social forces that it exploits. The improvement in wages in the West opened new markets to the expansion of capital; yet it was not brought about by the strategies of capital, but by workers' struggles. In the same way, an improvement of growth in the South might well open markets to capital from the North, but it has to be imposed by the countries of the Third World against the strategies of the West.

A second series of arguments stresses the — real — transformations which, operating at the level of expanding productive forces, seem to challenge autocentred accumulation and the functions of the bourgeois national state at the very centre of the system. No doubt imperialism such as Lenin knew and described it was marked, among other things, by the violent conflict of national imperialisms, a conflict that was the source of two world wars in our time. No doubt it is difficult today to imagine a repetition of a political conflict of such violence between the US, Europe (or the Europes) and Japan. Economic competition, which remains very real, is certainly attenuated by the common fear of the 'socialist threat'. In addition, at least until the 1970s, it was subject to the constraints of the hegemony of the US, which was then accepted.

But does this mean that the stage of imperialism has been 'overtaken',[15] that we are moving towards an 'ultra-imperialism' united by the interpenetration of capitals, these having already lost their national character? We do not think that to be the case. First, and foremost, because the key feature in imperialism is not the conflict of imperialisms, but the contrast between centre and periphery, which has reached a stage making the crystallisation of new capitalist centres impossible. But this contradiction, far from being attenuated by the weakening of the conflict of imperialisms, is on the contrary sharpened by the 'common front' of the North (against the South and the East). Second, because we are still very far from the time when a world state (even one limited, of course, to the capitalist North) has taken over from national states. The national state is, to date, the sole framework within which major social and political conflicts are settled. Moreover, this specific contradiction between capital — whose globalised dimension is effectively much more marked than it was only half a century ago although appropriation and control of capital have remained largely national — and the state — which for its part has remained strictly national — is the distinguishing feature of the crisis of our times. Attenuated by the hegemony of the US which enabled the American state to fulfil in part the functions of a 'world state' (the global policeman), this contradiction resurfaced with redoubled strength once that hegemony began to decline, that is when the US ceased to be the sole source of innovations and ceased to be capable of performing the functions of global policeman. The Reaganite counter-offensive, on which we have written elsewhere, does not basically alter this evolution.

There then remains the third series of arguments which, precisely, stress what is new — or allegedly new — in the South. We are told that new 'semi-peripheries' have emerged that are already in the process of constituting themselves into new capitalist centres (Brazil, South Korea, etc.), putting a final end to the existence of the now shattered Third World. Without going back here over the question of the diversity of the periphery — a commonplace that has been true at all times over the last four centuries — we would like to point out simply that it has not yet been established that the 'semi-peripheries' in question are effectively, and successfully, constructing bourgeois national states capable of controlling internal accumulation and subordinating their external relations to that accumulation, i.e. of escaping the heavy constraints of adjustment to the demands for the expansion of capital of the central monopolies. But, we are told, this construction is now pointless, since the national state is itself being diluted in the centres themselves. It would then be

8

necessary to show that the society of the 'semi-peripheries' in question is becoming more like that of the already constituted centres, in the global perspective of this homogenised capitalist world of the future that is coming into being. No such thing has been demonstrated or is even feasible, because the processes of social change under way in the foreseeable future are so divergent in the two areas. Once again, analysis of real contradictions and their own dynamism is replaced by the *a priori* vision of a harmony that has overcome those contradictions. Let us suppose the problem settled.[16]

The unequal character of capitalist expansion, which cannot be overcome in the framework of that expansion, thus objectively requires the reconstruction of the world on the basis of another social system; and the peoples of the periphery are forced to be aware of it and to impose it, if they wish to avoid the worst: and the worst might go even as far as genocide: the history of this expansion is there to testify strongly that such a threat is quite real.

But such a challenge to the capitalist order from revolts in its periphery obliges us to rethink seriously the question of the 'socialist transition' to the abolition of classes. Whatever people say about it, and however many nuances are made, the Marxist tradition remains handicapped by the initial theoretical vision of 'workers' revolutions' opening up, on the basis of at least relatively advanced productive forces, a transition which is itself relatively rapid. Such a transition is moreover seen as being marked by democratic rule by the popular masses which, while it is still described as 'dictatorship over the bourgeoisie' (through the means of a proletarian state of a new type rapidly beginning to wither away), is still considerably more democratic than the most democratic of bourgeois states.

Reality of course is not quite like that. All the revolutions that have proclaimed themselves anti-capitalist have so far occurred in the peripheries of the system; all have found themselves confronted with the problem of developing the productive forces and the hostility of the capitalist world; none has achieved any form whatever of real advanced democracy; all have strengthened the statist system. So much so that, more and more frequently, doubt is being expressed about their being described as socialist and their prospect of ending up one day, however far off it may be, with the true abolition of classes. For some (we are not among them and we have criticised their theses), they are even simply specific forms of capitalist expansion.[17]

The essential issue is of course not to characterise these systems, but to understand their origin, their specific problems and contradictions, and the dynamic processes that they open up or close off. By approaching them from this angle, we have reached the thesis that these are popular national states and societies. And we have reached the conclusion that this popular national phase was unavoidable, imposed by the unequal character of capitalist development.

As a result, these systems are effectively confronted with the task of developing the productive forces and are based on social forces that do not accept the thesis that this development could be obtained by a mere adjustment in the framework of world capitalist expansion. They are the product of revolutions carried out and backed by those forces revolting against the effects of the unequal development of capitalism. As a result, these systems are contradictory and conflict-laden

9

combinations of different forces, three in number it would seem. Some, socialist or potentially such, reflect the aspirations of the popular social forces that were the source of the new state. Others, capitalist, reflect the fact that at this stage of the development of the productive forces capitalist relations of production are still necessary, and that therefore they have to find real social forces to sustain them. But the existence of these capitalist relations must not be confused with integration into the world capitalist system. For the state is there precisely to isolate these relations from the effects of integration into the system dominated by the capital of the central monopolies. As a result, the third set of real social forces that are at work here, which we describe as statist, has its own autonomy. It is not reducible either to the disguised form of capitalist relations (as statism effectively is in the capitalist Third World), or to a 'degenerate' form of socialism. Statism represents its own real and potential social forces.

The state here then fulfils specific functions, different from those that it fulfils in the capitalist centres and peripheries. It is the means of national protection and affirmation, that is the instrument of what we have described as 'delinking', in the sense of the subordination of external relations to the logic of an internal development (which is not simply capitalist). It is the site of the — conflict-laden — regulation of relations among the three tendencies that we have identified.

Obviously, this state is not the same from one end to the other of the 'socialist' world. It is itself the product of specific concrete histories, themselves in dynamic evolution, through which combinations between the conflicting forces mentioned, peculiar as to time and place, manifest themselves. But these are always strong states, precisely because they are 'delinked'.

We re-situate the perspective of the 'democratic question' in this framework. For particular complex reasons that have to do with the history of Marxism, which we have analysed elsewhere,[18] these systems are scarcely democratic, to say the least, despite their material achievements in favour of the popular masses and despite the eventual support that the masses may give them in varying and variable degrees. But the problems with which these societies are confronted can only be overcome by a democratic development. It is so because democracy is an unavoidable condition, necessary in order to ensure the efficiency of a socialist social system. That is not the case in capitalism: here democracy only functions when its potentialities are emasculated by the 'majority consensus' produced by the exploitation of dominant central positions in the world capitalist system. That is why bourgeois democracy — limited as it is, as Marx analysed it (and this critique remains wholly correct) — is only possible in the central capitalist countries. In the periphery, it is impossible or, in its limited expressions produced periodically by the impasse of peripheral development, vulnerable in the extreme. Conversely, social relations based on the cooperation of workers and not their subordination with a view to their exploitation, are unthinkable without the complete expression of democracy. Will the countries of 'actually existing socialism' as they are called, reach this stage? Or will they enclose themselves in the impasse of its rejection?

It is precisely here that we once again encounter the basic question of internal factors. Here and not in the capitalist peripheries where the autonomy of the internal factor, while it of course explains past history (peripheralisation), is today very greatly attenuated by the weight of external constraints. Conversely, in the popular national states, the internal factor has again become decisive. In this sense, it is being rediscovered that there is no historical inevitability. By internal factor, we mean here of course the dialectic of the threefold contradiction mentioned above.

Why then has the Third World not — or not yet — embarked on this path, the path of the construction of a popular national state? Why is it assiduously trying to construct a bourgeois national state in imitation of that of central capitalism? Of course, this situation is not the product of ideas without any social base; it is the expression of certain social classes and strata with a bourgeois vocation, which dominated and still dominate the national liberation movement (i.e. the revolt against the effects of the unequal development of capitalism) and the state that emerged from it. History teaches that the bourgeoisies in the periphery have attempted this construction at every stage of world capitalist expansion, naturally in forms appropriate to their time. Just as it teaches that in the last analysis these attempts have always been frustrated by the combination of external aggression and the internal limits peculiar to those attempts themselves. These are moreover themselves largely the objective product of the peripheral condition, even if they have more remote historical roots. Elsewhere, we have described the 'Bandung era' (1955–75) as a global attempt by the contemporary Third World that had this nature and pursued this goal. The 'recompradorisation' that follows on from failure — and which is continuing during the present crisis — testifies to the historical impossibility of the project.[19]

The thesis of unequal development is thus not an economistic thesis based on an exclusive analysis of the mechanisms of the reproduction of 'economic inequality', as is unfortunately too often believed. It is a thesis that is situated on the total and complex level of historical materialism, thus making it possible to situate the role of the state in the 'question of development'. This role is decisive; but it can only be properly fulfilled if the state in question is national, popular and not bourgeois. So we propose to call it thus, and not socialist. Not that it is pointless to retain the perspective of the ultimate objective, the abolition of classes. On the contrary, the chances of the socialist forces operating within the national and popular society depend on the forceful expression of that objective. But we think that it is better to describe societies by the name that corresponds to their reality rather than by the nature of some project they might have. As for the description 'national', it is there to remind us that 'delinking' is necessary and that it makes it impossible to envisage a strategy aiming at the immediate passage, or in stages, from globalised capitalism to a socialism itself globalised. The passage demands a previous destruction of the order based on the capitalist–imperialist centralisation of the surplus (of surplus value and of all the forces transferring value), in favour, immediately, of a decentralisation of it to the level of the popular states. The autonomy won back by this 'delinking' then makes it possible to abolish the specific contradiction born of the unequal development of capitalism, and thus create the conditions for a later recentralisation, in a not yet foreseeable future, on the basis of a globalised classless society.[20]

In a certain sense then, the unequal development thesis demonstrates that the East–West contradiction and the North–South contradiction are of a similar nature, since they are both the expression of the impasses of capitalism.

## Notes

1. For our analysis of the failure of development in Africa, see several of our works some of which are already old: Samir Amin, *Trois Expériences Africaines de Développement, le Mali, la Guinée et le Ghana* (Paris, 1965); Samir Amin, *Le Développement du Capitalisme en Côte d'Ivoire* (Paris, 1967); Samir Amin and C. Coquery, *Du Congo Français à l'UDEAC* (Paris, 1970); Samir Amin, *The Maghreb in the Modern World* (Harmondsworth: Penguin, 1970); Samir Amin, *Neocolonialism in West Africa* (Harmondsworth: Penguin, 1973).

See also our 'Introductions' to the books by Lamine Gakou (*Crise de l'Agriculture Africaine* (Paris, Silex 1984); English translation, *Crisis in African Agriculture* (London, Zed 1987); Bernard Founou-Tchigoua *Les Fondements Economiques de l'Economie de Traite au Sénégal* (Paris, Silex 1981); and Bourges and Wauthier *Les Cinquante Afrique* (Paris, 1979).

See also our articles: 'Pour une stratégie alternative de développement en Afrique', *Africa Development*, no. 3, 1981; 'Développement et transformations structurelles, l'expérience de l'Afrique 1950–70', *Tiers Monde*, no. 51, 1972; *Du Rapport Pearson au Rapport Brandt*, 1980; 'Les limites de la révolution verte', CERES, July 1970; 'The Interlinkage Between the Agricultural Revolution and Industrialisation', *Africa Today*, 1986.

2. For a critique of the World Bank's report, see: Samir Amin, 'Critique of the World Bank report entitled "Accelerated Development in Sub-Saharan Africa"', *Africa Development*, vol. VII, nos. 1–2, 1982; Samir Amin, *Is Self-reliant Development Possible for Africa?*

3. For an analysis of economistic alienation and civil society, see: Samir Amin, *Unequal Development* (New York, Monthly Review 1976) ch. 2; Samir Amin, *Class and Nation* (New York, Monthly Review 1980) ch. 1.

4. Mahmood Mamdani, 'The Agrarian Question and the Democratic Struggle', *Bulletin of the Third World Forum*, no. 6, 1986.

5. Amin, *La Déconnexion* (Paris, La Decourt 1985) p. 334.

6. For a distinction between peripheries and backward centres, see: Amin, *Unequal Development*, ch. 4; and Amin, *Class and Nation*, ch. 4–6.

7. Amin, *La Déconnexion*, ch. 1, pp. 54–73.

8. Concerning autocentred development and the national bourgeois state, see: Amin, *La Déconnexion*.

9. Ibid.

10. This is also the viewpoint expressed by Serge Latouche, *Faut-il Refuser le Développement?* (1986) who agrees with the criticisms made of Western economic and social thought (including Marxism) by Islamic fundamentalists. We have expressed our reservations about these theses in writings in Arabic to which reference is also made in *La Déconnexion*. The challenge of imperialist capitalism cannot be met by a 'culturalist nationalist withdrawal', but by a direct confrontation within a universalist socialist perspective, but one that is not 'Western-centred' in the way in which, it is true, the dominant currents of Marxism have interpreted this perspective.

11. Thesis of Amin, *Class and Nation*, ch. 6.

12. Here I agree with the criticisms that Tamas Szentes, *Theories of World Capitalist Economy* (Budapest, 1985) makes of I. Wallerstein about semi-peripheries. See Amin, *La Déconnexion*.

13. I agree here too with Szentes' view of the importance of the imperialist break (see Amin, *La Déconnexion*). But I have some reservations about Andersson's thesis, presented and defended by Szentes, suggesting a distinction between the stage of the 'world capitalist market' (before imperialism) and that of the 'world capitalist system' (which is claimed only to have existed since the late 19th century). See Samir Amin, *Imperialism and Unequal Development* (N.Y. Monthly Review) part IV; *Class and Nation*, ch. 6; *Unequal Development*, ch. 4.

14. See: Samir Amin, 'Développement autocentré, autonomie collective et NOEI', *Africa Development*, vol. III, no. 1, 1978; Samir Amin, 'Le NOEI et l'avenir des relations économiques internationales', *Africa Development*, 1, 1978; Samir Amin, 'La crise, le Tiers Monde, les relations Est–Ouest et Nord–Sud', *Nouvelle Revue Socialiste*, September–October 1983; Samir Amin, *ll ya trente ans, Bandung* (Cairo: UNU, 1985).

15. See references in note 14.

16. Amin, *La Déconnexion*, ch. 1, pp. 54–73.

17. See our critique of Bettelheim and Warren, Amin, *La Déconnexion*, ch. 4. See also our articles: 'Expansion or Crisis of Capitalism', *Contemporary Marxism*, no. 9, 1984; *Third World Quarterly*, no. 2, 1983; 'On the Transition to Socialism', *Scandinavian Journal of Development Alternatives*, 2, 1983.

18. Amin, *La Déconnexion*, chs. 1, 2 and 4. See also: Samir Amin, *The Future of Maoism* (New York, 1983).

19. See Amin, *Il ya a trente ans, Bandung.*

20. That leads to our thesis 'Revolution or decadence', the conclusion of our book *Class and Nation*.

# 1 Introduction

by Peter Anyang' Nyong'o

The year 1985–86 was not the best for Third World dictators and their military warlord henchmen. In April 1985, the Nimeiri regime in the Sudan collapsed in the hands of a popular uprising organised by trade unions, students, traditional political parties, some members of the intelligentsia and sections of the armed forces. In July of the same year, Milton Obote escaped to Zambia from Uganda, leaving behind a regime beleaguered from within and without, and a situation in which the National Resistance Army, in collaboration with the National Resistance Movement, did not find it too difficult to put together a governing coalition from among the popular forces that spontaneously rose up against the *ancien regime*. In February 1986, both Ferdinand Marcos and Jean Claude Duvalier (Baby Doc) sought political asylum abroad with the help of the Reagan administration as the peoples of the Philippines and Haiti finally said 'enough is enough' to decades of dictatorship.

With the history of dictatorship now behind them, a *Newsweek* commentator observed that, now that democracy was to be restored under Corazon Aquino's presidency, the Philippines should now be able to deal seriously with their many socio–economic problems. The Philippines had been plagued by problems of economic backwardness not so much because they lack the necessary resources and human willpower for 'economic take-off', but more because the political leadership has been more interested in graft, waste and the stashing of the country's wealth into personal investments and foreign accounts than in promoting indigenous processes of accumulation in response to popular needs. When the Filipino people resisted and rebelled against these leaders, the US was quick to come to the defence of the regime and to provide it with more military hardware and electronic gadgets with which to oppress and control the popular masses even more effectively and efficiently. Marcos might have been a devil as far as the Filipinos were concerned, but that was no reason for the US State Department to abandon him; he was still a devil they knew and one who could look after US national interests in the Philippines.

In Africa, Asia and Latin America, repressive, authoritarian and dictatorial governments, out to defend the interests of small cliques holding political power while running down their economies, seem to be getting the support of foreign governments simply because they are friendly to such governments. In the case of the US, both Jeane Kirkpatrick and Henry Kissinger have justified such policies in very clear terms. They draw distinctions between what they call 'traditional and revolutionary autocracies'. Traditional autocracies are authoritarian regimes of the right, such as that of the former Shah of Iran, Marcos of the Philippines and Mobutu of Zaire. Revolutionary autocracies are what American governments have always referred to as 'totalitarian regimes'; Cuba under Castro; Nicaragua under the Sandinistas; and Ethiopia under Mengistu Haile Mariam. Traditional authoritarian governments, Kirkpatrick and Kissinger argue, are less repressive than revolutionary autocracies, more susceptible to liberalisation and hence more compatible with US interests. It therefore follows that US foreign policy should be geared towards maintaining a close relationship with such regimes while carefully husbanding them towards a democratic future within the US sphere of influence. As far as the 'totalitarian regimes' are concerned, no matter what genuine efforts they may make towards some social transformation of a popular type, priority must be given to their political destruction before the US can give them any economic assistance. In either case, US foreign policy is not geared towards helping the popular masses; it is geared towards achieving its own national interest goals on a global scale.

If the Filipino and Haitian experiences are anything to go by, it is the power of the people, unleashed by broad-based movements of a popular alliance type, that can restore democracy in a country run down by a dictatorship and not the fine reasonings of a Kirkpatrick or a Ronnie on horseback. After all, as far as the people are concerned, an autocracy or an authoritarian government are basically the same thing: they both deny the people their basic human rights; they are both a bunch of no-gooders who have very little respect for people's needs; they both undermine the legitimacy of the state and endanger social progress; they are both kept in power by the might of foreign powers. But a people's struggle for democracy and sovereignty comes not from the genuine grievances it holds against such regimes, nor from the prodding and help by external Good Samaritans, but from its organised and systematic efforts to get rid of such regimes and replace them with consciously designed democratic ones. Whether these efforts are successful is a different matter; but that the efforts must be conscious and purposeful is a lesson to be learnt from both the Bolshevik Revolution[1] and the discussions in the *Federalist Papers*.[2]

Ferdinand Marcos was forced out of power not because the US finally released a programme of liberalisation for the Philippines, but because the popular movement there elected Corazon Aquino against all odds to the Presidency. In the same manner, Nimeiri was forced out of power in the Sudan not because the US benevolently decided to dump him in the interests of the Sudanese people, but because the National Alliance for National Salvation mobilised the popular masses to force the establishment of a Transitional Military Council with a strict one-year mandate before the end of which general elections would take place and democracy could hence be restored. In both cases, the mobilised popular masses were prepared even to sacrifice their lives for the sake of creating a democratic society so as to ensure both basic human rights and viable socio–economic development in the interest of the popular classes.

In October 1985, a dozen or so African scholars came together under the umbrella of the United Nations University's African Regional Perspectives

Programme on 'Transnationalization or Nation-Building' to study and discuss one specific problem, *Popular Alliances and the State in Africa*. It occurred to these scholars that, while a great deal of attention had been paid to the economic aspects of the African crisis, little attention had been given to its political aspects. People talk of politics only glibly, perhaps during break time at conferences organised by UN agencies to discuss the crisis. Where any mention had been made of the politics of the crisis, for example in the World Bank Report (1981),[3] it had mainly been in economistic and technocratic terms. Thus the World Bank sees the political crisis as that of a state that has bitten more than it can chew: instead of engaging in economic activities through parastatals, the state should now withdraw and confine itself to those activities it is most traditionally qualified to undertake in a free-market economy, those of providing and running the physical and social infrastructure, maintaining law and order and guaranteeing a sound policy framework for capital accumulation.

While claiming to be the most far-reaching policy document for Africa's development during the next twenty years, the Organization of African Unity's *Lagos Plan of Action* (LPA)[4] itself does not even bother to deal with the question of state power, yet it expects the African state to be the nationalist entrepreneur which will turn the backward and stagnating African economies around along the path of a collective self-reliant development towards sustained progress. One of the fundamental issues of the African crisis is that, during the first twenty-five or so years of independence, African policy-makers failed to grasp the structural character of the environment they were dealing with nationally and internationally. Those who exercise state power act in specific national and international contexts in which that power responds to concrete social forces. The state is not a neutral actor in society responding to mere reason or the logic of development. The state does not simply identify the 'needs of the day' or the pre-requisites of an alternative scenario of development after a careful bureaucratic analysis and then proceed to implement appropriate developmental programmes. It is the contending social forces, interested in the implementation of such programmes which, after a successful political battle over the control of state power, will use this power to see such programmes through.

The capacity of the state to intervene in economic development as envisaged in the LPA, or to provide greater latitude for market forces as advocated by the Berg Report, is heavily conditioned by the constellation of socio–economic forces facing it nationally and internationally. These forces constitute the context in which political power is exercised, and hence the extent to which programmatic philosophies, ideologies and ideas become operational. The state is a set of power relations that emerges historically to orchestrate the reproduction of social relations in society. As such, it is important to remember that the state has never been purely or simply a security organisation or a tool of domination of one class over others. The state is a system which organises the co–existence of diverse social forces within society under a particular framework of social domination and strives to provide the *modus operandi* for an orderly change in society. That is why its legal, repressive, bureaucratic and ideological institutions and apparatuses are quite often the easiest to identify with state power. The existence of the state results from

16

a sequence of historical developments and cumulative experiences through which it gradually acquires attributes that, in any given historical moment, show a distinct level of development in terms of both the character of politicial organisation and the level of acceptance of state authority— the level of political consensus — in society.

Perhaps, as has been suggested in some literature, it would be more appropriate to speak of 'stateness' to refer to the degree to which a system of political organisation and public authority has concretised this set of properties so vital in reproducing social relations in a socially stratified society. As society changes in historical terms and acquires greater pluralism through stratification, and as people come to experience social problems which require various types of political arrangements for their resolution, so does the nature of social domination tend to change and hence the nature of the state. The role of the state as the focal point for social cohesion and social engineering is particularly important in societies that have not had time to melt and merge into solid nations where the people have some historical and collective memory which may help explain away certain conflicts and rationalise or justify political and social domination. Weak and young states, lacking time-tested legal frameworks and political cultures for conflict regulation, are likely to be very brittle in attempts at conflict resolution.

In Africa, therefore, the nature of the state can be understood only from an historical and sociological analysis. While states existed in pre-colonial Africa, the modern state is a 'hand-me-down' phenomenon in many respects. It does not only have continuity with its colonial predecessors in terms of concrete institutions and apparatuses used by ruling regimes in exercising political power, but the kinds of social relations it needs to sustain in the day-to-day reproduction of society are still very much part of the mode of production dominant in colonial society. What is being observed in Africa today is that — given its class content, historical heritage and the global context of its current operation — the state is losing or has lost both the ability and the capacity to undertake the socio–economic programmes necessary for the continued reproduction of the capitalist mode of production. A few indicators will suffice to illustrate this crisis of the state and social reproduction.

At the very bare minimum, a large number of African states cannot even maintain and reproduce their own bureaucracies: civil servants are often not paid for months, armies and policemen rely on highway extortion to obtain their monthly wages, government offices are falling apart, water and telephone systems do not work, and national airlines cannot even respect their own tickets. At a much higher level of analysis, we may argue that the state is suffering from a generalised fiscal crisis. This crisis begins to manifest itself more dramatically when heads of state accept as valid currency only those legal tenders emanating from the industrialised world, and treat with contempt banknotes bearing their own heads. But the crisis really originates from the economy of exchange — which the state superintends — and not the economy of production — which is yet to establish firm roots in Africa. Once the exchange relations between the neo-colony and the capitalist world system deteriorate, remedies predicted upon 'balance-of-payments crises' cannot redeem the crisis; they can only ameliorate it at the margins. In order to arrive at long-term solutions, the state must confront the problem of production, the problem of generating enough social surplus from within to ensure not only the expanded reproduction of capitalism itself but also the sustained reproduction of the state and its bureaucracy.

Several questions are therefore well worth asking: What needs to be done? How can the state in Africa acquire (re-acquire) the capacity to undertake programmes of positive social transformation? What type of state would this be? What kinds of social forces would exercise state power to accomplish this alternative scenario of socio–economic development? To what extent would mere 'bureaucratic rationalism' bring about a socio–economic transformation responsive to popular demands and needs?

The problem of production cannot really be confronted unless the problem of the *direct producers* is dealt with as Mahmood Mamdani points out in his essay. And this should not be approached purely in economistic terms, but in what we may choose to call *contextual terms*, the context in which these producers operate politically and ideologically as well as economically. From the other essays it would seem very clear that the foundation of this context can be traced to the struggle for independence. During this struggle, the popular masses were inspired into political action by their resentment of the colonial political economy: forced labour, racial discrimination, forced production of cash crops for which they were paid very little or nothing at all, land thefts, and so on. Democratic ideals, aimed at the democratisation of society at all levels, propelled them to demand political sovereignty, in other words independence. Newspapers, trade unions, political parties and co-operative societies all demanded the same thing: independence.

It is not as if the popular masses were involved in self-deception: they obviously were not. The first independence governments were democratically elected and moved fast to deal with the popular demands that informed the struggle for independence. It is not by mere chance that in every African government there was a ministry dealing with economic planning and development, placing a lot of emphasis on *rural development*. It was assumed that the appropriate response to popular demands was *development*; that development could be *planned for*; that planning essentially involved the optimum utilisation of available domestic and foreign resources to achieve certain growth targets; and that for the majority of the popular masses to benefit, these growth targets had to be in the rural areas, hence rural development.

However well-meaning an African government was, the very nature of the exchange economies limited the extent to which it could generate internal resources for purposes of domestic accumulation or development. Thandika Mkandawire[5] has clearly shown how African governments engage in programmes of economic nationalism, complete with the nationalisation of foreign companies, when their foreign exchange kitty is heavy. As soon, however, as the foreign exchange resources get depleted, such governments are forced to pursue conservative programmes of development which frequently involve acceptance of IMF austerity measures. Further, the use to which state power is put by both the bureaucratic and comprador bourgeoisies may also seriously undermine the viability of domestic accumulation and further compromise the state with imperialism. This is much more clearly demonstrated when both the World Bank and the IMF advocate the privatisation of public enterprises. The comprador bourgeoisie obviously favours privatisation; the bureaucratic bourgeoisie is ardently opposed to it, and the reasons behind the two opposite stands are interesting to decipher.

The compradors will argue that privatisation will bring efficient use of resources, cut down costs and losses, save the state from engaging in what it is not qualified to do, ensure profitability and perhaps generate more resources for the state through taxation. The bureaucratic bourgeoisie will argue that privatisation is reactionary, anti-nationalistic, pro-imperialist and even anti-people; what is needed is not privatisation but more efficient functioning of public enterprises under its hegemony. The reality, however, is that as long as the economy remains neo-colonial, as long as the neo-colonial state remains what it is, and as long as the economy remains essentially an exchange-oriented economy, neither privatisation nor so-called 'more effective and efficient running of public enterprises' under the hegemony of the bureaucrat bourgeoisie will take Africa anywhere. Let us turn to the political question, the question of the nature of the neo-colonial state, accumulation and development.

If we assume for the moment that we do understand how the structure of dependence limits the extent of domestic accumulation within the neo-colony, we shall come to realise that even within these limits, the lack of accountability of those who control state power has meant that more positive social transformation and more auto-centred processes of accumulation have not been initiated. One should recollect, and carefully reflect upon, the reasons why, in the *Federalist Papers*, Hamilton, Madison and Jay laid so much emphasis on the need for checks and balances for a state which superintends capitalist development. It should be of importance, in analysing the role of the state in capitalist development in Africa, to note that the *Federalist Papers* went much further and discussed how popular participation (though the blacks were never part of the 'people' until much later) in governmental affairs was necessary to ensure that government was not only responsive to the concrete needs of the governed, but that wielders of political power did not engage in personal excesses. The threat to which the marriage of personal interest with public office would put the reproduction of a whole society was clearly felt by the Federalists, and they counselled conscious social engineering to avoid this.

At the centre of the failure of African states to chart viable paths for domestic accumulation is the problem of accountability, the lack of democracy. The people's role in the affairs of government has diminished, the political arena has shrunk, political demobilisation has become more the norm than the exception in regime behaviour, social engineering for political demobilisation (i.e. repression) is the preoccupation of most governments; all this has come about to cement one notorious but common aspect of all African governments: the use of public resources as possibilities for viable indigenous processes of development is neglected or destroyed altogether. *There is a definite correlation between the lack of democratic practices in African politics and the deteriorating socio–economic conditions.*

If governments are not accountable to the people they govern, then they are very likely to engage in socio–economic practices which are not responsive to people's needs. Questions of development and problems of economic crisis cannot therefore be meaningfully discussed without discussing problems regarding the nature of state power, the form of popular participation in the processes of government, and the question, therefore, of democracy. The state cannot just acquire or re-acquire the capacity and ability for positive socio-economic transformation: *it has to be somebody's state*. It must be a state responsive to the demands of the social forces that provide it with its power base, its legitimacy, its ability to hold social conflicts in check and its capacity to ensure the reproduction of society as a whole.

The essays published in this book approach this issue with the underlying concern of trying to understand whether the present political atmosphere in Africa is conducive to any kind of development of a positive kind, socialist or capitalist. *Prima-facie* evidence would tell us that it is not: if so, what kind of political context is needed for dealing with the present crisis? Is it our role as social analysts to provide an appropriate political recipe? Why is it that the popular masses which took such an active part in the national democratic struggles for independence no longer matter in the contemporary political arena? Is capitalist development in Africa compatible with the flourishing of popular democracy or is it because there is no development of capitalism that popular democracy is also suffocating? To what extent have the popular classes continued to struggle for both democracy and development? What explains the reluctance or inability of established regimes to respond to popular demands for much more meaningful social transformation? Have military coups produced regimes which do better, as far as the popular masses are concerned, than those overthrown? Can military rulers lead revolutions necessary for the democratisation of society and greater social progress? Should people, in the final analysis, obey governments which, rather than ensure social progress, merely oppress and terrorise them? What form should the people's revolt take if it is to serve their interests in a long-term perspective?

These questions cannot be answered without defining the precise relationship between politics and economic development in contemporary Africa, the basic task which this volume seeks to address. African governments have neglected this linkage by asserting that political stability and order — not democracy — are the preconditions for economic growth and prosperity. To the contrary, the position taken by all the essays in this book is that political liberties and the accountability of the state to the people (in particular the popular classes) is a precondition for material progress. Political liberties need not be sacrificed in return for economic benefits; in other words, authoritarianism, even in return for stability and economic prosperity, is ultimately unjust. This is an old premise in bourgeois political theory going at least as far back as J. J. Rousseau's *Social Contract*.[6] It is amplified in that recent and widely-acclaimed version of social justice under a social contract system advocated by John Rawls in his *Theory of Justice*.[7] It must, of course, be added that neither Rousseau nor Rawls ever justified 'the democracies of the few' that tend to be typical of certain Western political systems where structures of opportunity limit the extent to which the voice of the popular masses can really be effective in the political processes. If Marxian analyses of the sort included in this book have any additional contribution to make to this insight, it is along the lines of Marx himself in the *Economic and Philosophical Manuscripts of 1844*.[8] The message Marx delivers here is the following: instead of counterposing a trade-off between economic prosperity and political liberty, socialism points the way in which people can be *both* free and prosperous. In Africa today, broadly speaking, the popular classes lack both freedom and prosperity.

The basic themes, therefore, on which these essays focus are the following. First, the progressive degeneration of the state in Africa accompanied by the shift towards authoritarianism. This has tended to degenerate further into what Odera Oruka[9] calls 'state terrorism' as the neo-colonial state becomes weaker and weaker with the 'withering away' of its fiscal base. A weak and disorganised state, such as that of Mobutu's Zaire discussed by Nzongola Ntalaja, cannot repress with sophistication: it tends to rely more on terror, naked force and sheer blood-letting.

Second, the emasculation of the popular classes not only because the bourgeoisie needs a tight political control over them so as to ensure a certain model of accumulation but also because, in a weak state, popular participation in politics is by itself a threat to 'public security'. That means, of course, that accountability is grossly undermined and the state easily gets away with murder.

Third, the problem of the *international linkages* that keep weak states, even the ones which terrorise their own people every day, in the business of being legal sovereign states which have the right to do whatever they do because nobody should interfere 'in their own internal affairs'. Even without invoking the sovereignty principle, external forces keep such states in business by giving them loans, providing them with arms, signing friendly treaties with them, and so on. The extent to which international interests provide maternal care to conflicts generated in Africa as a result of state-sponsored terrorism is substantial.

Finally, these essays are concerned with examining the people's stand amid this crisis. When the people take the initiative in their own hands, when they rebel and resist, how do they do it? How do they struggle? How do they confront state power — internally and externally — and what explains their successes and failures? The essays observe that there has been one common denominator in the people's stand in post-colonial Africa: *that of popular alliances and popular coalitions* against oppression and exploitation. There have been problems of mobilising and sustaining popular alliances as the cases of Ghana and Sudan show. Such problems are of two types: those *internal* to the alliances themselves turning on ethnic, religious, regional, ideological and gerontocratic issues; and those *external* to the alliances which include the politics of the conjuncture, the material conditions under which they operate, the power of the state to repress, organise, disorganise and co-opt, and international linkages and pressures.

The role of the military in popular struggles for democracy, given the historical evidence in Africa that the military has been able to 'steal the revolution' from popular movements (as in Liberia under General Doe), or to attempt to emasculate the movements and restore the *ancien régime* in a new guise (as in the Sudan after Nimeiri), or make a revolution of its own by gunning its way to power (as in Ethiopia), is of prime importance in these discussions. The Ghanaian experience shows that a popular revolution can follow many twists and turns. What begins as a process of political change promising some positive outcome to the popular masses can become so reactionary in its consequences that the same popular masses may begin longing for the 'good old days' of conservative regimes, including colonialism itself. As the regime becomes more and more bankrupt in terms of ideas for positive social transformation, so does it grow richer in revolutionary slogans, billboards and attire. A basic general question is posed: to what extent can a military regime, given the nature of African armies as they are and as they were inherited from colonial times, undertake processes of social transformation favourable to the masses after a military coup?

It is to be noted that the military is itself part of the institution of the state whose civilian members the soldiers drive away from state power; so, when soldiers take over political power, the state remains as before. It is also to be noted that soldiers are themselves a part of the petty-bourgeois strata which compete for, and alternate in, the occupation of positions within the state. A coup may therefore result in a new configuration of forces occupying the executive branch involving not only soldiers but also other civilians — Marxist–Leninist intellectuals included — using the military as a bridgehead to get into the executive branch. The military regime may not live to honour and defend the interests of such elements; *a priori*, there is no way of telling how a military regime will behave once in power with respect to satisfying the constituency from which it gets or expects support. But the use of Marxism to rationalise repressive military regimes has obviously done a disservice to, and undermined the credibility of, both socialism and the revolutionary intelligentsia who join such regimes to make revolutions.

Further, the military is a special extension of dependency relations between the neo-colony and the outside world in technological, financial and intellectual terms. Foreign military training frequently means well-entrenched ideas among the decision-making echelons within the military which, because of the expertise they have in defending the state, may make them exceptionally authoritarian and resolute in thinking that they, and only they, have solutions to socio–economic problems. In perceiving issues in terms of technocratic expertise, discipline and precision, soldiers may not be patient with their civilian counterparts once they involve themselves in the day-to-day running of government after some brief training or orientation. Moreover, where they are handicapped by lack of knowledge and inability to grasp the intricacies of government and conflict resolution, command is likely to be their way out. Thus discussions may be kept to a minimum, popular participation held at bay and government becomes the affair of even more closely-knit groups than it ever was under the most authoritarian civilian regime. Emmanuel Hansen goes even further with this argument: 'conventional' military regimes, he contends, cannot, by their very nature, defend and sustain popular democratic political cultures. The ability to surprise and cheat both friends and foes alike becomes the mechanism by which the military skilfully wields power; the impact and use of surprise attack becomes a method by which insiders are exposed as 'betrayers of the revolution' when programmes fail and scapegoats are needed on which the responsibility and blame for failure is to be heaped.

Why, then, do progressive forces (or the left), leaders of the popular alliances struggling for the democratisation of society, join military regimes? What do they expect to achieve? What do they actually achieve?

The essays in this book present *three* distinct cases where the left has joined military regimes and attempt to provide reasons why this was done. The case of Liberia is one in which, once the *subjective* conditions began to ripen for the democratisation of society led by mass-based movements, the military intervened to take the initiative from these forces and 'make its own revolution'. Representatives of the popular movements were then invited into the government to give it credibility internally and externally, to teach the soldiers the appropriate popular slogans, limericks and even political economy, and then finally to be discarded when the soldiers no longer needed them. In other words, once the army felt secure in power, it quickly discarded representatives of the popular forces precisely because the latter, organisationally, were a threat to it.

The second example is that of Ghana. The Ghanaian left genuinely entertained desires for progressive changes in society. But it was precisely because it was weak organisationally that it felt it needed the umbrella of a military regime to put into practice its ideas. This was a case of trying to make a revolution within state power belonging to somebody else, and it is no wonder that the left was so easy to manipulate and dispense with at the pleasure of the men in uniform.

The Sudan presents a different strategy by the left. This strategy has involved pushing for regime change in coordination with segments of the army (patriotic officers) but maintaining the organisational autonomy of the popular forces while still struggling to dismantle the *ancien régime* and establish a popular democratic regime.

At the root of the strategic political mistake that the left has been making in joining military regimes is the conception of 'state power' as something that can be changed and be put to more progressive use once 'left personnel' occupy key positions in the state apparatus. This strategy by the left of making the revolution can be described as the equivalent of the Africanisation programmes of the sixties which assumed that appointing African managers and directors to some *key companies* would lead to the indigenous control of the commanding heights of the economy. This tendency sees the neo-colonial state itself as central to transforming social relations. What the state needs is just more forward-looking personnel, more individuals committed to the cause of the people. The left thus seeks to join the ruling class, and to create more and more spaces within it through the tactic of placing more left individuals in important state positions so as to incrementally establish left hegemony within the state. This argument was once eloquently advanced by some left individuals who joined the Amin regime. The consequences, to those individuals and to Uganda, have been sufficiently recounted by Mahmood Mamdani in *Imperialism and Fascism in Uganda*.[10]

To assume that popular politics can be incorporated into state-organised politics, and that the state will champion popular causes even though the popular forces do not control state power, is both utopian and adventurous. Such adventures have led the left to disastrous ends in places like Ghana; they continue to plague struggles for democracy by popular forces all over the continent. What, then, should be the correct approach towards state power by those forces waging the democratic struggle?

Lenin argued that the revolutionary forces cannot just lay hold on the state machinery and use it for their own ends; the first task is to *smash* the inherited state machinery, beginning with its apparatuses of repression, and then to create a new state commensurate with the demands of the revolution. That the Bolsheviks, in 1917, smashed the Tsarist state and created Soviets instead is a historical fact; but whether they succeeded in making a successful socialist revolution based on Soviet power is still controversial.

A similar approach of smashing state power in making popular democratic revolutions is emerging in Africa, not only in the protracted struggles in the Sudan but also in the more recent dramatic example of Uganda. In both cases, threats of counter-revolution are still very prominent. But these are post-independence examples of people's struggles for a second independence. The litmus paper of their success will be the extent to which they will manage to smash the neo-colonial state and erect a popular democratic state instead. The NRA's kiss of death may yet prove to be its hurry to make all kinds of unholy alliances in order to form a government. Again, it is the impatience of left forces to get into positions of political power, rather than first build social power among the people, which remains a plague of revolutionary or potentially revolutionary movements in Africa. That, again, is why particular attention should be paid to the history of the United Democratic Front and other popular movements in South Africa: to what extent will they struggle and conquer political power without any compromises with neo-colonialism?

We do not mean to paint a scenario full of pessimism. However repressive regimes have been in Africa, and however successful they might have been in defeating popular attempts at democratic change as the case of Congo (Brazzaville) shows, the people's impulse to struggle for freedom and social justice can never completely die. This struggle may take decades, but it will always be there, being expressed in different forms at different times: a hunger protest by the imprisoned, street riots over food prices, a people's boycott of dirty public transportation, demonstrations against racial discrimination, work stoppages and strikes by workers for better conditions of service and livable wages, and so on. Even in situations where the popular masses have enjoyed the benefits of economic growth but at the expense of their democratic rights, e.g. Malawi and Kenya, injustices inherent in such systems still lead to sporadic outbursts of discontent. Although the state in such situations has adopted reasonably sophisticated methods of both co-option and repression, issues of legitimacy as a result of limited political participation and lack of public accountability still undermine the capacity and authority of the state to rule.

Questions of development cannot be settled through technocratic arguments; development is, by its very nature, a political issue. The kind of development that will respond to Africa's problems must focus on problems affecting the popular masses: unemployment, food imports, illiteracy, malnutrition, poor health, inadequate recreation facilities, and so on. All these have to do with the ability of an economy to generate enough social surplus to be deployed into productive activities that generate employment and other basic needs within the home market. A state that will plan for this inward-looking, self-centred and self-sufficient development must be a state controlled by the popular forces and accountable to them. It cannot be somebody else's state and yet be expected to be people-oriented. Such a state can only be born as a result of a popular democratic revolution.

Even social democracy did not come to the European popular classes on a silver plate; they struggled for it and forced the European bourgeoisies to concede to and reckon with their social power. Yet today, in the Third World, an idea is making its rounds that well-reasoned position papers submitted to the North will lead to a restructuring of the world economic system in favour of the wretched of the earth in the South. This hope for a global social democracy, initiated by debates around a new international economic order, must now be re-examined critically in the context of popular struggles in the South for real sovereignty, national liberation, democracy and socialist revolution. The agenda, perhaps, will no longer be set by discussions in international fora but more by the changes occurring in the Third World as a result of the revolt of the popular classes.

## Notes

1. See E. H. Carr, *The Bolshevik Revolution, 1917–23* 3 vols. (Harmondsworth: Penguin, 1966).

2. A. Hamilton *et al.*, *The Federalist Papers* (Middletown: Wesleyan Press, 1961).

3. World Bank, *Accelerated Development in Sub-Saharan Africa: An Agenda for Action* (World Bank: Washington, 1981).

4. The Organization of African Unity, *The Lagos Plan of Action* (OAU: Addis Ababa, 1980).

5. See Thandika Mkandawire, 'African State Responses to Economic Cycles and Economic Crises', *Eastern Africa Social Science Research Review*, vol. I, no. 2, 1985.

6. J. J. Rousseau, *The Social Contract* (Harmondsworth: Penguin, 1964).

7. John Rawls, *Theory of Justice* (Cambridge: Harvard University Press, 1971).

8. Karl Marx, *Economic and Philosophical Manuscripts*.

9. See, for example, Odera Oruka, 'State Disarmament: A Question for Regional Security and Military Disarmament in Africa', *Philosophy and Social Action*, vol. VIII, no. 3, 1982, p. 21 (New York: International Publishers, 1967).

10. Mahmood Mamdani, *Imperialism and Fascism in Uganda* (London: Heinemann, 1983).

# 2 The State, Development and the Need for Participatory Democracy in Africa

by Harry Goulbourne

Undoubtedly, one of the main characteristics of the state in independent countries in Africa has been the overwhelming presence it has sought to effect in nearly all areas of social, economic and, of course, political life. This feature of the post-colonial state on the continent has been repeatedly commented upon both as a matter for theoretical discussion as well as an issue for publication. It has been unfortunate, however, that the general concern over questions of democracy and active participation which was so central to the struggle for political independence, has been absent from general discussions; at best this concern has been given low priority. The principal aim of this chapter, therefore, is to attempt to reintroduce into the debate over the future of Africa some legitimate questions regarding democratic institutions and citizenry participation in the *res publica*. These questions will of necessity be linked to what is usually seen as the central problem facing all societies in Africa as she approaches the twenty-first century, namely, the question of development.

A general discussion of this kind is likely to irritate some who are intensely engaged in the day-to-day activities of coping with the practical problems of management and politics, particularly in those states where leaders are genuine in their attempts to overcome pressing problems with very limited resources. The discussion is also likely to irritate those who are of the dubious persuasion that only the specific, the concrete, blow-for-blow experiences of the peoples of the continent warrant discussion and that there are no worthwhile general remarks to be made about the collective experience of the continent. It is my view, however, that generalised statements about the African condition are warranted, *per se*, and, second, that the experiences of the past two decades or more of independent governments on the continent call for general comments of the kind which came out of the struggle for independence itself, such as, for example, Fanon's *The Wretched of the Earth*.[1] Of course, one assumption here is that the common colonial experience, the fight for independence, past and present forms of oppression and exploitation, etc., of the continent's peoples not only mark off the African collective experience but also constitute a common basis for continental action and coordination, and therefore, invite general comments. Such an approach to, or view of, Africa as we approach the end of one and the beginning of another century, in no way belittles the specific or particular experiences of people or peoples in any one or other country today. In short, the aim in this admittedly general essay is to pull

26

together some overall trends so as to form an individual statement about the continent.

I am also very much aware of the legitimate hostility which a piece of this kind may evoke, since I am not directly engaged in the day-to-day struggle for Africa. But in this regard I would wish to stress one point only: the concern over the past, present and future of Africa has long been the business of the African peoples, at home and in the diaspora, albeit in different degrees, for the better part of the post-Renaissance period during which Europe (and her diaspora) have been in a continuous unequal relationship with Africa. These comments are, therefore, made in the spirit of this historical concern for the continent.

## Democracy and control

In the dialectics between democratic practice and political control there is always a severe tension. This tension is sometimes expressed in terms of which set of principles should take precedence over the other — increased popular participation, for example, or greater efficiency. During times of war, national emergencies, sudden crises and so forth, the emphasis on *control* is usually considered to be the proper one; in times of normalcy or stability good management is often contrasted with inefficiency, which is sometimes believed to be the result of active democratic participation. Democracy is sometimes seen as costly, time-wasting; central control as efficient and cost-effective. Democracy and control are not, therefore, complementary, but more often than not contradictory phenomena in any social order.

The outcome of this tension in country after country in independent Africa over the past two or so decades has been that control has won out over active popular participation in those countries where identifiable political structures are evident. In these states the overriding concern has been to effect means of tight control over the activities of citizens, and political creativity has been exhibited chiefly in the construction of means to eradicate or at best limit and curtail democratic participation. In other words, the widespread concern over the generalisation of democratic participation of people who fought for independence against the various colonial powers who carved up Africa before and after the Congress of Berlin in 1883, have had little effect on the new political institutions and forms of political practices which have emerged since independence. In the making of a new Africa in the post-independence period, questions relating to the continuation and strengthening of active citizen participation in national or local affairs have been too easily elbowed out of the legitimate frame of urgent and immediate concerns. The refining of methods of control has been, in general, the prime consideration. Before proceeding with the discussion in terms of focusing on such concepts as democracy, participation and the like, it may be useful to consider briefly the opposite of these (which should make the task of definition itself easier as the argument develops) in terms of the anti-democratic political tradition which has been fostered.

First, the general problem may be approached from the perspective of the state forms and regime types which have emerged during the last quarter of a century or so in which most African colonies became independent states. Almost without exception, the states in post-colonial Africa have moved rapidly in an interventionist direction. Of course such a development is in no way unusual, because this course has also been taken elsewhere, both under conditions of advanced and underdeveloped capitalism. It is sometimes assumed, even after the debates over the capitalist state from the late 1960s and throughout the 1970s, that the state in advanced capitalism is, or used to be, of a non-interventionist nature in terms of having significant inputs in the regulating of the economy and the perceived proper relationship between groups and individuals in civil society and the economy. This is not and never was quite the case. The widespread practice of the capitalist state has been first to establish the basic ground rules for peaceful market relations (free labour power, the growth of commoditisation, etc.) as well as to assist in the construction of the material infrastructure necessary for capital accumulation. Later on the capitalist state became more directly involved with both the social arrangements between individuals as well as the productive capacity of its territorial base. Thus, in the early phase of capitalist development the state was the principal protector of the emergent bourgeoisie, and as capitalism evolved a highly complex social division of labour along with an integrated social and economic system, the political became more and more intertwined with these. It is therefore interesting that the liberal phase of the capitalist state (chiefly in Britain) has for so long been taken to be the typical or preferred form for the state in capitalist societies. The basic point, however, is that the fact of interventionism which characterises the state in independent Africa is far from being unique, with respect to the state in advanced capitalist societies.

The same is true with respect to the state in countries which are ostensibly socialist. In these situations the state has come to be expected to be highly centralised because of the emphasis on highly centralised and controlled planning since the Bolshevik experience under both Lenin and Stalin in the Soviet Union. The question of the nature of the form of this kind of socialist state is in some respects less problematic than in capitalist societies where the liberal tradition has taken hold; interventionism is taken for granted. Of course, such highly centralised states as in the present East Europe and elsewhere pose questions of a profoundly democratic nature for the more general socialist vision of a greater, not a less, democratic social order. At present, however, these questions are not generally and directly faced in Africa because, despite profession of socialism, the central problem in terms of political norms has to do with the very basic question of traditional rights being enjoyed by ordinary citizens. Undoubtedly, however, the centrality of the state in some ostensibly socialist states has much the same effect as the highly interventionist states in Africa, namely, the drastic curtailing of basic political and civil rights of citizens.

The post-colonial state in Africa, then, moves along a regularly beaten path of development: it is highly centralised, overbearing and restrictive in its operations. It seeks to concentrate state power in one or two state institutions and to make this power available to the executive arm of the government; often this means one person and/or the very small group of men around him. The interventionist state in Africa attempts to curtail and restrict the social life of citizens, often employing the most draconian and sometimes petty means available. In the economic sphere, this type of interventionist state attempts to effect near total control over all economic activities. The attempt usually takes different forms: sometimes the state claims that it is nationalising industrial, agricultural, commercial, etc., enterprises for the good of the country as a whole; at other times the state simply assists private capital to function more efficiently; and there are also situations in which the state's various institutions are so many bodies for the syphoning away of public funds into private hands. In terms of politics, the state generally outlaws all legitimate oppositional voices and even gestures; it denies, in general, even the minimum space for political discussion by citizens, thus effecting the very opposite of what were fought for during the nationalist period.

Nonetheless, the state in Africa is not identical to the interventionist state either under conditions of advanced capitalism or the socialist states of East Europe and elsewhere. In the first place, the state in nearly all African countries lacks the technological basis for an efficient participation in the social and economic life of society. In some academic and political circles the view is often expressed that failure to implement what would appear to be sound policies rests largely with administrators who lack motivation and know-how. It is true of course that these are too often unfortunately absent, but one basic aspect of the problem is the lack of an appropriate technological foundation which provides its own momentum for efficiency. Declarations, exhortations and so forth have not overcome this very real physical drawback with respect to the implementation of public policies. In the political sphere, this inefficiency is often the saving factor with respect to the lives and freedom of citizens. In other words, if the interventionist state in African countries were able to execute efficiently most of what leaders and regimes desire, then many of these states would have to be regarded as being fascist states. Paradoxically, therefore, it is sheer inefficiency which sometimes acts as protection against arbitrary treatment by one or the other state institutions and leaders. The reports rampant in January and February 1986 of General Okello's government troops looting and laying the countryside bare as they retreated from Kampala were, sadly, not unusual because these men had the wherewithal to enforce their will cruelly.

Democratic institutions and practices cannot be taken for granted in any society in which these are upheld, however imperfectly. People have had to fight for their establishment, defend them and ensure that they were constantly reaffirmed. In some places the right of citizens to express themselves freely is sometimes seen as a right given by the state and may therefore be withdrawn at any given time by the president or the government of the day. This view informed a letter some months ago by a Tanzanian student studying abroad to the editor of the government-owned *Daily News*. The letter objected to the publication of a witty column by one of the paper's reporters. The student was particularly concerned about a journalist being critical of leaders in a newspaper owned by the government; the reporter was abusing the right to write given by the government.

The view that citizens have rights separate and apart, independently of the state, and that the government derives its legitimacy from the people, are not sufficiently ingrained into the social, ideological and political fabric of many societies, at least not to the extent of ensuring that in general the government respects the necessary space between the state and civil society. But, if in some societies the rights of citizens need to be defended, in too many countries on the continent these rights still need to be established. In too many countries the very wherewithal of either the means to establish or defend democratic participation is absent.

This means that the first generation of post-colonial leaders in Africa has failed in one of the most important and far-reaching tasks of this era in the history of Africa — development of democratic institutions and modes of conducting public affairs. The first generation of leaders had a unique opportunity to set in motion the further development of democratic institutions, practices and conventions. First, there was the tremendous enthusiasm of the people for building a new social order, an enthusiasm born out of the struggle for political independence and which was still buoyant in the years immediately after independence. Second, the first generation of leaders throughout the continent enjoyed an authority which went beyond that derived from popular elections, etc.; they nearly all enjoyed something of what Weber called charismatic authority by virtue of being the leader who had challenged the colonial power and forged the path to political independence.

If the failure to develop or encourage a democratic political tradition seems an unimportant point, then it is worth considering for a moment the persistence of political institutions and modes of political behaviour once they are established in any society. For example, the convention of addressing the US president as plain Mr President rather than his excellency, or in some such grand manner, has lived on since the founding fathers decided that it smacked of royalism and the old Europe to refer to the President as anything else. A new state needs to establish conventions and, these being what they are, succeeding generations tend on the whole to follow them. Although there is at least one notably potential exception, it must be said that the possibility of a tolerant, participatory political tradition emerging and developing in the continent as a whole seems very bleak indeed. The founding fathers have long ago jeopardised this possibility which was present at political independence.

The tradition of intolerance, refusal to concede that a person or groups may have views contrary to those of leaders which may at the very least be worth hearing, have helped to make the state of even more central importance than would otherwise have been the case. In its attempt to intervene in all aspects of social life, the state not only becomes increasingly menacing, it also becomes crucial for any person and group with a project of any kind. Having no clearly defined boundaries beyond which it would be reluctant to exercise its authority or interference, the state becomes a major hurdle or obstacle in nearly every walk of life. It is not only that the boundaries between state and civil society are thereby blurred, but the expected space between institutions within the state disappear and the determined individual or group must be prepared to face the state in a hostile manner, even with the most innocent project. The depressing results are either that the individual or group must become outlaws, men and women operating outside the (arbitrary) framework of the law and bureaucratic politics, or they challenge the legitimacy and authority of the ruling group through one or the other of the very state institutions (usually the military).

In such a situation it becomes necessary for ambitious men with whatever project either to have direct access to the ruling clique or to have direct control of the instruments of the state themselves. Energies get dispersed; the development of the division of labour so necessary in the building of modern societies is frustrated because the businessman must be more of a politician than is usual and the politician must be more of a businessman than he might otherwise be. And, of course, neither set of activities gets done efficiently because there is an absence of definite purpose in most cases: leaders are sometimes neither businessmen nor politicians.

Before continuing with some of the implications of excessive state control it is pertinent to return to the central point at this stage of the discussion, namely, the question of how to understand the interventionist state in Africa. It must now be clear from what has been said so far that, irrespective of how states may describe themselves, we need to consider, independently, whether their labels are useful with respect to their actions. In other words, are these states to be accepted as being in the typical mould of 'capitalist' or 'socialist' etc. states or are they representing new forms which analysts need to pay attention to? For example, perhaps apart from the interlude in the late 1970s of the Emperor Bokassa of the Central African Empire, all African leaders in the post-colonial period have declared themselves at one point or another to be socialist. It is tempting to say that these declarations meant nothing since they certainly did not describe very much or indicate a great deal about the intentions of most of these governments, but it could be argued that the declarations by themselves indicated that leaders and their regimes felt that they had to respond to the popular demands for democratic participation and a fairer distribution of national resources. In any case, the word socialist has not been descriptive of these states, and in general the societies in which they have sprung up retain their underdeveloped capitalist characteristics as well as the highly undemocratic political forms inherited from colonialism.

The outstanding institutional feature of these interventionist states remains the prevalence of what has been described as 'presidentialism'. Basically the phenomenon of presidentialism involves the centralisation of state power in the hands of president and/or his office. The incumbent is supposed to represent the people as a whole in nearly all matters relating to the country. Nonetheless, many presidents derive their authority not from any popular electoral mandate but through sheer incumbency. There is the case, for example, of one country which is generally regarded as being comparatively democratic, in which the sole political party puts forward one candidate for election to the presidency. But where there is only one candidate for election to a post it is a well-known electoral practice that there is no need for election, and the candidate is returned and is deemed to have been unopposed. This is also supposed to demonstrate his popularity in the country, and the newspapers usually hail his election as a great victory. In that country, as in some others, presidents have never actually gone to the country for popular election because candidates have never been opposed, it being illegal to put forward a candidate from outside the *de facto* single party which becomes the *de jure* sole political party.

We are of course familiar with the development of the phenomenon of presidentialism on the continent since independence: the leader of the nationalist

31

movement soon after the hoisting of the new national flag declares himself president, abolishing any distinction there may have been in the transition to independence between different institutional sources of power (such as between prime minister and president). In effect the president becomes a 'king' sometimes for a term of years, sometimes indefinitely. Where the leader fails to become president almost immediately after independence, this delay is usually due to some particular problem, as is the case in Zimbabwe today where two or more parties vie for power. And in such a situation the conditions to be overcome are presented by the regime as the main issue in national politics. In Uganda under Obote's first presidency, the main problem was seen as the independence of the Bugandans; in Zimbabwe, it appears to be the existence of ZAPU; and there have been plenty of similar examples over the last twenty years or so in different parts of the continent. In some cases the new president is merely the military leader trying to establish a base or a political legitimacy for his despotic regime, as is the very recent case in Doe's Liberia.

The types of regimes which have emerged in Africa in the post-independence years have generally complemented the interventionist state form that has developed over the years. But whereas presidentialism has been a unified pattern throughout the continent, regimes have varied significantly from place to place. And such variations have sometimes marked major differences between countries such as, say, Tanzania and Kenya or the Ivory Coast and Nigeria. The variety of types of regimes to be found include the multi-party parliamentary (such as Zimbabwe, Senegal), restricted parliamentary, despotic, military, one-party, disintegrated authority and of course the cases of South Africa (which some would say is a colony) and Namibia.

Much of what I have said so far applies to states with identifiable structures, and there are those in which it would be difficult to identify any permanent structures at all. For example, at the present time, in the sad and depressing cases of Uganda, Chad and, to some extent, Ghana, it can hardly be said that they are in the same category or categories as the majority of states in the continent. These are examples of disintegrated states where the drift beyond any common sense of values, law, order and the absence of stability are such that it is difficult to speak of there being a 'state' at all either in the Weberian sense in which authority is exercised within definite territorial boundaries and the state possesses a monopoly of force within such boundaries; or yet in the Marxist sense in which the state is not merely a set of formal institutions but also and perhaps more importantly an ensemble of social relationships. As for the multi-party, parliamentary regime type, this can hardly be said to exist: at best there is the one-party dominant regime (such as Senegal); the unique situation of Zimbabwe is unlikely to last for very long in the face of ZANU's intention to create a one-party state either before or after the Lancaster House Agreement period runs out. In this regard, however, the case of South Africa, once majority rule is established, may be hopeful not only in terms of the country having the basis for multiparty democracy, but also because there will then be the conditions whereby the question of open and free political life can be introduced into the region.

Overall, therefore, the continent's leaders have generally opted for types of regimes which promise to provide effective control over political life as well as society in general. In this regard military rule and the one-party system have been the most attractive to leaders. In the case of the military, politicians are provided with perhaps the most effective (after the despotic?) regime, in terms of brute force and the convenient abolition of any democratic participation and procedures. The military regime, then, has proven itself over the years to be the most direct answer to impatient men eager to assume the reins of formal state power and this is not only true for men of a military background, but also for civilian politicians for whom the division between military and civilian is very blurred. It should be noted however that the predominance of the military in political life on the continent reflects also a widespread frustration with civilian authorities over inefficiency, corruption (as in Ghana and Nigeria throughout the years of their independence) and sometimes the ruthless manipulation of ethnic, tribal or regional differences. Nonetheless, although military rule usually promises quick solutions and ready courses of action, it also usually tends to compound the very problems it claims to wish to redeem the country from. Apart from its inability to stimulate the enthusiasim of the people and its inability to stem the tide of corruption — in short, its inability turn the country around and bring democratic participation into existence — the military's principal weakness is that it cannot provide regimes with the necessary political legitimacy for good government. Military regimes are essentially non-democratic and they eschew uncontrolled, voluntary participation. Consequently, instead of resolving the problems in any way, they generally compound them.

The one-party regime has so far been the organisational expression of the most stable and acceptable type of regimes on the continent. If only for this reason the single-party system in Africa is worth more than mention; but it deserves attention also because it represents the type of regime which has so far come closest in some particulars to effecting a modicum of democratic participation in some of the countries on the continent.

Essentially, the one-party system provides leaders with a relatively democratic organisation which may be used to rouse, exhort and encourage people towards desired ends and also allows for a limited degree of participation in public affairs by ordinary citizens. In these ways the contradictory urges on the one hand of the people for democratic participation and on the other hand of leaders to effect tight control may be accommodated in the same body. The party comes to express the contradictory nature of politics whilst at the same time establishing a framework within which leaders need not feel too threatened, especially since the party is usually fashioned in the image of the leadership. The point, then, is not that the party is a democratic institution; on the contrary, it is designed both in terms of its actual structure and in terms of its philosophy to effect control and limit democratic participation. Despite this, however, the party sometimes develops to become a body through which astute individuals and/or groups may achieve a very slight degree of active participation, particularly in matters which are not perceived by the senior leaders to be in any way a threat to their positions in the party or government or country at large. The single political party, therefore, may reproduce a government's political legitimacy whilst effecting the kind of tight control over politics and state institutions which political leaders desire.

Where the nationalist leader stands out head and shoulders above other senior figures in the leadership, the single political party, representing the leader in organisational terms, develops to become the institution which is regarded to be supreme over all other institutions of state and eventually over vast areas of civil society. The political party in Africa is very innovative in its design as well as in its spread: it is not restricted to any particular area of political or even social life, it reaches out in all directions, at least in terms of its rhetoric and its broad intentions. It therefore performs ideological as well as repressive tasks (à la Althusser)[2]; it is at once part of the state and of civil society. Where the single political party functions comparatively efficiently it is therefore more than a political party in the sense that it is not restricted to what would be ordinarily regarded as the political sphere or to what Nicos Poulantzas would have called the sphere of politics.[3]

In Africa, then, the political party unlike, say, parliament has again demonstrated that it is capable of adjusting to new conditions. It is therefore this organisation that is used by astute politicians to consolidate their hold over other state institutions such as parliament, the civil service (where this is reasonably achieved), the heads of parastatals, the government itself. The political party is therefore perhaps the only institution of state which enjoys, first, the organisational capacity to integrate diverse contradictory elements and is therefore pre-eminently useful in conditions of constructing 'new states' and/or new 'nation states'. Second, it is perhaps the only institution in the post-independence period which can claim to any significant degree to be comparatively indigenous (due largely to its adaptability). The other institution which relates to the modern world and to indigenous values, the Church, is not an overt state institution (Althusser notwithstanding) and therefore does not have the same clout in the political arena as the political party. And, finally in this regard, the political party is the central formal institution which was closely wrapped up in the nationalist struggle for political independence; and this itself endows a significant degree of legitimacy, particularly in an arena in which there are not very many semi-political, professional, or associational groups.

But just as it is a mistake to see the state as an independent force standing over society, so too is it a mistake to regard the party as an independent political unit or force within or outside the state. The important point here is that the party tends to perform its task under the direction of the political executive. Therefore, it is in those countries on the continent where leaders genuinely wish to establish a mix of democracy with widespread central control, in which we find the party situated as a buffer between the repressive institutions of the state and civil society. One-partyism and benevolent presidentialism tend, therefore, to go hand in hand where the political leadership is serious about its business and therefore allows for a modicum of participation.

Even in this situation, however, the cumulative effect of the development of the post-colonial state in Africa has been the relative absence of politics in the sense that open, free discussion about politics or public affairs cannot be taken for granted. State reprisals follow the most trivial, ordinary statements about matters of general public interest. The public tends to hear of decisions reached behind closed doors but presented as being democratic decisions. This presents a major problem for political analysts of African development — the exaggerated problem of how to analyse what Bachrach and Baratz called 'the second face of power' with respect to decision-making.[4] We hear of decisions and, if an analyst is sufficiently close to the centres of power or is willing to speculate and press questions like the journalist, then he or she may be able to hear what amounts to circumstantial rumours of how this or that politician acted, thought, was rebuked, and so forth, but none of these are expressed in the open. It is therefore very difficult to analyse political phenomena in Africa.

But the destruction of the birth of democracy in post-independent Africa was accompanied by a number of spurious arguments presented by prominent nationalist leaders. In other words, instead of using their immense authority to further the development of democratic sentiments, democratic practices and institutions, the first generation of post-independence leaders threw their weight behind the construction of a variety of repressive systems and used their authority to justify these new forms of repression.

First, the universal argument was that, being new states engaged in the process of nation-building, the unity achieved during the nationalist struggle for political independence should be maintained at all costs. It was as if, whilst the people wanted to advance to the aims of that struggle, leaders wanted to consolidate whatever they thought they had won for themselves and wanted the people to be less demanding. National unity was pitched against open politics; it was seen as a choice between the one or the other. The declared search for consensus which presumably formed the basis of national unity, was short-circuited and a 'unity' imposed from above through the repressive state institutions. Sometimes this unity — which, of course, served to hide real and substantial differences — was defended or justified as being socialism and, therefore, those who were ostensibly against unity were also, by force of the argument, against the ideals of socialism. Altogether, it was a convenient way of sidestepping questions regarding democracy, participation and genuine nationbuilding; that is to say, creating conditions within which individuals have the right to disagree without recourse by leaders to the use of state violence against them.

A second argument which was sometimes advanced was that the institutions and beliefs which are generally accepted as being the essential elements of democracy are colonial in character, or, in any case, came from the former imperialist countries and are, therefore, if only presumably by association, unacceptable. The argument, of course, conveniently ignores the fact that it was not part of the experience of colonial Africa to enjoy the democratic forms and practices of the former imperialist countries, and therefore, the experience of these practices and institutions cannot be described as 'colonial'. Second, these are not the products merely of the imperialists; they are the results of protracted class struggles in the very heartlands of the imperialist centres themselves. Simply because a thing comes from the imperialist countries themselves, it is not sufficient cause to assume that it is not worth emulating.

But a basic misconception in this form of argument needs to be stated more clearly and rejected. This is the deep-rooted assumption that what we generally refer to as bourgeois freedoms and democracy are entirely of the making of this

35

class; the traditional democratic rights of freedom of assembly, worship, freedom to publish, freedom of speech, etc. are seen as 'bourgeois' and, therefore, if only by implication, can be justifiably dismissed. These rights and freedoms which have come to define democracy to a significant degree are not, however, entirely of the making of the bourgeoisie and are therefore not entirely 'bourgeois'. It is from this perspective, then, that the socialist vision sees democracy of the 'bourgeois' period being transformed, advanced and added to so as to generalise socially these freedoms and rights and to rid them of the 'bourgeois' entanglements which make it difficult to realise them to their full potential.

A third reason usually advanced, coherently or otherwise, during the construction of the would-be monolithic and certainly excessively repressive state in Africa in the post-colonial period was that to effect rapid development it was necessary first to put controls in place. This argument maintained that much political disputation was bound to result in distraction from the main national effort, namely development. According to this view, it seemed that leaders and their regimes would be taking the question of national development seriously and therefore it was legitimate or reasonable to consider putting aside some less pressing issues in pursuit of the universal goal and development, understood in a largely if not exclusively material sense only. In this way the questions of development and democratic participation were presented in the sharpest possible way by regimes themselves. And it was not too difficult to see the partial truth of the situation they describe. Certainly there has been the fact that the new states in Africa have been suddenly confronted with a number of major problems which most other states faced in different historical periods and were able to address one at a time. For example, there have been the problems of national integration, the making of new political institutions and the forging of a national consensus over, sometimes, basic issues. Second, in parts of the continent, leaders and their regimes had to confront both the very pressing problem of physical intervention by the fascist government of South Africa and, until the revolution in Portugal and the independence of Angola and Mozambique in the mid-1970s, the might of that last colonial power, supported by NATO.

A second set of reasons which would appear to justify the argument that, if rapid development were to take place then it would be as well to put aside the question of democratic participation, arises from the general view that democracy and development are in any event contradictory elements. The argument seems to run something like this: a poor country cannot afford to dissipate its energies in the niceties, or luxuries, of allowing all and sundry to put their views about national matters when the task of prosecuting development is the national project over which independence was fought. In any event the argument implied that the forms of democratic participation seen in the countries of the former colonial power fell short of true democracy.

A second aspect of this argument is that in any event democracy is not a necessary condition for development. Now there has never been general agreement on the question of whether development is necessarily preceded by active participation or whether the reverse is the more correct order. There are historical cases to support either side of the argument: in some societies development and democratic participation went hand in hand with each other; in some other societies, the one went before the other. In still other societies (admittedly few and far between) democratic participation and institutions were present long before the kind of rapid economic development necessary to transform society.

The question of the relationship between democracy and development with respect to Africa is not really a question to be answered by reference to general principles alone. The specific experiences of the people in the different countries who fought for independence, whether peacefully or by means of war, point to one important fact, namely that during that struggle a high degree of popular democratic participation occurred and the contention here is that this experience was the historical basis from which democracy on the continent could have emerged. It is still the historical experience from which democratic patriots may one day draw their inspiration when they come to construct a democratic social order in specific countries. It might be added at this point that in any event the decline of democracy in the name of rapid economic development has been futile because this development has not been achieved after over twenty-five years of political independence on the continent.

## Underdevelopment and participation

The explanation of the development of an uncompromising, intolerant and repressive political tradition in Africa cannot, of course, be restricted to the justifications offered by leaders and their regimes. These must be set against the objective conditions in which leaders operate and which set the material limits on options available to them. As noted earlier, these do not, contrary to the views of some leaders, necessarily mean that the chances of democracy being established in these countries were so very slim; nonetheless, it is useful to remind ourselves of these limiting or inhibiting conditions.

First, there can be little doubt that the underdevelopment of social classes in Africa has been an inhibiting factor on many aspects of development, including politics and the state. In the first place, before political independence there was an absence of a dominant bourgeoisie. The fight for independence was not therefore a struggle waged under the leadership of a national social class confident in its social and economic status and power and seeking political power to finalise the moulding of society and institutions in its own image. Although some nationalists were inspired by the struggle of the American colonials against Britain, the situation of Africa during the struggle for political independence was quite different from that in the British American colonies at the time of the Boston Tea Party or at the signing of the Declaration of Independence in the 18th Century. There, as Charles Beard[5] argued, the emerging dominant class of settlers came to a point where political independence was important for their further development; leaders of the rebellion were members of this dominant class. There was a quite clear economic basis for the rebellion from the point of view of this class. This was to be seen in the later debates both over federalism and between Hamilton and Jefferson over the course of development in the US.[6] The struggle for independence in Africa, on the other hand, had no such clear class economic interest in view, largely because the emergent incipient dominant social class was so much less developed.

37

The class which was catapulted into positions of power after independence was, in general terms, rather ill-formed, economically weak and often fragmented through ethnic, racial, regional, etc. loyalties and identities. The claims of the class on the offices of the state were based almost entirely on the grounds that there ought not to be foreigners ruling over the population — a justified political or moral claim. But this political nationalism did not always go far enough to bring into question other related issues such as economic control and distribution within the specific countries. Nationalism, however, gave control of the state to this class and nationalism was to become the mainstay of this first generation of post-independence leaders. If the colonial power could be successfully challenged through nationalism, perhaps critics of the leader and his regime could also be silenced by appeal to nationalism. Nationalist sentiments such as unity against the enemy, which were of pre-eminent importance in some countries during the struggle against the colonial power — and, in the post-independence period, a leader's appeal for 'unity' — could stand out against all other voices; national 'unity' was deemed more important than discussion over alternatives. When we consider the manifold problems the majority of states are facing in terms of internal disruptions, civil wars, frequent coups and the like, the argument about national unity justifying the silencing of discordant voices is seen for what it often is in reality — a hollow claim.

Of course, apart from the broad force of nationalism, there were a number of important strategic positions which assisted the emergent petty-bourgeoisie in its accumulation of political power. There was the position of physical proximity to the colonial city. This proximity would benefit tribes, occupational groups or ambitious individuals. The general and relative absence of a firm economic base to the new formal ruling classes of Africa, particularly immediately after independence, led not to the realisation of Cabral's[7] rather utopian hope that the middle classes would commit class suicide, but, rather, to the more expected course of development — rapid class differentiation.

In this process of development, public office becomes the means whereby a base in the economy can be carved out by hitherto ill-formed social elements bent on rapid class transformation. These elements are then committed to the project of creating conditions for their own development. This takes different forms in different countries. In some it is the path of state capitalism, characterised by excessive central regulation of the economy in the name of socialism — for example, in Tanzania particularly between 1967 and 1985, but there are plenty of other examples. In other countries the process sometimes takes the form of uncompromising private accumulation, also using the state; for example Kenya and Ivory Coast are often seen in this way. In still other instances, the process was carried out on the basis of widespread warlordism and each strong man helps himself to whatever he can from for example the national purse or direct expropriation from peasants; Uganda since 1971, Ghana, and Nimeiri's Sudan are not bad examples of this form of 'development'. Whatever the course of development, the political profile comes to look depressingly alike in the majority of cases: 'socialism' here, 'capitalism' there, but the remarkable thing is that the overall picture is very much the same for the continent as a whole with respect to this large matter of class development and the utilisation of the instruments of the state. In saying this, I do not wish, however, to include all developments, some highly commendable, in countries such as Tanzania, Kenya and the Ivory Coast, with the almost totally deplorable situations in some countries such as Uganda under Amin, Obote and Okello and the Sudan before the overthrow of Nimeiri in early 1985.

In the endeavour to create conditions for their growth, the incipient petty bourgeoisie in African countries have attempted to use whatever aids they could. One of these has been the image/example set by the departing political order — namely the despotic model of government. Central to this model was, of course, the governor. It has variously been argued that in parts of the ex-colonial world (for example the Anglophone Caribbean) people have not had the opportunity to look back in their history at alternative political forms (an absence of autochthony) whereas in Africa this has not been the case. There may be some truth in this assertion but what is perhaps much more interesting in the case of the continent, and so often overlooked, is the fact that leaders in Africa generally have done nothing more than revert to the example of the former colonial executive system as the model from which to build a new political order. This system had at its very centre a governor whose personal, political will and preferences were largely important in the determination of state action within a general framework established by the imperial power in the metropolis and conditioned by the particularistic interests in the colony, which had partly been responsible for the establishment of the colony in its political and military frame in the first place. In general terms, therefore, it may be pointed out that, just as the colonial governor and his executives were the central piece of a political order, so today is the president and his coterie of experts both national and foreign. The contradictions of power flow through the office of the president where states can be clearly identified and it has no place where states can hardly be said to be in existence.

The essential difference between the colonial and the independent political orders is that the latter has a basis of political legitimacy whereas the former never had, other than the act of conquest and the white man's burden — which he had himself chosen to carry in the first place. The extent of the legitimacy is of course being constantly questioned and challenged in most of the continent, leading to constant eruptions, civil wars and disturbances, so that the continent and her people have not been able to settle down to the main tasks of constructing a viable order and one relevant to the need of the continent since the beginning of the process of political independence. The tragic situation of Ghana, which achieved political independence first, illustrates clearly the case of the continent in the most dramatic way. Nkrumah's political kingdom has not led to all things being given unto the ordinary man and woman who fought for political independence and the expected coming of a new deal or a fair deal or the beginnings of a good society. None of these come forth as promised at the dawning of the new day in the 1950s and the 1960s. Political order has been at best intermittent and political legitimacy, at least since Kofi Busia, if not since Nkrumah himself, tenuous.

To speak of a low level of class development with respect to the dominant class is also to comment on the conditions of the dominated classes. The working classes in

Africa have not successfully developed political forms of expression independent of the dominant class, which is itself engaged in its own construction. In at least one respect this is a little surprising because, although the social and technological forces in Africa have not been developed to the extent of making these divisions very clear, they have nonetheless been enough to make it possible for the working classes and the peasantry to stake an independent claim for themselves. If we consider for a moment the articulation of class interests in Europe at a time when there was no model to look at, the emerging working classes were able to ensure that the development of such forces as democracy, participation, and ideology did not develop independently of their own class interests, thereby modifying important aspects of bourgeois class society. In Africa the only significant input of the working classes has been one largely wrapped in the ideological rather than the political reality of regimes — namely, the postulation of the ideology of socialism as the official ideology of the vast majority of states. In other words, it may be argued that the acceptance of such a posture reflects the influence of labour but this of itself is very little because it does not get reflected in the actual policies of most governments/regimes. Expressed yet another way, it could be said that whereas the petty bourgeoisie has gained much from political independence, those who joined in the fight for it (peasants and workers) have gained comparatively little in the overwhelming majority of cases. They have been used as cannon fodder and consequently the new social order does not reflect the total span of contributions and may not do so for some considerable time to come.

Low class development, therefore, has not only affected the behaviour and practice of the dominant class in the making but also the political agenda of the dominated classes in post-independence Africa. Because of the delayed development and differentiation of social classes, as well as the opportunities available for would-be leaders of the dominated classes, individuals with leadership qualities and vision became entrapped by the nationalist vision of a new Africa which was itself none too clear. What was, however, clear about this vision was that the sky was the limit for those individuals who had such capabilities, provided they became part of the project of constructing a new dominant class. This development has been the most significant of all changes that have taken place in most countries on the continent in the post-independence period, and it is likely to continue to be so for perhaps a considerable time.

Finally, in a discussion of this kind, it must be made clear that these developments are taking place within the framework of dependence bred of underdevelopment, itself the result of imperialism. The extreme dependence of the continent as a whole on external forces has conditioned developments within specific countries and also given Africa a certain uniformity. For instance, even the continent's most devout, serious and thoughtful leaders (such as Nyerere) have nearly all failed to effect the developments which they promised would transform the lives of ordinary people. This fact holds not only for allegedly super-inefficient socialist regimes (such as Tanzania's) but also for supposedly healthy capitalist countries (such as Kenya). External capital's relations with specific countries have not been significantly different; the primary concern has been over the rate of returns on investment although, of course, the degree of availability and reliability of a country's infrastructure have sometimes given the edge to one country over a competitor for foreign investors. In general terms, therefore, it would be true to say that the options available to regimes and leaders in Africa over the past quarter-century have not been too promising with respect to development of the productive forces. And it is because of this that we sometimes need to moderate our views of the catalogue of failures which are the result of the post-colonial period when seen as a whole. A brief look at the limited options available to leaders and regimes helps to illustrate the qualifications we must be prepared to make when assessing the first quarter-century of post-colonial developments (or non-development) in specific countries.

The most obvious option available after political independence was that of developing the export sector of agriculture. This option was, and continues to be, supported by the argument that runs along the following lines: newly independent African countries are poor and need to earn their way in the world (true); one way of doing this is to increase production of agricultural goods which are not grown in industrial countries, but which have large markets for such products (also true); the money earned in these markets will pay for the goods necessary for consumption and perhaps the beginning of the transformation of the technological base of these economies. So far the last expectation has failed to materialise. The reasons for this have been repeatedly set out by leading Third World politicians and intellectuals and perhaps most clearly by Julius Nyerere: the costs of imported manufactured goods have continued to increase whilst the more these economies produce by way of improvements in agriculture the less they receive on the world market.[8] It is as if developed capitalist countries have found a way to arrest the tendency for the rate of profits to fall partly by political means — these countries are able to set the price of manufactured as well as imported agricultural goods through control of the market-place and support of their governments. By the same process, the expected benefits from greater productivity are reversed because African countries, like other Third World primary-goods-producing countries, constantly need to produce more and more but receive less and less through adverse terms of trade. The problem then gets compounded by natural events such as droughts or too-heavy rainfalls. As a result, whilst *industrial* Europe, America and Japan destroy, export or give as aid some of the abundance of the food they produce annually, *agricultural* Africa produces increasingly non-essential agricultural and horticultural goods for these parts of the world and imports foods from these same industrial countries. In this situation consumer idiosyncracies can have drastic and immediate effects on conditions in the continent: a slow-down in the consumption of coffee, sugar or tobacco, and many economies are adversely affected.

A second option adopted by some regimes has been the development of industry through import-substitution. Not only has this option been limited by rising import costs (of raw materials or semi-finished goods) but also by lower levels of productivity in these countries, and therefore the pushing up of costs for consumers. The protection that industries usually enjoy (being 'infant industries') is generally abused by manufacturers, partly to overcome the high levels of theft, low productivity, breakdowns, etc. at work and partly because they are still operating in the spirit of the merchant capitalist who believes that wealth (usually his) is created

41

by buying cheaply and selling expensively on the market.

The last and apparently most promising option may be more of an intimation or an invitation than a reality: the possibility of becoming a producer of heavy industrial goods (such as steel, shipbuilding, etc.). In other words, some of the older industries move from the developed capitalist centres due to high wage bills, etc. to where labour is cheaper and more manageable. Several factors, however, militate against this path of development taking place. First, up to the present time there has been a deeply in-built racist factor in the determination of investment by capitalists: it is relatively easy to invest in the white commonwealth but a disinvestment in non-white countries occurred at various points in the development and decline of the empires of the last century. For most of the present century investment in South Africa has been high particularly since the firm establishment of the apartheid state since World War II and it is to be pondered whether this will be so once majority rule is established. This perception has also been wrapped up with the question of the West's defence. Thus whilst it was possible for the Americans to invest heavily in Europe and Japan after the last World War, they were and are not willing to do so in parts of the Third World — including non-white dominated areas in Africa. I have already spoken of the inefficiency of post-colonial societies in Africa and this too militates against foreign capital investment on a scale that would make a difference in the development/underdevelopment equation. Nor are these states sufficiently competitive with those of South East Asia in the area of efficient state control to attract foreign capital on a scale that would make a difference to the present state of affairs. In any event, multinational companies are finding the southern states of the US attractive for investments because of the absence of unions and the availability of cheap labour. The enlargement of the EEC to include Spain, Greece, Portugal and Turkey may very well result in much the same line of development.

The limitations of these options are further complicated by outside political interference in the continent's affairs. In the first place, the rivalry between the US and the USSR impacts negatively on African countries and regimes as these superpowers vie for political influence and military strongholds in the regions of the continent. Not surprisingly, their interests, rarely — if ever — coincide with those of the people of the countries in which influence or strongholds are established. Cliques close to the centre of state power are assisted by the presence of either of these superpowers. And no sooner do these cliques upset their Soviet or American friends than we hear of coups in the name of the people, democracy or common sense. Either or both superpowers tend to be in the thick of regional problems such as the Congo in the 1960s, Angola since the 1970s and Uganda. There is therefore something of a new division of Africa in the post-World-War II period, a division between the Soviet/Eastern bloc and US/NATO interests.

This new division is of course superimposed on the older divisions along European imperialist lines — principally French and British. Further, both France and Britain maintain their own national interests in different parts of the continent, sometimes in conflict with the US and sometimes in concert. For example, during the presidency of Jimmy Carter, the US seemed willing to allow and encourage France to develop her policeman role in the continent, but as rivalry between the US and the USSR intensified in the Indian Ocean, the US moved to establish its own presence in Mombasa.

The Amin regime in Uganda was a good example of the havoc which can still be caused by the rivalry between the two international blocs. In 1971 Milton Obote was overthrown by Idi Amin with, it is widely believed, British and Israeli support at a time when Obote was critical of Edward Heath's government's supportive policy of the racist and fascist South African regime. Soon, Amin fell out with the Israelis and the British over the expulsion of the Asians among other matters. Libya and the USSR now had their opportunity to move in and did so. Thus, by the late 1970s, Amin could attack the Kagera Salient in Tanzania with Soviet weaponry and the war which ensued threw the Tanzanian economy into deeper crisis. This provided the World Bank, the IMF, etc. with the opportunity to press for Tanzania to cut back on the state's expenditure on social services such as health care, education, food subsidies, etc., Tanzania having spent an estimated $500m in the war and therefore being in urgent need of foreign currency. In short, the interference in the affairs of the continent by the superpowers and their friends has nearly always boded ill for specific countries, and sometimes it appears as if whole regions will drift into a state of chronic Balkanisation.

In these conditions, well-intentioned leaders are likely to find their options to be extremely illusory indeed. The superpowers have made it clear that in the hostile international environment, which is so important for weak and poor states, they must be seen to be for or against one of the super blocs. This imperative imposes severe limitations on the space available to leaders on the continent. These limitations usually move from being apparent to being very real indeed whenever leaders attempt to follow a non-aligned path in international affairs and even in purely national matters.

Therefore the old question of whither Africa not only continues to be very relevant but becomes more urgent.

## The way forward?

The question of the direction or directions in which Africa should go as she approaches the 21st Century is very much an open one as citizens and leaders ponder the cul-de-sac into which the first generation of leaders have led the continent. This is of course an important question which will affect concerned individuals outside the continent, particularly in the diaspora, but it is the peoples of the continent who will have to make the necessary difficult choices for Africa's future. However, in the effort to deal with some of the pressing day-to-day economic problems the countries of the continent face, consideration of her most fundamental problem of political leadership may be too easily swept under the carpet. In other words, such is the present variety of pressing issues to be dealt with that many leaders, sincere citizens and even more cautious observers take the view that the continent's problem is essentially for instance the shortage of foreign currency, or drought, or flooding.

My contention, however, is that the single most important problem facing the continent at the present time is the nature and quality of political leadership. The winning of political independence was such a rapid and dramatic development that for some time observers seem to have felt that the political question for the continent had been resolved. After over a quarter of a century of political independence, however, there can be little doubt that there is a pressing case for some old questions to be raised afresh in the light of the immediate past and with an eye to the imminent future. I would suggest that foremost on any such agenda must be the question of a new political discussion over the condition of Africa as a whole. In the remainder of this paper I would like to turn attention to two aspects of this larger question.

The facts of size, resources (or lack of them), duplication of goods for a world market, common set of needs and so forth continue to suggest that the only way out of the cul-de-sac is either greater regional cooperation or continental federation/union. It is rather paradoxical that at a time when nearly all major blocs of the world are getting close to overcoming minor differences in order to confront large, common problems, African countries continue to break into, or threaten to break into smaller and smaller units still facing the big problems, with less and less resources. If continental unity, the great dream of pan-Africanism, is unrealisable in the near future, the more readily acceptable option of regional cooperation should be pushed towards regional unity; Economic Community of West African States (ECOWAS) and Southern African Development Co-ordination Conference (SADECC) may be relevant beginnings. It is something of a paradox that Africa, due to her common problems, the unity of her peoples, etc., is looked at as a totality and in some ways tends to confront the world as a totality, but that she is rippled with internal divisions emanating largely from the strong sense of national identity which has been created under colonialism and since political independence.

An act of unity on this scale would have the effect, in a comparatively short time, of resolving a number of today's pressing problems for the continent. In the first place, the continent could face the developed world with a common set of policies which would enhance the strength of particular states rather than undermine their sovereignty, as at present. Second, it goes without saying that resources could be better used: for example, the abundant water of Tanzania and Uganda could go to drought-stricken areas; plans could be drawn up to resolve issues which are today treated as national problems but which are in fact international. I am very aware that I am not saying anything here that the pan-Africanists did not make clear, as for example in Kwame Nkrumah's *Africa Must Unite*.[9]

The abolition of 'national' boundaries would also help to bring into focus many of the continent's problems. For example, the question of refugees, inter-tribal linkages, smuggling of market products from one country to another, the separation of peoples from each other, etc., would be abolished. This would leave a generation of Africa's leaders at all levels of society to begin the construction of a more just social order and it could then be said that the continent had reached a very definite stage in its development. After all, one of the main lessons of the post-colonial period so far has been the inappropriateness of national boundaries. They are nearly all false and people, perhaps correctly, have not always felt bound to respect them. The multinational states of the continent — and they are nearly all multinational states — would be truly multinational in the sense of one state at the centre being responsible for a multiplicity of 'nations'. The present states need not give up their identities entirely and the variety of peoples seeking 'national' independence, or trying to assert their identities and who are not being stifled through the formal, assumed, but really quite mistaken, 'nationalism', could do so without engaging in civil wars. The advantages of continental or at least regional unity at the political level are obviously immense and it is a sad day when narrow, so-called nationalism, or, to be precise, false nationalism, is made to silence those voices which call for a greater Africa. It is of course true that nationalism based on the territories formed under colonialism achieved certain salutary objectives, such as the winning of independence, but like a spent booster rocket in space flights, this kind of nationalism based on false boundaries and premises, it will be found, is now a spent force and is therefore no longer in Africa's best long-term interests. It may, however, help to maintain the present largely parasitic petty bourgeoisie in power throughout the continent and also perpetuate the tendency towards civil war, constant warlordism and the depressive propulsion of the continent towards forming *a fourth world*. To move towards cooperation and unity and to abolish the present national boundaries involves a major political step which is far more difficult than the struggle for political independence.

The second but equally important, if not more important, matter which must be high on the agenda for discussion regarding the future of the continent is of course the question of democratic participation. The question of participation, however, should not have to wait for there to be regional or continental unity before being addressed.

In other words, this question can and should be addressed immediately, within the confines of the present state. In this debate over democracy the accent will necessarily be on meaningful participation by citizens in the affairs of public importance. This does not mean, however, that the forms of participation which will emerge will be the same as have been institutionalised in the liberal and social–democratic societies under advanced capitalism nor will they necessarily be like those of Eastern Europe. The forms that the new democratic order will take cannot and should not be predicted by any one group or other; it will not come spontaneously, but it should not be forced.

An example may be in order at this point. In the early 1960s Julius Nyerere was very concerned about the question of democracy in Tanganyika because in the elections in the years leading to independence all seats for the legislature were won by his party, TANU. He correctly saw this as a kind of critique of the Westminster model of a two-party political system; there was no need for the usually expected 'government' and 'opposition' sides in the legislature. In Nyerere's early essays on democracy in Africa, he developed a critique partly based on this experience of Tanganyika's politics in the years of decolonisation and the first years of political independence.[10]

To institute a form of democratic participation which could be said to be relevant to the country's experience, Nyerere gave political and constitutional status to the one-party system. Democratic participation was to be introduced in the country through the single party. In doing this, the country's leadership was not ridding the political scene of opposition forces as has been the case in other parts of the continent. Thus, as much as I would counsel caution over the introduction of the single-party system — partly because it puts a stop to any type of democratic alternatives, stifles a political system and is essentially anti-democratic — I have to admit that the fact of a one-party system in Tanganyika did not, at least at first, inhibit active political participation by citizens in such matters as elections and over political discussion; it may even have enhanced democracy. Indeed, the electoral rules introduced in the country have generally gone some way towards enhancing democratic participation. For example, the practice of presenting two candidates to the electorate in the contest for seats in the legislature is commendable; another example of this kind is the discouragement of the use of local languages during election campaigns and the promotion of the national language, Kiswahili, for political discourse. My very guarded statement here about these aspects of the one-party system in what is now mainland Tanzania does not mean that the negative features of this system must be seen as part of the desired new democracy. For example, the emasculation of the legislature by the party, the fact that there is only one candidate for the presidency, and the continuation on the statute books of the Preventive Detention Act are some of the features which belittle the positive aspects of the political system. The point that I am trying to make is simply that a serious attempt to interpret national conditions and adopt forms of representation which are relevant are important, and this kind of creative political skill is sadly lacking today in Africa.

Although the forms of participation which may be best suited to particular conditions on the continent must come out of the experience of the peoples of the continent, it must be fairly clear that the desired order must include some of the historical and therefore now universal rights which have been won in the fight against people's inhumanity to each other. In this respect I do not hesitate to say that the right to hold and express opinions contrary to those of the state, of regimes and leaders; to assemble freely and organise within the framework of the law: to publish contrary opinions about public affairs, to suggest alternative political strategies, and to expect the protection of the state itself from arbitrary arrest and abuse of power are rights to be upheld. These rights, it is true, were established largely in the struggle between the emergent bourgeoisie and the decaying feudal classes in Europe, but their extension and consolidation involved not only these classes but the working classes too and because of their historical importance these rights have become the common heritage of humanity. With the winning of political independence from the former colonial powers, the people of Africa laid claim to these rights; to surrender them to the state is to deny a birthright. These rights are not therefore entirely 'bourgeois' as some people may think. And even if they are bourgeois, surely Lenin's dictum — better bourgeois civilisation than barbarity — is apt, although he was, of course, referring to conditions in Czarist Russia.

At a practical, day-to-day level, the achievement of restoration of people's rights and placing again on the political agenda the question of African unity will be extremely difficult. These tasks call for a number of developments occurring simultaneously and for active engagement between intellectuals and the mass of the people. In the ensuing dialogue there will need to be an awareness of issues and questions which transcend the present national boundaries — in the way that nationalist leaders were able at various stages of the struggle for independence to make the questions of the day transnational questions. In other words, there will be the task of transcending the narrow confines of a spent nationalism.

## Conclusion

In conclusion, therefore, the point can only be repeated that in the needed debate over the future of Africa the question of democratic participation, historically defined, must be at the centre of both discussion and planning. In this next phase in the process of the liberation of the continent, some of the concerns of an earlier generation of pan-Africanists should be restored to a place of prominence. Failure to address the questions of democratic participation and greater cooperation or unity may well mean that Africa will continue along the downward slide to further underdevelopment as the rest of the world moves in the other direction.

## Notes

1. F. Fanon, *The Wretched of the Earth* (Harmondsworth: Penguin, 1963).

2. L. Althusser, *For Marx* (London: Verso, 1979).

3. N. Poulantzas, *Political Power and Social Classes* (London: NLB, 1973).

4. P. Bachrach and M. S. Baratz. 'Two Faces of Power', *American Political Science Review*, vol. LVII, no. 3, 1963, pp. 632–42.

5. C. Beard, *An Economic Interpretation of the Constitution of the United States* (New York: Macmillan, 1961).

6. See A. Hamilton, J. Madison and J. Jay, *The Federalist*, J. E. Cook (ed.), (Middletown: Wesleyan University Press, 1961).

7. See, for example, A. Cabral, *Revolution in Guinea* (London: Stage One, 1969).

8. See, for example, Fidel Castro, 'How Latin America's and Third World's Unpayable Foreign Debt Can and Should be Cancelled and the Pressing Needs for the New International Economic Order' interview granted to the Mexican daily, *Excelsior* (La Habana: Editoria Politica, 1985).

9. K. Nkrumah, *Africa Must Unite* (New York: International Publishers, 1970).

10. See, for example, J. K. Nyerere, 'Democracy and the Party System' in (J. K. Nyerere, ed.) *Freedom and Unity* (Nairobi: Oxford University Press, 1967).

# 3 The State and Popular Alliances: Theoretical Preliminaries in the Light of the Moroccan Case

by Abdelali Doumou

## Introduction

Historically, periods of societal crisis progressively generate a 'defetishisation' of social reality.[1] Social reality becomes transparent and offers peoples the opportunity to grasp the social fact of emancipation.

But the present crisis is accompanied by a singular failure both of social projects launched by established political regimes and the rival ones — emanating from political forces seeking social change — which have so far run up against a constant demobilisation of the popular masses. The fact is, paradoxical though it may seem, that the present crisis of African states does not seem to be generating popular processes of social change.[2] How is such a paradox to be explained?

An attempt to answer this question calls for an analysis of social classes and the state. This chapter is limited to an analysis of the state which will seek to apprehend the mechanisms of social ordering by looking at the state functions aimed at the production and reproduction of the existing conflict-laden class system, the socio-economic structure that underlies it, and the cultural and ideological factors that condition and hamper the phenomenon of social mobilisation.

This choice follows from the observation[3] that, in peripheral social formations, social differentiations result not from relations within a 'civil society' but from relations with the state. Current debates about the peripheral state[4] have made some progress in apprehending the nature of the state.

These various analyses of the globalisation of the state have, when applied to states in the periphery, however, a number of inadequacies because as a result of being inherently capital-centred, some of the hypotheses propounded do not stand up to historical analysis. Because the capitalist historical era is always determinant in these analyses, they fail to take note of the fact that contemporary state structures in the Third World are also the heirs of a 'pre-capitalist' history. Our purpose here, however, is not to conduct a historical analysis but simply to set out the principal terms of the theoretical problematic of the peripheral state before going on to debate the case of Morocco.

## The problematic of the peripheral state: some hypotheses

Contemporary peripheral states seem to be the product of a double 'historicity'. First, they are the product of their own particular (pre-capitalist) history which is

48

evidence of the variety of pre-capitalist 'political societies'; second, of the universal history of these states which gives them their common capitalist essence consequent upon their integration into the world capitalist system.

For various historical reasons,[5] this double 'historicity' has produced, in Africa, state structures that are homogeneous in their class nature (the content of the state) and heterogeneous in their form (political regime) proceeding, usually, from distinct historical epochs.

According to this thesis, contemporary African state structures are not solely the product of their integration into world capitalism (as the capital-centred approach to the peripheral state claims), but the result of a historical evolution in which the capitalist (and colonial) era is but one component. For several African states (including Morocco), colonisation was only the culmination of a long process of integration already underway for at least a century.[6]

This hypothesis, however, has to deal with the question of how to periodise the 'opening up' of African economies to capitalism. From what point can one speak of a particular articulation of African states on the centre states giving them a capitalist-type class nature?

Some writers hold that the very thesis of the opening up of some African economies after 1850 (J. L. Miège, 1961) needs to be seen in context, since this 'sudden opening up' was only the end result of a much older process of integration.[7]

Conversely, it is necessary and instructive to take account of the colonial period if the analysis relates to the phenomenal form of the peripheral state. Is the colonial state a negation of the 'traditional' material aspect of African states or is it the combined product of two (traditionally modern) material aspects? How are these two historically conflicting materialities articulated?

Analysis of the functions of the state in Africa (regeneration of capital and legitimation) should lead to emphasising their particular features (at the level of their content and their specific articulation). To grasp these particular features requires studying the socio-economic base of politico-religious and socio-cultural life in a peripheral social formation on to which a political regime has been grafted.

While in the developed capitalist countries the development of capital, in its initial stage, was moved by historical factors which worked in the direction of identifying the social space with the 'nation' (what is usually described by the expression 'homogenising dialectic of the nation-state'), it is different in the period of the reproduction of capital at the international level (the imperialist stage) when this reproduction meets with an obstacle: the recalcitrance of a 'non-capitalist' social world.

The particular feature of the situation of the peripheral social formations which have been victims of this process lies in the fact that the social classes — newly created or remodelled — that mediate this process of conquest of the social space by the space of capital, are obliged to develop a favourable social framework: 'the nation'. But, in most African societies, this process of 'nation-building' meets with obstacles. The paradox in Third World countries is that states exist, but states in quest of a nation.

Analysis of the underlying social structure of African states cannot be separated from study of their socio-economic strategies.

In dependent social formations, economic and social differentiations result not from relations within a 'civil society' (which seems to be the case in the social formations of the developed centre) but from relations with the state. It is for this reason that the formation of social groupings called 'classes' in the periphery occurs, in the last instance, not through social diversification from below, but through cooptation from above. The peripheral state constitutes the principal mechanism of this cooptation[8].

If, today, in some underdeveloped countries (the most industrialised ones), the state seems to represent a class, this was not the case in the past, neither is it always the case in the least industrialised underdeveloped countries where the state seems to generate the class which is deemed to identify it: the state thus seems not simply to be the guarantor of capitalist relations of production but also and above all the producer of such relations. The peripheral state, 'fully a state', has its own logic; political power as it is exercised there has its own properties: instead of the groups in power producing an ideology of legitimation (as was the case in the states in the centre) this ideology is encapsulated through the state in the various social spheres. While in the state in the centre, the autonomy of the state apparatus in relation to the bloc in power is only relative, for dependent societies, the state has a function that objectively alienates it from the bloc in power as a whole, since no social force, however powerful, can aspire to a hegemony sufficient to alienate state power from the state itself. Whence the importance of socio-cultural factors which condition social struggles and alliances.[9] The importance of this dimension arises from another one, that the economic domain is not obscured by a 'fog as thick as that given out by commodity fetishism in industrial society'. It should be pointed out in this connection that one of the hypotheses of the theory of the derivation of the state[10] (dominating the current Marxist debate on the capitalist state) rests on the fact that it is 'commodity fetishism' in capitalism which constitutes the material basis of the 'illusion' about the state. Commodity fetishism' thus makes it possible to make the state appear as an instance above social classes.

However, given that this fetishism depends on how generalised commoditisation has become, and that the specificity of the genesis of Third World states and the particular place they occupy in the world economy tend to give their political regimes particular characteristics, this proposition seems to refer above all to the developed industrial states. The result is that deduction of the state from the category capital is not relevant for the case of underdeveloped countries where the capitalist mode of production is not the product of contradictions internal to these societies but has in a sense been parachuted in from outside. This situation has several implications: exchange value cannot constitute, by itself, the basis of social cohesion; it cannot generate a reification of social relations such that it can constitute the material and central element of the perception of the state as something other than what it is. It can then not provide, except partially and contradictorily, the basis for legitimation on to which the political regimes could graft themselves. These latter will seek legitimation for their action through forms of personal dependence, direct submission, and moral and religious legitimation, i.e. in their own cultural resources.

These points raise questions about the nature of the complex relations that exist between the state and the ruling class in dependen

In most African states, the practice of political regim
analysis, by a structural tendency for the contradict
requirements of social reproduction — the regeneration of capit
— to reappear.

If this contradiction was blurred in the past through projects of social
(development of agrarian capitalism, development of Import Substit
Industrialisation (ISI), etc.) made possible and encouraged by the 'classic
international division of labour which reconciled development of capital and
legitimation, at present the state, lacking opportunity as a result of the effects of the
crisis of world capitalism,[12] is paralysed as a result of its inability to ensure the
regeneration of capital without engendering a loss of legitimation calling the
existing political regimes into question.[13]

How acute this contradiction is varies, however, from one society to another, as a
function on the one hand of what social alliances are available (either by
relaunching traditional social alliances or establishing new ones that depend on the
relations of force between the social classes involved) and what can be drawn from
the cultural stock (of legitimation) on the other. It is on this level where the impact
of the historical depth of some African states brings traditional reserves of
legitimation[14] on their role in social reproduction.

Otherwise, how can such a situation be explained? Whatever the response given,
it is, in our opinion, secondary to a systematic analysis of the function of
legitimation of the political regime as well as its articulation on that of the
regeneration of capital.

The study of this 'historicity' leads, necessarily, to highlighting the particular
features of the functions of the peripheral state (content, articulation and limits),
the material basis of legitimacy (the economic, politico-religious and socio-cultural
dimensions) on to which the political regime is grafted as well as the social structure
that underlies it. Highlighting these particular features throws light on the
contemporary political history of Third World countries. In Africa, the
contradiction between legitimation and regeneration of capital seems to have been,
until now, blurred over in favour of legitimation and to the detriment of capital
accumulation and democracy.

Thus, one of the particular features of the development of peripheral capitalism
is that so far it has not been able to promote a process of political development. The
recent reintegration of 'civilian segments', under the impact of semi-industrialisa-
tion, has created the illusion of an emancipation of 'civil society' from the state.
Whence the recent infatuation of Third Worldist intellectuals for 18th century
theories and for debates on democracy.[15] In the 'political societies' of the Third
World, social demand makes democracy a pre-requisite of any project for society,
and the current weak attempts at democratisation are an attempt to reduce the
pressure of this growing social demand.

But these ideas and this demand are not accompanied by an effective lessening of
statism in Third World countries. On the contrary, peripheral societies seem to
persist in their high degree of heterogeneity and this continues to impose the state as
the necessary principal instance for the reproduction of the socio-political system.

51

...d to the growth of the role of the
...ole of the political and ideological
...the state remains the cornerstone of
...hat the recent neo-liberal attempts in
...will not escape the phenomenon of
...of the same kind in other times. The
...number of societies appears more as an
...st of legitimation that is lacking than an

## ... the two myths of the 'nation-state' and 'co...

While there is agreem... ...e principle that the process of globalisation of the
capitalist system seems to be accompanied by a globalisation of political
institutions and a cultural model, it must however be asked whether the
hierarchical ordering of the 'capitalist world-economy' into centre, semi-periphery
and periphery is not reflected at the level of the forms of social organisation in a
'composite' typology of states. In this typology the various degrees of 'national
integration' — and hence of correspondence between the two entities, state and
nation — would lead, if not to rejecting the use of the concept of 'nation-state', then
at least to showing its inadequacy to account for the reality of the state in dependent
social formations.

### The nation-state in dependent social formations
Most analyses of the contemporary peripheral state are based on the assumption of
the 'nation-state'.[16] Our purpose is to suggest that this historical category (the
nation-state) is — when applied to the social formations of the Third World —
problematic. After presenting a number of components of what is usually called
'the theory of the nation', we shall emphasise that the foundations on which the
peripheral state rests are complex and specific since they derive from socio-cultural
formations that — in several aspects — fall outside the West-centred criteria of the
definition of the nation.

For some who are nostalgic for the colonial regime and theorists of 'neo-
colonialism', the historical category of nation is one of the numerous creations of
the 'genius' of the West. For them, the countries of Asia and Africa have
experienced this historical category only recently and from outside.[17] For other
Marxist authors, of whom Stalin is the precursor, the nation is 'an historically
evolved, stable community of language, territory, economic life, and psychological
make-up manifested in a community of culture'.[18] Among the four criteria
suggested by Stalin, community of economic life seems to constitute the base-line
from which the nation draws its full social cohesion.

Such a definition of the nation, which has inspired numerous Marxist authors,
corresponds rather to the historical experience of Europe (including the Soviet
Union). In this case, Marxist theorisings about the nation take on a West-centred

52

spirit, neglecting the Afro-Asian countries 'except to consider them as simple variants of bourgeois nations, or as "pre-nations" in the process of evolving'.[19]

That is why it is necessary to ask, from a Marxist viewpoint, about the place the problem of the nations of Africa and Asia occupies and how, from this viewpoint, the process of formation of these nations can be interpreted.[20]

Concerning sub-Saharan Africa, a long discussion was initiated by *Marxism Today* (London) in which Potekhin[21] discussed whether it was possible to talk of nations before the development of capitalist relations of production. The author suggested, following Stalinist logic, that the essential element that marks the birth of nations is the formation of a capitalist market. This amounts to considering, by analogy, that the process of formation of nations in sub-Saharan Africa and other 'Third World' countries is incomplete. In *Main basse sur l'Afrique*, Jean Ziegler specifies that 'the usual way of looking schematically at the national phenomenon includes the following three paradigmatic concepts:

– The view of history shared by the majority of the members of the nation, and . . . which arouses, in every class of a given population, the will to struggle and live together, to form a nation . . . In this sense, on the national project, the view of history is trans-class, trans-ethnic and trans-regional.

– The territory is given . . . It expresses materially and sensually . . . the feeling of national identity. Myths legitimise it, the origins of the nation are rooted in it. The territory records, memorialises and celebrates the memory of the nation.

– Language is the privileged instrument by which the nation imposes its new consciousness. Like the territory, it pre-exists the nation but it is not given in the same way . . . Its spread is the result of national integration . . . .[22]

This leads other authors to extend this thinking by asking: 'Can the African state be understood in such a way, even superficially? In other words, does the African state live up to this image of the nation-state? African sociological reality plainly suggests otherwise'.[23]

In the Arab–Aslamic social formations, the essential problem posed to Marxists is to know how to conceptualise both the national reality of the Arab world (*al Umma al 'Arabiyya*) and that of the various countries comprising it (the Tunisian, Egyptian, Moroccan, etc., 'nation'). Samir Amin perfectly expresses this concern when he writes: 'From the Atlantic shores of Morocco to the Persian Gulf, from the Mediterranean to the centre of the Sahara and the upper Nile, a hundred million people speak the same language, listen to the same radio programmes, read the same books and see the same films. They have all been oppressed by the same European imperialism during the contemporary period. Nevertheless, when one asks one of them: "What is your nationality?" not one will spontaneously answer "Arab"; the reply will be "Moroccan", "Egyptian", "Yemenite", etc. Do these hundred million people form one nation, the Arab nation, as the contemporary ideologues of Arab nationalism assert — even granted that this nation is still in the course of formation? Or do they make up fifteen different, albeit related, nations, as orthodox communism has long claimed.'.[24]

For a long time, Arab Marxists provided only a partial response to this question in favour of the first term (the Arab nation) through the definition of 'the democratic path for the Arab liberation movement as a whole'.[25] It is Egyptian

Marxists[26] who deserve the credit for having been the first to have attempted to conceptualise this 'political dualism' of Arab-Muslim social formations. The 'nationhood' of the Arab countries derives in their view from a 'two-tier nation'.[27] For the case of the Maghrebi Arab countries, many Marxist authors are agreed on the recent and incomplete character of the process of formation of nations.

In the case of Morocco, the issue has barely been raised, the question of the nation having never been the object of a full-fledged analysis.[28] The concern is beginning, however, to be felt — albeit implicitly — in some recent analyses.[29] That is why we feel it important to try and bring out the conception (the definition) of the nation that Abdallah Laroui seems to adopt for the case of Morocco. In doing so, an initial difficulty arises: Laroui has no theory of the nation, at least no systematic one. The author is moreover explicit on this point; he specifies early in his book that: 'it is not a matter of asking the question: did a Moroccan nation exist before the present century?'.[30] However, Laroui observes also that 'every nationalism works on some sort of raw material or other, and it is precisely the Moroccan raw material that we wish to describe'.[31]

From Laroui's description, an approach emerges: the elements of analysis used by the author attempt to demonstrate the existence of a 'Moroccan organism'; it turns out that these elements coincide perfectly with the West-centred criteria of the definition of the nation. Does this mean that this 'Moroccan organism' that Laroui speaks of was building a nation? That is what we shall try to bring out by a reading of Laroui's work.

In fact the underlying purpose of Laroui's analysis is to demonstrate the existence of a 'Moroccan organism' equipped with a certain homogeneity in the pre-colonial Moroccan social formation. Evidence of this is first the plan he adopts to set out his first part, the headings of which are in this connection extremely significant: 1. The bases of Moroccan society; (i. A people; ii. A Moroccan economic market; iii. A territory). 2. A king, a government; 3. Local authorities. 4. An ideology, a culture.[32]

These various elements making up the first part of the plan adopted by Laroui correspond to the definitional criteria of the nation is perceived in Marxist theory.[33] Is this a simple formal coincidence? That is what we shall try and disprove by examining what Laroui writes of these various elements constituting the 'nation'.

Thus use of the term 'people' instead of 'populations' in the plural is a first bias of the author. In order to demonstrate the existence of a Moroccan people, the author writes about dress: 'what interests us is not so much the degree of uniformity within geographical Morocco as the difference that separates Moroccan dress from the dress to be found to the east and south outside Morocco'.[34]

What interests Laroui is demonstrating the specific features of 'national dress': 'Over and beyond undeniable regional variations', he writes, 'the important fact to stress is that the traditional Moroccan dress instantly distinguishes those who wear it from their neighbours to the east'.[35] Which means that regional variations are insignificant compared to the differences that exist beyond the national borders.

When he deals with the problem of language, Laroui's comments are similar: the community of language is affirmed: 'suffice it simply to emphasise what emerges clearly from travellers' accounts: at the time there did not exist any linguistically, politically, economically autonomous region that could provide the basis of an entity within or on the fringes of what is today Morocco'.[36]

The community of economic life constitutes, in the author's opinion, another homogenising factor in Moroccan society, which leads him to write: 'in all the small centres, the traveller finds the same imported goods as in the large ones. The image of a true circuit takes shape when a single centre is linked to two major towns or when several radiate from one large town: Demnat, Beni Mellal, Tazenakht around Marrakesh; Sefrou, Ouezzane, El Ksar around Fez'.[37]

When he touches on the question of territory, the author writes: 'one can speak, as we have seen, anthropologically, of a territory of the *balgha*, the *ksa*, and tea, which, in the east, ends where the use of sandals and boots, cigarettes and coffee begins'.[38]

After this initial survey Laroui concludes by spelling out that: 'the aim, more modest, was to have an idea of the mobility of Moroccans in a more or less fixed framework, with a de facto differentiation and a feeling of specificity not only vis-à-vis Europeans, but also vis-à-vis neighbouring Muslims, whether living under Muslim or non-Muslim rule'.[39] In the same spirit, the author stresses the material framework of national identity in pre-colonial Morocco by writing that 'the elements brought together in this chapter, ranging from observations by journalist-ethnographers to correspondence by diplomats, the number of which had to be reduced, show quite clearly that there was no contradiction between loyalty to Islam and loyalty to territory, and that nothing in the history of Maghrebi Islam was opposed to a slow differentiation along given ethnological, economic, and linguistic lines thus forming the material framework of a national identity'.[40]

Analysis of the *makhzen*, its structure (army, bureaucracy and orders) and its relations with the rest of society, constitutes another level of perception of the 'homogeneity' of Moroccan society: 'There was no group', writes the author, 'urban or rural, which did not recognise, whether it liked it or not, an aspect of the sultan's authority. Of course, the state as order, rationality, form, was not isolated within the *makhzen*. The sacred, the religious, the civil, the military were still juxtaposed in it, if not indiscriminately mixed up together'.[41] The author adds in the same vein: 'symbol and personification of every aspect of authority, the sultanate was both solid and fragile, abstract and yet indispensable. That this point of unity exists, there can be no doubt, since even those who defined themselves for a time against it nevertheless remained prisoners of its logic'.[42] This analysis of the *makhzen* leads the author to raise the problem of the existence of a nation-state in pre-colonial Morocco: Laroui wonders whether one can 'speak of a state, of a society, words which have acquired a precise meaning in modern times?' and replies 'if we speak of a constituted system, it is mainly to emphasise that everything was ready for a state and a society, in the true meaning of the terms, to emerge, as happened elsewhere, and to refute the idea of a "host of autonomous tribes"'.[43] How is such a quotation to be understood if it is not that Laroui is attempting to understand 19th century Morocco on the basis of the 'nation-state' dialectic, which he refers to as the 'precise meaning' that the words 'state' and 'nation' have acquired in 'modern times'.

Even when the author integrates local rulers into his analysis, it is not so as to show in what the Moroccan social formation failed to meet the criteria of the category 'nation-state', but so as to insist on the importance of the integrative mechanisms that make these local rulers a vital part of the 'Moroccan organism'.[44] 'This co-existence', he writes, 'between the *makhzen* and local rulers denotes a tendency towards communal synthesis: this dialectic of temporary opposition and transaction, of violent rejections and mutual attraction, is the best proof of the existence of a Moroccan organism'.[45]

If the Marxist authors as a whole considered here seem to use the same approach based on the assumption of the 'nationhood' of Afro–Asian socio-cultural formations, they however part company on two levels. First, at the level of the use of the criteria underlying the definition of the nation: is the community of economic life criterion determining or not? How is 'community of economic life' to be defined? Does it completely overlap with the capitalist national market as Kozlof or Potekhin assert? Or can it arise in other earlier forms predating the development of capitalism (as Samir Amin seems to maintain for the Arab nation.)[46]

Second, at the level of the forms assumed by the 'nation' concretely: oneness or duality of the 'nation'?

Nevertheless, it should be pointed out that all the theorisings previously presented originate in a West-centred approach according to which Afro–Asian social formations could only be understood in terms of 'nation'.

This approach has the major defect of extrapolating historical criteria (community of economic life, psychological community, etc.) whose place of birth, form and content are the particular product of European experience. The logical end-result of this 'analogism' is to relate the birth of capitalism to that of the nation.

Furthermore, the various analyses pass silently over the specificity of the relations between the two entities 'state' and 'nation'. The relations between the state and what is called the 'nation' do not have the same forms in the 'Third World' as they do in the West. In fact, in the developed capitalist societies the state appears as the emanation of the nation as a result of the existence of a system of generalised identification, civil society being wholly integrated economically ('free' labour market, generalised exchange circuit), institutionally (trade unions, parties, parliament, sporting and artistic associations) and culturally (generalisation of a single consumption model, a unified education system, etc.).

In this context, the construction of the national state was based on a mode of social self-perception imposed by a minority (the bourgeoisie) and internalised by the population as a whole. The generalisation of this consciousness went hand in hand with the advances of socio-economic integration that characterise ascendant capitalism 'if the nation-state is necessarily, in its completed form, a bourgeois state, it is however the fruit of a slow conflict-laden convergence of a certain accumulation of capital, a given development of techniques of production, a transformation of institutions, and a shift in the orientations of the movements of ideas'.[47]

It is this slow process of dialectical convergence (laden with conflicts) that the 'nation-state' seizes, when the historic occasion arises to make itself into the sole political instance aspiring to total control.

Thus nation and state were built, in Europe, like the two terms of a dialectical process of multiple convergence and creativity: 'the nation, a fundamentally exclusive concept, in/and through its relationship with the state, homogenises within frontiers, violates or sustains the particularities and integrates the subject sub-groups . . . in this slow process, ideology and the production of relations of production and violence, armed or latent, are exchanged and fuel each other in a dialectic in which the complementarities are always dominant and the incompatibilities secondary and thus retrievable'.[48]

However, in most of the peripheral states that currently exist in the world state system, the process of state-building seems to have nothing at all to do with the 'state-nation' dialectic. In the countries of the so-called Third World the 'state-nation' relation is specific: it is the state which elaborates and presides over the realisation of the 'project-nation'[49] in 'a-national' socio-cultural formations. In other words, 'the juridical existence of the African state is not to be called into question; history, via human will, has so decided. And yet, does the African state exist sociologically? The concept of nation, attached to that of state, does not fit the African state'.[50]

In that case, in a large number of underdeveloped countries, the construction of a 'nation-state' remains an incomplete and reversible process, the 'nation' being, still, a project to realise: 'Not only do the "nations" that are the presumed content of the various borders established over the last twenty years not exist in reality, but also their construction seems to be running into insurmountable obstacles'.[51] As Houphouet-Boigny put it: 'We have not inherited a nation, but an artificial state born of colonisation. It takes years to make a nation.'[52]

Samir Amin's conception of the nation seems to rest essentially on two theses. The first involves a break with the capital-centred definition of the nation. This latter 'is a social phenomenon which can appear at every stage of history'. It is not necessarily concomitant with the capitalist mode of production. The class that controls the state apparatus and ensures economic, political and cultural unity is not necessarily bourgeois. His second thesis consists in stressing that the nation is a reversible process: it can develop and grow stronger or, on the contrary, it can break up and disappear, according to whether the social class in question reinforces its unifying power or loses it altogether. In the latter case, the homogeneity of the society declines and a conglomerate of ethnic groups comes into being; these ethnic groups may aspire to constitute one or several nations if the historical conditions allow one social class to realise its 'project-nation'.[53]

These two hypotheses make it possible to understand why the attempts at nation-building — in Morocco or in the rest of the Arab world — have never gone very far (except in exceptional and very short periods), not only because they were prevented by foreign designs, but above all because the level of development of the productive forces never allowed the extraction of sufficient surplus to establish the class attempting to build the nation.[54] This class remained the prisoner of its capacity to capture a surplus externally through long-distance trade. The 'project-nation' was, then, handicapped by this characteristic of the ruling class in pre-colonial Morocco.

The same hypothesis seems to be valid for the period of the integration of the Arab world into the capitalist system: the new social class — latifundist bourgeoisie or commercial bourgeoisie — could lay no claim to any hegemony because of its economic, political and cultural dependence.[55]

It was not this new class that ensured the economic and political unity of the country. Those functions were fulfilled by imperialism, by resorting to the militarisation of political regimes in the Third World and to violence. The weakness of this class manifested itself as a weakness of national integration. That is why all attempts at nation-building were to remain embryonic and incomplete in most so-called underdeveloped countries.

### 'Ethnicity', an 'a-national' socio-cultural reality

An alternative explanation stresses the importance of ethnicity as the dominant socio-cultural reality in a-national social formations. According to this conception (constituted) ethnicity has often been looked upon as an outdated left-over, an exotic curiosity and often as a problem that upsets the advocates of 'nation-state determinism'. In fact, it is argued, ethnicity constitutes an aspect[56] — and not simply a residue — of the present socio-cultural dynamic.

In this perspective, analysis of the state in general and of the peripheral state in particular cannot be separated from a study of the specificities of the socio-cultural formations that constitute its sociological base. To analyse the peripheral state is also to analyse the socio-cultural structures that underlie it.[57]

Such a position is disturbing (politically, be it understood) since by putting in the forefront the variety of the socio-cultural formations in the countries of the so-called Third World, it undermines the 'accomplished fact' of the 'nation-state'. This approach consists in giving socio-cultural categories (ethnic, religious, linguistic, etc.) their proper place in the dialectic that everywhere brings them into opposition to the 'modern state'.

From the preceding discussion it follows that ethnicity is an integral part of the African cultural personality, a reference point, a symbol of dignity and collective solidarity. These comments are not at all designed to propose the false alternative of national-state structure or ethnic socio-cultural structure; it is obvious today, more than in the past, that no formation can replace state organisation. On the contrary, these comments have as their purpose to integrate an important dimension that explains, largely, the passivity — or the reticence — of the popular masses with regard to the 'societal projects' proposed by the 'popular vanguards'; this approach is especially relevant in the context of the minority problems that are tearing most Third World societies apart, thus posing the urgent question of knowing: should one collaborate to strengthen the allegedly national framework of the present oppressive state? Or should one struggle to break up centralised power in the hope of eliciting the autonomy of minorities in revolt? Far from claiming to provide a response to such a broad question, our aim is to pose this often overlooked problem correctly while specifying that one of the major limitations of the dominant Marxist analyses in the dependent societies, is that it is conducted in 'simplistic' terms of 'class contradictions', the 'abolition of class exploitation', etc. neglecting the complexity of these phenomena in specific social formations where social conflicts are shot through and intensified by other forms of discrimination, inequality and oppression based on ethnicity, language, religion, customs, etc.;

whereas it is precisely this incompatibility between the 'project-nation' of the ruling class and the specificities of the social formations that constitutes one of the principal causes of the crisis of the state in most Third World countries.

A second, no less important, cause of the crisis of the peripheral state — offering another level of perception of the limits to the application of the category 'nation-state' to dependent societies — lies in the fact that every social formation in the Third World, even if 'fully committed to the reproduction of capitalist relations of production . . .', 'is not obscured by a fog as thick as that emanating from commodity "fetishism" in an industrial society'.[59]

### From commodity fetishism to state fetishism

In peripheral social formations, exchange not being generalised (its diffusion being incomplete and specific), exchange value cannot, on its own, constitute the basis of social cohesion. It cannot then generate a reification of social relations such that this can constitute the material and central element of the perception of the state as something other than what it is. Nor can it provide, except partially and contradictorily, the basis for legitimation on which the political regimes could be grafted. These latter will seek legitimation for their action through forms of personal dependence, direct subordination, and moral and religious legitimation, that is by drawing on their own cultural stock. The commodity, identified with the aggression of which it is the product, is rejected in favour of a return to religion and the values of the past, which instead of being 'values to retreat into' become 'values by which to act' through which social cohesion is established.[59] In that situation, analysis of the process of social reproduction in Third World social formations involves elucidating the problem of the fantastic character of social relations, the problem of religion and, beyond that, the problem of symbolic practice and ideology in general.

In *Capital*, Karl Marx explained the content and origin of the fantasmic character of the spontaneous representations that individuals make of the essence of commodities, money, capital, wages, etc.[60] In the representations everything is presented back to front, relations between individuals appear as relations between things, and what is cause appears as effect.

In the *Critique of Hegel's Philosophy of Right* (1842), Marx analyses political fetishism using the concept of 'alienation'. Fetishism is perceived through awareness of the separation of the individual from its object. This separation is such that the object, although created by the subject, makes itself autonomous and ends by dominating the subject.

Such an analysis is wholly applicable to the state, and one talks of state fetishism 'whenever a product of social acts tends to take on an autonomous existence, seems to detach itself from social relations, takes on the appearance of a reality endowed with an activity of its own which then governs the relations under consideration'.[61]

In the social formations of the 'Third World' — because of the incomplete and particular character of the diffusion of capitalist relations of production — it is other forms of fetishisation of social relations that underlie these mechanisms of reversal of cause and effect: an 'imaginary being', a god, appears as the living unity of a community, the source and condition of its reproduction and well-being. 'State fetishism', then, only draws its strength from the cultural resources of legitimacy on which political regimes rest (the ideology of negritude in Africa, Islam in Morocco, etc.). In the Arab-Islamic social formations, 'state fetishism' is not the product of an 'economic fetishism'; it is the product of the Muslim individual's idea of the state, that is the illusion that the state transcends worldliness and functions as a spiritual entity; an illusion produced by Islam as a 'reaction of revolt' against the worldliness of the state.[62]

Religion, in these societies, constitutes the principal mechanism by which the objective conditions of social life take on a fantasmic character. For it (religion) 'is at once a form of presentation and of presence of this structure accompanied by a form of action on it, representation and action, which are such that, at the very moment that social structure appears in the consciousness and offers itself to action, this structure becomes an object of theoretical misunderstanding and the illusory purpose for practical action. The invisible articulation of social relations, their inner basis and their form, which is both present and dissimulated in its mode of presentation, become the site where man is alienated, where real relations among men and among things are presented reversed, fetishised'.[63] In this context religious practice offers 'really a form of action, a political practice on the specific social contradictions continuously engendered by their mode of production and social existence, constantly threatened with fission and disaggregation'.[64]

It follows that, unlike in the central capitalist countries, these structures cannot be assimilated solely to the economic form of their expression; social reproduction cannot be confused with economic reproduction. The particular status of 'the economic' makes it impossible to assume 'commodity fetishism' in the peripheral social formations since, despite a dominance of commodity relations, 'the economic' is not a 'fetish' insofar as it does not constitute the exclusive system of behaviour and representation of social life.[65]

On the basis of a small personal survey carried out in a small village in the Haouz (Oulad Zarred in the Kelaa Seraghna region) we have been able to observe that despite the succession of drought years (seven years in succession), the inhabitants remain attached, by tradition, to cattle herding. This latter is an unviable economic operation since for the most part a milch cow brings in, at best, seven or eight dirhams a day but consumes about 20 dirhams a day. This small example shows that economic calculation and rationality are not the norms that govern the behaviour of most Moroccan peasants.[66]

For its part, the state — out of concern for legitimation — encourages this sort of thing. In the same region, the granting of consumer credits is accompanied by a postponement of repayment dates.

These various comments are an attempt to explain why it is the politico-ideological mechanisms that largely preside over the process of social reproduction in peripheral social formations; in most of the so-called underdeveloped countries, what is called the 'economic system' functions in a context of 'chronic crisis'[67] compared to the norms of central capitalism.

### Comprador character of the bourgeoisie

One of the principal manifestations of the non-existence of a material basis of legitimation in peripheral social formations is the particular nature of the bourgeoisie. This class, with its limited ability to bring about a transformation of economic and social structures and its incapacity to bring about the auto-dynamic development engineered by the French, English or other bourgeoisies, constitutes a characteristic trait of peripheral capitalism, and one that is universal.[68]

The crucial point here is to examine the manner in which this inability and these limitations of the bourgeoisie are reflected in Moroccan reality as a result of its dependence vis-à-vis foreign capital, rather than to debate this class's precise nature. The different terms of this debate, despite the fact that they situate the problematic of the 'characterisation' of the Moroccan bourgeoisie at a strictly conceptual level[69] (comprador bourgeoisie or national bourgeoisie[70] or 'non-bourgeois bourgeoisie'[71], etc.) are at one in stressing the class's weak dynamism and the fragility of its internal basis for accumulation.

These characteristic traits of the Moroccan bourgeoisie reveal the weakness of a material basis of legitimation of the state:[72]
– Weakness of national private investment in the FBCF;
– Weakness of the productive character of national private investment;
– Dependence of the Moroccan bourgeoisie on international capital and the world market;
– Dependence of the bourgeoisie on the state.

Several writers see this situation as one in which the state is attempting, through a large public sector, to make up for this weakness of national private capital in order to constitute a material base of legitimation for itself. But an analysis of public interventionism — at the level of both the means of finance that it requires and the feeble results that it is achieving in the area of capital accumulation — reveals that the public sector, far from playing the role assigned to it at the level of discourse as a 'crutch for capital', is participating in the reproduction of the existing model of accumulation[73] for several reasons:

– The structure of public expenditure by the state which is only the expression of its 'ideal project of social ordering' testifies to its weak productive effect.[74]

– The majority of public enterprises contribute little or nothing to capital accumulation (except perhaps for the OCP and the ONIS) as a result of the 'patrimonial conception' that the political regime has of the public sector[75] where this latter is perceived not as a support for the development of productive capital but as a patrimony belonging to a social stratum.

## The Moroccan case

Here we shall discuss only two aspects in order to illustrate the discussion above. These are the tremendous slowness of the development of commodity and capitalist relations, and the contrasting legitimacy that the political regime enjoys, up to a certain point.

**Slowness and particular features of the diffusion of capitalist relations of production: the case of the Moroccan economy**
One of the principal characteristics of the Moroccan economy lies in the weakness

61

of the diffusion of capitalist relations of production. There are several indicators to back up this hypothesis: the importance of 'not specifically capitalist' forms of production, the persistence of 'traditional' agricultural techniques, the weak impact of agricultural credit in the enlargement of commodity relations, the weakness of the wage-earning sector and the home market, etc.

a) The weakness or importance of mechanization in agriculture constitutes an indicator of the rate of the spread of capitalist relations of production. In fact, if we agree with Lenin that 'the application of machinery in agriculture is of a capitalist character, i.e., leads to the establishment of capitalist relations',[76] it appears that, in the case of Moroccan agriculture, this process remains severely limited.

Thus, simple observation of the present state of production techniques in agriculture reveals that the wooden plough, the scythe and animal energy remain the dominant means used by the Moroccan peasant.[77] Mechanisation, while it constitutes a real process, is progressing very slowly. From 1956 to 1978, the number of tractors rose from 532 to 2,592 only (a factor of four in 22 years), that of straw presses increased less, rising from 89 to 142 (a 60% increase) while over the same period the number of combine harvesters declined from 487 to 226 (see Table 3.1).

In addition, this mechanisation affects only the capitalist forms of agricultural production (about 40% of cultivated land) and conceals a general phenomenon of the low development of the productive forces in Moroccan agriculture overall (7 million ha). By way of illustration, of the total number of agricultural holdings, fewer than 15% currently have access to mechanical energy.[78] Furthermore, from 1956 to 1977, only 482 state engineers and veterinarians were trained, for a rural population numbering some 11 million (1977), which is one engineer for every 22,821 peasants.[79]

b) The preponderance of 'non-capitalist' forms of agricultural production in the arable areas provides a second indicator revealing the slowness of the spread of the capitalist sphere of production. In fact, over five million hectares out of a total arable area of seven million hectares make up the so-called collective lands given over to food crops. The five million hectares occupy almost 80% of the rural population.[80] Even taking the more optimistic figures of the 1973–1974 agricultural census, it appears that over 56% of farms under five hectares are marginal lands of very low productivity and specialised in food grains, accounting for 50% of our potential grain production.[81] On these farms, the dominant form of production is still governed by kinship relations. Subsistence farming remains the principal purpose of production and exchange.[82] Even the exchange economy is only concerned, in this setting, with subsistence problems: 'whereas the farmer in the capitalist system is absorbed in thinking about market prices, the family farmer,' writes P. Pascon, on this subject, 'when he turns, in part, to the exchange economy is haunted by the number of mouths to feed and the manpower he has available to him'.[83]

This quantitative preponderance of 'non-capitalist' forms of agricultural production conceals a qualitative dominance of capitalist forms. The articulation between the two does not however seem to be 'temporary', that is destined to disappear and give way to the exclusive development of capitalism. The reality is

**Table 3.1**
**Sales of agricultural equipment 1956–1978 (in units)**

| Year | Agricultural tractors | Combine harvesters | Straw presses |
|------|------|------|------|
| 1956 | 532 | 487 | 89 |
| 1957 | 910 | 232 | 44 |
| 1958 | 1,335 | 48 | 9 |
| 1959 | 760 | 107 | 12 |
| 1960 | 665 | 147 | 19 |
| 1961 | 475 | 115 | 28 |
| 1962 | 601 | 41 | 30 |
| 1963 | 452 | 67 | 15 |
| 1964 | 623 | 177 | 58 |
| 1965 | 805 | 144 | 14 |
| 1966 | 968 | 104 | 35 |
| 1967 | 1,058 | 81 | 161 |
| 1968 | 2,286 | 56 | 32 |
| 1969 | 1,618 | 366 | 111 |
| 1970 | 1,912 | 257 | 61 |
| 1971 | 1,526 | 198 | 52 |
| 1972 | 1,487 | 209 | 84 |
| 1973 | 1,612 | 218 | 120 |
| 1974 | 1,784 | 125 | 125 |
| 1975 | 2,706 | 158 | 155 |
| 1976 | 2,083 | 118 | 315 |
| 1977 | 2,835 | 235 | 374 |
| 1978 | 2,592 | 226 | 142 |

*Source: La vie économique*, op. cit., p. 6;
*Le Maroc agricole*, no. 105, March 1978, p. 8.

much more complex since the slowness of the integration of 'traditional' forms of agricultural production into capitalism is to be explained, in large part, by the role those forms play in the legitimising system of the political regime. The leaders themselves are fully aware of this role: 'covering a large area [the communal forms of agricultural production] are important to the Moroccan economy for two reasons: they make a not insignificant contribution to supplying the country, particularly in grains, and they provide a living for a large proportion of farmers'.[84]

These few data on the importance of 'non-capitalist' forms of agricultural production testify to the slow rhythm of the development of capital.

c) Agricultural credit is supposed to be a special factor, diffusing capitalist relations of production. It is intended to fulfil this function at three levels:

– Agricultural credit involves putting into circulation large sums of money and by so doing contributes to the development of commodity and monetary relations;

– It also contributes to a certain development of the productive forces to the extent that it promotes the purchase of agricultural equipment.

– It obliges the peasant to subordinate his production to the market so as to provide himself with the liquid cash necessary for repayment of debts.

But an analysis of the evolution of agricultural credit[85] in Morocco reveals the weakness of its effects on the generalised diffusion of capitalist relations of production.

The first reason for this weakness is the selective character of this credit. The fact is that while the amount of credits increased by about 152% between 1962 and 1977,[86] it was the minority of big landowners engaged in capitalist forms of production who benefited. The 1978–1980 plan itself recognised this phenomenon; in it it is stated: 'During the five-year period (1973–1977), 200,000 farmers were able to benefit from agricultural credit loans, or about 10% of the total number of farmers, which is of course relatively few'.[87]

The second reason stems from the very nature of the use made of agricultural credit. Neither in its orientations nor in the 'reaction' it provokes among the peasants does the application of agricultural credit obey any capitalist logic.

In this respect, what is most striking is the channelling of credits essentially towards the purchase of consumption goods. This comment can be backed up by the preponderance of short-term credits granted by the CNCA. For 1973 the Bank of Morocco reports that the CNCA shared in almost 70% of the distribution of short-term credits, a rise of 7.7% over the previous year; this trend was apparent throughout the whole credit sector in Morocco since 'credits for two years or less constituted 71% and medium- and long-term credits 29% instead of 67% and 33% a year earlier'.[88]

d) The evolution or intensity of the development of the wage relation in the principal sectors of the economy constitutes another factor making it possible to access the limits on the enlargement of capitalist relations of production within the Moroccan economy.

Thus, in the industrial sector, industry's contribution to total employment virtually stagnated between 1960 and 1977; it represented 10.2% in 1960, 10.5% in 1971 and 11.8% in 1977. In the rural areas, the slowness of the diffusion of the wage relationship was still more pronounced as Table 3.2 shows.

From this table it emerges that:

– The percentage of wage-earners in the rural areas remains low: 20% in 1960, 21% in 1971, 21.7% in 1977. This clearly reflects the weakness of the spread of the wage relationship as a specifically capitalist relationship in the rural areas.

– The share of 'traditional' forms of agricultural production remains overwhelming: it was 69.5% in 1960, 75.4% in 1977. This figure, which includes 'self-employed' and 'family helpers', becomes larger if one takes into account seasonal workers who represent two-thirds of wage-earners.

Furthermore, even taking the case of agricultural regions where the capitalist form of production is most widespread, there too the low level of wage-earning can be observed. In the case of the Gharb, Lazarev reports that only one household in five is wage-earning on a permanent or part-time basis in farms alone. This ratio is 1:4 in the Meknès region.[89] The share of the agricultural sector as a whole in total wage employment has actually declined, dropping from 32.4% in 1960 to 28.5% in 1970.[90]

64

**Table 3.2**
**Employment in the rural areas (October 1977) (in '000 of individuals)**

| Year Category | 1960 Numbers | % | 1971 Numbers | % | 1977 Numbers | % |
|---|---|---|---|---|---|---|
| Employers | 177 | 9.6 | 57 | 2.9 | 57 | 2.7 |
| Self-employed | 814 | 44.4 | 837 | 42.1 | 877 | 41.5 |
| Wage-earners | 366 | 20.0 | 419 | 21.1 | 458 | 21.7 |
| Family helpers | 461 | 25.1 | 672 | 33.8 | 716 | 33.9 |
| Situation not stated | 16 | 0.9 | 3 | 0.1 | 4 | 0.2 |
| Total | 1,834 | 100 | 1,988 | 100 | 2,112 | 100 |

*Source:* Boutata. M.. 'Les problèmes de l'emploi au Maroc', in *La crise, l'alternative*. Ed, Al Bayane. Rabat, 1980, p. 253.

These data illustrate undeniably the 'lopsided' character of the move towards the wage relationship, and this is so even in the regions 'really' subordinated to capital.

e) The smallness of the home market is a further indication of the weakness of the diffusion of capitalist relations of production since 'the issue of the home market simply does not arise as a separate, self-sufficient problem not depending on that of the degree of capitalist development. The home market appears when commodity economy appears; it is created by the development of the commodity economy, and the extent of the social division of labour determines the level of its development; it spreads with the extension of commodity production from products to labour-power, and it is only to the extent that the latter is transformed into a commodity that capitalism embraces the production of the country'.[91]

In Morocco, the economic effects of the smallness of the home market are officially recognised. Thus, we can read in the 1973–1977 plan that 'the smallness of the home market does not make sufficient development of our industry possible. Despite the existence of a potential market of more than 15 million inhabitants, habits of subsistence in the rural areas and the slow growth of real incomes considerably reduce the real market. We must therefore export in order to be able to increase the activity of this sector of the economy and thus create jobs. The incomes procured by these new jobs will in turn enlarge the home market'.[92]

In fact, in the Moroccan social formation, the existence of a large sector of formal subordination ('non-capitalist' forms of production) is indicative of the importance of subsistence consumption. The share of this latter in the rural areas in 1971 was 50% for grains and grain-based products, 24.6%, 19% and 14% respectively for fats, vegetables and meat.[93]

On the other hand, the under-remuneration of labour in agriculture constitutes the second factor explaining the smallness of the home market. Table 3.3 reflects this situation.

The various elements described above testify to the particular features of the functioning of the 'law of capital' in peripheral social formations. These various factors — reflecting the weakness of the material base of legitimacy of the Moroccan political regime — explain why capital is shored up by the state, as part of its efforts to establish 'national unity'.

The scale of state intervention is to be explained, in this framework, by the particular character of social reproduction. The weakness of the material base of legitimation rules out any "fetishisation" of social relations; whence the recourse by the state — at the level of its legitimising function — to 'political fetishism'.

**Table 3.3**
**State and remuneration in rural areas**

*Temporary jobs*
a) less than 2 dirhams          11
b) 2 dirhams and above          27
c) 3 dirhams and above          24
d) 4 dirhams and above          16

*Permanent jobs*
e) 5 to 8 dirhams               16
f) 8 to 10 dirhams               4
g) 10 dirhams and above          2
                               ___
                               100

*Source:* P. Pascon and M. Bentahar, *Etudes sociologiques sur le Maroc*, op. cit., p. 200.

## Some hypotheses on the state and social alliances in Morocco

Analysis of the Moroccan state reveals a 'lack of correspondence' between its outward form and its real nature.[94]

This 'lack of correspondence' is the product of the complex history of state structures in Morocco. A systematic study of the history of these state structures (pre-colonial, colonial, and post-colonial) would reveal one major fact: the continuity of the 'traditional' system of political domination represented in a particular form of the Moroccan state (i.e. the existing political regime) and based on the dominance of the 'land-power' relationship in the production and reproduction of the Moroccan social formation. It should be recalled in this connection that colonisation did not hamper the formation of landholdings by the landed oligarchy that had been in progress for centuries in the pre-colonial period,[95] 'quite the contrary, not only did this class not lose most of the advantages that it had acquired by the beginning of the 20th century, but it took advantage of its collaboration with the colonial system to develop its situation and among other things to consolidate its pre-1918 landholdings'.[96] On the subject of this continuity in political and economic domination by the landed oligarchy, Lazarev notes that the lists of landowners in 1960 show that they were the same names except for a few newcomers, and that there are elements of continuity between the administration of the *makhzen* and that of the higher administration of independent Morocco.[97]

However, this same analysis also shows an important change in this continuity: the presence of a new mode of exploitation giving the state a capitalist essence.[98] This double form of existence of the state is the expression of the two essential components of every class society underlying state organisation; exploitation as the process by which class society tends 'to assure social subsistence', and domination, which defines the forms in which this exploitation is maintained and accepted.[99]

Concerning the pre-capitalist Moroccan economic and social formation, most of the 'historic discourses' on the state testify to the 'co-existence' of two principal forms of social organisation: a tribal form of organisation and another 'makhzenian' form.

An examination of the articulation of these forms of social organisation with the Moroccan pre-capitalist social formation makes it possible to distinguish three principal paradigms.[100]

– The colonialist paradigm[101] establishing relations of externality between the two forms of social organisation.[102]

– The neo-Khaldunian paradigm[103] stressing on the contrary the relations of complementarity between these two forms.

– The paradigm of the 'nation' based on the thesis of the unity of the Moroccan socio-political system in which the 'tribal fact' and, more generally, 'the local rulers' constitute a simple component of this system.[104]

These various approaches to the Moroccan state and society, despite their divergences, reveal the existence of a political system that, in our view, colonisation did not fundamentally alter.[105]

The colonial period did not mark a break with the past, for two reasons. First, the relatively short duration of colonialism, comparing Morocco to Algeria and other countries in 'Black Africa'. Secondly, and more importantly, the very nature of the system, the colonial state, allowed all the administrative machinery of the *makhzen* to continue to exist and maintained the traditional élites of the country (great *caids, zawiya* chiefs) in office.[106]

### Nature and form of the Moroccan state: a contradiction?

The distinction between state and political regime makes it possible to conduct the analysis of the Moroccan state at two levels: at a logical level through deducting its nature from the constituted world economy (CWE); at a historical level through looking at the concrete characteristics that the state (the political regime) assumes in a given historical context.

In fact the social changes that have occurred in the Moroccan economy and society over a century take on two closely related forms: growing statisation of the economy[107] and capitalisation.[108]

The development of landed capitalism (which is reflected in a process of capitalisation of urban and rural property rent, encouraged by the state) made this conciliation-adaptation possible during an initial period covering the decade 1960–1970 when a series of crises (internal and external) clearly showed its social and political limits. Analysis of the function of regeneration of capital reveals, during this period, a preferential treatment of landed capital (land and property) at the expense of industrial capital.

67

This preferential treatment is perceptible at several levels.

– In the agricultural domain, water policy,[109] the role of the CNCA,[110] as well as that of the fiscal system[111] are evidence of a regime aiming at the development of agrarian capital. These choices proceeded from a will (or a concern) to develop capitalism while at the same time reproducing the 'traditional' social space which underlies the political regime; choices which had no chance of being realised except through the transformation of the landed oligarchy into an agrarian bourgeoisie.

– In real estate, comparison of the Real Estate Investment Code and the Industrial Investment Code reveals the preferential attitude the state adopts towards the development of the real estate sector.[112]

– So far as concerns industry, many indicators reveal a 'calculated indifference' on the part of the 'authorities' vis-à-vis the development of industrial capitalism.[113]

This particular nature of the function of the regeneration of capital (development of landed capital) is the logical product of the contradiction between the extended reproduction of capital and legitimation.

An option in favour of the first term of the contradiction would have implied a development of industrial capitalism and, hence, engendered a crisis of the political regime which draws its legitimacy from the 'traditional social space' (industrialisation presupposes a restructuring of the agrarian structure — an agrarian reform — and the formation of a significant home market through a policy of income redistribution which is harmful to the interests of the 'dominant segments' of the rural social space). Concerned with subordinating its practice to the requirements of legitimation, the political regime set itself the task of erasing the contradiction in favour of the second term; the regeneration of landed capital constituted the means of reconciling reproduction of capital (a demand imposed by the articulation of the Moroccan state with other states in the framework of the constituted world economy) and reproduction of the 'traditional social space' (the source of legitimacy for the political regime). Thus the function of the regeneration of capital seems to have as its objective foundation the function of legitimation.

We should however specify that the interest given by the political regime to its traditional space does not concern solely the 'economic and political élites' (the landed oligarchy) but the whole of the rural social space. It is in this perspective that the components of the agrarian policy aiming at controlling the rural areas must be interpreted.

'Operation ploughing'[114], 'national promotion'[115], the system of agricultural 'small credit'[116] are so many different aspects of public intervention which are evidence of the primacy accorded by the political regime to the function of legitimation.

The 1970s constituted a period in which the lack of correspondence between the nature and form of the state produced sharper and sharper contradictions in a socio-historical context of internal political crisis (of legitimation) coupled with a world conjuncture of economic crisis.

This context was reflected at the level of the class struggle by growing 'frictions' among the various social factors.[117]

In this context, several attempts at 'readaptation' were, once again, undertaken by the government (Moroccanisation,[118] egalitarian discourses, 'industrialisation',[119] etc.).

Nevertheless, analysis of public practice — distinguishing the level of discourse from the strictly practical level — reveals a continuity in the logic that has hitherto underpinned this practice. But this is a continuity that is increasingly shaken by the sharpening of internal contradictions.

Whence a question of very great current concern: are these various attempts at re-adaptation really indicative of a potential for rupture? Or are they mere changes in continuity? The difficulty of answering such a question does not however prevent us from observing, without ignoring the possibilities of reverses, on the basis of certain data, the emerging trend in social reality. Two key facts support this view: the modesty of the results and the selective character of Moroccanisation[120] and the limits of the state's 'industrial policy'.

In fact the results of Moroccanisation (which has in any case been called into question by the new investment code[121]) and the limits of the state's industrial policy are evidence of a continuity in public practice, despite the vague attempts at restructuring apparently underway since 1973. Analysis of the achievements shows that it is light industries that have enjoyed virtually all public investment.[122]

More recently, the promotion of small and medium enterprises (PME) seems to constitute a step backwards. It is in fact no such thing if one attempts to grasp the true socio-political determinants of this 'promotion' through an analysis of its nature and results.

In this last perspective, the policy of 'promoting small and medium enterprises' looks more like an attempt by the state to open up its social space to certain social strata (a fraction of the petty bourgeoisie) in an economic and social context of world crisis reflected, at the political level, in a more or less relaxed conflict between the state and certain segments of the 'ruling class'.[123]

In fact the current crisis of agro-export activities on the one hand, and the textile and leather industry on the other produced by the crisis in the central economies, has led to a loss of legitimacy among certain fractions of the bourgeoisie with regard to public interventionism.

In this context the state — realising the risk of its social space shrinking — is turning to an economic policy aimed at enlarging it to previously excluded social strata. That, in our opinion, is one of the principal reasons for the existence of the 'promotion of small and medium enterprises', rather than any will to industrialise the country; the results of this policy which seems to affect and benefit primarily the non-industrial small and medium enterprises, bears this out.[124]

Even concerning the small and medium industries which have benefited from this policy, their orientation by the state into agro–industrial activities constitutes another confirmation of this trend towards the transformation of the landed oligarchy into an 'agro–industrial bourgeoisie'.[125]

## Conclusion

In this sense, the Moroccan state is the product of various periods of this historical evolution: pre-colonial, colonial and post-colonial. Taking account of the capitalist era alone to understand the Moroccan state is a 'capital-centred reductionism' which cannot throw light on the impact of 'traditional' mechanisms which are still at work in shaping its functions (functions of legitimation and the regeneration of capital). The capitalist nature of the Moroccan state — conferred by its participation in the world state system — is articulated, contradictorily, on a function of 'traditionalising' legitimation. This function's dominance at the level of the process of social reproduction sets objective limits to the function of the regeneration of capital. The resulting slow and specific diffusion of capitalist relations of production is reflected in the weakness of the state's material basis of legitimacy.

Conversely, the approach to the state suggested in this paper has the advantage of being able to provide an important explanatory element of the mode of development of capitalism in Morocco and consequently of the form of underdevelopment; and to do so by relating the 'lack of correspondence' between the (capitalist) nature of the Moroccan state and its particular phenomenal form (the 'neo-patrimonial' political regime) on the one hand and the real estate mode that the development of capitalism assumes in Morocco (development of export agriculture and property speculation) to the detriment of the development of industrial capitalism on the other.

Starting from this approach, the present crisis of the state in Africa seems to be the manifestation of a *structural tendency towards the resurgence of the contradiction between the two requirements of social reproduction: the regeneration of capital and legitimation.*

While being a structural effect, it was possible to gloss over this contradiction in the past thanks to projects of 'social ordering' (development of dependent agrarian capitalism, of ISI, etc.) made possible and encouraged by the 'classic' international division of labour, which reconciled the development of capital and legitimation. At present, the state, running out of possibilities as a result of the effects of the crisis of world capitalism, is struck with a double paralysis: its inability to ensure the regeneration of capital without engendering a loss of legitimacy dangerous to existing political regimes.

## Notes

1. Defetishisation (in the sense of demystification) refers here to the fact that the illusion according to which social reality appears as something other than it is, is severely challenged in periods of crisis.

2. Even where there have been some slight attempts at social change, signs of them being reversed are apparent today, which removes any illusions about the consolidation of the popular content of these experiences.

3. The historical relevance of such an idea was confirmed by a concrete analysis of relations between state and dominant classes in Morocco. See A. Doumou, *De la problématique de l'Etat périphérique. Essai d'interprétation de l'intervention de l'Etat marocain*, Rabat, 1984.

4. The question of the state in dependent societies constitutes a very recent concern in the Marxist theory of development and underdevelopment. In this connection see the recent systematic studies devoted to the question by H. Alavi, 'The state in post-colonial societies: Pakistan and Bangladesh', *New Left Review*, July–August 1972; A. G. Frank, 'La crise économique et l'Etat dans le Tiers monde', in *Perspectives Latino–Américaines*, 1, October–December 1980 (Ed. Anthropos). The important contribution (but one not translated into French) by Latin American authors seems equally to date from the last decade if we believe P. Salama's presentation of the debates on the question of the state in Latin America in 'Au-delà d'un faux débat', *Actes du XLIIe Congrès International des Américanistes*, Paris, 29 September 1976, published with the assistance of the Fondation Singer Polignac. As for 'conventional' development theory, the question of the state is now being re-examined, having been originally discounted as being outside the methodological purview of its whole problematic. In fact, even establishment authors who have never dealt with the state are beginning to ask themselves 'Do we need a theory of the state?', *European Journal of Sociology*, 1977, cited by Philip Resnick in 'Search of a theory of the modern state', paper presented to the 19th World Congress of the International Political Science Association, Moscow (USSR), 12-18 August 1978.

5. G. O'Donnell, 'Formation historique comparée de l'appareil étatique dans le Tiers Monde et changement socio-économique', *Revue Internationale des Sciences Sociales*, 4, 1980, p. 773.

6. See in this connection for the case of Morocco: J.-L. Miège, 'L'ouverture', in *Le Maroc et l'Europe*, PUF, 1961; C. Lazarev, 'Aspects du capitalisme agraire marocain avant le protectorat', in *Problèmes agraires au Maghreb*, CNRS, 1977. M. Kenbib, 'Structures traditionelles et protection diplomatique dans le Maroc précolonial', in *Structures et cultures précapitalistes*, Anthropos, 1981.

7. For example, the evolution of the sugar industry in Morocco is indicative of this integration. On this see P. Berthier, 'L'archéologie, source de l'histoire économique: les plantations de canne à sucre et les fabriques de sucre dans l'ancien Maroc', *Hesperis Tamuda*, 1966; 'L'ère d'ouverture sous M. Ben Abdallah', manuscript n° 981 entitled 'Natijatou al ijtihad fi al mouhadanati ou al jihad', edited by Ahmed Ben Mehdi el Khoggal on the sultan's orders. N° 981 BGSA.8. See K. Vergopoulos, 'L'Etat dans le capitalisme périphérique', *Revue Tiers–Monde*, vol. XXIV, 93, January–March 1983, p. 45.

9. For a study of the mechanisms by which the fields of the economic (particular diffusion of capitalist relations of producton) and the socio-cultural (importance of ethnic, religious and other relations) condition social struggles and alliances, see in particular:

10. See E. B. Pasukanis, *La théorie générale du droit et du marxisme*, Ed. EDI, 1970; J. Holloway and S. Picoiotto, 'Etat et capital: le débat allemand sur la "dérivation" de l'Etat', *CEP*, 10, 1980; H. Hirata 'Les recherches marxistes sur l'Etat contemporain: deux lectures', *CEP* 26, 1977; J. S. Gonzales, 'La question de l'Etat dans les pays capitalistes sous-développés. Quelques problèmes de méthodes', *CEP*, 13-14, 1980; F. Mellah, *Les espaces du prince*, op. cit.; M.Carnoy, *The State and Political Theory*, Princeton University Press, 1984.

11. See P. Salama and G. Mathias, *L'Etat surdéveloppé*, Découvertes, Maspero, 1983.

12. For the states of North Africa (especially Tunisia and Morocco), the crisis in relations with the EEC, accentuated by the entry of Portugal and Spain, are

indicative of the exhaustion of the classic mode of their integration into the world capitalist market.

13. The social and political reservations encountered in the implementation of austerity policies recommended by the World Bank and the IMF are clear expressions of this contradiction (Morocco, Tunisia, Sudan, etc.).

14. See J. Habermas, *Raison et Légitimité*, Payot, 1978.

15. In Latin America, the activities of CLASCO (notably a seminar on the social sciences confronting the challenge of the 80s, Mexico, 1981, organised by Unesco) which brings together institutions and researchers are an illlustration of this. In Africa, during the second congress of the IAS, held in Dakar in December 1983, it was unanimously agreed that democracy is a socio-economic imperative.

16. See Abdelali Doumou, *De la problématique de l'Etat périphérique. Essai d'interprétation de l'intervention économique de l'Etat marocain*, ch. 1, forthcoming, Editions Publi-Sud, Paris, 1986.

17. See A. Doumou, *De la problématique*, op. cit., pp. 22 et seq.

18. J. Stalin, *Marxism and the National Question*, International, 1942.

19. See J. Chesneaux, 'Le processus de formation des nations en Afrique et en Asie', *Pensée*, 119, February 1965, p. 74.

20. One of the first to have raised the fundamental question of the 'nation' from a Marxist viewpoint was J. Suret-Canale, in *Présence Africaine*, February–May 1959.

21. See Potekhin, 'De quelques problèmes méthodologiques pour l'étude de la formation des nations en Afrique au Sud du Sahara', *Présence Africaine*, 17, 1958.

22. See J. Ziegler, *Main basse sur l'Afrique*, Paris, Le Seuil, 1978, pp. 35-38.

23. See G. P. Tchivounda, *Essai sur l'Etat Africain post-colonial*, Paris, LGDJ, 1982, p. 56.

24. See S. Amin, *The Arab Nation*, Zed Press, 1978, p. 10.

25. See Khaled Bakdash, *Ittijahan fi'l-'haraka al watanyya al 'Arabiyya*, Beirut, 1959.

26. It is in Egypt that Marxists have faced up to the theoretical problematic of the nation most systematically, perhaps because of the antiquity of certain Egyptian 'national traditions', or of the relative novelty of the Arab dimension in Egyptian social life.

27. This formula was suggested by A. Abdel Malek in his introduction to 'La pensée arabe contemporaine', 3rd cycle thesis, Paris 1964 (substantially in English as *Contemporary Arab Political Thought*, Zed Books, 1983).

28. It is not a mere coincidence that most of the works devoted to pre-colonial Morocco do not raise this problem; it is because it is assumed that the problem of the state has been eliminated. See for example: K. Allioua, 'L'Etat marocain anté-colonial', 3rd cycle thesis, Ecole des Hautes Etudes, Paris, 1980; D. Benali, 'Essai d'analyse de la formation économique et sociale marocaine précapitaliste', state thesis in economics, Grenoble, 1976; M. Ennaji, 'L'expansion européenne et le Maroc du 16e au 18e siècles', DES, Rabat, 1981.

29. See A. Laroui, *Les origines sociales et culturelles du nationalisme marocain 1836–1912*, Maspero, 1977.

30. Ibid., p. 27.

31. Ibid.

32. See the table of contents in Laroui's book, op. cit., pp. 477-479.

33. See Stalin's definition above.

34. See A. Laroui, *Les origines*, op. cit., p. 32.

35. Ibid., p. 33.

36. Ibid., p. 40.
37. Ibid., p. 52.
38. Ibid., pp. 56-57.
39. Ibid., p. 65.
40. Ibid., p. 66.
41. Ibid., p. 124.
42. Ibid., p. 127.
43. Ibid., p. 124.
44. See the analysis of the role of the brotherhood in ibid.
45. Ibid., p. 190.
46. S. Amin, *The Arab Nation*, op. cit., p. 81.
47. See T. G. Pangalos, *Les espaces du prince*, PUF, 1978, p. 77.
48. Ibid.
49. There is often a tendency in the Third World to confuse a purpose of the state: 'the creation of the nation' (which is why we prefer to speak rather of 'project-nation') and the intrinsic content of the social formations which is 'a-national'.
50. See G. P. Tchivounda, op. cit., p. 36.
51. See *Les espaces du prince*, op. cit., p. 78.
52. See interview granted to *Paris–Match*, 15 August 1980, n° 1629, p. 9.
53. See S. Amin, *The Arab Nation*, op. cit., p. 81.
54. Ibid. p. 82.
55. 'One of the characteristics in which we can see the absence of a national construct is the fundamentally foreign nature of the culture of the local bourgeoisie . . . the ruling class uses the language of the old colonial masters while the people continue to speak the vernacular. How can we speak of nation and national culture under such conditions?' S. Amin, *Class and Nation*, Monthly Review Press, 1980, p. 175.
56. The Hausa grouping, with its 25 million members and its economic, political and linguistic position, is one of the most important forces in Black Africa, and the Biafran crisis put it in the headlines; this is evidence of the importance of this fact. See G. Nicolas, 'Organisation sociale et appréhension du monde au sein d'une société africaine', thesis for doctorat d'état, Bordeaux, 1969 and 'Fondements magico-religieux du pouvoir politique au sein de la principauté haoussa du Gobir', *Journal de la Société des Africanistes*, 34, 2, 1969.
57. 'Thus, although state and nation are not identical, the national phenomenon cannot be separated from the analysis of the state.' S. Amin, *Class and Nation*, op. cit., pp. 19-20.
58. See *Les espaces du prince*, op. cit., p. 94.
59. See P. Salama and G. Mathias, *L'Etat surdéveloppé*, Maspero, 1983.
60. K. Marx, *Capital*, vol. I, ch. 4.
61. See H. Lefebvre, *De l'Etat*, 10/18, 1976, vol. 2. p. 123.
62. See A. Laroui, *The concept of the state* (in Arabic), Arab Cultural Centre.
63. M. Godelier, *Horizon, trajets marxistes en anthropologie*, Maspero, 1977, vol. 1, p. 134.
64. See M. Godelier, *Horizon*, op. cit., pp. 41 et seq.
65. P. Pascon, *Le Haouz de Marrakech*, INAV, Rabat and CNRS, Paris, 1977, vol. 2, pp. 593-594.
66. See also ibid.
67. We adopt a broad meaning of the word 'crisis'; it does not here describe a simple 'temporary dysfunction' of capitalism taking the form essentially of

inflation and unemployment (which seems to be the case in the developed capitalist countries currently); the term 'chronic crisis' here describes a structural situation of most 'underdeveloped' countries characterized by a low level of economic integration (persistence of a large sector of formal subordination, absence of a true capital market, etc.) weakness and fragmentation of local capital, importance of unproductive accumulation, etc.

68. Concerning the characteristics of this class, see especially S. Amin, *Unequal Development*, Monthly Review Press, 1976, pp. 338 et seq.; *Class and Nation*, op., cit., pp. 74 et seq., pp. 131 et seq. See also A. G. Frank, *Lumpenbourgeoisie and Lumpenproletariat*, Monthly Review Press, 1972; E. Mandel, 'Classes sociales et crise politique en Amérique Latine', *CEP*, 16-17; September 1974; Mahmoud Hussein, *Class Conflict in Egypt: 1945–1970*, Monthly Review Press, 1973; A. Touraine, 'Les classes sociales dans une société dépendante', *Tiers-Monde*, XVI, 62, April–June 1975.

69. Thus running a very great risk of glossing over the real problem which is that of grasping the nature of the economic, political, ideological, etc., behaviour of this class.

70. 'The weight of the oligarchy that monopolizes the most profitable lines of business, the movement to the concentration and centralization of capital, the close dependence of these strata on the banks (for credit) and the administration (markets, licences, etc.) create within them a situation of unease and frustration, expressing itself up to a certain point in nationalist-type demands and in a relative hostility to the oligarchy', Aziz Belal, 'La bourgeoisie marocaine est-elle ou n'est-elle pas?', *Lamalif*, 136, 1982.

71. 'In short the bourgeoisie of the Third World is not bourgeois (in the Marxian sense); it is bourgeois in its caricatural mimicry in the area of consumption, but it is not capitalist by its role in the accumulation process or by its political and ideological practice; its development is maintained by statism in its various forms', H. El-Malki, 'Dépendance et problématique de la transition', *RIPEM*, special issue, June–December 1980, p. 217.

72. Here we shall simply list these elements and for analysis of them refer to A. Doumou, *De la problématique*, op. cit., ch. III.

73. See A. Berrada, 'Secteur public et formes indirectes de la dépendance', *Al Assas*, 17, December 1982; Chiguer, 'Le secteur financier publique marcain de 1904 à 1980'. DES, Rabat, 1981.

74. For an analysis of the role of the public sector, see A. Doumou, op. cit., ch. IV.

75. Ibid.

76 See Lenin, *The Development of Capitalism in Russia*, Moscow, Foreign Languages Publishing House, 1956, p. 76.

77. See P. Pascon, *Le Haouz*, op. cit.

78. See D. Guerraoui, 'Dualismes agraires et développement rural', thesis for doctorat d'état es-sciences économiques, Lyon II, 1982, p. 338.

79. See D. A. E. Mara, 'Données essentielles sur le secteur agricole'.

80. See D. Guerraoui, op. cit., p. 349.

81. See 'Le recensement agricole 1973–74', *Libération*, January–February 1981, p. 8

82. P. Pascon, 'Segmentation et stratification dans la société rurale marocaine', in *Recherches récentes sur le Maroc moderne*, BESM 1979.

83. P. Pascon, 'Considérations préliminaires sur l'economie des exploitations

agricoles familiales', *RJPEM* (Rabat), 3, December 1973, p. 83.

84. *Plan 1978–1980*, p. 174.

85. For this analysis see A. Berrada, *Le crédit agricole au Maroc de 1917 à 1977*, Rabat, 1979. See also T. Masmoudi, *Le crédit agricole,*, BMRR, Casablanca, 1982.

86. See A. Berrada, op. cit.

87. *Plan*, op. cit., p. 137.

88. See *Rapport de la Banque du Maroc, exercice 1973*, p. 140.

89. G. Lazarev, 'Changement social et développement dans les campagnes marocaines', in *Etudes sociologiques sur le Maroc*, p. 138. (The figures date from 1966.)

90. See 'Etude de Dar Al Handsah, croissance et transformations structurelles de l'industrie marocaine 1968–76'.

91. See Lenin, *The Development of Capitalism in Russia*, op. cit., pp. 48-49.

92. See *Plan 1973–1977*, vol. II, p. 372.

93. See D. Guerraoui, op. cit., p. 391.

94. See A. Doumou, *De la problématique*, op. cit.

95. For the precolonial period see essentially G. Lazarev, 'Remarques sur la seigneurie terrienne au Maroc', in *Structures et cultures précapitalistes*, Paris, Ed Anthropos, 1981 and 'Aspects du capitalisme agraire au Maroc avant le protectorat', *A. A. N.,* CNRS, XIV, 1975.

96. See G. Lazarev, 'Aspects', op. cit., p. 87.

97. See G. Lazarev, op. cit., and P. Pascon, *Le Haouz*, op. cit.

98. See below, discussion of the function of the regeneration of capital of the Moroccan state. The analysis of the concrete manifestations of this function is evidence of the particular features of the capitalist nature of the Moroccan state which proceeds from the lack of correspondence of its two levels of existence (nature-form).

99. See Foessart, *Les Etats*, vol. V, Paris, Seuil, 1981, p. 9.

100. We prefer the concept of paradigm to that of discourse for two principal reasons. The pejorative aspect with which the term discourse is perceived and which arises form the strong ideological connotation given it in everyday language. Freed of linearity and the 'positivism' which underlies it in grasping the evolution of knowledge (see essentially T. S. Kuhn, *The Structures of Scientific Revolutions*, Chicago, 1962), the concept of paradigm has the relevance of accounting for the emergence, evolution and crisis of a 'system of thought', providing that the criteria defining this latter are first defined.

101. We have brought together under this heading simply to be systematic both what is called colonial ethnology and segmentary analysis. For colonial ethnology see especially: Eugène Aubin, *Le Maroc d'aujourd'hui*, Paris, 1904; A. Bernard, *Le Maroc*, Paris, Ed. F. Alcan, 1921; H. Terrasse, *Histoire du Maroc*, Casablanca, Ed. Atlantides, 1950; R. Montage, *Les Berbères et le Makhzen dans le sud du Maroc*, Paris, Ed. F. Alcan, 1930. For segmentary analysis see especially E. Gellner, *Saints of the Atlas*, London, Weidenfeld and Nicholson, 1969; D. M. Hart, 'Segmentary systems and the role of the fifths in rural Morocco', *Revue de l'occident musulman et de la méditerranée* (Aix-en-Provence).

102. See the discussion of the relations between the *blad siba* (dissident tribes) and the *blad makhzen* (central government) in the above-cited works.

103. We use the term 'neo' to indicate that we are referring, beyond the works of Ibn Khaldoun, to a number of contemporary writers who start from the tribe (in one or other of its dimensions: kinship, religion, etc.) in order to grasp the mechanisms

of reproduction — the forms of legitimation — of the pre-colonial Moroccan state. See M. Morsy, 'Comment décrire l'histoire du Maroc?', *BESM*, 138-139, 1979; and *Les Ahansalas, examen du rôle historique d'une famille maraboutique*, Paris–The Hague, Mouton, 1972; A. Hammoudi, 'Segmentarité, stratification sociale, pouvoir politique et sainteté, réflexions sur les thèses de Gellner', *Hespéris-Tamuda* (Rabat), XV, 1974.

104. See especially G. Ayache, *Le Maroc. Bilan d'une colonisation*, Ed. Sociales, 1950; G. Ayache, *Etudes d'histoire marocaine*, Rabat, Smer, 1979, A. Laroui, *L'histoire du Maghreb*, Paris, Maspero, 1975; and A. Laroui, *Les origines sociales*, op. cit.

105. See our discussion of the patrimonial state and its characteristics in 'Crises, réformisme et pénétration étrangère au Maroc' paper presented to the international seminar held at the faculty of letters, Rabat, Morocco, 'Réformisme et société marocaine au XIXe siècle', April 1983.

106. This colonial practice invented by Lyautey was scrupulously followed by all his successors. See *Lyautey l'Africain*, selected texts presented by P. Lyautey, 4 vols., Paris, Plon; and *Lyautey Maréchal, Paroles d'action, 1900–1926*, A. Colin.

107. This in no way signifies that this process is new. On the contrary, the makhzenian's monopoly of the economy was a major characteristic of pre-colonial Morocco. It is only the scale and novelty of the forms of this phenomenon which make the post-colonial period special.

108. By capitalization we mean the diffusion of capitalist relations of production; although this is real, it takes on particular forms; see *Le Tiers-Monde*, op. cit.

109. See *Plan 1968–72* in which 42% of state investment in agriculture was devoted to irrigation projects, *Plan 1968–72*, vol. I. p. 79. See also the report on the ORMVA, by the minister-delegate of the prime minister, November 1980; MARA, 'Données essentielles sur le secteur agricole', division des affaires économiques, April 1979; this report shows that between 1954 and 1984 14 dams were built or in progress. See, finally, Ben Elkadi, 'L'évolution de l'exploitation des réserves hydrauliques', INAV, Rabat, 1975–1976.

110. See especially T. Mesmoudi, *Le crédit agricole et le développement de l'agriculture au Maroc*, SMER, 1982 and A. Berrada, *Le crédit agricole au Maroc 1917-1977*, publication of the Faculty of Law, Rabat, 1980.

111. See A. Berrada, 'L'impôt agricole' *RJEPM*, 11, 1982.

112. See Maria Benbouchaib, 'Eléments d'analyse de la crise du logement à travers l'étude de la ville de Rabat', DES, Rabat, 1981, pp. 175 et seq. See also A. Berrada, 'La bourgeoisie immobilière, un enfant gaté du système fiscal'. *Al Assas*, dossier n° 1, 1983; and S. Benzamour, *Essai sur la politique urbaine au Maroc 1912-1975*, Ed. Maghrébines, Casablanca.

113. The rejection of the 'industrialist' 1960–1964 plan and the secondary character of industry in the framework of the 1968–1972 plan are significant in this respect.

114. See A. Belal, *L'investissement au Maroc (1912-1964)*, Ed. Maghrébines, Casablanca, 1980; and M. Fadili, 'L'Opération labour', Rabat, CEDES, 1961.

115. See A. Belal, op. cit.

116. In recent years as the economic and social crisis worsened in the rural areas (for a host of reasons), the CNCA inaugurated an agricultural credit scheme for consumption by small peasants.

117. See the hostile attitude of the bourgeoisie to the development of statism in Morocco. Seminar on Agriculture, Marrakesh, 1981; and the national seminar on

economic take-off and social development, Casablanca, 1982.

118. See law n° 1-73-210 of 26 Moharem 1393 relating to the exercise of certain activities (*BORM*, n° 3149 of 7 March 1973).

119. For a detailed analysis of the industrial options of the 1973–1977 plan, see H. el Malki, *L'economie marocaine, bilan d'une decennie: 1979*–1980, CNRS, Paris, 1982.

120. An analysis of Moroccanisation reveals the partial character of this operation. Industry is the sector where the rate of Moroccanisation was the weakest. See 'Premier bilan de la marocanisation sur le plan juridique, économique et social', Ministère du Commerce et de l'Industrie, 1977; and El Aoufi, 'La marocanisation et le développement de la bourgeoisie', DES, Rabat, 1979.

121. See Industrial Investment Code, adopted 15 June 1982, BNDE.

122. See H. El Malki, *L'économie*, op. cit.

123. See the discourse of the agrarian fraction of the bourgeoisie at the seminar on agriculture, Marrakesh, February 1981.

124. See Abdurahmane Farhloumi, 'Vers un système d'aide intégrée à la petite et moyenne industrie au Maroc', Mémoire du cycles supérieur de l'ENAP, December 1981. See also Abdeslam Idrissi, 'Les PME au Maroc: le rôle des PME dans l'industrialisation', Mémoire de DES, Rabat 1982.

125. Ibid.

# 4 Contradictory Class Perspectives on the Question of Democracy: the Case of Uganda

## by Mahmood Mamdani

The contemporary crisis in Africa is having a contradictory political effect. On the one hand, one witnesses an increasingly narrow factional control over state affairs so that even a mere cabinet reshuffle becomes a violent affair; on the other hand, as this same crisis leaves ever-widening sectors of society without the possibility of organised political participation, a general demand can be heard in the chorus of dissatisfaction: a demand for broader participation in state affairs or, in a word, a demand for democracy.

While a number of writers[1] have correctly warned against the attitude in certain circles that dismisses the question of democracy as a mere 'bourgeois' question, an attitude implying that it should be of importance only to the bourgeoisie and its sympathisers, it is time also to heed an opposite warning. For yet another tendency is discernible today, one that eulogises democracy only in the form conceptualised by the bourgeoisie. By casting a halo around one single demand — that for a multiparty system and free and fair election — as the sum and substance of the democratic process, its net effect is to call for a 'democratic opening' so narrow that it would grant meaningful freedom only to rival bourgeois factions, while leaving popular classes beyond its pale.

The assumption behind such a conception is that there is only one form of democracy, and that either we struggle for it or we remain with the narrow dictatorship of a bourgeois faction. What this hides is that, even on the question of bourgeois democracy, there are different and contradictory perspectives, in the final analysis reflecting different class positions. One point of this chapter is to discuss two such contradictory perspectives in the contemporary African context.

To bring to life the debate around this question, one needs to look at democracy as more than an artifact or a set of formal institutions. For if democracy is to be an activity of meaning to all classes in society, and in particular to the popular classes, then its form and scope must indeed be meaningfully related to the living conditions of these same classes. In other words, a discussion of the political form of the state cannot be divorced from an analysis of existing production relations. In the contemporary African context, this means linking the question of democracy first and foremost to an analysis of the agrarian question. Any popular discussion of the issue must recognise that at the heart of the question of democracy lies the peasant question. While this essay will discuss contradictory perspectives on the democratic struggle with specific reference to Uganda, I hope its general significance to the

78

broader African scene will not be obscured.

## Unequal and exploitative relations in peasant society

Beginning in the 1960s, a fairly substantial literature built up on the analysis of the labour reserve economies in southern Africa.[2] Seeking to explain the crisis of peasant small commodity production, these writings successfully pointed out that this crisis could not be understood without focusing on the relationship of peasant households to large-scale capitalist enterprises, since the former functioned as labour reserves for the latter. Its singular merit was to focus discussion of the crisis on the relations of production in society.

The same, however, cannot be said of the literature on the current crisis of peasant small commodity production in Africa outside the labour reserve economies. Writings on this subject have been characterised by two predominant tendencies.

In the main tendency, there has been a shift of focus away from relations of production to relations of exchange. Lines of debate have been drawn within these shared parameters: is the crisis primarily the result of external exchange relations (adverse terms of international trade leading to unequal exchange and flow of value to imperialist centres) or of internal exchange relations (unfavourable terms of trade between agriculture and industry reinforced by adverse and overvalued exchange rates)? On one side stand the proponents of dependency theory, on the other the technocrats of the World Bank and the IMF.[3]

No doubt, this has been a worthwhile debate, shedding much light on the terms of integration of peasant producers into wider markets, both local and international. And yet, its focus has been on relations through which value is *transferred*, not on those through which it is *produced* and *appropriated*. Without an analysis of production relations that shape the very character of peasant productive activity, it is not possible to get to the roots of the agrarian crisis.

In contrast, the second tendency does indeed begin with an investigation of relations of peasant production. But the analysis — best characterised by the writings of Goran Hyden[4] — is heavily coloured by results of previous investigations into the agrarian question in Asia and Latin America, where the agrarian question was synonymous with the land question and agrarian relations with landlord/tenant relations. This is why, as he confronts the Africa of small commodity producers, and finds that except in small patches (the largest being Ethiopia) the peasant in Africa does not confront an immediate social overlord, and that land here is not a scarce commodity, Hyden concludes that indeed in most of Africa the peasant is free, unexploited, 'uncaptured'. In his futile search for a Latino–Asian-type reality in Africa, Hyden even fails to identify the relations that do obtain in the Africa of small commodity producers, let alone analyse them.

To consider the agrarian question to be synonymous with the land question is to generalise from one concrete historical situation to others. Such an analysis cannot possibly capture the real content of these other historical experiences. It can only characterise them through formal analogies with the 'original' experience — that here the peasant confronts no social overlord, that here there is no land question — as Hyden understands the Africa of small commodity producers by formal analogy with the Latino–Asian experience.

To go beyond the limitation of these two tendencies — one that is confined to the analysis of exchange relations, and another that tries to investigate production relations through formal analogies with an earlier historical experience — I shall begin by posing one single question: *Why do peasants enter into unequal, exploitative relations?*[5] The answer leads one to recognise the variety of production conditions faced by peasant households.

The unequal relations that peasants enter into have a *dual* character about them. One set of relations is the product of social relations obtaining in the villages. They are entered into because of the force of objective circumstances. In the sense that there is an absence of any *direct* compulsion, and only in this sense, these relations can be said to be entered into 'voluntarily'. Their starting point is the unequal position of peasant households and their result is to deepen the differentiation internal to the peasantry. What are these objective compulsions that peasants face?

In the Ugandan situation, broadly speaking, one can speak of two different contexts: where landlordism combines with an acute land shortage (mainly Buganda) and where the peasant confronts neither an immediate overlord nor an acute shortage of land.

The main location of landlord–tenant relations in contemporary Uganda is Buganda. The history of these relations dates to the 1900 agreement whereby pre-colonial landlordism was restructured by the grant of miles of land to a class of British-connected landlords. A tenants' movement in the 1920s compelled the colonial state to introduce rent control legislation, the 1928 Busulu and Envujjo Law, setting a limit on both the ground rent (*obussulu*) and the commodity rent (*envujjo*) a landlord could demand from his tenant. Since the law only covered existing tenancies, the passage of time loosened its effect as population increased and new lands were brought under cultivation, which landlords could sell or utilise as they wished.

It was, however, the 1975 Land Reform Decree of the Amin regime which gave a new lease of life to landlordism in Buganda. By abolishing the 1920 Busulu and Envujjo Law, and by turning the landlords into lessees of the state and the tenants into sublessees, it removed the protection of the law from the tenant, and left rent in each case to be worked out by the pull and push of class relations on the ground.

**Table 4.1**
**Average Landholding by Strata in Kitende Village**

| | |
|---|---|
| Landlord | 4 Sq. miles |
| Rich Peasant | 2.17 acres |
| Middle Peasant | 1.08 acres |
| Poor Peasant | 0.66 acre |

The effect of this history can be seen on the distribution of land in one village in Buganda in 1983. The data have been culled from a larger study on the agrarian question in contemporary Uganda.[6]

It is clear that the rural poor in Kitende enter into exploitative relations because of one predominant fact: they are land-poor.

Production conditions in the bulk of the Ugandan countryside are quite different. Here, there has been no history of landlordism. In the colonial period, land was relatively sparse, and access to it governed by customary tenure. And yet, in spite of the absence of land shortage, a differentiation can be observed amongst the peasantry, leading the rural poor into exploitative relations 'voluntarily'. To understand the reason behind this, *it is necessary to go beyond the formal ownership of the land to the capacity of each stratum of the peasantry actually to bring the land under cultivation*. Table 4.2, taken from the same larger study referred to above, summarises production conditions obtaining in a village in the northern part of Uganda.[7]

**Table 4.2**
**Peasants' Access to Land, Labour and Implements by Strata in Amwoma Village**

| | Land (in acres) | | Labour* | Implements | |
|---|---|---|---|---|---|
| | *Owned* | *Culti-vated* | | *Hoes* | *Ploughs* |
| Poor and Lower Middle | 4.26 | 1.92 | 2.59 | 1.74 | — |
| Middle (Average & Upper) | 4.20 | 3.00 | 3.90 | 2.40 | 0.4 |
| Rich | 18.75 | 6.08 | 4.50 | 2.50 | 2.0 |

\* To calculate the labouring strength of a household, I have given one point to all those aged 12 and above, 0.5 to those 8 to 12 and 0.25 to those between 5 and 8.

Why is it that poor and lower-middle peasants who own as much land as do the rest of the middle peasants (4.26 as opposed to 4.20 acres) are in a position to cultivate only 65 per cent (1.92 as opposed to 3.0) of the land compared with the latter? The decisive difference lies in their respective access to instruments of labour. Though its labouring strength is 2.59 on the average, a rural poor family owns only 1.74 hoes and no plough. This means at no time are there sufficient hoes to utilise family labour to capacity. My point is simple: though not land-poor, a rural poor family in this case must enter into unequal relations because it is implement-poor.

The unequal relations that peasants enter into 'voluntarily' develop in relation to each of the forces of production: land, labour and implements of labour. Land may be rented or 'borrowed'. In the former case, payment is in cash; in the latter, in kind. Labour power may be sold openly as wage labour, or the sale may be disguised through a host of communal labour-sharing arrangements, which have an unequal result because they are now carried out between households in unequal positions. Similarly, implements of labour — ploughs — may also be rented or 'shared'.

This set of unequal relations, 'voluntarily' entered into, develops relatively spontaneously. Their starting point, more often than not, are past co-operative relations that have evolved around the sharing of scarce resources such as labour or its implements. Since sharing can confer equal benefits only when organised between households of roughly equal standing, its continuation between households in increasingly unequal positions gradually subverts its contents, turning it into a mechanism for a transfer of surplus labour from poorer to richer households.

In contrast, peasant households in these villages enter into yet another set of relations, all of them the result of direct pressure from above. Since none of these are 'voluntarily' entered into — in the sense that compulsion in this case is direct and not indirect — each requires at least a complement of extra-economic coercion to be effected. The source of these compulsions is either the state itself as an organised power or state-connected institutions (the Church, the ruling party) or individuals. These involuntary practices take on a variety of forms, ranging from forced labour to forced contributions, forced enclosures, forced crops and forced sales.

*Forced labour* is organised by the hierarchy of local state officials (chiefs) and is usually legitimated as a continuation of the traditional communal labour for communal interest (*Bullungi Bwansi*). The difference is that the source of these demands is no longer the local community but local state organs. Similarly, the officials in command are not community leaders elected from below but state officials appointed from above. In practice, these demands can cover projects for community use like clearing a road or a well, repairing or building a school or a dispensary. But they can also cover such activities as working in the gardens of the Church or of individual chiefs, or building sheds for local political rallies.

*Forced contributions*, taking the form of financial exactions or collections of a portion of the harvest or simply a chicken, can also be demanded as the occasion arises, be it the construction of a local presidential lodge or a local party headquarters, the purchase of a bus for the local school or the payment of tithe to the Church at harvest, Christmas or Easter time.

*Forced enclosures* are of particular relevance in those parts of the country where landlordism was absent and customary tenure supreme. The 1975 Land Reform Decree took away legal recognition from all forms of customary tenure, turned the peasant into a tenant of the state, and gave local District Land Committees the power to transfer land from customary tenants not 'developing' it to those with the capacity to do so. Ostensibly designed to clear the ground of all pre-capitalist obstacles to capitalist development in agriculture, the real result of the decree was to pave the way for the penetration of capital into the countryside, not to organise production but to monopolise exchange.

*Forced crops* and *forced sales* have a parallel history. The history of export crops in the colonies is well known, as is the element of compulsion in their introduction. The continued expansion of export crop production is continually the subject of moral exhortation from above. At crisis times, however, exhortation gives way to compulsion. 'Grow More Cotton' and 'Grow More Coffee' campaigns are put under the command of local state officials. Enforcing sales are a whole range of parastatals — from the Coffee to the Cotton to the Tobacco Marketing Boards — having the right to purchase and market export crops.

This, then, is the galaxy of compulsions forced on the peasantry from above. There is, of course, quite a diversity in the specific mix in which these practices appear in each locality: here the Church may be a preponderant force, there it may be the ruling party, and in yet a third locale it may be state agents who are the direct source of coercion. Together, however, this set of direct compulsions from above constitutes a web of coercive practices choking peasant productivity and creativity.

In sum, then, peasant productive activity is shaped by *double* exploitative relations. Those 'voluntarily' entered into are a result of objective circumstances faced by different peasant strata, underlining the differentiation internal to the peasantry, either because of unequal access to land or to implements of labour. These relations are also internal to the peasantry. They constitute the stuff of petty exploitation of the rural poor by the rural rich. In contrast are those relations imposed on all strata of peasants from above. The involuntary character of these relations is underlined by the fact that none of them can be effected without the direct use of political power, i.e. extra-economic coercion.

The role of political (state) power in both instances needs further clarification. Certainly, the reproduction of commodity relations between different strata of the peasantry — those I have characterised as 'spontaneous' and 'voluntary' — is not possible without the state power ensuring the continued functioning of commodity markets (in land, labour or its products) through legal guarantees: most importantly, through guaranteeing the sanctity of private property and of contracts. And yet, the difference with the relations directly imposed from above, those entered into involuntarily, is that in this latter case political power directly functions as an economic force. This is the meaning of saying that, in this second instance, the compulsion required is not simply economic, but extra-economic.

To these two sets of unequal relations, those entered into 'voluntarily' and those involuntarily imposed, there correspond two distinct forms of capital accumulation. The result of 'voluntary', 'spontaneous', unequal relations is the path of capital accumulation *from below*, through peasant differentiation, as one stratum enriches itself at the expense of another, giving rise to a village bourgeoisie out of the ranks of the rich peasantry. This is a long-run and gradual process, whose starting point is the process of production itself and whose focus is competitive market relations. But the significance of this tendency is eclipsed by the second form of capital accumulation. More recent, this is the path of accumulation *from above*. Its starting point is a political connection. Its reproduction requires an element of extra-economic coercion, even if as a complement to market relations, so as to give it a monopolistic character. Whether the resulting accumulation is by the state power itself (as with state marketing boards) or by individual capitalists, it cannot be overemphasised that the common denominator in this case is a political connection, ensuring direct access to the machinery of extra-economic coercion.

It is this second path to capital accumulation that represents the dominant tendency in the countryside today. Its carrier and beneficiary is not the village bourgeoisie, but the 'external' bourgeoisie. This bourgeoisie is the result of a concrete historical process, whose market character is that political power paves the way to wealth generation, a fact already observed in a growing body of literature.[8] In the next section, I shall review the process of its development, and thereby of the increasing weight of extra-economic relations in agrarian relations, in the context of the deepening crisis in Uganda.

## The bureaucratic bourgeoisie and agrarian capitalism in Uganda

An understanding of the development of the bourgeoisie requires viewing it as part of the broader process of class formation. In contrast to the Asian and Latin American countries colonised prior to this century, the bourgeoisie in African countries bears the hallmarks of a fairly distinctive process of development.

Before I begin, however, a clarification is in order. My interest here is not in underlining the *functional* (economic) character of this bourgeoisie, i.e. whether its operations have predominantly a merchant or an industrial character. The point of the analysis, as will become clear, is to underline the *political* characteristics of the bourgeoisie.

My starting point is the colonial period. In this era, the continent was divided into two; settler and non-settler colonies, or colonies of occupation and colonies of domination. In the settler colonies of the north and the south, the function of a bourgeoisie developed by and large on a sector of the European population that originated from the imperialist country itself. In the non-settler colonies of the east and the west, the colonial power drew a sharp line of demarcation between their political and economic agents. While 'indirect rule' was mediated through indigenous chiefs, market relations were mediated through an immigrant bourgeoisie imported from older colonies, usually from India (to eastern Africa) and Lebanon (to West Africa). Of these colonies, it was only Nigeria which developed a substantial indigenous bourgeois stratum in the colonial period.

My point, then, is that an indigenous African bourgeoisie has for the most part been a very recent, post-independence formation. In its creation, the direct employment of state power has played a central role. Conversely, a state connection has been vital for an individual to become a member of this class and to prosper as one. This is why it is correct to say that the key *internal* characteristic of members of the indigenous bourgeoisie has been a close *individual–state connection*. This is the first imprint of the history of capitalist development in Africa on its bourgeoisie.

Secondly, to the extent the continent has a bourgeois tradition, it is essentially *a comprador* one. Right from the 18th Century, the European slave trade created a class of intermediaries. These were men who already had a commanding economic position and an access to means of coercion, attributes they could turn to profitable activity as the European slave trade turned to gigantic proportions. In the 18th Century, this class flourished all along the western coast, from Angola to Senegal.[9]

With the further penetration of the world market along the African coast (east and west) in the 19th Century, the comprador acquired greater significance. Of particular interest in this period was the gun trade, what with imported guns helping to forge new empires (Samori Toure in the West African savanna or Tippu Tip on the Upper Congo) and to strengthen existing ones (Buganda). But, whether they dealt with guns or groundnuts or slaves, this is the period in which the comprador class acquired its greatest significance in African history. Its members vied with one another to be recognised as the foremost agents of one foreign state or another.

Their fortunes, however, reversed with the intrusion of colonial rule in the later 19th Century. Generally hostile to indigenous compradors, colonial powers cut them off from any potential role as a national bourgeoisie in the new era. To the extent that their replacements from the imperialist countries or the older Asian colonies have contributed to a bourgeois tradition on the continent, it has been almost a onesidedly pro-imperialist and anti-national contribution. While the settler bourgeoisie was openly hostile to the possibility of independence, seeing in it the realisation of a rival claim to political power, the immigrant bourgeoisie from the older colonies was at best marginal to the national movement.

As we shall see concretely in the case of Uganda, only after the Second World War, when confronted with a hostile political situation, did colonial powers reassess their policy and groom an indigenous bourgeois class, a function that was immediately passed over to the World Bank and allied 'aid' agencies following independence. The second imprint of the history of capitalist development on the African bourgeoisie has been to give it a predominantly *comprador* character in its external relations.

It is the internal characteristic of this bourgeoisie, that its members have needed an individual state connection to enter the ranks of the bourgeoisie, which is of particular concern so far as the subject-matter of this essay is concerned. Its recent origin means that its internal composition is very much in a state of flux, more so than market competition would normally account for in a bourgeois class. It is not just that the African bourgeoisie does not possess the commanding presence in the economy that the hegemonic bourgeoisies of the Western countries do; it is also that members of this class in Africa usually lack even the independent property base and the concomitant strength that its counterparts in Asia and Latin America do possess. This is why the development of the African bourgeoisie has had a more top-down character than anywhere else. Here, state property precedes individual property. A state position acts as the lever for capital accumulation rather than being a reward for it. A brief look at the history of the Ugandan bourgeoisie will help underline this point.

In any meaningful sense, the development of an indigenous bourgeoisie in Uganda must be dated from the colonial reforms of the post World War II period. This same period saw the rise of a mass-based militant nationalist movement. And it is the growing strength of this popular movement, illustrated by the general strike of 1945 and the peasant uprising of that same year and 1949, that underlined for the colonial state the necessity for an indigenous bourgeois social base in the colony. The point of the post-war reforms was to create the rudiments of such a bourgeoisie through state action. The same political power which in an earlier period had been used to put an artificial brake on the process of class formation was now used to artificially accelerate that same process.

The post-war period had also a second significance. The worsening crisis of British imperialism provided the impetus for the development of a small but significant state industrial sector. Surplus funds from the export of peasant-grown cotton and coffee by state-controlled marketing boards were utilised to set up a number of import-substitution industries, mainly in textiles and food processing and canning, under the umbrella of a single parastatal, the Uganda Development Corporation (UDC). In practice, each of these investments was effected through a UDC partnership with the local Asian bourgeoisie and foreign capital. Being the core of the state sector, the marketing boards and the UDC became the springboard for the growth of the indigenous bourgeoisie after independence.

The transfer of political power could not but accelerate the process of the development of an indigenous bourgeoisie. And yet, throughout the first Obote regime (1962–71), the centre of gravity of the local bourgeoisie remained within its immigrant wing. This was in spite of the mix of 'Africanisation' and 'nationalisation' measures which, since they affected internal trade more so than export–import or industries, turned into a crisis mainly for the Asian petty bourgeoisie. Neither the Asian bourgeoisie nor foreign capital was substantially affected by these measures.

The real turning point in this process came with the Amin expulsion of the Asian minority in 1972. More than any other single event, it was this which marked the watershed in the development of the indigenous bourgeoisie. The top-down character of this development was further reinforced by the fact that the properties acquired from the expelled section of the bourgeoisie, whether industrial or real estate, were distributed by the state. It made a political connection key to membership in the indigenous bourgeoisie. In popular parlance, this whole group which came to acquire wealth via a political connection came to be known as the *mafuta mingi*.

But the necessity for a direct political connection did not simply become the pre-history of this class, its starting point, a pad from which its members launched themselves into autonomous operations in civil society, acquiring predominantly the character of a privately-based bourgeoisie. Barring a few notable exceptions, their hold over the wealth so acquired continued to remain tenuous. The state power kept the bourgeoisie on a tight leash, orchestrating a series of 'redistributions' of the same properties after periodic intervals. In the eight years of the Amin regime, there were no less than four such 'redistributions'.

This trend did not halt with either the two Uganda National Liberation Front (UNLF) governments, nor with the Military Commission, nor with the second Obote regime. To begin with, each of these regimes carried out its own 'redistribution'. One still came into wealth by way of a political connection, rather than vice versa. My point is quite simple: the indigenous bourgeoisie that developed after the post-war period, and really after the 1972 expulsion, did so mainly in a top-down fashion, not so much through competitive accumulation in the market, but more through access to state resources via a state position or connection. The methods characteristic of its accumulation practices were naturally a combination of corruption and coercion, the former in relation to state resources, the latter in relation to private resources.

My specific concern here is really with the penetration of capital into the countryside. Although numerous and assorted examples of this can be gathered from earlier periods, the real benchmark is once again the Amin period. From this point of view, no single state action has greater significance than the 1975 Land Reform Decree. In overriding all forms of customary tenure protecting usufruct rights of peasants, this decree paved the way for the legal movement of state bureaucrats and state-connected capitalists into their 'home areas' to demarcate and enclose large pieces of land, the point being to use land titles to get a mortgage for substantial sums to move into transport and trade. Since the allocation of land was done by District Land Committees, staffed by local state officials, what mattered was not the validity of one's claim but the strength of one's political connection.

The Administrative Reorganisation that had preceded the Land Reform Decree should indeed be seen as its administrative complement. With each province placed under the direct control of a military governor, the muscle was now available to give teeth to the Land Reform Decree. Not only could the military bureaucracy oversee the 'reform' of land ownership, it could also organise periodic campaigns to 'Grow More Cotton' and 'Grow More Coffee'.

The above was one side of the movement. Its other side was a sharp cut in peasant incomes as both state assistance to peasant agriculture and state-determined prices for peasant export crops declined sharply. The former reduced the *social* returns of the peasantry, the latter undermined *individual* returns of peasant households. The overall context of this development was a shrinking state budget from which ever larger portions were claimed for coercive purposes.

State aid to peasant agriculture has a dual character. Technical assistance to peasant agriculture, going under the name of 'extension services', is designed to ensure the reproduction of its technical basis over the long run. On the other hand, social services — medicine, transport, education — to the countryside are designed to ensure the social reproduction of the peasantry over the long run. A sharp decline in both shifted the burden of their reproduction directly onto the shoulders of the peasantry. Whether to be freshly constructed, repaired or simply to be operated, schools, dispensaries and transport services came to rely heavily on self-help measures. No wonder there came to be a corresponding increase in forced labour and forced contributions in the countryside over the past decade.

Finally, real prices for export crops grown by peasants came down sharply throughout the last decade, being the lowest they have been in the history of export agriculture in Uganda. In the case of robusta coffee, the source of nearly 90 per cent of export income since the 1970s, the share of the world market price paid to the peasant grower came down from an average of 40 per cent in 1953 to around 19 per cent in 1983.

While these trends could be discerned in the Amin period, they really culminated in the IMF programme of 1981–4 in the second Obote regime. The state budget shrank dramatically, giving the *coup de grâce* to both extension and social services. In spite of the illusion of steeply rising shilling prices for peasant export crops, tumbling exchange rates and a galloping inflation really meant a continued decline in real returns.

This double movement, on the one hand the accelerated movement of capital into agriculture (through forced enclosures and the monopolisation of trade in food staples) and on the other the reduction to a trickle of both state services (leading to an increase in forced labour and forced contributions) and returns for state-marketed crops (accomplished through forced crops and forced sales), had one overwhelming consequence: *a growth in the element of extra-economic coercion.* Without grasping this fact, it would be difficult to understand the character of the state power in Uganda — the subject I turn to in the next section — let alone formulate demands for the democratisation of that power.

## The State, the popular classes and democracy

To understand the basic character of a state, it is necessary to grasp the character of the basic political relation in a society, that between the state (the rulers) and the popular classes (the ruled). The question of the relation between the state power and the ruling class as a whole (the bourgeoisie), formulated in contemporary literature as the question of the 'relative autonomy of the state', though important, must be ranked as a question of second importance. I shall begin with the latter question first.

There is always a tension between the particular and the general interests of a class. In the case of a ruling class, it is state power which enforces on its individual members and factions a compliance with their general interests. It is to these interests that we give the name of political interests. So long as a ruling class possesses muscle, stamina and vision, 'politics in command' must be its slogan.

The most important aspect of the relation between state power and the individual members and factions of the ruling class is that the former enforces a minimum collective discipline on the latter, a discipline to ensure the reproduction of essential conditions of production. What other sense can one make of Marx's analysis in *Capital* of the reports of English factory inspectors and the subsequent factory legislation on the working day, child and female labour, etc. — at a time when the greed of individual capitalists threatened to drain the life blood out of not only existing but also future generations of the English working class — except that of enforcing a collective recognition on the English bourgeoisie of its general interests in contradistinction to its private and particular greed?

No such discipline, however, is possible without the state having a 'relative autonomy' from bourgeois factions. For unless class imperatives prevail over factional considerations, the continuation of bourgeois rule must itself stand in jeopardy. This fact stands highlighted at no other time than in a crisis. And it is precisely in a crisis — if that crisis is to be resolved in favour of the bourgeoisie — that the bourgeois state must exhibit the greatest possible 'relative autonomy' *vis-à-vis* all partial bourgeois interests.

Let me now return to my earlier discussion of the political characteristics of the bourgeoisie in Africa. Now, the fact that a state position or connection is a necessary springboard for membership of the bourgeoisie gives a life-and-death character to political struggles within it. A political position does not simply reinforce a pre-existing economic base or open up new opportunities where old ones already existed; it is in fact the very foundation of economic prosperity. A downturn in political fortunes almost mechanically leads to a similar downward shift in accumulation opportunities.

This is why internal bourgeois struggles in Africa are routinely waged with an intensity not known in many other places; why opposition is normally construed as treason and criticism as sabotage; why elections, whether single or multiparty affairs, are usually a predictable hoax; and why the typical method of resolving contradictions inside the bourgeoisie is a coup, not an election. Even the most substantial bourgeoisie in Africa, that of Nigeria, has been unable to organise a bourgeois democracy in 'its' own country. 'Democracy in one country', as long as the comprador and bureaucratic bourgeoisie control state power, is perhaps impossible to realise in Africa.

All these characteristics are even more sharply accentuated in the Ugandan case. Here, more than anywhere else, the contradiction between indigenous bourgeois aspirants and immigrant bourgeoisie exploded as an antagonism in 1972. Whereas everywhere else the tendency was to resolve this contradiction through an alliance worked out in the course of a protracted struggle, in Uganda the resolution was more or less at a stroke as the immigrant bourgeoisie was expelled in 1972. As a result, in Uganda more than anywhere else, most members of the bourgeoisie have yet to develop an autonomous base in civil society; correspondingly their very survival has depended on sustaining an individual state connection. The resulting intense factionalism inside the bourgeoisie, and its petty bourgeois hangers-on, has been further reinforced by their comprador orientation. As each faction looks for an external sponsor, the rivalry between the sponsors is in turn reproduced internally, pulling rival factions in diverse directions.

The collapse of a common discipline, the victory of partial over general interests, is the clearest sign of the crisis of the Ugandan bourgeoisie, whereby factions jostle for control over key state positions and institutions to advance their private interests. The results are clear in both the relations internal to the bourgeoisie and in its relations to the producers of wealth.

Instead of the state power disciplining bourgeois factions in the name of a general interest, one hallmark of the crisis is that various factions begin to reproduce inside the very organs of state power, and particularly inside its repressive organs, stripping each of its internal discipline and dissolving each from within into so many repressive instruments of so many rival factions.

This same victory of particular over general rationality can be observed in the relation with the popular classes, especially the peasantry. As I commented earlier, the activities of individual capitalists, no matter how rapacious, are in normal times always counterbalanced to a degree by state programmes that seek to ensure the reproduction of human and technical conditions of production through social and extension programmes. The collapse of the latter through the Amin and the second Obote regimes in Uganda suggests the emergence of a sort of looting capitalism, moving from one political crisis to another, but as yet incapable of resolution, however partial, from above or below.

It is down below, on the ground so to speak, that one glimpses most clearly the relation between the rulers and the ruled, underlining the basic character of state power. It is here that one can discern the lines of continuity in the organisation and exercise of state power, undisturbed by the 'political storms in the sky above', from the colonial to the neo-colonial period, from one successive regime to another. Sure, there are changes, but they resemble more a slight shift of emphasis here, another there, like ripples in the bedrock of government and administration. So, for example, while the second Obote regime continued the emphasis on 'Grow More Coffee' and 'Grow More Cotton' campaigns, its implementation was no longer in the hands of local military officers but in those of local administrative officers. But the basic character of the administration, military or civilian, remained unchanged. Similarly, while successive regimes after Amin wore civilian masks, and each vied with its predecessor in claiming the mantle of 'democracy', the extremely undemocratic character of local state organs continued unchallenged and undisturbed.

In times of civilian rule, the local exercise of state power is primarily through its administrative and judicial organs. In practice, there are no autonomous local political bodies: administration and politics are fused into one. The administrative organ — often called 'local government' — is a hierarchy of chiefs below a District Commissioner. As in colonial times, it is appointed from above, never elected from below. But could it be expected to be otherwise given that it is this same hierarchy of chiefs that implements the whole gamut of coercive practices from day to day?

Local judicial organs, too, are integrally connected with the practices of extra-economic coercion. For if a peasant fails to pay the full annual tax assessed on him by the July deadline, it is the lowest grade magistrate who — without trial — sends him to jail for a minimum of three months. Should he fail to pay that same tax upon release, he is jailed yet again. The same happens should a peasant fail to perform the labour or pay the cash he is asked to 'contribute' towards a 'development' or a 'community' project by his local chief. In that case, local authorities would simply seize something of equivalent value — say, a cock — from his possession, whether he consented or not. And should he be too poor to own anything of value, he would then go to jail.

Jail, of course, is not just a place of confinement, not even primarily so. It is rather a place for protracted, continuous forced labour. Prisoners are pressed into labour teams, either for use by local state officials or for hire by local capitalists. Being subject to greater control than wage labour, such captive labour is highly competitive in the rates at which it is offered, thereby undermining and depressing prevailing rates in the labour market.

I believe that when a person is confined by state authorities without due process, even without a trial, the correct legal term for it is not 'jail' but 'detention'. It is then no exaggeration to say that what exists in the countryside for its vast majority — the rural poor — is not any form of rule of law, with however many infringements, but a blanket regime of preventive detention.

Local administration and local judiciary are that part of the colonial heritage so carefully nurtured by successive post-colonial regimes. The specific innovation of the Amin regime was to create District Land Committees — the seat of forced enclosures — through the 1975 Land Reform Decree. It is yet another comment on the nature of the post-Amin regimes that no one even dared question this decree, let alone repeal it! It was part of the Amin legacy that was incorporated into the new order.

It is these three institutions — local administration, local judiciary and the District Land Committee — that constitute the heart of the regime of labour controls, the sum total of coercive practices, in the contemporary Ugandan countryside. While multiparty elections were introduced after the fall of the Amin regime, these organised instruments of local power, instruments through which rulers discipline and tame the ruled, remained steadfast on the ground. It is their demise that would pull the rug from under the feet of the comprador/bureaucratic bourgeoisie. And precisely for that reason, their demise would be resisted tooth and nail by this same sector of capital.

The above discussion should allow us to highlight a point of more general significance. Where direct force is an integral part of production relations, no consistent democracy is possible. One condition for a democratic political life is that direct producers be free of direct constraint, that is, extra-economic coercion. Bourgeois democracy is predicated on contractual relations between exploiter and exploited through the market-place — where a worker may 'choose' to sell his labour power to an employer or a peasant may 'choose' to sell his crops to a buyer and not on direct compulsion from above.

This requires a relative separation of economics from politics, of the market from the state. It requires that the relations between the exploiters and the exploited be relatively separate from those between the rulers and the ruled, that force not be integral to production relations, but only 'weigh in the balance' to ensure that market freedoms and class relations are indeed reproduced.

None of this, however, would be possible in the Ugandan case without an end to extra-economic coercion and the emergence of 'free' producers. For only then can the direct producer function as a free agent in the market place. At present, however, the persistence of extra-economic coercion shapes the character of state power in neo-colonies like Uganda, underlining the element of continuity with the colonial state.

The conclusion drawn above can be reinforced and broadened by reference to the experience of democratic struggles in the West. A short note will suffice.

From the standpoint of the subject-matter of this essay, two salient features from the Western experience merit attention: one objective, the other subjective. In the case of ancient Greece, even when democratic freedoms went beyond propertied classes, their exercise was limited to the ranks of 'free' producers. Slaves and serfs always remained beyond the pale of a democratic political life. While the fluctuating scope of organised democratic life in ancient Greece reflected the outcome of political struggles at home, there was one line of demarcation that always remained rigid: that between 'free' and 'unfree' producers.

The experience of later bourgeois democracies also underscores the same point. Not until the end of extra-economic coercion in production relations — or, to put it differently, not until the end of primitive accumulation at home — could democratic freedoms be exercised by those outside the propertied classes. This is not to say that state power never interfered with the 'freedom' of direct producers. It did, especially outside the sphere of market relations whenever there was an attempt to exercise freedom collectively. Thus, state intervention was more the rule than the exception in the history of trade unionism. In short, the state played an active role in shaping collective forms of organisation to suit the demands of bourgeois hegemony. And yet, at the level of market relations, the contrast with preceding periods was that the individual direct producer operated as a free agent. This, then, is precisely my point. No consistently democratic organisation of state life is possible unless direct producers are free of extra-economic coercion. The *objective* precondition of a democratic political life is the emergence of 'free' producers, whether peasants, artisans or proletarians.

Of course, democracy did not automatically or mechanically follow the emergence of 'free' labour. It had to be won from below. This *subjective* aspect of the Western democratic experience has perhaps an even greater relevance for us today.

In the ancient world, the contrast between Greek and Roman experience is particularly illuminating.[10] In Rome, unlike in Greece, the upper classes were able to divide, contain and tame those below, particularly through the institution of patronage, which tied individuals and sections from the lower classes to the coat tails of upper class patrons. In Rome, those down below hoped to better their conditions through expectation of charity from above. In Greece, on the other hand, there was no such insidious institution as that of Roman patronage. If anything, the tendency was for leaders from the upper classes to be disciplined by the organised intervention of masses from below. The lower classes, unlike in the case of Rome, pinned their hopes on winning rights through a struggle from below. Greek democracy could not be without this perspective of a struggle for *rights* from below; in contrast, the absence of democracy in Rome was very much anchored on the expectation of *charity* from above.

The same conclusion can be drawn from the experience of later bourgeois democracies. Every reform that broadened the scope of democratic life to include larger sections of the popular masses was the result of sharp struggles from below. In England, for example, the bourgeoisie conceded the parliamentary reform of 1852 only when faced with the spectre of revolution. It was the fruit of Chartist agitation, and not of ruling-class magnanimity or ruling-class conspiracy.

Our experience in Africa has been no different. The introduction of multiparty elections in the post-war period cannot be understood as simply an initiative on the part of colonialism. It was in fact a response to popular struggles — in Uganda, the workers' general strike of 1945 and the peasant rebellion of that same year and 1949 — a minimum concession through which the ruling power hoped to contain the maximum demands of organised nationalist agitation.

My point remains. Whenever it has shown a measure of consistency, bourgeois democracy has not been the achievement of the bourgeoisie. It has always been a fruit of the organised struggle of popular classes. Without grasping this historical lesson, it is not possible to arrive at a suitable perspective on the question of democratic struggle in the contemporary world.

### The Bourgeoisie, The Popular Classes and Democracy

After the fall of the Amin regime, from the various UNLF regimes to the second Obote regime, the primary public political issue in Uganda was that of democracy. All organised parties to the public discussion were agreed regarding the essence of democracy as a multiparty system with free and fair elections. It is within this shared context that arguments raged as to whether the 1980 'umbrella' elections envisaged by the UNLF constituted an infringement of democratic rights or whether the subsequent 1980 elections organised by the Military Commission were indeed free and fair. While the discussion below focuses on the specifics of the Ugandan context, its relevance to the discussion of the democratic struggle in other African countries should be quite clear.

More eloquent than the points of disagreement between various parties were the moments of silence they shared. For it underlined their shared premise, their common ground. The discussion on democracy, on how state affairs may be organised, was confined to central state structures, and particularly to its political organs: the presidency and the parliament. There was no discussion on whether local state structures must allow for democratic control by working people in the countryside. And certainly none at all on whether broader changes were needed in agrarian relations for that silent majority of society, the peasants, to have a meaningful participation in the country's political life.

This is why the points of agreement between the feuding factions were more telling than their points of disagreement. It indicated that all parties shared, consciously or not, a narrow conception of democracy, one that could have meaning only to a minority in society.

To make this point clear, it needs to be placed in the context of a discussion on contradictory perspectives on the democratic struggle — one narrow, the other broad — in terms of how each would conceptualise the democratic struggle, as regards both its demands and the methods of their realisation.

The narrow perspective on the *content* (demands) of the democratic struggle is well illustrated by the premises shared between the contending parties in Uganda in the post-Amin period. Its limits are those of formal liberal democratic reforms: free and fair elections in the context of multiparty competition. It is not that these are not important. They are. The real point, however, is that they are of significance only to those classes already free from extra-economic coercion in the process of production: the bourgeoisie, the petty bourgeoisie and, at most, the working class. Not only does it leave out of consideration the largest section of society, the bulk of its producers of wealth, the peasantry; the resulting political competition is also limited to an arena defined by the demands of struggles internal to the bourgeoisie. That is why this narrow demand must be characterised as bourgeois.

A struggle that aims for democratisation of the political life of the majority of society must simultaneously aim to create the pre-requisite for such a reform. This pre-requisite is an end to the regime of extra-economic coercion that stifles the peasantry. This is nothing short of a demand for a transformation in production relations. Furthermore, no such change can be effected without the democratisation of local as well as central state organs. This means, at minimum, a thorough-going reform of local government, local judiciary and local land allocation/control bodies.

93

Closely connected to the issue of the demands of a struggle is that of *method* by which it is waged. From a bourgeois perspective, democracy is expected to be an achievement of the bourgeoisie. Such a perspective then naturally gives the leading role in the democratic struggle to bourgeois opposition movements, not only to set the goals of the movement in a narrow way but also similarly to define its method of organisation — *from above* — thereby ensuring the continuation of bourgeois control over the movement of popular classes. No matter what the language of its articulation — 'socialist', 'nationalist' or otherwise — such a perspective ends up confining the organisation and the activity of popular classes within parameters defined by the imperatives of intra-bourgeois factional rivalries.

In contrast, a popular perspective must raise the question of breaking this hold. Its starting point must be to ensure that the creativity of popular activity and popular organisation is not hemmed into the limits set by the requirements of factional struggles inside the bourgeoisie. This requires nothing less than the perspective of organisation *from below*, which in turn is not possible without raising those demands of direct significance to the popular classes below.

The key popular demand in the present situation is one that concerns the peasantry. Not because the peasantry is itself capable of transforming national political life, but because no popular urban force — the working class included — can expect to influence meaningfully the direction of political events without breaking the political hold of the bourgeoisie over the peasantry.

The two perspectives outlined above are contradictory in that they would have opposite results. Narrow demands and top-down methods end up strengthening bourgeois rule. Broad demands and bottom-up methods end up weakening that same rule and building the autonomy of popular forces. The former will give us a sham democracy; only the latter can ensure a consistent democratic reform.

# Notes

1. I. G. Shivji (ed.) *The State and the Working People in Tanzania* (Dakar: CODESRIA Book Series, 1985); C. Y. Thomas, *The Rise of the Authoritarian State in Peripheral Societies* (New York: Monthly Review Press, 1984); E. Wamba-dia-Wamba, 'Struggles for Democracy in Africa; The Case of the People's Republic of Congo', *Philosophy and Social Action*, vol. X, nos. 1–2, 1984.

2. G. Arrighi, 'Labour Supplies in Historical Perspective' in G. Arrighi and J. Saul (eds.) *Essays on the Political Economy of Africa* (New York: Monthly Review Press, 1973); C. Meillessoux, *Maidens, Meal and Money* (Cambridge: Cambridge University Press, 1984); H. Wolpe, 'Capital and Cheap Labour in South Africa: From Segregation to Apartheid', *Economy and Society*, vol. I, no. 4, 1972.

3. A recent article by Michael Lofchie attempts to sum up this debate, in the process giving detailed citations on the relevant literature. It, too, however, remains trapped within the same narrow perspective. See M. F. Lofchie, 'Africa's Agrarian Malaise', in G. Carter and P. O'Meara (eds.) *African Independence: The First Twenty-five Years* (Bloomington: Indiana University Press, 1985).

4. See G. Hyden. *Beyond Ujamaa in Tanzania: Underdevelopment and Uncaptured*

*Peasantry* (London: Heinemann, 1980) and by the same author, *No Shortcuts to Progress: African Development Management in Perspective* (London: Heinemann, 1983).

5. See also how H. Kuchertz handles this question in the case of the peasant 'work-parties' in Mpondoland, South Africa in his article 'Work-parties in Mpondoland', *Africa*, vol. 55, no. 2, 1985.

6. See M. Mamdani, 'Towards an analysis of the Agrarian Question in Uganda: A Preliminary Report', *Journal of Peasant Studies*, 1987.

7. Ibid.

8. C. Y. Thomas, *The Rise of the Authoritarian State*; I. G. Shivji, *Class Struggles in Tanzania* (London: Heinemann, 1976).

9. For an excellent and detailed discussion of the 18th and 19th Century processes of class formation in Africa, see Bill Freund, *The Making of Contemporary Africa: The Development of African Society since 1800* (Bloomington: Indiana University Press, 1984).

10. See, for example, de Ste. Croix, *The Class Struggle in the Ancient Greek World* (London: Duckworth, 1981).

# 5 The Experience of Struggle in the People's Republic of Congo

by E. Wamba-dia-Wamba

Discussions about democracy in Africa, the lack of it, the need for it, but also the rejection of it, have become in vogue. People are demanding democracy in Africa against what, for example, H. Odera Oruka calls 'state terrorism'[1] among other things.

Experiences and practices of democracy are historical. Democracy emerged, developed and changed historically. This history is often neglected and democracy is often reduced to one or the other form it acquired historically. Concrete attempts at struggling for democracy in Africa itself are not studied in their very limitations. Theoretical disputations (at most scholastic) in search of relevant or appropriate democratic schemes for Africa on the basis of ignorance of those attempts will not lead to sensible results. After all, it is through concrete struggles for democratic rights that the African peoples' subjective element, their political capacity to have control over their life process, is developed.

Debates gravitate around a series of arguments, both pros and cons, on both sides: that of the regimes in power (whether self-declared socialist or capitalist) and that of anti-neocolonial regime movements. These arguments can be dealt with, beside their critical analysis, by examining concrete struggles for democracy in Africa. A few recurrent themes, for purposes of illustration, are worth mentioning.[2]

The dominant theme is based on what could be termed constraints or requirements of economic development. Since the basic task, for Africa, is one of 'coming out of economic backwardness', notions of democracy are said to be incompatible with this task because democracy aims at 'sapping discipline', 'scattering the nation's forces and inviting anarchy'. Democracy is counterposed to economic development and consequently rejected as 'a luxury that the African masses cannot afford'. Organic intellectuals (A. Smith, R. Malthus, D. Ricardo, etc.) of the industrial bourgeoisie saw economic development as conditioned by mass poverty. Development was seen as a function of the creativity and the propensity to save of an entrepreneurial minority, and mass poverty was claimed to be inevitable. Intellectuals of the African regimes see it as conditioned by authoritarian rule. The failure by the state authoritatively to *capture* 'free predominantly peasant masses of people' is claimed to retard development. Backwardness, ignorance and untruth are seen to lie outside of the state.

The reductionist theories equate 'democracy as a whole' with bourgeois democracy and opportunistically exaggerate the limitations of democracy in bourgeois society to reject it under the pretext that 'democracy can only be fake bourgeois democracy'. The struggle for 'socialist' society is thus claimed to be incompatible with all notions of democracy and the 'need for the iron fist of the proletarian dictatorship' (equated with sheer authoritarianism) is invoked in order to justify the extensive repression. It is well known that 'official socialism in Africa is basically authoritarian and professedly anti-democratic'.[3]

On a similar line of thought, apologists for existing African regimes claim that the struggle in Africa for democratic rights (freedom of the press, of association, of aesthetic taste, etc.) is either 'bourgeois' (in which case 'reactionary') or 'elitist' (in which case 'foreign' to the African peoples' profound aspirations). The absence of any form of democracy — restricted, bourgeois or otherwise — is thus seen as superior to bourgeois democracy! This is but a rationalisation for authoritarian rule.

Self-styled left or revolutionary groups also advance the same sort of arguments to dismiss the struggle for democracy in Africa. It is clear that, by so doing, those groups are either unaware of discussions on political strategy and calculation in proletarian struggles and Marxism (from Marx, Engels, Lenin to Mao Zedung) or they do practise an authoritarian alternative. Marx, Engels, Lenin and Mao Zedung emphasise[4] the role of the bourgeois democratic revolution in facilitating and deepening the proletarian struggle for power. According to this line of reasoning, only a bourgeois–democratic post-colonial period as a precondition would facilitate proletarian revolution in Africa. Classical Marxism has certainly held various, even contradictory, points of view on this question; but it has never rejected the role of bourgeois democracy. 'The winning of bourgeois democratic rights', wrote F. Gitwen, 'represents a contribution to the struggle for socialism, overcoming the existing practice of total censorship and prohibition of organisation opens up broader possibilities for revolutionary struggles and helps to eliminate the limitations imposed by clandestine struggle'.[5] The recent history of protracted splitting of party formations has shown that a political strategy developed clandestinely is often extremely centralist, undemocratic, elitist and authoritarian.

Of course, it is important not to view the struggle for bourgeois democracy as an ultimate objective:

> The struggle for bourgeois democratic freedom is waged in the correct perspective only when posed as stepping stone, as a useful and necessary step for the proletariat's struggle for power, for the destruction of the state and the creation of a new society[6]

Even bourgeois democracy is not a simple gift; it must be struggled for and won by the proletariat.

Other important theories of democracy are based on the philosophical thesis of *African exceptionalism*. This is shared by both left and right, anti-colonial regime groups as well as apologists for the regimes and of course those of imperialism.

Theoreticians of Euro-Communism (claimed also to be based on European exceptionalism), for example, claim that the demand for democracy is not relevant for masses of the underdeveloped countries due to their level of development. Santiago Carrillo, for example, wrote in his *Euro-Communism and the State* that 'to demand pluralism in countries like Vietnam is like braying at the moon'.[7] The ontological fact of multiple different realities is here reduced to an attitude. And Jean Ziegler, in his *Contre l'ordre du Monde, Les Rebelles*,[8] develops a similar thesis, namely that anti-democratic actions of the juntas in Africa are justified; while these acts may be considered undemocratic and paternalistic in Europe, they are not so in Africa, Latin America and Asia, due to their level of development and their difficult tasks of eradicating misery, providing food to the starving people, developing productive forces and creating powerful states. Constraints linked to the existing state of oppression and exploitation are invoked to deny the masses of people of those countries the right to demand broad democratic rights, to justify paternalist tendencies on the same basis as that of the balance sheet analysis used to support colonialism. Socialism in Africa can thus be without democracy even if this is unthinkable for socialism in Europe! Since the workers are not really in power, without democracy what guarantees are there that technicist or technocratic task-oriented politics will serve the interests of the workers and the large masses of people? And is it not the case that the way out of economic backwardness is via a revolution assuring power to the masses and a qualitatively different kind of democracy? The claim that the 'level of development of the productive forces' is responsible for either the absence of democracy (low level) or its presence (high level) has become a dogma that needs reexamination. Was the level of development of the productive forces in Ancient Greece higher than that of Europe of the Middle Ages? This important question cannot, unfortunately, be dealt with in detail here. Fredy Perlman has examined this question very satisfactorily.[9]

Apologists for the so-called 'regimes with a socialist orientation' even deny, on the same basis, the possibility of socialism in Africa, and defend repressive states provided that these claim to practise 'socialist orientation' and ultimately give themselves a state-created 'vanguard party'. Theoretical treatment of the so-called 'socialist orientation' in Africa has been extremely naive and unconvincing. The socialist character of a regime or state has tended to be reduced to mere formalism of ideological proclamations and the regime's ties with the Soviet camp rather than based on concrete tasks carried out by those countries of 'socialist orientation'. The 'vanguard' character of a party has tended to be viewed in terms of the mere party form, i.e. the structural arrangements of party components and the formal ideological rhetoric.

Democracy, whether seen as (1) a mode of government, (2) a mode of class domination, or (3) a mechanism of union (community or people's solidarity) and conciliation, implies a *de facto* division, a fractioning of the organic community, the existence of 'individualistic' individuals (individuals freed from past traditional or social ties), i.e. the existence of classes and class struggles. It is, indeed, ideological class struggles which move apologists for neo-colonial regimes to deny the existence of social classes in Africa. Nobody, in a truly classless community, would be busy denying the existence of social classes! The dissolution of the primitive community gave rise to ancient democracy for example in Greece; the dissolution of the feudal society in Europe led to bourgeois democracy (made possible by, among other things, intense workers' struggles and the availability of black slaves and later on colonies and neo-colonies). Apologists for the one-party state system precisely deny the existence of classes, class struggles, division or fractioning of the African community (the ontological fact of pluralism) to reject the demand for democracy (i.e. the right of organisation of political parties, of dissent and of assembly and association). The thesis of 'one classless community' led to the thesis of 'one people', 'one party', 'one leader, father figure, father of the nation'; the 'oneness of the community' is equated with the 'oneness of the community's interests'. Moreover, when class differentiation, becoming increasingly blatant, is admitted, it is asserted that 'the differentiation of classes in Africa does not imply diversification of interests let alone opposition of interests'.[10] Often reversing the order of causality, a plurality of parties is claimed to cause class antagonisms which must be avoided (rather than 'resolved') with a one-party state system. Even if democracy does not entail the plurality of political parties, does the denial of the right to organise imply a restriction of people's rights, a form of negation of democracy? Does one party guarantee people's unity and solidarity? Should this not be put to free discussion by the large masses of people rather than the state deciding on it for them once and for all? 'The whole idea of opposition', said President Kaunda,[11] 'is alien to Africans'! Thus, all forms of protest — from workers' strikes to demands for democracy — are seen as being fomented by foreign agents.

While those same apologists talk a lot about the 'specific form of democracy of the African traditional society', the teachings of the 'community palaver'[12] — the equivalent of a mechanism of conciliation — are never taken up. Let me bring out at least some of them.

1. Popular consensus is never reached through silence, since silence is complicity, an obstacle to the democratisation process.

2. Democracy is also the free collective and individual exercise of speech by the entire community and each of its members. It is the complete release sanctioned by the palavering community of each person's whole physical being: one's senses, one's gestures, etc., so as never to restrain any aspect whatsoever of one's creativity. The integral freedom of speech within the community also requires and stimulates very attentive listening to one another and thus the mutual respect for the right of each to speak, whoever he or she may be. The palaver demands that the bad guy be listened to so that his bad word is dealt with and he himself is cleansed.

3. The true leader is the one that listens to those spontaneous and varied voices of the community tirelessly, attentively and with respect for even the most insignificant meaning, before refining what has been said into directives. It is not for the leader to silence this speaking. It is the task of a cadre, the *Nzonzi*, to eliminate any obstacle to clarification, to democratisation, to simplification, to the creative spontaneity of the community, to the spiritual stimulation of the community as a whole, to the people's grasp of what is new, to community life; the cadre enhances the community life process, not its destruction. The *Nzonzi* are literally 'speakers', masters of the clarification of speech. They function as competent handlers of dialectics; they are, therefore, dialecticians. They can and do make use of rhetoric but they are not above all rhetoricians. They are very able detectors of the divisive 'bad word' and stimulators of the palaver and they help to assure that it does not degenerate into violent antagonism. They know how to make very severe criticisms without offending or silencing the one criticised: it is crucial that the latter continues

to speak. The *Nzonzi* are thus the cadres of the popular democracy organised through the palaver. There are those who emerge and discover themselves competent *Nzonzi* through the very dialectics of the palaver. This is why, in order to be a good *Nzonzi*, one must know how to *listen* attentively and tirelessly, to *pick up* rapidly the essence of each word spoken, attentively *observe* every look, every gesture, every silence, and *grasp* their respective significance (their target) and at the same time to elaborate, in conformity with the axioms of popular wisdom (ideology), arguments to counter these unjust positions and/or to reaffirm or reinforce correct positions. The *Nzonzi* is thus a thinker engaged in mental dialogue interacting in words and gestures with the members of the community organised in a palaver (in the process of community unification through struggle) successively and simultaneously to seek out and destroy the 'bad word' exposed as a thesis deviating from the ancestral line.

The role of the *Nzonzi* is not to take sides openly with a thesis of a member of the community but to assure that the criticism and self-criticism are carried out according to the ancestral procedure of mass democracy. It happens at times that the various *Nzonzi* may be placed on two strong opposed sides or camps which are formed in the very process of the palaver. In any case, a *Nzonzi* who shows himself *to be blind to the correctness of the theses* put forward by both sides is seen to have been corrupted and as a result to be unable to act as a true specialist in ideological clarification and to have become a mystifier (*Nzonzi za luvunu* — lying Nzonzi). He is thus transformed into a target of the palaver.

The collective self-criticism is carried out under the intellectual (dialectical) leadership of the *Nzonzis* who articulate positions and counter-positions in relation to the theoretical, ideological and symbolic requirements of the palaver. The *Nzonzis*, by using all sorts of stylistic turns of phrases, symbolic analogies full of imagery, songs etc., express more clearly the 'correct theses', those which reflect the political and ideological line of the ancestors as well as the 'deviationist theses'. The intellectual and symbolic gymnastics directed by the *Nzonzis* are aimed at leading the holders of 'erroneous theses' to admit publicly, not by use of physical or moral threat or by witchcraft (spiritual terrorism), but solely by generalised collective debate, that they deviate from the 'community right line'. If these elementary teachings were taken seriously by our regimes, our present communities would be very different.

These are but a few themes and arguments one is often confronted with. Clearly they can only be clarified, refuted or deepened with sound theoretical analyses and concrete case studies of the African peoples' struggles for people's power.

Theoretical analyses would include such topics as: (a) the complete history of democracy in its various phases — from ancient democracy, post-feudal bourgeois democracy, post-fascist social democracy to 'proletarian democracy' in post-revolutionary societies; (b) specific implications for proletarian democracy of the 'crisis of Marxism' (for example the crisis of the conception of representation in politics); (c) the critical analysis of theories of democracy in Africa.

From ancient Greece to the bourgeois world, democracy developed out of class struggles as a *concrete form of class rule*. Democracy, in its various historical forms, has partially been a strategical way of politically organising (demobilising) some dominated groups within the ruling class or dominated classes (whose support is needed for the legitimation of class rule) to be associated in the intense exploitation of one section of society excluded from 'real humanity'. Democracy has been a form of class leadership, developed through class conflict, of the ruling class *vis-à-vis* ruled classes. Its content has depended on the quality of the struggles of the ruled classes against domination (i.e. their capacity for autonomous self-organising).

Ancient Greek democracy was based on the exploitation of slaves whom Aristotle described as 'animated machines' or 'speaking instruments'. The social group of the so-called 'free people' were democratically made to approve the class exploitation of slaves by their 'slavemasters'. The claim by Socrates that even slaves could philosophise, in other words were real people, was one of the crimes that led to his execution by the Athenian authorities.

Bourgeois democracy developed on the basis of intense exploitation of black slaves (slave trade), the murdering of native Americans, and later on, the colonising of non-European peoples. Bourgeois-dominated classes were democratically entertained and associated — no matter how marginally — in the exploitation of classes and peoples excluded from genuine humanity (in the imperialist bourgeois epoch: excluded from civilisation and 'universal history'). Of course, this form of class rule took shape through intense class struggles, especially those of the working class. While democracy is, from the point of view of the ruling class, a process of legitimising its class rule, it is, however, from the point of view of the classes that are ruled a process of restraining class domination (which divides the community) by strengthening community solidarity. Bourgeois democracy is necessarily limited: it excludes large sections of people from 'humanity' and makes exploitation politically bearable.

Post-fascist social democracy was a concrete form of bourgeois class rule that developed out of class struggles that led to the defeat of the proletariat of Western Europe. The proletariat was again made to be associated in the class exploitation of colonies and neo-colonies. Indeed, even 'communist parties' favoured colonial and neo-colonial domination.

Following the emergence of 'new bourgeoisies' in post-revolutionary societies, attempts at achieving 'proletarian democracy' through proletarian cultural revolutions, for example — a form of an integral community or anti-class rule aimed at ultimately abolishing class domination and exploitation — have been shortlived. At stake, of course, has been the crucial question of the *Marxist conception of representative politics*. How can Marxism grasp and master in its development, the correct relationship between the large masses of people, the proletariat, the party (as an 'advanced detachment of the proletarian class') and the state that is to wither away? These are crucial questions needing a lot of research and critical political analysis that only a team of committed intellectuals can carry out. I want, as a beginning, to devote the rest of my discussion to the concrete case of struggle for people's power in Congo–Brazzaville.

## The Case of Congo–Brazzaville[13]

The People's Republic of Congo is one of the African countries with a one-party state system, having adopted 'scientific socialism' (since 1963) and 'Marxism–

Leninism' (since 1968). Two of its presidents (Fulbert Youlou and Yhombi-Opango) have so far been forced to resign through direct (Youlou) and indirect (Yhombi) people's mass revolutionary pressure. Congo has experienced practically most of the problems related to the question of democracy in Africa. Can a one-party state system be democratic? Can a military coup be progressive and lead to a democratic regime? What are the fundamental conditions of existence of democratisation of the state? Is socialism through a military coup possible? Can trade unions lead a powerful mass movement to a bourgeois democratic regime or any other democratic regime? What constitutes a people's capacity for democracy? What determines the character of the state — whether it is democratic or undemocratic? Can the state be transformed from within? Can a truly revolutionary party of labour be created by the state? Can the people succeed in transforming the state before they have mastered the imperialist domination of their economy? These and other issues were confronted by the revolutionary mass movement in Congo. Whatever the character of the historical outcomes of the people's struggles confronting those very issues, they can indeed throw some light on the concrete possibilities for resolving them.

Congo became independent on 18 September 1961 through a well-prepared imperialist scheme of French neo-colonialism which had former priest Fulbert Youlou as the first President. Through his party, UDDIA (union for the defence of African interests, actually functioning as the union with imperialism for the defence of French neo-colonial interests), Youlou succeeded in taking over the leadership of the mass movement then dominated by Andre Matsoua's religious messianic movement. French official support and open backing by Western business circles were decisive in this regard. Some of the democratic rights (of organisation of trade unions, youth associations, etc.) won by the masses of the Congolese people in the colonial period were not overturned. In fact, confrontation by the masses of people against Youlou's regime was over those very rights. In line with the need for consolidation of the neo-colonial state, this regime sought to curtail people's initiative and to organise their systematic *passivity*. For example, the right of free association and organisation independently of the state had come under systematic and severe attack by the regime.

Youlou's regime was particularly reactionary, repressive and pro-neo-colonialist French interests. Its programme, marked by a frantic anti-communism (especially of the anti-Lumumbist variant), tribalist political strategy, opposition to 'positive neutralism' in foreign affairs and to the Casablanca OAU group, close ties with the secessionist Moise Tshombe, and rampant corruption, gave free hand, in economic policy, to foreign capital and organised people's exploitation and repression. Three years of Youlou's regime pleased only former colonialists and neo-colonialists; the masses of the Congolese people progressively organised through trade unions (African General Confederation of Labour, African Confederation of Free Trade Unions and African Confederation of Christian Workers) and independent youth movements (Union of Congolese Youth, Christian Working Youth and Protestant Student Youth) taking up the struggle against the regime and very soon started demanding and agitating for its overthrow.

To strengthen its power and break up the mass resistance movement, the regime tried to unify trade unions into one state trade union and youth movements into the state-based UDDIA youth movement. It sought to introduce strictly individual membership of UDDIA in a *de facto* one-party system rather than on the basis of organisations demanded by trade unions and youth movements. At issue again was the recognition or non-recognition by this state party of the right of organisation of independent trade unions and youth movements and the need to have a specific political position even inside the state party. How can the people maintain their initiative in a state party?

The most radical trade union (African General Confederation of Labour) tried to organise for the unification of the trade unionist movement on a different basis, independently of the state, against the Christian section (African Confederation of Christian Workers) which correctly continued to agitate for its autonomy at all costs.

On those two specific fronts, the regime failed to break up and in fact radicalised the people's mass resistance. The regime sought new 'political pretexts' to divide and hit the people's mass movement led by trade unions solidly supported by the radical youth movements and progressive intellectuals. The regime claimed, for example, to have discovered a 'communist plot' to overthrow it; it used this as a pretext to isolate and destroy the radical tendencies in the African General Confederation of Labour (CGAT), the Union of Congolese Youth (UJC) and the student movement. State repression and censorship were thus unleashed and the people's rights of association, organisation and public assembly won during anti-colonial struggles were denied.

Against the stepping up of state repression leading to the arbitrary arrest and killings of trade union leaders, for example, the mass movement increased its pressure on the state and developed into a powerful popular movement — known as the movement of the 'trois glorieuses' — which in 1963 (13–15 August), through a general civil insurgency (an uprising initiated by a strike of 35,000 workers called by trade unions and bringing together workers, peasants, students and progressive intellectuals), succeeded in forcing Youlou's repressive regime out of power. Not even the French army, still stationed in Brazzaville, dared to intervene to save the pro-French neo-colonial regime, as the whole population seemed so determined and so united against it. Even neo-colonialists felt that such an intervention was likely to precipitate a civil war. The initiative to transform the character of the state, so it seemed clearly, belonged to these rebelling masses of people who unfortunately had no political revolutionary leading core.

The powerful revolutionary movement had no real political strategy of transformation, by steps, of the state and society, i.e. no real organised political alternative (a conception of a new society and state). People wanted a new regime, a better regime — that was all; they had no clear political conditions or directives. Trade-unionist leaders soon realised that trade unions, as such, cannot provide political leadership to a powerful mass revolutionary movement. The youth section — influenced by progressive intellectuals — had only one political project: to enter into the state apparatus and transform the state from within.

A revolutionary mass movement without a party working out a strategic programme — dealing with the contradiction between state repression and mass resistance — for the seizure of state power and the transformation of the state cannot even organise for and win a long-lasting democracy. But a party outside of a mass revolutionary movement degenerates into a state-like bureaucracy.

Indeed, decisions on the spot were taken *democratically*, a committee for the merger of the trade unions was, for example, democratically formed. And to deal with the lack of an organ of political leadership, a Conseil National de la Révolution (CNR) was created. Only a minority, African General Confederation of Labour (CGAT), in the trade-unionist movement, had any clear idea of a class party. The great proletarian cultural revolution in China introduced an important distinction in this matter.[14] Revolution is the overthrow of one form of state and its replacement by another form. The party is the revolution plus communism. It deals not only with the state in its present phase, but also that of the following phases. There are, in fact, revolutionary situations without any party and Marxist parties which are not revolutionary. A revolutionary party is not necessarily a communist party. The proletarian class party is revolutionary and communist. In other words, a powerful mass movement leading to an overthrow of a form of state and its replacement with another form may exist without having been led by a party. A party, when it exists, and when it leads such a movement, is a revolutionary party. It is not automatically a communist party unless it leads a movement towards the protracted overthrow of successive forms and phases of state and the latter's withering away, i.e. towards communism. Besides leading the movement of the overthrow of the state in the present phase, a proletarian class party leads the movement that transforms the state in its successive phases as well. The nature of a proletarian class party depends on the relationship it has with the mass movement, the party process and the state process. Conceived as a bureaucratic organ of political leadership, a party cannot be both revolutionary and communist, both leading the overthrow of the state in its present phase and strengthening community solidarity against the state process up to communism. A revolutionary party that becomes a state structure after the overthrow of one form of state, despite possible claims of being a proletarian class party, proves thereby to be the opposite of a communist party. The movement could not have made this important distinction.

To avoid the possibility of bloodshed, the movement called on Massamba Debat, an experienced politician, a former minister of Youlou's government who had resigned earlier to protest against the regime's orientation, to head a new government and arbitrate among the contending social forces. He was seen as an honest politician. Against the politics of undemocratic representation of Youlou's regime, the movement came back to another politics of representation which turned out to be difficult to control. Already, French colonialists were quite satisfied with and relieved at the movement's choice of the head of the new government.

The trade-unionist leadership remained outside the new government. The youth section of the movement saw this as a major political blunder on the part of the trade-unionist leadership. On the contrary as will be seen later, a strong independent trade-unionist movement is more effective in determining the democratic character of the state than the simple entry into the government of trade union leaders.

To fulfil the need for a political party, a National Revolutionary Movement (MNR), a mass political organisation, was created through a constitutive congress. The organisational aspects were dominated by former bureaucrats around Massamba Debat, so much so that 'scientific socialism', adopted by acclamation as the doctrine of the movement, was not even mentioned in the act of creation of the MNR.

By the same logic, all the youth movements were regrouped into a youth movement, the National Revolutionary Youth Movement (JMNR), and a Civil Defence Organisation, an embryonic people's army or militia. While all this was taking place in a fairly democratic kind of way, the right of organisation independently of the state was already being undermined. Without explicit recognition of this right — then taken for granted — the democratic character of the regime would soon be curtailed.

The balance of social forces which gave rise to the new regime proved to be very unstable. The MNR regime was based on the alliance between an administrative bureaucracy dominating the government, the increasingly radicalised trade-unionist movement, the youth movement (the JMNR and Civil Defence), and Marxist intellectuals. French imperialism still controlled the economy. Through the mass movement pressures and the presence of 'reformists' and 'socialists with Marxist rhetoric' in the state apparatuses, important decisions were nevertheless made: the educational system was divided from the churches (reducing the anti-communist, obscurantist religious tendencies passing through the school system); imperialist military bases were closed and the army democratised; a 'women's revolutionary union' was created by the state (the first public recognition of the need to take up the women's question); one state trade union, the Congolese Trade Unionist Confederation (CSC) was created; diplomatic relations with socialist countries (including China) were opened; and a state economic sector was established. Needless to say, the state-created mass organisations, controlled from above, tended to function as state instruments to contain the mass resistance movement. Moreover, all these decisions, slightly curtailing the revolutionary momentum of the mass movement, were unable to offset radically the imperialist domination of the economy; the latter's structures remained completely integrated into the French neo-colonial system. Economic aid through cooperation with socialist countries, insufficient to start with and bureaucratically disposed of, was unable to uproot the French and American overpresence in the economy. To deal with those basic issues, a strong mass revolutionary movement and a clear strategy ('economic guerilla calculation') was necessary.

Those contradictory tendencies, exacerbated by the anti-democratic attitudes of the 'socialist forces' in the regime, soon led to a crisis of the new regime. Indeed, the 'socialist forces', strongly influenced by Marxist intellectuals (Ndalla, Noumazalaye, etc.), had no clear ideas about the politics of reform: they tended to see things in terms of 'either everything or nothing'; their understanding of the transformation of the state from within consisted in driving 'non-socialists' out of the state apparatus. Struggles in the state were reduced to struggles by 'socialist elements' to occupy 'strategic' state places: these included also those places and positions in the party and the trade union both of which had been transformed into state agencies

105

(the distinction between party in power and party as a state structure was nonexistent). Those 'socialist elements' thus tended to be hostile to the right of people to organise independently of the 'scientific socialist regime'. The demand for this right was seen, of course, as reactionary. Socialist planning tended to be viewed as a process of planning by the state of every aspect of people's life, i.e. a process of statisation tending towards the destruction of civil society. The contradiction between the state and civil society, typical of specific relations in production, is resolved by extending the state over civil society without dealing with the dominant relations of production. The solution to the limitations of state planning was again to call for more state planning. Ultimately, the claim was made (by P. Lissouba) that the main problem was the fact that the Congolese people as a whole were not ready for rigorous planning. In brief, statism was seen to be revolutionary if the state apparatus was occupied by socialist elements. Socialist politics, said to be necessary to 'radicalise the revolution', tended increasingly to be conceived as a coup clearing the state apparatus of 'non-socialist elements'.

The sad consequence was that apparently only non-Marxist elements were advocating a bourgeois democratic regime, and the struggle for democracy, so closely linked then with non-Marxists, was seen as a reactionary project. Marxist elements were somehow unable to see the necessity of bourgeois democracy for the process of proletarian class differentiation from other classes, so as to allow the proletariat to develop a class capacity to organise a political alternative. This cannot be done through state agencies. This may also explain why Marxist elements were putting so much weight on their clandestine relation with the so-called 'progressive section of the army's officers' (N. Gouabi and Raoul's group).

It was precisely the 'socialist forces' in the JMNR (led by its most radical fraction, the UGEEC — the General Union of Congolese Students and Pupils), in the Civil Defence, in the army officers' group and among some intellectuals which organised the coup d'etat which overthrew the Massamba Debat regime, the most potentially democratic regime the Congo has known. This was the only regime that came to power on the basis of a popular uprising and intervention of the broad masses in the political process. The regime to rule the Congo prior to this was a French imperialist puppet regime. All the regimes after Massamba Debat arose through military intervention and the complete demobilisation of the masses of people. Of course, this demobilisation started with that regime as all mass organisations became statised and progressive 'left' cadres entered the state apparatus and let themselves be cut off from the masses of people. At least at the beginning, with this regime, autonomous organising of the masses of people, independently of the state, was potentially possible.

Marien N'Gouabi, a self-styled Marxist and the commander of the armed forces, became the new head of state (on 4 September 1968); Marxism–Leninism was adopted as the doctrine of the new regime. The left elements of the mass movement were brought into the state apparatus to 'radicalise the transformation of the neo-colonial bureaucratic state and society'; and a new Revolutionary National Council (CNR) was created to serve as the necessary organ of political leadership. This new 'Marxist–Leninist' very quickly started making decisions which not only created tensions and conflicts among the 'socialist forces' in power themselves (affected probably by the Sino–Soviet split), but also led to a process of statisation (almost militarisation) of the whole civil society — never achieved before. The 'Civil Defence', the embryonic people's militia, was dissolved and integrated into the army. A new, more state-controlled, youth movement, the UJSC, was created to replace the JMNR, leading to a real state control of the mass movement. As could be expected, the trade unions and part of the UJC started opposing the new regime. To curtail this opposition, the state first dissolved the confederation bureau or executive committee of the only existing trade union (CSC) and subsequently completely eliminated the trade union itself. All independent mass political organisations were destroyed, and on 31 December 1969 a Congolese Party of Labour (PCT) was created by the state. The new regime increasingly adopted formal revolutionary symbols (the red flag, the international anthem, etc.) with no real Congolese social content. The party was later proclaimed a 'vanguard party'.

The ultimate consequence was that left elements in the state apparatus were basically cut off from the large masses of people. These responded with strikes, trying to defend their right; despite 'Marxist' state repression, workers' strikes and students' protests multiplied. Of course, the left elements believed that the presence of the rightist elements in the state was responsible for the state's repressive orientation. They sought to entrench themselves in the state and kick out, if possible, the rightist elements. Under Diawara's leadership they used the occasion offered by Kikanga's coup attempt to strengthen their power in the state. A new people's militia, armed with military material, was thereafter created; still state repression did not subside.

As if to consolidate this new 'Marxist–Leninist' state power, state links with reactionary regimes in neighbouring countries (Zaire, Cameroon, etc.) were created; new accords with such regimes were signed leading to exchanges of political prisoners (Mulele, for example, was extradited to Zairean authorities). Progressive militants of neighbouring countries (Cameroon's UPC cadres, Chad's Frolinat militants, etc.) were arrested in Brazzaville and handed to the regimes they were struggling against as goodwill for 'regional détente'.

Against these repressive state tendencies, people's struggles increased: they exposed more and more 'socialist forces' in the 'Marxist' regime. 1971 saw an important increase of popular struggles which increasingly embarrassed the 'left' within the PCT. An important strike of dockers took place in Point-Noire, the Congolese maritime port. In the nationalised sugar cane plantations of Jacob, strikes also took place about the same time as students organised in the UJSC staged demonstrations. The necessity for the state to control the situation against this threatening anti-regime mass movement divided the 'left' further and reinforced right-wing elements dominated by Marien N'Gouabi's cousin, Yhombi Opango, who threatened to stage a rightist coup. The 'left' was unable even theoretically to defend the autonomy of mass organisations, nor was it prepared to defend the right of the working class to strike even against a self-styled 'socialist' state employer. The 'Marxist' president N'Gouabi pre-empted this move by bringing Yhombi Opango back to a prominent position in the state as the army's chief of staff ultimately controlling the entire army.

On 22 February 1972, feeling politically threatened and still trying to transform the state from within, the left elements (under Diawara's leadership) tried an ultimate putschist action (a coup attempt) which failed. Rapid and stronger 'Marxist' state repression was thereafter unleashed: 2,000 people (all the left elements of the state-created 'vanguard party', and of the army) were arrested. Some elements (including Ange Diawara, J. B. Ikoko, Jean Claude Bakekolo, J. P. Olouka) escaped and went underground. They constituted themselves and their partisans into the so-called M22 movement giving rise to a *foco*-type armed maquis in the countryside.

This was an interesting historical development. It showed that Marxism, seen as a scientific or technological instrument, can lend itself to be used in anti-democratic practices. This is precisely one of the issues related to the so called 'crisis of Marxism'. Marxism, taken as a science above the large masses of people, becomes anti-democratic. While the Marxist left inside the state still held to its objectives — at least at the level of intentions — of destroying the neo-colonial bureaucratic bourgeois state apparatus and of democratising the army — still patterned after the French armed forces — it became increasingly unable even to guarantee its own physical safety under a regime it helped set up.

Democracy is won through mass-based struggles; it is not won by mere occupation of the state apparatus by 'socialist forces' cut off from the broad masses of people. Cadres that should have helped organise the masses of people politically still struggling spontaneously against state repression for their democratic rights, allowed themselves to be cut off from the masses and thus became, instead, hostages in and of the state. Instead of being an asset to the rebelling mass movement, they became its liability. Indeed, it was in the name of those cadres also that the 'Marxist' regime decided to unleash repression against the rebelling masses of the Congolese people, to organise their pro-state passivity.

It is important, however, to mention the fact that the left elements that went to the maquis organised an important network connecting their maquis with the working class, the peasantry and the youth. In this maquis they made an important self-critical assessment of their past practice. A document, *Autocritique du M22*, written in 1973 by Ange Diawara, and one of the most important documents of the revolutionary movements in Africa, says: 'it is not possible to struggle against the state apparatus from within unless one entertains reformist illusions or gives priority to an adventurist putschist strategy'.[15] Ange Diawara, a very strong and domineering personality, led the maquis. He was, until 1972, the strongest element from the south in a regime increasingly becoming dominated by people from the northern part of the country. He was the most important leader of the Civil Defence.

Unfortunately, it was too late; with the complicity of the Zairean state, the revolutionary network established by the M22 movement was dismantled and its leadership decimated. The bodies of the assassinated leaders were publicly displayed to frighten and discourage the mass movement.

A revolutionary movement, based on the proletarian class capacity to make history, requires a democratic social–political atmosphere to develop and truly arm the rebelling masses of people to be able to bring about a new alternative of politics, society and state. A few individuals, acting on behalf of the proletariat and the broad rebelling masses of people, cannot accomplish such a profound social transformation. To make a genuine contribution in this perspective, left elements must develop, in line with revolutionary politics, a genuine politics of reform. There is no real short cut. The obstacles to overcome are so overwhelming that a powerful mass revolutionary movement led by a real proletarian class with the capacity for social transformation of African neo-colonial societies is required to succeed. This capacity cannot be developed through a state self-declared 'vanguard party'.

The process of statisation and extreme state centralisation brought about by the failure of the M22 movement and the new waves of mass struggles of resistance from 1973 to 1977 gave rise to a series of political crises. Stalinist methods of 'cleansing or purifying the party' were often used: people, accused of 'blocking the Revolution', were constantly expelled from the PCT. In the same perspective and to 'radicalise the Revolution', the Political Bureau of the PCT was dissolved in 1975 and a special revolutionary committee of five people was created to 'give a new breadth to the Revolution'. Leaders of the trade unions, who supported a vast movement of strikes in public enterprises in 1976, were fired as part of the purification process.

In the midst of all these struggles, and as a result of those struggles and the impact of world economic crisis on this well-integrated imperialist system, an economic crisis of major gravity developed. By the end of 1976, N'Gouabi, unable to control the situation, became isolated. To break this isolation, he tried to use the tactic of 'democratic opening' towards former politicians, old leaders of trade unions or youth movements and other important figures (such as the Cardinal) to bring about a democratic front of national reconciliation ultimately regrouping all political forces in the country. In conjunctures of political crisis, 'democratic opening' may be a way of trying to keep one's power. 'Democratic opening' can become real only in a situation in which the rebelling masses of people are capable of organising themselves independently and thus of forcing the state to make it real. In a similar situation of economic catastrophe and political crisis, President Senghor used that same tactic in Senegal, leading to multipartism.

Of course, after having consolidated the right wing, considerably weakened the left of the regime and allowed tribalist politics to go deep, this 'democratic opening' came too late indeed. The northern tribalist group,[16] headed by Yhombi, felt threatened by N'Gouabi's move, rightly or wrongly interpreted as aimed at 'returning power to the southerners', staged, on 18 March 1977, a rightist coup. President N'Gouabi himself was killed as well as all the prominent politicians and personalities, such as the Cardinal and former President Massamba Debat, he had contacted in the 'democratic opening' exercise. As can be seen, the 'Marxist regime', with the kind of politics it incarnated, was clearly responsible for this ultimate development: *Qui sème le vent, récolte la tempête*; (who sows the wind, reaps the whirlwind); or, he who rides a tiger cannot dismount.

Under the pretext of overcoming the catastrophic economic crisis, the new regime's main task was to consolidate, concentrate and centralise further the state power into fewer and fewer hands. The Congolese Party of Labour — already a mere bureacratic state organ — was neutralised to the maximum as the right was unable to control it completely. All the other 'political forces', understood to have been the focus of the project of 'democratic opening and national reconciliation', were systematically and militarily dealt with. A military committee of the party (CMP) was created as the leading core of the military dictatorship. Many officers, unknown until then, rose up to the highest positions of the state apparatus. Faked trials were staged, followed by summary executions. The future of the mass movement appeared to be very bleak indeed; stronger state repression and censorship were unleashed. Attempts at the militarisation of the labour process were made.

Despite all the socialist rhetoric and all the talk about 'productive labour carried out with rigour', capitalists were still reluctant to invest. No real economic programme came out of this 'radicalisation of the Revolution'. In a few months, a process of Zaireanisation of Congo started taking place: increasing embezzlements of public funds, presidential privatisation of public funds, banishment of 'undesirable political elements' to their villages of origin, etc., were becoming common. Yhombi Opango, the new head of state, drew from the state coffers and for himself as much as 1.7 billion CFA in two years of power. Taking Mobutu as his model, he indulged in luxury extravaganzas for 'socialist transformation'. For the first time since Youlou, the salaries of state functionaries were not forthcoming — sometimes for months. Even imperialism could not condone this behaviour and wanted him removed.

Yhombi Opango, desperately trying to control all the power, tried by all kinds of pretexts to eradicate opposition (real or possible). This led to an intense political confrontation within the ruling elite which ultimately gave rise to Denis Sassou Nguesso's coup of 5 February 1979 which removed Yhombi Opango. As far as can be seen, no politico–ideological break took place, nor did any real curtailment of neo-colonialism come out of it. If anything more imperialist capital started flowing in again, especially after the discovery of new oil deposits, and reliance on France for the regular payment of civil service salaries increased. Congolese leaders have continued to exploit contradictions between Soviet superpower and French imperialism to bargain over the country's dependency, and it is to be noted that the currently economically catastrophic situation cannot really be improved outside a truly revolutionary involvement of masses of people in the process of the transformation of society.

To take up that challenge, the new 'Marxist–Leninist regime' tried to organise a new 'union of the left' composed of old left elements (connected with the 22 February 1972 purge) and new elements coming back from outside the student movement. Once again, the exercise of 'socialist transformation from within the state apparatus' re-emerged as if the *Autocritique du M22* never existed. Worse still, the left entered the state apparatus, this time with neither an independent programme nor a shared ideology: only an instinct of political and physical survival. With no real links with the mass movement whose organisations have been reduced to political silence, the left cannot really do much. It can only provide technical and ideological decor for the regime.

## Conclusion

Struggles for people's power in Congo have exposed the left opportunism and left extremism of the petty bourgeois Marxist intellectuals. They have exposed their tendency to practise statism; ultimately this statism has proved ineffective without some doses of the 'democratic opening'. Had the rebelling masses of people been correctly organised into independent mass organisations, when the left still enjoyed solid ties with them, the political space for institutionalised democracy, allowing proletarian class differentiation to take place, would probably have been achieved. The most important thing is that mass struggles for people's democratic rights, however spontaneous, continue.

## Notes

1. H. Odera Oruka, 'State Disarmament: A Question for Regional Security and Military Disarmament in Africa', *Philosophy and Social Action* vol. VIII no. 3, 1982, p. 21.

2. Most of what is said here has also been discussed by F. Gitwen, in his 'The Struggle for Democracy in Africa', *Ethiopian Marxist Review*, 1 August 1980, pp. 82–94.

3. *Ibid*. p. 82.

4. See for example: Peter Gibbon, *Political Strategy and Calculation in Classical Marxists*, unpublished MS., 1982.

5. Gitwen, 'The Struggle for Democracy', p. 86.

6. *Ibid*, p. 86.

7. *Ibid*, p. 86.

8. Jean Ziegler, *Contre l'ordre du Monde, Les Rebelles* (Paris: Editions Seuil 1982) especially his introduction.

9. Fredy Perlman, *Against History, Against Leviathan* (Detroit: Black and Red, 1983).

10. In *Présence Africaine*, no. 30, Paris, 1960; Also quoted by F. Gitwen, 'The Struggle for Democracy', pp. 87–8.

11. Quoted by Gitwen, 'The Struggle for Democracy', p. 90.

12. More details in E. Wamba-dia-Wamba: *Experiences of Democracy in Africa: Reflections on the practice of communalist palaver as a method of resolving contradictions among the people*, unpublished MS. The French original appears in *Journal of African Marxists*, no. 7, March, 1985, pp. 35–50.

13. Most of the material discussed here on Congo came from the following sources: Frank Tenaille, *Les 56 Afriques: Guide Politique* vol. 1 (Paris: Maspero, 1979) pp. 120–29; Hugues Bertrand, *Le Congo*, (Paris: Maspero, 1975); Jean Peter, 'Le Marxisme–Leninisme Tropical' *Le Perroquet*, nos. 29–30; the unsigned article 'Congo: Le "socialisme" en question', *Libération Afrique*, no. 7, 1980; Woungly Massaga, *La révolution au Congo* (Paris: Maspero, 1974).

14. Paul Sandevince, *Notes de Travail sur le Post-Leninisme*, (Paris: Editions Potemkine, 1981) p. 14.

15. Quoted in *Libération Afrique*, no. 6, 1980, p. 7.

16. Referred to in some underground pamphlets: 'Deux lignes politique diametralement opposées au sein du comité central'; 'Qui est Yhombi Opango'; 'Ne Rien Cacher au Peuple' where they refer to the 'association of Kouyou Elders'.

## Other Important Works on Congo

Samir Amin and Catherine Coquery-Vidrovitch: *Histoire économique du Congo (1880–1969)* (Dakar: I.F.A.N., 1971)

Hilaire Babassana. *Travail force, expropriation et formation du salariat en Afrique noire* (Grenoble: P.U.G., 1978).

Pierre-Philippe Rey: *Colonialisme at Néo-colonialisme: exemple de la Comilog au Congo Brazzaville* (Paris: Maspero, 1971).

# 6 The Second Independence Movement in Congo–Kinshasa

## by Nzongola-Ntalaja

The first major resistance against the post-colonial state in Africa took place in Congo–Kinshasa (now Zaire) between 1963 and 1968. A mass-based movement for genuine independence, this resistance was the work of a popular alliance of workers, peasants, the unemployed urban youth, students, lower civil servants, and radical nationalist leaders.

This chapter is a historical study of the struggle between the state and this popular alliance, which designated itself and is better known today as the 'second independence movement'. The purpose of the study is to show the strengths and weaknesses of both the state and popular alliances within the socio-political context of neo-colonialism. The paper is based on my ongoing research on the national liberation struggle in Zaire, begun in 1969.[1]

The concept of 'second independence' was developed, not by social scientists, but by ordinary people in the Kwilu region of western Zaire. For the people, independence was meaningless without a better standard of living, greater civil liberties, and the promise of a better life for their children. Instead of making these promised benefits available to the masses, the politicians who inherited state power from the Belgians lived in much greater luxury than most of their European predecessors and used violence and arbitrary force against the people. For the latter, the first or nominal independence had failed. Their discontent with the neo-colonial state served as a basis for an aspiration towards a new and genuine independence, one that the 1964 insurrections were to incarnate.

These popular uprisings resulted in the control of nearly half the country by the popular alliance under the leadership of Lumumbist politicians. They constituted a revolutionary attempt to end injustice and the new social order favourable to the neo-colonial ruling class and its external backers or allies at the expense of ordinary people and their allies within the petty bourgeoisie. As such, they were a clear manifestation of the class struggle within a neo-colonial context, a struggle which is at once social and national, anti-capitalist as well as anti-imperialist.[2]

Unfortunately, the second independence movement was soundly defeated by the neo-colonialist forces, beginning with the US–Belgian intervention of 24 November 1964 at Kisangani (then Stanleyville), headquarters of the revolutionary government. Unable to defend itself against its own people, the neo-colonial state had to rely on mercenaries and imperialist forces for its survival. This was its only strength.

113

As for the popular alliance, the advantage gained through revolutionary mobilisation among all popular classes and strata and from spontaneous actions against a very weak state was soon lost as a result of crippling weaknesses. These included the absence of revolutionary intellectuals (except for Pierre Mulele, Laurent Kabila and a few others) in the leadership, the reliance on the eventually deceptive power of magico-religious beliefs and practices, the intrusion of ethno-regional factors in revolutionary politics and organisation, and the lack of preparation for a long, protracted struggle against a militarily superior enemy, whose arsenal included a CIA-organised air force of anti-Castro Cubans, white mercenaries, and metropolitan troops.

The analysis that follows is divided into two parts. The first part consists of an examination of the rise of a popular alliance in Zaire (then the Belgian Congo) in response to the oppressive colonial system. It provides the historical background necessary for understanding the major aspirations of this alliance and why it turned to a struggle for a second independence when those aspirations went unfulfilled after independence. The second part attempts to provide a succinct analysis of the second independence movement as the continuation of the struggle for genuine liberation and a better life. It examines firstly the transformation of the popular alliance as a result of decolonisation, giving rise to the major social cleavage around which the movement revolved, secondly the strengths of the movement *vis-à-vis* the neo-colonial state, and thirdly its weaknesses in the face of external intervention.

## The Rise of a Popular Alliance in the Struggle for Independence

The popular alliance that emerged as a second independence movement in post-colonial Zaire traces its origin to the anti-colonial struggle in the Belgian Congo, which succeeded in uniting all the social classes of African society in the fight for independence between 1956 and 1960. A brief analysis of this historical background is essential for any scientific explanation of the strengths and weaknesses of the revolutionary popular alliance during the 1960s and today.

To understand how all these classes came together for a common cause, it is necessary to look at the Belgian colonial system and its impact on Congolese society. Elsewhere, I have attempted to provide a detailed outline of the class structure of the Belgian Congo, together with a description of the position and role of each class within the colonial political economy.[3] My aim here is to look at the overall impact of colonialism and social change on the people of the Congo and at the factors underlying the alliance of the various social classes in the struggle for independence.

## Belgian colonialism and social change in the Congo

The Belgian colonial system represents a classic example of imperialist exploitation, or that of a colony that financed not only its own affairs but also the economic development of the metropolitan power. This basic characteristic of the Belgian colonial enterprise in our country was common to both the Congo Free State of King Leopold II of the Belgians and the Belgian Congo.[4] Whatever the claims made by the ideologues of the so-called *mission civilisatrice* concerning Belgian rule in the Congo, the main task of Belgian colonialism was to expand and consolidate Belgian

114

economic interests. In 1921, the then Belgian Minister of Colonies, Louis Franck, wrote that the first major goal of Belgium in the Congo was to develop 'the economic action of Belgium'.[5]

King Leopold II, as one Belgian historian has written, was a great capitalist who 'possessed the Congo just as Rockefeller possessed Standard Oil'.[6] This meant that the colonial enterprise had to be judged in strictly business terms, that is in terms of whether or not it was profitable. Leopold and his agents found that it was necessary to impose iron rule in order to accumulate wealth. When Belgium took over the running of the country from the king in 1908, the Belgian government had to operate on the basis of what had already been established economically and administratively since 1885. According to Roger Anstey,

> Belgium inherited, not only a colony, but a colony possessed of a certain structure. The elements of that structure were a sparse population and a battered customary society; a vast territory which had not been properly administered; a system of direct economic exploitation, or an unfettered variant of the concessionaire system, and, as a consequence at a further remove, abuse and atrocity. Thirdly, the fact that the Congo was a legacy meant that Belgium had no relevant tradition of policy to invoke, no positive aims regarding it.[7]

Contrary to those who, like Jean Stengers, argue that after 1908 'the special characteristics of the Congo Free State disappeared or were effaced, giving way to grey-haired orthodoxy' in colonial matters,[8] Anstey shows that the legacy of the Free State regime was crucial in determining not only 'the early lines of Belgian conduct in the Congo' but also the subsequent trends in Belgian rule. He writes that 'there was no major departure from the broad lines of the original Belgian comportment in the Congo which the legacy had done so much to determine, though certainly there was refinement of that comportment.'[9]

The first step towards this refinement, and one that was partially meant to mollify public opinion in Europe and North America, was the adoption of a colonial constitution, the *Charte coloniale*, which was drafted by men presumably committed to 'grey-haired orthodoxy' in colonial affairs. Of these men, one had once spent eight days in the Congo, and four had major interests in several Belgian companies with investments in the Congo. With a Catholic party in power in Brussels and with major companies represented in the colonial decision-making process, it was evident that the second Belgian regime in the Congo was going to rely on the unity of state, the Catholic Church and major corporations to continue the triple mission of economic exploitation, political and administrative oppression, and cultural oppression. More clearly than elsewhere, it was in the Belgian Congo — the 'model colony' of imperialist propaganda during the 1950s — that a perfect fit obtained between the 'colonial trinity' and these three defining characteristics of modern colonialism.[10]

The framework of social change in the Belgian Congo consisted therefore of the three key variables of economic exploitation, political repression and cultural oppression, and it was greatly influenced by the brutal legacy of the Congo Free State. Just as in the past, the country remained a major source of capital accumulation for the metropolitan power. Having provided the revenue for the construction of public buildings, highways and other public projects dear to its sovereign and sole owner in Belgium, the Congo was also able to bail the colonial power out of financial troubles during and after both world wars and to continue being a major source of investment capital and job opportunities for the Belgian economy.[11]

Such an arrangement meant that colonial administrators had to give as much attention to peasant agricultural production and labour recruitment for large companies and white settlers as they gave to maintaining law and order. This implied the necessity of having recourse to force and coercion, just as Free State officials had found it necessary to use violence against the people. Political repression was the answer for all those who, individually or collectively, refused to be exploited economically. Just as Free State agents had used the *chicotte* to whip those who rebelled against authority, colonial agents used the whip to humiliate people in public, treating even the very old as though they were still children. Although colonial administrators did not match the inhumanity of their Free State predecessors in their repressive acts, the end result was the same, namely, suffering and misery for countless mothers and children, whose husbands, sons and brothers languished in jail for no good reason.

During the early period of Belgian rule, the state relied on government by companies in those parts of the country where it could not establish effective rule. Contrary to what historians like Stengers have suggested, company rule did continue beyond 1908. Among the Kuba, for example, it remained virtually the same from 1905 to 1910. According to Vansina, this period of the rule of the *Compagnie du Kasai* in the Kuba Kingdom was a period of atrocities.[12] The company held a monopoly over trade, and the people had to sell rubber to it so they could pay their taxes. These were collected for the company by King Kot aPe, who played the role of company agent in order to maintain his throne. For its part the Company employed about 285 *kapita* or auxiliaries in 1908, who acted as armed rubber buyers and collectors, with one *kapita* per village. These African mercenaries managed to use their guns to oppress villagers, and force them to produce more rubber. During this same year, there was a food shortage and widespread hunger in the area.

In addition to using African chiefs and *kapita* as their auxiliary agents, the companies employed European contractors and Christian missionaries to recruit workers for them, a task with which they were greatly helped by the colonial administration. Until the 1930s, all Africans so recruited for work in the mining industry in Katanga (Shaba) went to this region by foot from as far away as Maniema, Kasai, and even Rwanda and Burundi. The Europeans, of course, were carried in hammocks and continued to be so well treated long after porterage was officially outlawed in 1926. The number of people who died during all these long marches and during the construction of railways still needs to be determined. Adults who were adolescents in the 1910s and 1920s have told many horror stories about the kidnapping of fellow villagers, the brutality of recruiting agents and work-gang foremen, and the manner in which people living along the railway lines were coerced into feeding those who worked on the railways.

State rule, when it was finally established at the local level, did not significantly differ from company rule. The state itself brought along with its rule new exigencies.

These included not only the usual economic demands involving labour and taxes but also a whole new set of regulations governing virtually all aspects of one's life. Crawford Young points out that the Belgian colonial state distinguished itself from other colonial systems by its deeper penetration and more inclusive organisation of the countryside:

> More familiar, and most unpopular, was the agricultural officer, of which there was at least one per territory, seconded by several African agricultural assistants and a network of *moniteurs* with rudimentary training to bring the administrative system in contact with virtually all the population. Legislation permitting 60 days per year (45 after 1955) of compulsory cultivation (or other public works) was generally applied until 1957 and was still legally authorised, although largely abandoned, in 1960.[13]

Just as it was done during the period of company rule, intimate contact with the population was best established through African chiefs. Initially, they were the only group with sufficient legitimacy to play the role of intermediary between their people and the colonialists. In reality, the work done by chiefs was essentially that of low-level officials of the colonial administration. It consisted chiefly of obtaining the people's compliance with forced labour, compulsory cultivation, conscription, labour recruitment and other state regulations. By fulfilling their colonial functions faithfully and by attempting to enrich themselves in the process through legal or extra-legal means, the chiefs eventually alienated themselves from most of their subjects. This was especially true for those who were mere colonial creations and lacked any claim to traditional legitimacy.

Despite the hard work in which they engaged, the peasants did not improve their material conditions of life during the 75 years of Belgian rule. Table 6.1 below shows the relative importance of the rural sector of the economy in the overall summary of the economic standing of the indigenous population during the pre-independence decade, the decade of rapid economic growth in the Belgian Congo.

**Table 6.1**
**Size of Enterprises and Personal Income (in million francs; 50f. = $1)**

|  | 1950 | 1954 | 1958 |
|---|---|---|---|
| (a) Gross national product | 30,480 | 49,350 | 55,850 |
| (b) Marketed product of indigenous enterprises | 3,600 | 4,950 | 6,230 |
| (c) (b) As percentage of (a) | 12 | 10 | 11 |
| (d) Value of indigenous commercial activity | 210 | 700 | 1,200 |
| (e) (d) As percentage of (a) | 0.7 | 1.4 | 2 |
| (f) (d) As percentage of (b) | 5.85 | 14 | 19 |
| (g) Monetary income of indigenous population | 8,780 | 15,910 | 20,330 |
| (h) Wages paid to indigenous population | 5,180 | 10,960 | 14,100 |
| (i) (h) As percentage of (g) | 59 | 69 | 69 |
| (j) (h) As percentage of (a) | 17 | 22 | 25 |

Sources: Fernand Bézy, 'Problems of Economic Development of Congo', in E. A. G. Robinson (ed.) *Economic Development for Africa South of the Sahara* (New York: St. Martin's Press, 1964) Table 8, p. 78; Belgium, Belgian Congo and Ruanda-Urundi Information and Public Relations Office, *Belgian Congo*, vol. II, Brussels, 1960, p. 78.

The low level of the marketed product of indigenous enterprises shows that although they were integrated in the money economy, the peasants did not enjoy an easy access to modern manufactured goods, because of their very low monetary income. And if African commercial activity was not limited to retail traders, the peasants' part in it was definitely very small. Peasant farmers nevertheless sold part of their food output in rural and urban markets, but the colonial administration kept agricultural prices low, in order to ensure a higher rate of investment through forced saving. Bézy explains the reasons for this anti-people policy as follows:

> . . . Congolese economic development has been financed to a large extent by the forced saving of a generation of workers, even of those of independent means. Indeed, economic policy has kept agricultural prices artificially low, for fear that a rise in the cost of living might bring with it an increase in wages. Thus, inflationary periods, as well as those following devaluation, have, until recently, always worsened the position of peasants and workers, thus increasing — temporarily at least — the possible mobilisation of forced saving.[14]

Thus, in addition to the accumulation mechanisms associated with the compulsory cultivation of export crops, the colonialists undermined the economic well-being of the peasants by depriving them of the ability to make a decent living through the sale of their food products. Their standard of living remained very low and, in many cases, their lot was worse than their conditions before colonialism. For them, economic and cultural changes were minimal and of little real value. The introduction of cash crops and plantations did not succeed in radically changing traditional social relations, partly because of the extractive nature of economic activities. The survival of traditional leadership with modern and traditional roles shows that the colonialist did not change African cultures significantly. They left rural society with almost the same level of economic and cultural life they found there when they conquered it, but in a shattered and chaotic state.

The major economic transformation involved those Africans living in the urban and mining centres. There, three new social classes emerged as a function of colonial capitalism and its contradictions. The first class is that of skilled and unskilled workers who constituted the modern proletariat of the Belgian Congo, one of the largest and most stable working classes in colonial Africa. The second class consisted of petty-bourgeois employees and entrepreneurs and included an elite group that came to be known as the *évolués*. As for the last class, or the lumpenproletariat, its appearance was inseparably linked to colonial urbanisation and the proletarianisation process. Its composition, then and now, consists of permanently urbanised and proletarianised masses who, unable to find wage employment or lacking the necessary skills or vocation for it, develop their own means of livelihood and survival in the underground economy and/or in criminal activities.

All three classes interacted with the peasants and shared with them the common grievances of the colonised concerning colonial oppression in general and economic exploitation in particular. More vividly than the peasants, they experienced economic inequality with the Europeans on a daily basis through the colour and wage bars as well as through the Manichean structure and life of the large cities and other urban centres.[15] African participation in modern economic activities not only widened the Africans' social space, with labour migrations, the workplace, trade unions and urban life bringing people of different ethnic groups together, but also created among them a sense of nationhood.[16]

The disparity between their life chances and those of the European intruders was a major source of irritation. In the Belgian Congo, the average annual income per capita was estimated to be $77 in 1956, but only $41 for Africans and $29 for the 9 million people in the rural sector.[17] In 1958, the Congolese share of the national income was approximately 58 per cent for some 13,540,182 people, while the European minority of 100,000 people had to itself over two-fifths or 42 per cent of this income. Economic inequality was therefore a salient factor in the colonial conflict. To wage their anti-colonial struggle, the people found a willing and interested leadership among the *évolués*.

## The Anti-colonial Alliance

How did this alliance between ordinary people and the educated elites or *évolués* come about and what did it represent? Two conflicting theses have been advanced in the historiography of African nationalism on the origin of the struggle for independence. In his otherwise excellent study of national independence movements, Rupert Emerson asserts that colonialism was a school for democracy — when in fact it was a school for tyranny — and that the largely illiterate masses of Asia and Africa had no clear understanding of the 'sovereignty of the people' as they were 'little aware of the complexities of the issues with which they were confronted'.[18] For him, only the educated elites were in a position to understand such issues:

> Colonial educational systems have frequently been attacked, with evident justice, for teaching the history of the metropolitan country or of Europe rather than local history — the stock image is that of children of French Africa or Madagascar reciting 'nos ancêtres le Gaulois' — but it was from European history that the lessons of the struggle for freedom could on the whole be most effectively learned. The knowledge of Western languages open up vast bodies of literature teeming with seditious thoughts which the young men who came upon them were not slow to apply to their own problems.[19]

Thomas Hodgkin rejects this viewpoint and its minimisation of the role of the masses in the African independence struggle, together with the idea that Africans could not learn the lessons of resistance to colonial rule from their own history:

> For large masses of Africans in a variety of colonial territories to say 'No' to the colonial system and 'Yes' to the ideas of 'freedom' and 'independence' it was not an essential pre-requisite that their leaders should have studied the Western political classics at Harvard, the Sorbonne, or the London School of Economics.[20]

Hodgkin supports Fanon's thesis that the masses, the peasants in particular, had a clear understanding of the critical issues, and that their attitude in the struggle for national liberation was more radical than that of their petty-bourgeois leaders, who tended to be more moderate and preferred constitutional bargaining to a people-based armed struggle.[21] He adds that

> Without the mobilization, and participation, of significant sectors of the 'the masses' — and in some critical situations, pressures on the national leadership to move more rapidly than it would have chosen to go — the African revolutions which we have experienced, and are experiencing, could never have occurred.[22]

The historical evidence from the Belgian Congo supports Hodgkin's thesis.[23] The 'educated elites' of this colony were people of relatively limited formal education. With few exceptions — the higher education of medical assistants and of leaders like Joseph Kasa-Vubu who had studied for the Catholic priesthood — the formal schooling of the overwhelming majority of Congolese nationalist leaders was limited to three or four years of secondary education. Patrice Lumumba, the leading nationalist leader, was an autodidact whose formal schooling consisted of only four years of elementary school and one year of technical training at a school for postal clerks.[24] Thus, of the 50 top political leaders or those who occupied strategic positions and played crucial political roles in the country during the four-month period between the May 1960 elections and the fall of Prime Minister Lumumba in September, 48 or nearly all of them were formerly petty-bourgeois employees (34 clerks, 7 medical assistants and other salaried employees in the state and private sectors). Only two had spent the greater part of their lives before 1958 as businesspeople.[25]

Rather than being the result of any inspiring reading of Western classics, the *évolués'* involvement in the struggle for independence was basically a continuation of their fight for equality of opportunity in the colonial political economy, where they experienced discrimination with respect to career and other economic opportunities, in addition to the daily humiliations of colonial racism. Their opposition to inequality, injustice and oppression was the critical linkage between them and the masses. For the protest of the peasantry against compulsory cultivation, forced labour and a heavy tax burden; the demands of the working class for higher wages and better working conditions; and the struggle of the lumpenproletariat for a right to earn a decent livelihood in the cities — from which the unemployed or *chomeurs* were frequently deported — had a common denominator with the cause of the *évolués*: they were part of the struggle for a better life socially and economically.

For all these classes, the colonial social structure represented the general obstacle to their quest for a better life and for the future of their children. To remove this obstacle and thereby realise their social and economic emancipation, it was necessary to obtain political emancipation. Although the dominant factor of discontent was economic, it became clear to most people that politics had to be the dominant organisational principle in the fight against colonialism along with its violence and racism. Against the opposition or indifference of reactionary elements within the petty bourgeoisie and among the chiefs, the popular classes and their petty bourgeoisie allies formed a united front against colonialism.

To explain the anti-colonial alliance, its underlying causes alone are not sufficient. It is also important to show its organisational potential. For the Congo, organisational possibilities or the necessary conditions of effective mobilisation and action included firstly the tradition of resistance dating back to primary resistance movements and to anti-colonial revolts since 1920, secondly the revolutionary potential of messianism, and thirdly the experience gained since 1944 in urban-based voluntary associations.

Primary resistance refers to the armed struggle waged by an African people or state against the colonial conquest and/or the imposition of colonial rule in its territory. Generally, this struggle was led by the rulers of the pre-colonial nations or territories, although there were cases in which the leadership of the resistance was taken up by professional warriors defending a conquest state or a trading frontier, and by religious leaders. Given the relatively short history of colonialism in Africa, memories of primary resistance did persist, and they were useful to modern mass nationalist movements in achieving a high level of mobilisation and emotional involvement in the independence struggle. As Fanon writes,

> the propaganda of nationalist parties always finds an echo in the heart of the peasantry. The memory of the anti-colonial period is very much alive in the villages, where women still croon in their children's ears songs to which the warriors marched when they went out to fight the conquerers.[26]

Historians have uncovered the evidence to establish such a connection between primary resistance and the national liberation struggle. The clearest connection in this regard is perhaps the one between the *Chimurenga* or the Shona/Ndebele war against colonial settlers in 1896–7 and the Zimbabwean war of liberation between 1972 and 1980.[27] In the Congo, nationalist mobilisation in areas like the Sankuru and North Katanga (now Shaba) benefited greatly from the tradition of anti-colonial resistance established since the 1890s in the heroic opposition of the Atetela and the Luba of Katanga (Shaba) to colonial occupation. These are also areas where the radical nationalism of Patrice Lumumba found a fertile ground, and which joined the Kwilu and the northeast in the second independence movement.

In addition to primary resistance movements, anti-colonial revolts in the form of peasant uprisings and urban rebellions did play their part in consolidating a tradition of resistance which proved useful to nationalist parties in a number of areas around the country. Peasant revolts against compulsory cultivation, taxes and other *prestations* required by the colonial state took place all over the country. The fear of such revolts was so great among the Belgians that they instituted three types of operation by the colonial army or *Force Publique* to deal with anti-colonial resistance: military occupation, military operation, and police operation. As the terms imply, occupation involved the placing of troops in a troubled area and requiring the population to feed them and to do whatever the troops ordered them to do, while the military and police operations involved simply putting down a rebellion and intimidating the population in order to keep it on its best behaviour, respectively.[28] A variant of the last two types of operation is what was known as the *promenade militaire*, which meant not a leisurely stroll by the military in the countryside but a veritable walkover by the *Force Publique* in its intimidation and/or repressive work *vis-à-vis* a defenceless population.

One of the major rural revolts was the Pende uprising of 1931 in the Kwilu region, which claimed well over 500 lives before it was put down.[29] It was directly tied to the colonial political economy in general and to the economic hardships caused by the oppressive concessionary system under the control of the *Huileries du Congo Belge* (HCB) and the *Compagnie du Kasai* in particular. Peasant unrest combined with discontent among company workers and the militancy of syncretic movements to make the Kwilu area one of the bastions of rural radicalism in the Congo. It is this radicalism that characterised the mass base of the *Parti Solidaire Africain* (PSA), one of the most radical of Congolese political parties, at least with respect to the wing led by Antoine Gizenga and Pierre Mulele. It was also in the Kwilu that Mulele later attempted to develop, between 1963 and 1968, 'the first real experience of revolutionary resistance in [post-colonial] Africa.'[30]

In the urban areas, the poor living conditions of ordinary Africans contrasted sharply with the luxury enjoyed by the European bourgeoisie, petty bourgeoisie and — in large cities and mining centres — labour aristocracy, made up of skilled workers. Africans were barred from stores and public accommodations reserved for Europeans and from the European section of town after 9 p.m., except for those who were domestics, policemen and sentinels, or had a special permit to be there. They were also required to carry passports for travel across provincial boundaries and restricted as to how long they could stay as visitors in urban and mining centres. Their resentment against the colonial system thus went beyond parochial issues of wages, promotions and working conditions, although these were certainly basic to the colonial conflict.

The tradition of resistance in urban areas involved mainly memories of army mutinies and of strikes and work stoppages among mining, industrial, transport and public sector workers. Before 1956, the year in which the independence struggle began, the most important urban rebellions were the December 1941 strike of *Union Minière* workers in Elisabethville (Lubumbashi), the February 1944 mutiny of the *Force Publique* garrison in Luluabourg (Kananga), and the November 1945 strike and demonstrations of dock workers in Matadi.

These rebellions were partially a result of the hardships imposed on the African population as part of the *effort de guerre* (or war effort) between 1940 and 1945. After their brutal suppression, the Belgians responded to their fear of urban unrest not only with the infamous *opérations policières*, mentioned above, but also with better economic and social services. Under the theory of Belgian paternalism, these were designed to keep the public eye on bread and circuses — and more specifically on bicycles, radios, gramophones and soccer matches — and thereby stem the tide of nationalism.[31]

Fortunately, the improved standard of living in urban areas could not quench the thirst for an even higher one. It only served to strengthen the people's resolve to do whatever was necessary to improve their lot. Moreover, urban development attracted large numbers of young people from rural areas and small towns to the large cities, where they eventually played a crucial role in the independence struggle. It was this lumpenproletariat, together with the working class, that initiated the major rebellion of 4 January 1959 in Leopoldville (Kinshasa), which led to the Belgian decision to grant independence to the Congo.

The second major contributing factor to mass political mobilisation was the work of African independent churches. These religious sects had sprung out of established churches with the aim of making the Christian message more relevant to people's concerns by finding the most appropriate means of resolving the contradictions of the contemporary world. Messianism or the prophetic vision of these religious movements posed a threat to both the traditional and colonial societies by its affirmation of the coming of a new social order: a world without witchcraft and other negative elements of village life, and without white domination. It was precisely this last aspect of the prophetic vision that the colonial state seized upon to unleash an unrelenting repressive campaign against the independent churches.

The most important of these churches and the one that made the greatest contribution to the nationalist struggle in the Congo is the *Eglise de Jésus-Christ sur la terre par le Prophète Simon Kimbangu* (EJCSK), founded by the Kongo prophet Simon Kimbangu in 1921.[32] After barely six months of a brilliant and dynamic ministry, the prophet spent the rest of his life (or nearly half of his 62 years) in jail in Elisabethville (Lubumbashi), from 1921 to 1951. In spite of imprisonment and relegation to remote detention camps all over the country, his followers continued his work clandestinely. They were eventually able to take advantage of a new political climate in the 1950s to come out of the underground and demand official recognition as a church. The persecution of Kimbanguists had as a consequence the politicisation of their movement, since they had to fight for civil liberties and democratic rights, beginning with the freedom of religion.

As a movement that arose among the Kongo, Kimbanguism had attracted large numbers of people in the Lower Congo (Zaire) region and in Leopoldville (Kinshasa). The anti-colonial radicalism of the *Alliance des Bakongo* (ABAKO), the party of Joseph Kasa-Vubu, was in many ways related to the revolutionary messianism of Kimbaguism, particularly at the grassroots. Wyatt MacGaffey reports that the two organisations had some similarities:

> Apart from its self-identification as a political party, Abako, with its utopian references to the return of a quasi-mythical Kongo kingdom, was clearly similar in some ways to Kimbanguism, and the membership of the two organizations overlapped extensively.[33]

This connection between ABAKO, Kimbanguism and mass radicalism illustrates the manner in which the anti-colonial alliance was formed by the combined effect of the tradition of resistance, the contribution of religious movements to the quest for freedom and justice, and the organisational experience gained in voluntary associations.

There were four types of voluntary association in the colony: ethnic associations, *évolué* circles or clubs, old boys' associations, and trade unions. The most important of these groupings were the ethnic associations, of which ABAKO was among the most prominent. They were initially created as mutual aid societies designed to help migrants from the same ethnic homeland or the same region cope with the challenges of urban life, or as organisations committed to the defence and promotion of the language, culture and interests of the group in a presumably

123

hostile environment. Given the ban on political activity until the municipal elections of 1957, the low level of trade union organisation due to Belgian paternalism and legal restrictions, and the elitism of the various associations of the *évolués*, the ethnic associations were the only medium where the interests of the vast majority of the colonised could be articulated. After the Luluabourg mutiny of 1944 and the emergence of the *évolués* as an elite group with national leadership aspirations, these associations formed the political base of the petty bourgeoisie.

Consequently, most of the nationalist parties were ethnically or regionally based. Many were either the ethnic associations themselves or coalitions of such associations constituted as parties, as in the cases of ABAKO and Moise Tshombe's *Confédération des Associations Tribales du Katanga* (CONAKAT), respectively. Others were organised in such a way that they absorbed, substituted themselves for, or worked very closely with, the ethnic associations. The best examples of this second category include Albert Kalonji's wing of the *Mouvement National Congolais* (MNC/K) which had an intimate relationship with the *Mouvement Solidaire Muluba* during the Lulua–Baluba war, and, on the other side of this conflict, the *Union Nationale Congolaise* (UNC), which was similarly related to *Lulua Frères*.

Among the major political parties, the notable exceptions to this pattern of ethnically-based parties were Lumumba's or the mainstream *Mouvement National Congolais* (MNC/L), Anicet Kashamura's *Centre de Régroupement Africain* (CEREA), and the PSA. Although the last two parties were regionally based, they saw themselves as having a national vocation and they were unquestionably supra-ethnic in a way that clearly distinguished them from parties like CONAKAT.[34] The only other major supra-ethnic party to resemble Lumumba's party in having adherents in all the six provinces of the Belgian Congo was the *Parti National du Progrès* (PNP). Unlike the MNC, however, this party had no mass base, and it was created at the instigation of the colonial administration as the party of the reactionary fraction of the petty bourgeoisie and the chiefs. Hence, the derogatory label it earned in the country as the '*Parti des Nègres Payés*'.[35]

These party alignments were very significant not only with respect to the positions of the leaders in the ideological split within the nationalist movement between federalists and unitarists and between moderates and radicals, but also with regard to the impact of this split on their followers. Thus, leaders of ethnically-based parties like Kasa-Vubu, Tshombe and Kalonji tended to be federalists and moderate, while those of supra-ethnic parties like Lumumba, Gizenga, Mulele and Kashamura tended to be unitarists and radical. It is not surprising, therefore, that the regions controlled by the moderates were not very hospitable to Lumumba and the Lumumbists, and were consequently left out of the struggle for a 'second independence' in the 1960s. It is to that struggle, and the nature of the popular alliance involved, that we now turn.

## The Second Independence Movement

The second independence movement was born barely three years after the country became independent on 30 June 1960, in response to the unfulfilled expectations of ordinary people concerning decolonisation. As these people had identified independence with both freedom from white rule and material prosperity, their petty-bourgeois nationalist leaders had cultivated hopes among the masses in the effort to enlist their support. But these leaders were primarily interested in replacing whites in the upper echelons of the state apparatus and using their control of the state to enrich themselves and to consolidate their power as a ruling class. The united-front character of the independence struggle had masked this fundamental contradiction of interests, expectations and perceptions between these two component parts of the anti-colonial alliance. For the masses, independence had failed, and the politicians had betrayed them. Their frustrated expectations materialised in a generalised contempt for the new rulers, whom they now saw as liars, and in a new socio-political movement for genuine liberation.

Whereas the moderate leaders abandoned the popular alliance to savour their victory over Lumumba and the radicals and to enjoy the fruits of independence, some of the radical leaders attempted to reconstitute the alliance in order to regain power and to realise the goals for which people had laid down their lives in the anti-colonial struggle. The most original of the attempts made in this regard was the revolutionary enterprise of Pierre Mulele, which involved the identification by a small group of petty-bourgeois intellectuals with the deepest aspirations of the people for genuine liberation — or what they called the 'second independence'. In the contemporary world, such a struggle poses a threat to both the neo-colonial state and imperialism, the first because it challenges the privileges of the national ruling class, and the second because decolonisation does not necessarily mean the end of imperialist domination.

## Decolonisation and the Transformation of the Popular Alliance

In the Congo (Zaire), decolonisation was a classic case of the transition to neo-colonialism, albeit one not as smooth as the polished architects of decolonisation would have liked to see.[36] Initially, it did not follow the usual script as a process of power transfer to a virtually hand-picked group of people who had undergone a necessary period of apprenticeship and who could therefore be trusted not to endanger the long-term interests of the departing colonialists in the country. In addition to being overwhelmed by the radicalisation of the anti-colonial struggle through decisive mass participation and rural radicalism, the Belgian colonialists were so overtaken by the events that they easily acceded to the militant demand for immediate independence.

The Belgian wager in all this was that Belgium would continue to run the country through its technical assistants, while the 'unprepared' Congolese, lacking trained cadres of their own, would be distracted by the prestige and perquisites of their political offices and contented to sign documents prepared for them by Belgians. After the impressive showing of the radical nationalist parties in the May 1960 elections, in which they won 71 of 137 seats in the lower house of Parliament,[37] it became apparent that the gamble might not work. A major stumbling-block to the Belgian strategy of neo-colonialism was Patrice Lumumba, along with the other radical leaders. Removing this obstacle meant that the Belgians and their allies were to do everything possible to prop up the moderate side of the major political cleavage within the nationalist movement.

As already indicated above, this ideological cleavage proved to be of major significance. The radicals were basically progressive nationalists who sought to create nationally-oriented mass-based parties, saw independence as an opportunity for some changes likely to benefit ordinary people economically and socially, and espoused non-alignment as their basic posture in international politics. They were emotionally committed to obtaining an authentic independence, both politically and economically, although they were not very clear on how to achieve this goal. Their popularity within the working class, the most politically conscious class among the masses, is best exemplified by the strong and consistent support that the important Luba-Kasai population of the mining and urban centres of Katanga (Shaba) gave to Lumumba, even after the split between him and Luba leader Albert Kalonji had become final in late 1959.

The moderates enjoyed strong support from Belgian and other Western government and corporate circles. This support was clearly revealed at the very beginning of the transitional period when the Belgian official charged with the supervision of the transfer of power, African Affairs Minister Ganshof van der Meersch, made the surprise choice of Kasa-Vubu as prime minister designate on 16 June 1960. This nomination was surprising because the MNC/L had a working majority in the Chamber of Deputies, compared to only 12 seats for ABAKO. The hope that Kasa-Vubu might succeed in rounding up enough coalition partners to form the government was a harbinger of the difficulties that the Belgians and their allies were going to create for Lumumba in the weeks ahead.

Kasa-Vubu having failed to form the government, the task of putting together the first national government was finally and rightly entrusted to Patrice Lumumba. After the usual compromises of parliamentary democracy, he succeeded in forming a broad-based government, and threw the support of his radical coalition behind Kasa-Vubu's bid for the ceremonial position of head of state. Unfortunately for Lumumba, this position was to be exploited by his external enemies in the first decisive battle between moderates and radicals, and one that ended with the political and physical elimination of Lumumba himself. With the support of Belgium, the US, the UN and others, the moderates won the battle in all its stages: the Kasa-Vubu coup of 5 September 1960 with the crucial and active support of UN representative Andrew Cordier, a US citizen, which consisted of the illegal dismissal of Lumumba as Prime Minister; the first coup by Joseph-Désiré Mobutu, then colonel and chief of staff of the *Armée Nationale Congolaise* (ANC), on 14 September 1960; Lumumba's arrest by Mobutu's troops while he was attempting to run to the Lumumbist stronghold of Stanleyville (Kisangani), on 30 November 1960; and his assassination at the hands of the secessionist leaders of Katanga on 17 January 1961.[38] It is now a well-known fact the US Central Intelligence Agency (CIA) was intimately involved in the plot to assassinate Lumumba.[39] The alliance of the moderate leadership with US imperialism was thus sealed with Lumumba's blood.

The anti-colonial alliance was being drastically transformed by these neo-colonialist victories, which included the secession of the mineral-rich province of Katanga in July, and that of the diamond region of South Kasai in August 1960. The moderate leaders who were involved had clearly opted for an alliance with imperialism against the best interests of their own people. The setbacks to the national liberation struggle and Lumumba's assassination gave rise among his followers to the first organised opposition to the neo-colonial ruling class, whose major centres were Leopoldville (Kinshasa), Elisabethville (Lubumbashi) and Bakwanga (now Mbuji-Mayi). The Lumumbist opposition was led by Gizenga, Lumumba's vice-premier, who became head of the rival central government in Stanleyville in late 1960. His top aides included Christophe Gbenye, Interior Minister in both the Lumumba and Gizenga governments and Lumumba's successor as national president of the MNC/L, and Pierre Mulele, Education Minister in these governments and later on the envoy to Cairo.

The Lumumbists moved so fast in expanding their control and authority in the eastern part of the country, with spectacular military victories in the Kasai and in northern Katanga that the leaders of the central government in Leopoldville rushed to conclude a military alliance with the very secessionist forces against which they were supposed to be fighting in Katanga and in South Kasai. On 27 February 1961 Interim Prime Minister Joseph Ileo, Katanga President Tshombe and South Kasai President Kalonji signed in Elisabethville what became known as the 'Leopoldville–Bakwanga–Elisabethville axis' military accord.[40] This was followed by regular meetings between Mobutu and the secessionists in Brazzaville and in Elisabethville, where another military agreement was signed in July 1961.[41] The threat of a Lumumbist victory was finally averted when the US-sponsored manoeuvres of the UN Congo Mission (ONUC) succeeded in the formation of a national unity government under Cyrille Adoula in August 1961. Weissman cites a former US Embassy official according to whom the whole process was 'really a US operation but using outstanding UN personalities'.[42]

In spite of the hopes generated by the entry of Gizenga, Gbenye and others into the Adoula government, the latter was unable to resolve the contradictions between the major fractions of the new ruling class. The Adoula government was unable to achieve a lasting reconciliation with the Lumumbists because it was basically a puppet government, taking its directives from the US Embassy in Leopoldville and responsive to the pressures exerted on it by General Mobutu and his Binza group. This was a politically powerful clique named after a suburb of the capital where its principal members met and had private residences. It derived its power from the control of the central state machinery, particularly its key organs, then as now closely linked to external sources of assistance and pressure: the military (Mobutu), the security police (Victor Nendaka), internal affairs (Damien Kandolo), the National Bank (Albert Ndele), and the Ministry of Foreign Affairs (Justin Bomboko).

The Binza group worked closely with both President Kasa-Vubu and Prime Minister Adoula in their common struggle against the progressive nationalists. They were supported in this endeavour by the US and other Western powers. Weissman has shown that the American government 'not only supported Adoula, it was, in many different ways, part of his government.'[43] And if Adoula had any difficulty understanding this connection, the ever-reliable Binza group was there to make sure he understood what needed to be done. The immediate task was to eliminate the most prominent Lumumbists from the political scene and, with them, the 'Communist menace' that their presence meant to US foreign policy-makers like G. Mennen Williams, Assistant Secretary of State for African Affairs in the Kennedy and Johnson administrations, who abusively referred to the Gizenga regime as 'the Communist-supported Stanleyville secession'.[44]

In accordance with American wishes, the Lumumbists were systematically eliminated from the political scene, beginning with their titular leader Gizenga. He was arrested in January 1962 and relegated to the island prison of Bula-Bemba until July 1964. He has lived in exile since his release. Other Lumumbists were eventually coopted, dismissed from the government, confined to minor positions, or went into exile voluntarily by the end of 1963. By then, the anti-colonial alliance had already broken down with the birth of a new class, the moderate-dominated and externally-backed ruling class of the post-colonial state. Within this new order, the major social cleavage consisted of two antagonistic class alliances, to wit, the new class and the imperialist bourgeoisie, on the one hand, and the popular classes, the student movement and radical nationalist leaders, on the other. Virtually all of these leaders came from the Lumumbist coalition comprising the MNC/L, the PSA, CEREA and the Katanga cartel of anti-secessionist parties. Some of them regrouped in 1963–64 to provide the leadership for the second independence movement.

## The Second Independence Movement and the Neo-colonial State

The fundamental contradiction between the popular alliance and the state in post-colonial Africa has to do with the capitalist nature of the state and its neo-colonial tasks. The most important of these tasks are the preservation of a country's position in the international division of labour as a supplier of raw materials and cheap labour, the expansion within its borders of a market for luxury goods, sophisticated technologies and turnkey investments, and the suppression of revolutionary ideas and movements likely to challenge this arrangement. The neo-colonial situation thus involves the uninterrupted exploitation of the country's resources by the international bourgeoisie, but this time in collaboration with the national ruling classes. The primary mission of the latter is to maintain the order, stability, and labour discipline required to meet the country's obligations to the international capitalist system. The essential reality of this situation, according to Jean Ziegler, resides in 'tensions between a dissatisfied people and rulers essentially conservative, concerned above all with the preservation of their acquired privileges'.[45]

Zaire, then Congo-Kinshasa, is the first country in Africa where this situation gave rise to a national liberation struggle within the neo-colonial context. The struggle itself was spearheaded by a mass-based socio-political movement seeking to overthrow the neo-colonial state in order to replace it with a people-oriented state, under the control of a reconstituted popular alliance led by revolutionary nationalists. This movement had an authentically African and mass character, and virtually all of its guiding ideas and themes were essentially the intellectual production of the masses. These included their notions of state officials as 'liars' and as the 'new whites', the theoretically rich concept of 'second independence', and various magico–religious ideas concerning warfare.

Rather than being the product of pure imagination, these notions were grounded in the material reality of their life experience since independence. For example, during the electoral campaign of 1960, the politicians had promised everything under the sun, including more jobs, higher wages, higher prices for the peasants' cash and food crops, and free and better social services. Some demagogues went so far as to promise the white man's house, car and other belongings. Three years after independence, it was the same politicians who now occupied the mansions and nice cars that once served their European predecessors, and who oppressed the people just as the colonial officials had done in the past. They were the 'new whites', privileged, demanding, and oppressive, in addition to being 'liars' in the sense that they had no intention of living up to the fantastic promises they had made to the people. For the latter, therefore, the first or nominal independence had failed. The time had come to fight for a second or genuine independence.

Translated into the language of political economy, this means a revolutionary class struggle by the popular alliance against the neo-colonial state controlled by a power bloc comprising the metropolitan bourgeoisie. Such a struggle is in the final analysis a struggle for national liberation. According to Amilcar Cabral, national liberation in its fullest sense is a revolutionary process involving the complete overthrow of imperialist domination in its colonial as well as neo-colonial form.[46]

A relatively high level of political consciousness was fairly well developed among the urban youth and among the people generally in those areas that were heavily politicised by the parties of the Lumumbist coalition such as the Kwilu, where the concept of 'second independence' originated. The task of revolutionary intellectuals was simply that of systematising the popularly-produced notions and ideas into the language of 20th Century revolutionary thought and politics. Needless to say, the people's vision of a future of equality, justice and material prosperity was not new. It had already been given expression in various ways, notably in anti-colonial revolts and through the activities of religious movements. As Badiou and Balmès suggest with respect to the ideological resistance of ordinary people in general, the ideas of the popular classes against exploitation and oppression do not remain dormant until there appears a class capable of guiding their materialisation.[47] For the masses, too, have their own organic intellectuals.[48] However, the popular rebellions through which their ideas and mass sentiments are expressed have very little chance of changing the system radically in the absence of modern organisational resources necessary for a long and difficult struggle, including a well-informed conscious element or leadership capable of analysing the balance of forces correctly and of charting the appropriate course of action. In the Congo, the only group that was well placed to play this vanguard role was that of progressive Lumumbists.

Thus, the political defeat of the Lumumbists in 1962–3 was a great blow to the popular alliance, as ordinary people were left with no organisation to speak on their behalf. The only exception to this was the *Union Générale des Etudiants Congolais* (UGEC), a national student organisation founded in 1961 to fight tribalism and to promote the nationalist ideals that Patrice Lumumba had championed. Until it was banned by the Mobutu regime in 1968, UGEC remained the most stable and most vocal legal opposition grouping in the country. Its three national congresses, held in

1961, 1963, and 1966, represent three important phases in the development of a socialist consciousness within a predominantly elitist and careerist university student population.[49] Because of the limitations imposed on its political action by elitism and careerism, UGEC was incapable of assuming the leadership of the mass movement.

Like the student movement, the labour movement was unable to organise the masses politically. Its leaders were basically reformists whose overall political activity smacked of economism and opportunism. Like most UGEC leaders, they have since been coopted by President Mobutu to serve at the highest levels of his regime.

Given this leadership vacuum, the masses had to await the regrouping of the most revolutionary-minded Lumumbists to find the leaders who were ready to guide them in the struggle against the neo-colonial state. Interestingly, the very period of the political defeat of the Lumumbists in the externally-orchestrated political manoeuvres of the First Republic coincided with the period of the multiplication of the number of provinces from 6 to 21 between 1962 and 1963. The creation of new provinces had once again raised people's expectations with respect to the promises for a better life made to them by the politicians in 1960. As these politicians fought each other for power and influence and spent their limited financial resources in enriching themselves, dispensing patronage and, rather infrequently, paying state employees, these lofty goals were simply forgotten. Instead of improving, all social services deteriorated. Instead of more jobs, wage employment became extremely rare, thus contributing to adding thousands of school leavers and rural migrants to the ranks of the urban lumpenproletariat. In addition to these privations, the people were subject to unhealthy living conditions, a skyrocketing inflation due to the shortage of essentials and to speculation, and all kinds of extortion by security forces and other state employees.[50]

The result was a widespread popular discontent with the new provincial governments and, indirectly, the central state power which sustained them. This discontent served as a basis for an aspiration towards a new or real independence, an aspiration that the 1964 insurrections were to incarnate.[51] Generally known as 'rebellions', these popular insurrections can best be described as a revolutionary attempt to end injustice and the new social order favourable to the neo-colonial ruling class at the expense of ordinary people.

The struggle was led by two interrelated but independent organisations: the Kwilu maquis under the leadership of Pierre Mulele, and the eastern front under the *Conseil National de Libération* (CNL). This was an organisation of Lumumbist parties, including Mulele's own PSA/Gizenga,[52] whose major objective was to overthrow the Adoula regime. The essential difference between the two consisted in the more radical aims of Mulelism, which had a comprehensive programme of social transformation, as compared to the narrow class interests of the top CNL politicians managing the eastern front from exile in Brazzaville or from the relative safety of liberated Stanleyville.

## Mulele and the Kwilu Maquis
Pierre Mulele was the first prominent Lumumbist to return to the country and the

first person to launch a revolutionary struggle against neo-colonialism in Africa.[53] After nearly 15 months in Cairo as the external representative of the Gizenga government, Mulele went on to spend the next 15 months in the People's Republic of China, where he received his training in revolutionary guerilla warfare between April 1962 and July 1963. Returning to the Kwilu through Leopoldville, he spent nearly six months laying down the groundwork for a revolutionary struggle and training the first group of partisans. His teachings, as found in the lecture notes of some of his cadres, display a successful attempt at a systemisation in Marxist–Leninist–Maoist terms of the egalitarian, ascetic, communitarian and other ideas of ordinary people in revolt against exploitation, conspicuous consumption, and oppression. State employees, teachers, students, and the unemployed urban youth joined peasants in what became a profoundly popular and rural insurrection.[54]

After several encounters with the repressive machinery of the neo-colonial state in late 1963, a fully-fledged guerila war was launched in January 1964. The Mulelist forces succeeded in controlling a major portion of the Kwilu province. Unfortunately, they depended so much on Molotov cocktails, hunting rifles as well as other traditional weapons, and such small quantities of modern arms and ammunition as could be captured from the enemy that they were not in a position to expand and hold on to the territory under their control. They never succeeded in capturing Idiofa and Gungu, the two major urban centres in their operational zone, nor in expanding this zone beyond the areas occupied by the two ethnic groups constituting the initial base of the insurrection, the Mbunda (Mulele's ethnic group) and the Pende (Gizenga's group).[55]

With all these limitations, the core of the Mulelist maquis remained more or less intact until November 1967, and Mulele himself survived all counter-insurgency drives aimed at dislodging him from the Kwilu bush, where he spent five full years, from August 1963 to August 1968. In spite of a promised government reward of approximately $10,000 for information leading to his capture, dead or alive, not a single soul was found to betray him. It was only after he had gone to Brazzaville for medical treatment and for purposes of regrouping that the Mobutu regime lured him back to Kinshasa with false promises of national reconciliation. Under pressure from the Brazzaville authorities, who did not wish to have him on their soil, and hesitant about seeking political asylum in another country far away from the guerillas he had left behind in the Kwilu, Mulele returned to Kinshasa, with false hopes of resuming the struggle clandestinely. He was assassinated on 3 October 1968. His murder by General Mobutu and his colleagues marked the end of the first phase of the second independence movement.

There are many lessons to draw from Mulele's revolutionary enterprise. Suffice it to say here that the choice of his own region of origin as a revolutionary base, the lack of external sources of military supplies, and the absence of a dependable rear base in the neighbouring countries turned out to have the most negative consequences for the struggle. Although it did appear sensible for all revolutionaries to start the struggle in their own areas with the aim of eventually merging all of the revolutionary bases in a truly mass-based national struggle, the fact that a revolutionary leader of Mulele's stature was to be mainly identified with his own and allied ethnic groups proved detrimental to the struggle, as other groups were encouraged to feel excluded from it by the enemies of the revolution. In the contemporary world, a revolutionary group facing a militarily superior enemy cannot hope to succeed without access to external sources of essential supplies, lethal and non-lethal. These are some of the lessons that future leaders of revolutionary struggles in Zaire will do well to ponder.

### The CNL and the Eastern Front

The Conseil National de Libération was founded in Leopoldville on 3 October 1963, four days after President Kasa-Vubu dismissed parliament for the second time during his tenure as head of state, so that he, Adoula and their Binza allies could exercise power unfettered by legislative overview and by the probing and critical eye of the Lumumbist coalition. The CNL moved to establish its headquarters across the river in Brazzaville, where a popular revolution had overthrown the reactionary regime of Abbé Fulbert Youlou and brought a more progressive regime to power in August 1963. Here, the CNL sought to attract support for its struggle from the progressive and socialist countries.

Unfortunately, the CNL became well known not so much for its seriousness and unity of purpose but for ideological differences and personality conflicts among its top leaders. A group of revolutionary intellectuals from the PSA/Gizenga trained in China defended a mass line identical to that of Mulele, who had already started his maquis when the CNL was created. This group was opposed to a more moderate MNC/L group led by Christophe Gbenye, the nominal MNC/L leader, whose radical credentials were already in doubt since he signed the arrest warrant against Gizenga in January 1962, in his capacity as Interior Minister in the Adoula government. Gbenye and his friends wanted to enlist the support of progressive elements in the international community for another attempt at a government of national unity or 'public salvation' in Leopoldville, but one controlled by the Lumumbist majority in the Parliament. That majority had been shown to be more fiction than fact when the US-sponsored manoeuvres of 'outstanding UN personalities' had found enough Lumumbist and PSA/Kamitatu politicians ready to be bought so they could support Adoula against Gizenga in July–August 1961.

To the ideological split between those who opted for armed struggle and those who wanted to pursue the game of parliamentary politics was added a number of personality conflicts, the most significant of which opposed MNC/L leaders Gbenye and Davison Bocheley. The latter joined the PSA militants to form what became known as the CNL/Bocheley, which was interested in developing a broad-based guerilla struggle by linking the Mulele maquis to revolutionary fronts to be created in the east and elsewhere in the west. However, an attempt to establish a maquis in the Lac Leopold II province and from there link up with Mulele ended in failure.

The CNL/Gbenye, on the other hand, was preoccupied with recapturing power in the vast area of the country formerly under the control of Lumumbists and covering more than the entire eastern half of of the country minus South Kasai and the southern portion of Katanga. This is basically what the Gbenye group accomplished in 1964 when, under the pressure of people like Gaston Soumialot and Laurent Kabila, it decided to use violence. These two leaders were sent to

Burundi in January to start preparations for an armed conflict in the east. The insurrections which they helped organise began three months later on 15 April, with the first victory against Mobutu's army being registered on 15 May when Soumialot's forces took over the city of Uvira.

Here, as in subsequent encounters with the ANC, entire cities and regions were literally handed over to the *simba* (lions) or partisans, who had virtually no arms. Their basic arsenal consisted of magico–religious resources that supposedly ensured their invincibility. These included an immunisation ritual with drops of magic water called '*mai Mulele*' (or 'Mulele water'),[56] various fetishes, and the observation of a strict code of conduct involving sexual abnegation and dietary restrictions. The belief in their invincibility — in the notion that bullets hitting them would turn into water or return to hit the source — was so widespread that a simple announcement of their imminent arrival over the wire or by other means of communication provoked such a panic among government troops that they ran away, leaving their arms behind to be picked up by the *simba*.

The rapid breakdown of state authority throughout the entire region created an administrative and military vacuum that the CNL had to fill with its *Armée Populaire de Libération* (APL), under the command of General Nicolas Olenga. Within two months and a half, the APL was in control of North Katanga, Maniema, Sankuru, the entire Eastern province and portions of Equateur province. The major victory came on 4 August 1964, when the APL conquered Stanleyville. A month later, Gbenye established a people's republic there on 5 September, with himself as president, Soumialot as defence minister, and Olenga as commander in chief of the armed forces. By the end of September, half the country and seven of the 21 provincial capitals were under the control of the APL.[57]

This spectacular success on the eastern front was short-lived. With few exceptions, the APL-controlled cities were lost as easily as they were originally conquered, thanks to the effective counter-insurgency measures taken by the US and its allies in order to save the moderate regime in Leopoldville. The rapid disintegration of the mass movement in the east pointed to its major limitations as a revolutionary attempt. These included a leadership that was theoretically and ideologically bankrupt, the absence of an adequate preparation for a long, protracted struggle, the lack of discipline among the nationalist youth groups or *jeunesses* constituting the bulk of the APL rank and file, and the sinister role of ethnicity.

Preoccupied more with regaining the power they had lost to the moderates than with organising a genuine revolutionary struggle, the Lumumbist leaders of the eastern front clearly lacked the will and the ability to play the role of revolutionary intellectuals. Their goals, as exemplified by the kind of rule they set up in Albertville (Kalemie), Kindu, Lisala, Stanleyville and elsewhere, were not that different from those of the new ruling class in Leopoldville and in moderate-controlled provincial capitals. The following assessment of the brief tenure of the CNL regime in the east by Jules Gérard-Libois gives an apt description of some of the major weaknesses of the eastern front:

The revolution also soon ran into trouble from within its own leadership. The common phenomenon in the Congo of fragmentation and conflict among leaders and groups was once again repeated. . . . all these negative features were powerfully enhanced, with more arbitrary arrests and ruthless repression, with hoarding by some leaders, with the demagogic exploitation of xenophobia and primitive beliefs, and with a reckless wastage of young lives in ill-prepared operations.[58]

More successful militarily than the Kwilu maquis, the eastern front privileged militarism over politicisation, and preferred action over reflection. Given the lack of political preparation, the spontaneous mobilisation of partisans and the rapid turn of events, CNL leaders were not in a position to control their middle cadres effectively. These cadres were recruited among clerks, primary school teachers, ex-soldiers, ex-policemen and leaders of the *jeunesses*. For most of these partisans, as for their leaders, the concept of 'second independence' meant their turn to enjoy the fruits of independence formerly monopolised by the reactionary politicians they had removed from power. The idea that the new order was to serve all of the people was lost in a youthful population given to excesses of brutality and savagery once it fell under the influence of hemp. This lack of discipline was a critical factor in the progressive alienation of the masses from an army that they had considered as their liberator from the brutal and repressive ANC.

Finally, as in the Kwilu, the ethnic factor was an important determinant of participation in the struggle, given the pattern of regional and local politics that was part of the political equation since 1960. Mobilising people against incumbent politicians of groups other than their own was relatively easy, since these people could claim with some justification that the politicians had discriminated against them on ethnic lines. However, if ethnically-inspired killings took place, the masses did also execute people of their own ethnic group who were correctly or incorrectly identified as 'intellectuals', 'reactionaries' or PNP members. Obviously, this class dimension of the struggle tended to be relegated to a secondary position because of the rapidity of events, the lack of adequate political preparation and education, and the opportunism of leaders like Gbenye, Soumialot and Olenga. It was also their neglect of the class basis of the movement that made it harder for them to anticipate the hostility of US policymakers towards them and the latter's determination to destroy this potential challenge to the neo-colonial state.

## The Second Independence Movement and Imperialism

The second independence movement was the single major threat to the neo-colonial state after the elimination of Patrice Lumumba and his followers from the political scene. Gérard-Libois describes the reaction of the new ruling class to this ominous danger as follows:

In order to meet this challenge, it subdued its own internal conflicts and changed its Prime Minister, resorted to the help of South African, Rhodesian, Belgian and German mercenaries, and relied upon Belgian high-ranking officers to organise and coordinate military aid. After the reconquest of Stanleyville and the ruthless repression meted out in rebel zones, the ruling group long seemed to hesitate as to the policy it should pursue — whether to seek a new understanding with the other African states, or to continue repressive policies in the Congo with the help of Mike Hoare's mercenaries. The dilemma was resolved by the Army, whose leaders seek to gain popularity by attacks on corrupt politicians and by some measures of reform.[59]

The change of prime minister was engineered by Belgium and the US. The repeated defeats of Mobutu's army before the *simba*, the impending departure of UN troops by 30 June 1964, and the continuing threat of an invasion from Angola by Moise Tshombe's Katanga gendarmes called into question the very viability of the Adoula regime and its ability to correct the deteriorating security situation. The solution adopted was to set up a provisional government of 'public salvation', bringing together old secessionists, moderates and radicals in a cabinet headed by Tshombe. The former Katanga leader had made himself invaluable not only by the implied threat of his army of gendarmes and mercenaries, but also by a clever strategy of contacts with all sectors of political opinion, including negotiations with the more moderate CNL/Gbenye through Thomas Kanza. André-Guillaume Lubaya, a member of the CNL/Bocheley, became Health Minister in Tshombe's government. According to Tshombe, Kanza would have become his foreign minister had it not been for President Kasa-Vubu's objection, due to the latter's long-standing feud with Kanza's father Daniel.[60]

Long before Tshombe and his mercenary army became a useful tool of imperialist counter-insurgency, the CIA had since early 1964 started to conduct a major paramilitary campaign against the Kwilu and eastern insurrections. According to Weissman, this campaign lasted for nearly four years and included the use of Cuban and European mercenaries to fly T-6 training planes, T-28 fighter planes armed with rockets and machine guns, C-47 military transport planes, H-21 heavy duty helicopters, and B-26 bombers.[61] The US airforce gave critical air support to government troops and mercenaries, in addition to dropping napalm and other deadly killers on the people.

After the fall of Stanleyville to the insurgents, the pattern of imperialist counter-insurgency changed to include both covert and overt forms. Weissman describes them as follows:

Four American C-130 military transports with full crews and parachutist 'guard' arrived in Leopoldville, along with 4–5 B-26 bombers, ground vehicles, arms and ammunition. The Belgians also supplied equipment as well as 300–400 officers who assumed background roles of command and logistical support. Nearly all this overt assistance was on behalf of a 700 man force of South African, Rhodesian and European mercenaries which did much of the fighting as 'spearheads' of selected Government troops. . . . The Agency did supply more Cuban pilots for the B-26s which joined the rest of the CIA Air Force in support of the mercenary advance. (By January 1965, two additional T-28s were operating in the Congo as were 3–4 more B-26s apparently provided by Intermountain Aviation, a CIA proprietary).

As certain African countries began to ship arms to the rebels across Lake Tanganyika with apparent promises of Soviet replacement, the CIA engaged pilots and crews, reportedly South African, for patrol boat operations. A CIA front organisation, Western International Ground Maintenance Organisation (WIGMO) chartered in Liechtenstein, handled maintenance for the boats as well as the fighter planes with a staff of 50–100 Europeans. The WIGMO

135

mechanics and maintenance personnel enabled US and Belgian military personnel to escape direct association with air and sea combat operations; they also represented an attempt by the CIA to get away from its increasingly visible Cuban connection.[62]

A more direct intervention by metropolitan troops was deemed necessary to break the back of the insurrection in the east, by providing better support to the mercenaries and Belgian-officered government troops sent to reconquer Stanleyville. Thus, on 24 November 1964, a Belgo–American military intervention code-named DRAGON ROUGE took place at Stanleyville, with Belgian paratroopers being dropped over the city by US military planes. The intervention succeeded in ending Gbenye's People's Republic, and in opening the way for the final defeat of the Lumumbist insurrections for the second independence. The magico–religious arsenal that had worked so well against Mobutu's troops proved futile in the face of the more disciplined and sophisticated Katanga gendarmes, European and Cuban mercenaries, and metropolitan troops. Equally futile was the militaristic strategy of frontal attacks by thousands of untrained and poorly armed partisans, as they became easy targets for a well-armed enemy, using automatic arms, armoured vehicles and military aircraft.

The three top leaders of the Stanleyville regime — Gbenye, Soumialot and Olenga — went back into exile. They returned to Zaire in the early 1970s after the trials and tribulations of exile had made Mobutu's amnesty offers look attractive. Led by Laurent Kabila, the more progressive and revolutionary-minded CNL militants had by this time returned to the bush to continue the armed liberation struggle under a new party, the *Parti de la Révolution Populaire* (PRP). Conceived as a project in June 1966, the party was established on 24 December 1967, after a critical reappraisal of the errors of the CNL and the APL. The PRP sees itself as being engaged in a protracted struggle against a system that the insurrections of 1964 failed to destroy.[63] It has preserved itself through self-reliance, while lacking the means with which to break out of its isolation in the mountains of the Uvira–Fizi area along Lake Tanganyika. Like the Mulele maquis in the Kwilu, its longevity is a sign of its strength as well as its weaknesses. For if the Mobutu regime is unable to destroy the PRP maquis, the latter does not pose a major threat to the neo-colonial state and to imperialist interests in the country.

## Conclusion

A popular alliance of the African masses and the nationalist petty bourgeoisie arose to challenge colonial domination, along with its economic exploitation and racist oppression. The deepest aspirations of ordinary people for meaningful social change and material prosperity were exploited by the petty bourgeoisie in the interest of a mere Africanisation of the inherited state apparatus. Once in power, this class set out to transform itself into a state bourgeoisie and to enter into alliance with the international bourgeoisie at the expense of the masses.

Zaire is the first country in post-colonial Africa where this betrayal coincided with the assassination of the most prominent nationalist leader, Patrice Lumumba, thus creating the conditions for a new popular alliance between an outraged people and other radical nationalists. Pierre Mulele and other Lumumbists assumed the leadership of this alliance, a mass-based revolutionary movement for a second independence. They led it to spectacular victories over a disorganised neo-colonial state that was also lacking in legitimacy in the eyes of the people. Unfortunately, these victories were short-lived, as the neo-colonial state was able to summon to its side the full weight of imperialist counter-insurgency, against which the mass movement revealed a number of crippling weaknesses.

The struggle for genuine liberation was defeated between 1964 and 1968, but it is not over. New organisations have arisen and will continue to rise to pursue the revolutionary enterprise that Pierre Mulele began in 1963. So far, there is a paradox that the most militarily successful organisations, like the CNL/Gbenye and Nathanael Mbumba's *Front de Libération Nationale du Congo* (FLNC) — the group responsible for the Shaba wars of 1977–78 — are also those groupings that have done the least with respect to mass political education. On the other hand, the Mulelist and PRP maquis, where politicisation seems to have been highly advanced, remained for the most part low-level guerilla wars posing a limited threat to the neo-colonial state and requiring little in the way of external military assistance.

The challenge to Zairean patriots and revolutionaries is how to combine the virtues of politicisation with the ability to strike at the most vulnerable or strategic points of the neo-colonial state, so as to destroy the conditions which allow for timely and limited interventions by imperialism. In other words, such interventions must be rendered more cumbersome and costly. In this way, their perpetrators will be forced to explain to their national constituencies why they have to crush the legitimate aspirations of ordinary Africans for a better life by supporting corrupt and dictatorial regimes which show no concern for the welfare of their own people.

## Notes

1. Previous publications from this research include 'Les classes sociales et la révolution anticoloniale au Congo–Kinshasa: le rôle de la bourgeoisie', *Cahiers Economiques et Sociaux*, vol. VIII, no. 3, September 1970, pp. 371–88, also published in English as 'The Bourgeoisie and Revolution in the Congo', *Journal of Modern African Studies*, vol. VIII, no. 4, December 1970, pp. 511–30; 'The Authenticity of Neocolonialism: Ideology and Class Struggle in Zaire', *Berkeley Journal of Sociology*, no. 22, 1977–8, pp. 115–130; 'The Continuing Struggle for National Liberation in Zaire', *Journal of Modern African Studies*, vol. XVII, no. 4, December 1979, 595–614; and 'Class Struggle and National Liberation in Zaire', in Bernard Magubane and Nzongola-Ntalaja (eds.) *Proletarianization and Class Struggle in Africa* (San Francisco: Synthesis Publications, 1983) pp. 57–94.

2. This is the way in which the national liberation struggle is conceptualised by Amilcar Cabral, particularly in his classic essay entitled 'The Weapon of Theory'. For more on Cabral's theory, see my 'Amilcar Cabral and the Theory of the National Liberation Struggle', *Latin American Perspectives* 41 (Special Issue on Amilcar Cabral) vol. XI, no. 2, Spring 1984, pp. 43–54.

3. Nzongola, 'Class Struggle and National Liberation in Zaire'.

4. Also known as the 'Congo Independent State' (from the French *Etat*

*Indépendant du Congo*), the Free State was established as a sovereign entity in 1885. The country became a Belgian colony in 1908.

5. Louis Franck, 'La politique indigène, le service territorial et les chefferies', *Congo* vol. I, no. 2, February 1921, pp. 189–201.

6. Jean Stengers, 'La place de Léopold II dans l'histoire de la colonisation', *La Nouvelle Clio*, no. 9, 1950, p. 524, cited in Ruth Slade, *King Leopold's Congo: Aspects of the Development of Race Relations in the Congo Independent State* (London: Oxford University Press for the Institute of Race Relations, 1962) p. 176.

7. Roger Anstey, *King Leopold's Legacy: The Congo under Belgian Rule, 1908–1960* (London: Oxford University Press for the Institute of Race Relations, 1966) p. 261.

8. Jean Stengers, 'The Congo Free State and the Belgian Congo until 1914' in L. H. Gann and Peter Duignan (eds.) *Colonialism in Africa 1870–1960* vol. I: *The History and Politics of Colonialism 1870–1914* (Cambridge: Cambridge University Press, 1969) p. 289.

9. Anstey, *King Leopold's Legacy*, p. 262. For a similar viewpoint, see Michel Merlier, *Le Congo de la colonisation belge à l'indépendance* (Paris: Maspero, 1962) pp. 36–7.

10. The best analysis of these three defining characteristics of modern colonialism is to be found in Jean Suret-Canale, *French Colonialism in Tropical Africa* (New York: Pica Press, 1971).

11. On the economic value of the Congo to Belgium, see in addition to Merlier, Jean Stengers, *Combien le Congo a-t-il coûté à la Belgique?* (Brussels: A.R.S.C., 1957) and Pierre Joye and Rosine Lewin, *Les trusts au Congo* (Brussels: Société Populaire d'Editions, 1961). Walter Rodney, *How Europe Underdeveloped Africa* (Washington, D.C.: Howard University Press, 1974), p. 172, cites the following statement from a Belgian official on the Congo's contribution to the Belgian war effort in 1940–45:

> During the war, the Congo was able to finance all the expenditures of the Belgian government in London, including the diplomatic service as well as the cost of our armed forces in Europe and Africa, a total of some £40 million. In fact, thanks to the resources of the Congo, the Belgian government in London had not to borrow a shilling or a dollar, and the Belgian gold reserve could be left intact.

12. Jan Vansina, 'Du royaume Kuba au "territoire des Bakuba"', *Etudes Congolaises*, vol. XII, no. 2, April–June 1969, pp. 3–54; see esp. pp. 23–38.

13. Crawford Young, *Politics in the Congo: Decolonization and Independence* (Princeton: Princeton University Press, 1965) p. 11.

14. Fernand Bézy, 'Problems of Economic Development of Congo', in E. A. G. Robinson (ed.) *Economic Development for Africa South of the Sahara* (New York: St. Martin's Press, 1964) p. 82.

15. On the Manichean nature of the colonial situation, see Frantz Fanon, *The Wretched of the Earth* (New York: Grove Press, 1963) ch. 1.

16. Nzongola-Ntalaja, 'The National Question and the Crisis of Instability in Africa', *ALTERNATIVES: A Journal of World Policy*, Special UN Commemorative Issue, vol. X, no. 4, 1985, p. 542.

17. Fernand Bézy, *Principes pour l'orientation du développement économique au Congo* (Léopoldville: Editions de l'Université Lovanium, 1959).

18. Rupert Emerson, *From Empire to Nation: The Rise to Self-Assertion of Asian and African Peoples* (Boston: Beacon Press, 1962) p. 227.

19. Ibid, p. 53.

20. Thomas Hodgkin, 'The Relevance of "Western" Ideas for the New African

States', in J. Roland Pennock (ed.) *Self-Government in Modernizing Nations* (Englewood Cliffs, NJ: Prentice-Hall, 1964) p. 60.

21. Fanon, *The Wretched of the Earth*, pp. 92–102.

22. Hodgkin, 'The Relevance of "Western" Ideas', p. 61.

23. See, among others, Paul Demunter, *Masses rurales et luttes politiques au Zaïre: Le processus de politisation des masses rurales au Bas-Zaïre* (Paris: Editions Anthropos, 1975) and Herbert F. Weiss, *Political Protest in the Congo: The Parti Solidaire Africain During the Independence Struggle* (Princeton: Princeton University Press, 1967).

24. See Benoit Verhaegen, 'Patrice Lumumba: martyr d'une Afrique nouvelle', in Charles-André Julien et al (eds.) *Les Africains*, vol. II (Paris: Editions Jeune Afrique, 1977) pp. 185–219; reprinted in *Jeune Afrique*, 1 February 1978, pp. 69–96.

25. Nzongola-Ntalaja, 'Occupational Background of the Political Leaders of the First Republic', unpublished paper.

26. Fanon, *The Wretched of the Earth*, p. 114.

27. On the general theme of the connection between primary resistance and contemporary liberation struggles, see T. O. Ranger, 'Connexions Between "Primary Resistance" Movements and Modern Mass Nationalism in East and Central Africa', *Journal of African History*, vol. IX, no. 3, 1968, pp. 437–53 and vol. IX no. 4, 1968, pp. 631–41. The literature on Zimbabwe is too abundant to be cited in a single footnote. For a useful summary account of the war of liberation there, see David Birmingham and Terence Ranger, 'Settlers and Liberators in the South', in David Birmingham and Phyllis M. Martin (eds.) *History of Central Africa*, vol. 2 (London and New York: Longman, 1983), pp. 336–82, esp. pp. 369–82.

28. Ludo Martens, *Pierre Mulele ou la seconde vie de Patrice Lumumba* (Berchem, Antwerp: Editions EPO, 1985) p. 29.

29. Weiss, *Political Protest in the Congo*, p. 187. Martens, *Pierre Mulele*, p. 29, writes that although the official figure was 550, as many as 1,500 people may have died.

30. Jules Chomé, *L'ascension de Mobutu: du sergent Désiré Joseph au général Sese Seko* (Brussels: Editions Complexe, 1975) p. 191.

31. See Thomas Hodgkin, *Nationalism in Colonial Africa* (London: Frederick Muller, 1956) p. 52.

32. The EJCSK or Church of Jesus Christ on Earth by the Prophet Simon Kimbangu was granted official recognition by the Belgian colonial authorities 38 years later in December 1959, and it became a member of the World Council of Churches in 1969. It is perhaps the largest of African independent churches born within the colonial situation.

33. Wyatt MacGaffey, *Modern Kongo Prophets: Religion in a Plural Society* (Bloomington: Indiana University Press, 1983) p. 8.

34. Thus, whereas anyone living in the Kwango–Kwilu region and in the Kivu could become a member of the PSA and CEREA, respectively, membership in CONAKAT was basically contingent on being a member of one of the ethnic groups constituting the party, or being an 'authentic Katangan'.

35. Meaning, the 'party of paid niggers' or those who have sold out.

36. It was, as Verhaegen suggests from the standpoint of the Belgians, a 'failed decolonization', as it involved a shift of the major imperial centre for the country from Brussels to Washington. See Benoit Verhaegen, 'La Première République (1960–1965)', in Jacques Vanderlinden (ed.) *Du Congo au Zaïre 1960–1980: Essai de bilan* (Brussels: CRISP, 1980) pp. 111–37, esp. pp. 132–3.

37. The distribution of the 71 seats was as follows: MNC/L and direct alliances, 41 (33 + 8); PSA, 13; CEREA, 10; and the Katanga cartel of unitarist parties, 7. Although some of the PSA seats belonged to the more moderate Kamitatu wing of the party, Lumumba was still capable of obtaining a working majority in the Chamber of Deputies.

38. On Lumumba's assassination and the Congolese politicians involved in it, see G. Heinz and H. Donnay, *Lumumba: The Last Fifty Days* (New York: Grove Press, 1969).

39. There is now an abundance of information on the CIA plot to assassinate Lumumba. Basic references include US Congress, Senate, *Interim Report: Alleged Assassination Plots Involving Foreign Leaders*, by the Select Committee to Study Governmental Operations with Respect to Intelligence Activities, 94th Congress, 1st Session, November 20, 1975; the same committee's *Final Report: Foreign and Military Intelligence*, Book I, 94th Congress, 2nd Session, April 26, 1976; Madeleine G. Kalb, *The Congo Cables: The Cold War in Africa from Eisenhower to Kennedy* (New York: Macmillan, 1982); Richard Mahoney, *JFK: Ordeal in Africa* (New York: Oxford University Press, 1983); and Stephen Weissman, 'The CIA and US Policy in Zaire and Angola', in Rene Lemarchand (ed.) *American Policy in Southern Africa: The Stakes and the Stance* (Washington, D.C.: University Press of America, 1978) pp. 382–432.

40. Pierre Artigue, *Qui sont les leaders congolais?* (Brussels: Editions Europe–Afrique, 1961), pp. 92, 114, 218–219, and 363.

41. Chomé, *L'Ascension de Mobutu*, p. 112.

42. Stephen R. Weissman, *American Foreign Policy in the Congo 1960–64* (Ithaca: Cornell University Press, 1974) p. 147.

43. Ibid., p. 208.

44. G. Mennen Williams, 'U.S. Objectives in the Congo, 1960–65', *Africa Report*, vol. X, no. 8, August 1965, p. 16.

45. Jean Ziegler, *Sociologie de la nouvelle Afrique* (Paris: Gallimard, 1964) p. 12.

46. Amilcar Cabral, *Unity and Struggle: Speeches and Writings* (New York: Monthly Review Press, 1979) pp. 119–37.

47. Alain Badiou and François Balmès, *De l'idéologie* (Paris: Maspero, 1976) p. 91.

48. See Antonio Gramsci, *Selections from the Prison Notebooks* (New York: International Publishers, 1971) pp. 5–23, on the concept of 'organic intellectuals'.

49. On the elitism of university students and the political limitations of UGEC, see Jean-Claude Willame, 'The Congo', in Donald K. Emmerson (ed.) *Students and Politics in Developing Nations* (New York: Praeger, 1968) pp. 37–63; Wamba-dia-Wamba, 'Short Bibliographical Notes on the Congolese (Zairean) Revolutionary Nationalist Movement', unpublished paper; Makidi-ku-Ntima, 'The Role of Congolese Intellectuals in the Making of Neo-Colonialism: U.G.E.C.–Mobutu Alliance or the Story of the Odd Couple', paper presented at the 28th Annual Meeting of the African Studies Association, New Orleans, November 23–6, 1985.

50. On the inflation and its consequences, see IRES, *Indépendance, inflation et développement* (Kinshasa: IRES; Paris and The Hague: Mouton, 1968).

51. The most detailed account of these insurrections is to be found in Benoit Verhaegen, *Rébellions au Congo*, 2 vols. (Brussels: CRISP, 1966, 1969). Ludo Martens's *Pierre Mulele* is an excellent study of the revolution in the Kwilu, the most comprehensive to date and the best documented report we have on Mulele and his revolutionary work.

52. As distinguished from the more moderate and opportunistic PSA/Kamitatu.

53. The UPC movement in the Cameroon was also involved in a revolutionary struggle against neo-colonialism, but this was a continuation of a struggle for genuine independence that was aborted with the installation of Ahmadou Ahidjo in power in 1958 and the granting of a nominal independence in 1960 by the French, who also continued to lead the counter-insurgency drive against the UPC.

54. On the social origins of Mulele's partisans and cadres, see Herbert Weiss and Renny Fulco, 'Les partisans au Kwilu: Analyse des origines sociales des membres et cadres des équipes de base', paper presented at the International Conference on Rebellions/Revolutions in Central Africa, University of Paris VII, Paris, December 13–15, 1984.

55. For more on the negative consequences of ethnicity for the struggle, see Benoit Verhaegen, 'Le rôle de l'ethnie et de l'individu dans la rébellion du Kwilu et dans son échec', paper presented at the Paris conference (see note 54).

56. The initial successes of the Mulelist maquis in the Kwilu had created a veritable legend around Mulele's name and personality, giving rise to the identification of his name with the magic water. Although Mulele himself tolerated the use of fetishes by his partisans, there is no evidence that he either encouraged or believed in the power of magico–religious resources.

57. Verhaegen, 'La Première République', p. 126.

58. Jules Gérard-Libois, 'The New Class and Rebellion in the Congo', in Ralph Miliband and John Saville (eds.) *The Socialist Register 1966* (New York: Monthly Review Press, 1967) pp. 277–8.

59. Ibid., p. 271.

60. Moise Tshombe, *Quinze mois de gouvernement au Congo* (Paris: Table Ronde, 1966) p. 20.

61. Weissman, 'The CIA and U.S. Policy in Zaire and Angola', pp. 391–2.

62. Ibid., pp. 392–3.

63. B. Muhuni, 'Mobutu and the Class Struggle in Zaire', *Review of African Political Economy*, no. 5, January–April 1976, 94–8.

# 7 Challenging the Apartheid Regime from Below

by Horace Campbell

Twenty-five years after the Sharpeville massacre had placed the brutality of the South African state squarely into the consciousness of humanity, the South African Police mowed down blacks attending a funeral procession at Uitenhage on March 21, 1985. Four months later the regime of P. W. Botha declared a State of Emergency as the urban black oppressed challenged the survival of the present form of racial exploitation which is called apartheid. These twenty-five years marked the period of decolonisation in Africa. In South Africa the maturing of the confidence of the exploited black majority was witnessed. This confidence corresponded with a crystallisation of the working poor and a level of proletarianisation which supported the growth of new forms of social awareness among the blacks. The political correlate of this crystallisation was the flowering of organisations of youths, sports clubs, cultural groups, trade union and community organisations. These organisations merged into a popular alliance in 1983 called the United Democratic Front and forced the pace of political change in South Africa.

The levels of state violence in South Africa have been matched by the determination of the popular masses to resist the apartheid war machine. Throughout 1984 the South African state embarked on a programme of reform at home as it sought to tell the world that it was a peacemaker by signing the Nkomati Accord and the Lusaka Agreement. The leadership had been taken in by its own propaganda only to be brought back to reality by the day-to-day insurrectionary violence, uprisings, boycotts, rent strikes, industrial action, stay-aways, funerals and other forms of mass resistance to the repressive regime. The sustained uprisings made the question of South Africa the number one question of this decade as the issue of apartheid was debated in many international fora and demonstrators protested the Reagan administration's policy of 'constructive engagement' with South Africa.

At the level of international politics, apartheid was conceptualised to mean different things: for the United Nations, it was a crime against humanity; for the Organisation of African Unity and the Non-Aligned Movement, it was an affront to the dignity of the black person; for the social-democratic elements in Europe and the US apartheid was a barrier to the development of full capitalist relations of production in that part of Africa, and for the conservative forces of Reagan and Thatcher, apartheid stood as a force against communism and the Soviet threat to Africa. But for the vast majority of South African blacks, the question of apartheid had moved beyond the issues of racial segregation, Bantustans and pass laws, and had become a profoundly *social question*. The very organisation of society, the social despotism of the factory and the total dehumanisation of blacks meant that the present struggle was for a total redefinition of the purpose of life, the quality of life and the need for basic human rights. In effect, the present problems of apartheid meant that the solution to these social problems required answers beyond the question of majority rule and universal adult suffrage. And yet the political and ideological backwardness of the society meant that even those who considered themselves 'liberals' in South Africa opposed the granting of the franchise to all adults of voting age.

The social questions which impelled the masses had called into being new forms of organising and the mushrooming of popular groups in all spheres of life of the society. Out of this self-expression and self-organisation of the poor emerged a loose front — the UDF — as an alliance of over 600 affiliates and over two million adherents. Originally coming together to confront the 1983 reforms for a new constitutional dispensation, the UDF evolved in the midst of the uprisings to become a tremendous force in the politics of South Africa. When the regime murdered or arrested the bulk of the leaders, religious leaders emerged as important spokespersons for this alliance. The UDF did not set out to replace any of the banned liberation movements, but in the process of struggle the front began achieving a dynamic of its own. Through legal, political and industrial struggles, the UDF was acting as a school for a new generation of South Africans who were not afraid to confront the tanks, shotguns and rubber bullets of the South African Defence Forces.

The Boers, in a state of panic, used their last weapon as they occupied the townships and moved to arrest school children as young as seven years old. The Western media, immobilised by their inability to transcend the anti-socialist mania of the metropoles, lamely reported the war in the townships simply with a body count of those murdered in battle since August 1984. Yet the visual images of the repression relayed by satellite across the world sharpened popular anti-dictatorial consciousness in a period of counter-revolution.

The alliance of the popular masses in South Africa, fighting against an armed machine of the Boers, brought to mind the popular alliances which had been formed earlier this century — from the Popular Front which fought in the Spanish Civil War to the anti-fascist alliances in Europe during World War II. These alliances had served as important reference points for the leaders of the nationalist movements which emerged in Africa during the period of decolonisation. Guided by the dictum of positive action, the period of the transition from colonial rule threw up an alliance of workers, poor peasants, rich peasants, farmers, budding business persons, traders and the educated who wanted to end European overrule.

Forty years after the start of the process of decolonisation and the consolidation or disintegration of African states, there could be a revolution of the form and content of these alliances, even when the alliance took the form of armed guerilla struggles as in Algeria, Kenya, Mozambique or Zimbabwe. The nationalism which acted as an ideological cover for this alliance has been shattered by the process of class formation, crude enrichment and the intense struggles for political power.

Subsequent forms of ideological and political cleavages led to the disintegration of the pre-independence popular alliances. Schisms among the emergent ruling classes brought divisions among the producing classes to the point of civil wars or other forms of armed conflict which contributed to the strengthening of external domination of the continent. New alliances between the emergent ruling classes and foreign capital concentrated power in the hands of the petty bourgeoisie and local capitalists in the same proportion to the destruction of popular political expression and participation. The manipulation of race, regionalism, tribalism and other divisions among the people took priority over serious efforts towards social progress. Drought, famine, hunger and poverty became, after twenty years of independence, the most vivid expressions of neo-colonial politics. This expression was compounded by the international capitalist crisis which transferred part of the burden of recovery of capitalism onto the shoulders of the African poor through unequal trade, excessive interest on debts and other forms of exploitation. This crisis in Africa led the popular masses to seek new alliances and the potentialities of such alliances were demonstrated in the Sudan in April 1985.

To understand and underscore the process of the present alliance in South Africa is the task of this chapter. The present struggle in South Africa brings to the fore many questions with respect to the recent history of popular alliances and popular fronts. What are the social forces that aspire towards leadership within this alliance? What is the nature of the links between organised and unorganised toilers? What is the level of urban/rural imbalance and how does this affect its strategy and tactics? What is the leading theoretical/political line in this alliance? Does any one section seek ideological or political hegemony? What are the short-term and long-term objectives of this alliance?

All of these questions are conjunctural and pertinent when one hears the generalised demand for the dismantling of apartheid. Because this demand means essentially different things to different social forces it is necessary that these questions become part of the problem of those in combat. To end unemployment, poor housing, compound- and barrack-like existence; to gain proper health and safety at work, a living wage, decent and meaningful education and democratic political forms have all been mooted as the requirements of the poor in South Africa. For others the coming to power of a black political leadership would solve the social issue. Recent examples in Southern Africa showed that unless the direction of the struggle was to recapture the dignity of labour by transformation of the labour process, black leaders can be as effective as white leaders in defending transnational capital. Moreover, the two-stage theory of revolution or the conception of the development of the productive forces has in the past been articulated to defend the deepening of capitalist relations and state control over working-class organisations or other organs of popular power.

Thus, in the period of war, capitalist depression, monetary crisis and famine, international capital seeks new ways to spread consumerism and finance capital across Africa. The popular alliance in South Africa can be an instrument for the limited goal of sharing power or it can be geared for a prolonged struggle where the self-emancipation of the toilers will take them to higher levels of consciousness and struggle. In this there are both negative and positive lessons to be learnt from the recent alliances of the masses in Iran and in El Salvador. The El Salvador alliance of a political military front pushed the people forward in a unity in struggle which overrode secondary political differences.

The present self-expression of the South African masses bodes well for new political lessons where the voiceless millions begin to play the leading role in the struggle for human emancipation.

## The Racial and Social Components of Apartheid

In the Southern cone of Africa a new popular alliance is being fashioned to challenge the most repressive regime on the continent. The ruthless nature of South African capitalism had precipitated the first major anti-colonial movement as early as 1912 with the formation of the South African Native National Congress. Changing its name to the African National Congress (ANC) in 1923, the evolving political organisation assigned to itself the elementary task of creating one political movement which transcended regional, ethnic and class barriers among the blacks. Because the educated blacks were completely excluded from the circuit of accumulation by the rigid racial segregation, these elements dominated the political organisations of black people in South Africa.

When the stirrings of the anti-colonial movement signalled a 'wind of change in Africa', the National Party, which had come to power in 1948, articulated a set of principles strengthening racial segregation and domination and entrenching white minority rule and a legal framework of white domination which controlled the mobility and reproduction process among Africans. Apartheid as a doctrine codified and structured the relations of production with the use of brutal force, extra-economic coercion and dispossession to make cheap labour available to the white-dominated economy. A separate administrative structure established in the twenties and the system of African 'reserves' which had been given legal embodiment in the Land Acts of 1913 and 1936 became the basis of a Bantustan system where 24 million people, or 72 per cent of the population, were coralled into  the barren and infertile 13 per cent of the territory. In a twenty-year period up to 1984, as many as four million Africans were retribalised into so-called homelands, the legal name given to the Bantustans.[1]

By the end of the 1960s, when European colonial domination had been forced to change its form to economic exploitation, South African society was governed by the crudest forms of racist segregation and dehumanisation. Every sphere of human relations was governed by race: how and under what conditions people are born, where they live, where and if they go to school, the quality of housing, how they travel to work, what kinds of jobs they could do, the levels of skills which could be attained (job reservation), where they go to pray, where they carried out their sporting and cultural activities, and where they are buried. A battery of laws and regulations governed these relations to support a system built in the main on a migratory labour force. Masters and Servants ordinances and the pass laws defined the position of Africans in the labour process and influx control laws regulated their freedom of movement. The Group Areas Act, Native Land Act, Population Registration Act, Reservation and Separate Amenities Act, Liquor Act and Suppression of Communism Act are all part of the legal basis for the super-

145

exploitation of black labour.[2]

Political deprivation and the exclusion of blacks from all forms of legal assembly and organisation reinforced the power of racial capitalism. By the 1980s, in a society with over 30 million citizens, the whites, comprising 4.5 million or 15.5 per cent of the population, totally controlled political power and over 87 per cent of the land. The 24 million Africans were segregated into Bantustans and the urban townships from where they sold their labour. The coloured and Indian population were further segregated into their own residential areas and were treated as 'supports' to the Africans, thereby the system solidified a rigid system of racial classification and racial separation. White workers were mobilised by the ideology of the Afrikaans ruling class to provide for the complete separation of blacks and whites in all areas of social reproduction.[3]

The institutionalisation of racism in South Africa had guaranteed continuous forms of passive and organised resistance against the oppression of apartheid. Mass action, epitomised by the campaigns against the pass laws and the Defiance Campaigns of the fifties, had heightened the consciousness of the urban workers and gave rise to the Congress Alliance. Out of this temporary alliance of whites, Indians and coloureds, and the ANC, emerged the Freedom Charter and a decade of intense anti-apartheid activity in South Africa.[4] This politics of mass insurgency was shattered by Sharpeville. The growing divisions in the black liberation struggle had led to the formation of the Pan-Africanist Congress of Azania. Underground political work both in the communities and in the building of new cells to prosecute an armed struggle replaced the popular and open campaigns as the repression snuffed out a generation of leaders, imprisoned hundreds, including Nelson Mandela, and drove others into exile.

International capitals gave the Afrikaans leadership their stamp of approval by increasingly investing in apartheid during the 1960s and 1970s. A healthy competition between Britain, the USA and West Germany for dominance in the economy led the way for an increased flow of capital to South Africa. Total foreign investment in the country had reached only Rand (R) 3 billion by 1960 and after

**Table 7.1**
**South African Gross Domestic Product, end 1983, R million, 1975 prices.**

| Sector | 1982 | 1983 |
|---|---|---|
| Agriculture | 2,385 | 1,861 |
| Mining | 3,376 | 3,313 |
| Manufacturing | 8,009 | 7,478 |
| Construction | 1,298 | 1,296 |
| Trade, wholesale and retail | 3,863 | 3,891 |
| Financial services | 4,164 | 4,309 |
| Government services | 3,109 | 3,261 |
| GDP at Factory Cost | 31,223 | 30,201 |

Source: *Financial Mail,* 7 December 1984

Sharpeville fell slightly by 1963. But by 1970 foreign investment soared to over R5.8 billion, surpassed R7 billion in 1972 and by 1979 totalled R22.8 billion.[5] In the 1980s the US became the leading investor in apartheid with over $14 billion invested. The abundant mineral wealth and unlimited supplies of cheap, non-unionised and super-exploitable labour attracted capitalists from all over the world. The return on capital was frequently as high as 15–20 per cent per annum so that investors could often get the whole of their money back in only 5 or 6 years.

Foreign investment stimulated greater diversification and expansion of the apartheid economy so that by the end of the 1970s mining was no longer the leading pole of accumulation in South Africa. Although there are over half a million workers employed in the mining sector, manufacturing and finance have become the leading sectors of the economy.

These figures show that by 1982 manufacturing had become twice as important as mining in the South African economy with all the added implications for the working people. South Africa had become a booming industrial economy producing steel, motor cars, textiles, plastics, petro-chemicals, and armaments which utilised the most advanced technology available to the major transnational companies (TNCs) in Western Europe, North America, Brazil and Japan. TNCs expanded their subsidiaries with over 2,100 in 1980. These companies supported the efforts of the South African regime to intimidate and repress the peoples of the region and colluded to violate the UN mandatory arms embargo against South Africa.

Self-sufficiency in armaments provided a further spur to economic expansion as the regime embarked on a massive project of arms procurement and manufacturing. A state corporation, the Armaments Development Production Corporation — ARMSCOR — was established to produce weapons. ARMSCOR, with a multi-faceted web of subsidiaries and over 25,000 contractors, produced a wide range of weapons from the much-heralded 155 artillery, a wide range of munitions, air-to-air and sea-to-sea guided missiles, jets, electro-optics, computers, telecommunications equipment, rockets and pyro-technical products. It was from this industrial, scientific and technological base that South Africa developed the hydrogenisation of coal (SASOL) and, with the assistance of the West, built up a nuclear capability. With the open support of the Reagan Administration under the policy of 'constructive engagement', South Africa of the middle of the eighties ranked number ten in the hierarchy of capitalist arms manufacturers.

The very dynamic of industrialisation and technological development which arose out of the ideas of repression, domination and expansion undermined one of the key pillars of apartheid — the migratory system of labour. The military–industrial complex forced the pace of technological change so that the society required a much higher level of skill and training beyond the deformed and entrenched system of job reservation in the mines. Changes in the technical conditions of the labour process called into being a more stable and skilled black labour force and at the same time provided mobility for the white workers who increasingly occupied supervisory roles. This, together with their racist socialisation, sharpened their political and ideological identification with the ruling class. Differential wage rates and differences in the distribution of the social product were now the key pillars of apartheid in a system which affirmed that the worth and dignity of black labour was not the same as that of white labour.

This affirmation of white superiority was more explicit in the areas of social reproduction, in the fields of health, education, housing, transport, cultural amenities, pensions and social welfare. Apartheid was now becoming a profoundly *social* question inextricably bound to the race question, as the pass laws and forced removal ensured that labour did not really become free in South Africa. These social questions were compounded by the callous neglect of the environment evidenced by the boom in chemical and petro-chemical industries, which polluted the environment and impaired the health of the society. In the rural areas, hundreds of blacks die each year as a result of the use of illegal poisons and the mishandling of registered pesticides.[6] It was this totality of exploitation and repression which produced the present popular alliance.

## Preludes to the Alliance

The changing organic composition of capital led to changes in the composition, size, skill, stability and social weight of the working class. However, the transformation at the material level was not reflected in political or ideological changes in the ruling class. Vast resources were being allocated to implement pass laws and influx control while capital was attracting labour to the urban shanties to the extent that, by 1980, over 60 per cent of the workers were permanent residents in the poverty-stricken and overcrowded townships. Report after report detailed the levels of poverty of these townships. Even the most conservative estimates of the poverty datum line showed clearly the abysmal conditions of township life.[7] Through defensive action and other forms of struggle, the urban workers were struggling for their rights, especially those which occupied them on a day-to-day basis.

Significantly, the exiled liberation movements were battling for their own survival and did not yet develop a clear programme to champion the struggle around the social question of apartheid. Having conceived of their political programmes before the shift in the leading basis of capital accumulation, the contents of the demand for change remained within the conceptions of the era of nationalist politics. It was in this context that the workers were slowly evolving new forms of self-expression and struggle.

### From Durban to Soweto

This self-organisation and mobilisation of the urban workers arose out of the day-to-day degradation and humiliation at work and at home. Low wages, high prices, exorbitant transport costs are now acknowledged as being at the core of the massive Durban strikes between 1971–1973. The Durban strikes of 1973, in particular, marked a new period of class struggle as over 100,000 black workers struck for higher wages. The strike movement spread rapidly across the country from this industrial area which was a centre for the textile and metal industries. By 1970 there were over 165,000 workers employed in Durban:

The industrial workers in Durban tended to be concentrated in large factories and the strike movement swept rapidly from one industrial area to another. The mass strikes in Natal Province demonstrated the unity of the black working class across divisions between migrant and urban workers, between different industries and even between industrial and agricultural workers.[8]

These mass strikes won substantial increases in wages and the success stemmed from the organisational strength and techniques used during the confrontations with capital. Strikers refused to elect a leadership thus immunising themselves from the effects of victimisation and cooption. They avoided all formally constituted representative bodies and relied on the sharp demonstrative shock of a short withdrawal of labour to gain concessions from employers rather than entering into negotiations or protracted confrontations.[9]

Far-sighted elements in the capitalist class perceived the potentialities of the self-organisation of the working class and they spearheaded the call for an industrial framework where black workers could organise freely but with rigid state control of trade unions. This search by capital sharpened after the massive stay-aways which formed part of the Soweto uprisings in 1976 and 1977.

### Soweto

Soweto, like Sharpeville, became a symbol of the black liberation struggle after the youths and students took on the armed power of the state to oppose the educational component of apartheid. Numerous accounts of the uprisings testify to the levels of spontaneity and the fact that the leadership came from a new generation which had come to maturity long after Sharpeville.[10] Students' protests in the schools formed part of a wider protest against the social inequalities of the society. Spurred on by the victories of Africans over colonialism in Mozambique and the defeat of the South Africans in Angola in March, 1976, in June the students of Orlando West led the opposition to the attempt by the regime to reproduce knowledge through the medium of Afrikaans.

This attempt was to reinforce an educational system which reproduced the ideas of black inferiority. The educational system reproduced the alienation, deformities and racism of the system and the content of education preached the values of individualism and progress through hard work. These ideas and values stood in direct contradiction to the concrete realities of the students' existence. A march by students to protest this contradiction and the imposition of Afrikaans was met by armed police and at the end of the day at least a score of youths were shot dead.

The revolt spread rapidly across the society as the police responded with total violence, so that by the end of the uprisings over 284 has been killed and over 2,000 injured.[11] The events of Soweto and its aftermath are too well documented to bear repetition here. What are of significance are two factors: (a) the growth of the student–worker alliance and (b) the impact of black consciousness on black political culture in South Africa.

It was in this period of the Soweto uprisings that the successes of the stay-aways imprinted the strength of the worker–student alliance. Slowly recognising the limits of their own ability to take on the might of the state, the students and youths developed and deepened links with the workers. These links were being fashioned even though the principal intellectual force among the students — black consciousness — was more occupied with questions of dignity and respect rather than questions of wages, safety, unemployment or compound housing.

Black consciousness became an essential element of black liberation struggle as the educated youths and students stridently sought to assert their isolation from white forms of cultural and political dominance, including the perceived role of radical/liberal whites in the anti-apartheid movement. This consciousness and its impact on organisations and movements provided the foundation for a divergent understanding of South African political economy, history and culture and gave rise to various organisations and groupings until the banning of the Black Consciousness Movement (BCM) in October 1977.[12]

Despite the differences between the idea of black consciousness and the multi-racial principles of the ANC, many of the youths who fled South Africa joined the ANC and the PAC. There was a weak attempt to establish the BCM in Europe. Of those who remained some became careerists in professions like social work while the state imprisoned the activists or murdered the spokespersons of the movement like Steve Biko. The permanence of race consciousness as an aspect of the class consciousness of South African society meant that the ideas found a lasting place in the society. Many students had graduated to become teachers, lawyers, clergymen, trade unionists and journalists, and in 1978 an organisation was formed guided by the ideas of the BCM. This was the Azanian People's Organisation (AZAPO).[13]

**From Soweto to the UDF**

Because the racial and cultural alienation embedded in the educational systems was a permanent feature of apartheid, student protests became a fundamental component of the mass resistance from 1980 to 1985. During this period there was not a school term when a major boycott of schools was not in progress. Hundreds of thousands of young people across the country initiated protests against the contents of education, boycotted classes, left schools deserted and left some teachers in a real quandary as to their link to the struggle. In the historic year 1984 over half a million students in over 60 townships boycotted schools as the call for political and intellectual freedom merged with the generalised resistance against apartheid.[14]

Pupils demanded better and more relevant education, free and compulsory education for all, an end to the use of untrained and undertrained teachers, the scrapping of the age limit, the abolition of capital punishment, an end to sexual harassment of pupils and the right to elect democratically student representative councils. These demands conflicted with the basic thrust of capitalist education whether in its apartheid form or in the neo-colonial form. All over the country the students, through their organisations, the Azanian Students Organisation and Congress of South African Students (COSAS), formed liaison committees linking the struggles of the students to those of the workers. By 1983, COSAS had dropped its black consciousness stance and played a central role in the 1984 stay-away in the Vaal triangle. When the UDF was formed the worker–student alliance had deepened beyond the elementary links of 1976. The police continued to respond with repression to the point where in 1985 they were beginning to arrest pupils as young as seven years old. COSAS was banned during the State of Emergency of 1985.

During and even before the declaration of the State of Emergency, the determination of the youths to confront rubber bullets, teargas and armoured vehicles with sticks and stones helped to define the limits of the military power of the war machine. Unlike the previous generation which had gone into exile after Soweto, this new social force played the leading role in the insurrectionary violence which swept the society. Guided by an amalgam of ideas, the ANC, the AZAPO, black cultural identity, Rasta and socialism, the youths were slowly rising above the regional and tribal differences which had been supported by the segregated tribal-based housing locations. Moreover, these youths, in forcing the pace of change, were in the forefront of a search for an education system and an embryonic intellectual culture which reflected their real conditions.

Hitherto, the intellectual culture of the society had been dominated by whites (both conservatives and Marxists) — and members of this generation were now concerned with formulation of an ideological heritage and with questioning themselves and their knowledge in relation to the concrete realities of their daily lives.

Imperialism has recognised the tremendous energy of the youths and is now working overtime to train a new generation of leaders in the US and West Europe. In 1981 the US Congress passed legislation that provided $4 million yearly for undergraduate and graduate scholarships in the US for black South African citizens. 'Educational programs comprise a large portion of US Corporations and the AFL–CIO have programs to provide assistance in the training and education of South African citizens.'[15] This hasty programme to train and inculcate the ideas of capitalist individualism into the brains of a select few has had little impact on the youths as a whole. Yet this programme represents an important element of the long-term project of imperialism to defuse the intensity of the crisis in South Africa. This project lay at the core of the reforms and constitutional changes which at the same time helped to sharpen the popular alliance.

## The Search for Reforms

Space does not allow an elaboration of the pressures for reform by local and international capital. Codes of conduct and principles of labour–management relations were part of the thrust of capital which pushed the Afrikaans ruling class to make some reforms in order to stem the massive popular resistance. The Wiehahn Commission and the Riekert Commission were two initiatives by the state to subject the growing black trade union movement to greater legal and administrative control and to control the urban dwellers through definite channels of access to jobs and housing.[16] Billed by the media as reforms, these initiatives were lame attempts to come to grips with changing material conditions. The Riekert Commission was explicit in its recommendation to give the rising class of black professionals and traders a stake in the system of repression through community councils. The Black Local Authorities Act of 1982 was an attempt to cement the administrative and legal links between the state and the growing townships. Many power-seeking blacks who embraced this later version of indirect rule and joined the community councils paid with their lives as the uprisings of 1985 rendered the townships ungovernable.[17]

The question of the legal framework for industrial arbitration remains one of the vexing questions facing the urban working class. There is still no unanimity between black workers and their trade unions in their response to the decision by the state to bestow legal recognition to African trade unions which were illegal before the enactment of the Labour Relations Amendment Act of the same year. A recent volume of South African organisations has cited the different unions and their reasons for registration. Major strategic and tactical questions were raised by the package of concessions and control.[18] Questions relating to the power of the registrar of trade unions to intervene in the affairs of unions and the relationships between non-racial and all-black unions persist even though many conferences have taken place to create a federation of black trade unions since 1983. And, as in the fields of the reproduction of knowledge, the international labour centres of capitalism have brought to bear their vast experience in Africa in trying to sanitise trade union leaders with their conception of non-political trade unions.

The overt and covert attempts to control the trade unions through reforms were part of a wider effort of the Botha regime to develop a package of 'constitutional reforms'. This package, called a new constitutional dispensation, involved the selective integration of sections of the aspiring Asian and coloured classes into the state superstructure. A tricameral parliament reflected the specious set-up of racial separation even at the level of parliamentary representation. However, real power was still to be vested in an executive president who ruled through a defence-based State Security Council.

In essence, the reforms were designed to entrench apartheid and race domination and this was most explicit in that the Boers did not even make an attempt to coopt some blacks into this tricameral parliament. As a gesture towards ending the international isolation of the regime, these reforms exposed the backwardness of the political culture of the ruling class. But far more significant was the fact that the reforms articulated in 1983 were to be a smokescreen for greater repression and militarisation in a period when the South African state had intensified its repression at home and destabilisation abroad. The Nkomati Accord with Mozambique in 1984 formed an integral part of the war, repression and reform strategy. The United Democratic Front, which bore the brunt of the repression, published a pamphlet *Repression in the Midst of Reform* to show that in this period many organisations were banned, thousands were detained under section 28 of the Internal Security Act and more persons were charged with treason than at any other time in the history of South Africa. Heightened repression was one symptom of the deepening political crisis. Popular power in the streets shook the confidence of international bankers. Economic depression, strikes, unemployment and troops on the streets graphically exposed to the world the violence and repression of capitalism. It was in this period that the popular alliance of the oppressed deepened and took organisational form in the formation of the United Democratic Front.

### The United Democratic Front
The UDF was formed in 1983 in response to a nation-wide call for a united opposition to the constitutional proposals. As the social questions had sharpened, so had the organisational capacity of the oppressed. This was demonstrated by the

tremendous outpouring of support for the UD.... Plain, Cape Town. Two thousand delegates ... organisations had come together in the biggest rall... represented a plethora of workers, students' gr... organisations, religious groups, Free Mandela Committee... clubs, ratepayers' associations and political groups. (See Ap... of organisations that registered at the conference. Guided by ... racial imperatives of the Congress alliances of the 1950s, the UDF ...... ....ed by the experiences of the youths and workers whose confidence ...... out of Durban and Soweto. The UDF explicitly supported the aims of ... Freedom Charter but was never really an arm of the ANC, though there were in its ranks many veterans of the period of the defiance campaign.

The base of the social composition of the UDF reflected the expansion of the urbanised youth and working-class culture which had matured in the townships after 1976. The techniques of organisation and mobilisation, graphic posters, pamphleteering, films, video, mass meetings, and selective use of the media also corresponded to the new skills and confidence of black workers and their allies. In terms of the class outlook of the leaders, the known national leaders were from the budding black and coloured professionals, clergy, trade unionists, journalists and lawyers. In the communities and the civic organisations, there was a new cadre of full-time organisers who worked around the specific day-to-day struggles of the working people. Some communities had the resources to support full-time organisers. The commitment of the leadership ranged from those who were being pushed forward to the militant leaders who were based in the civic associations.

Democratic structures, mass participation and greater accountability were principles formulated in the day-to-day struggles. The UDF used the level of integration of the South African state to maintain a national body but with regional and local autonomy. Each organisation continued to mobilise in its own area and the differing experiences served to strengthen this front. The existence of a national and legal political organisation which had rallied the oppressed and their allies provided a boost to other unorganised sectors of the population such as farm labourers, domestic servants and the so-called squatters. The UDF did not have a clear strategy to organise all these forces and issued a basic strategy calling for: an end to forced removals, the release of Nelson Mandela and all political prisoners, the lifting of the ban on political organisations and persons, the ending of police harassment, the building of more homes, a stop to rent increases, the lifting of the freeze on township development and for the building of more schools and creches. This UDF charter called for a democratic, united and non-racial South Africa.

The UDF call for democracy did not specify whether it was seeking a modification of the class rule of the South African state, or a form of association or partnership with the ruling class, or the construction of a new social order. Because this conception of democracy was not specific, it allowed for unity of classes and the independence of the different organisations in the struggle against the state oppressions; it is within this broad alliance that the UDF acted as an umbrella and a kindergarten for the political development of the working class.

That the UDF was multiracial and declared for a united non-racial South Africa

153

...ve response from one of the surviving black consciousness ...s, AZAPO. This small group objected to the embrace of the UDF for the ...dom Charter, especially the conception that 'South Africa belongs to all who live in it, black and white'. A few months before the launching of the UDF, AZAPO had launched the National Forum Committee, another alliance of blacks which held that whites had no role to play in the struggle to liberate South Africa.[19] This disagreement between the declared representatives of the black consciousness movement and the mushrooming alliance within the UDF could not become primary as the problems of wages, rent strikes, school boycotts and stay-aways pushed the masses beyond the differences which had dogged the PAC and the ANC for two decades. And the fact that the UDF sought to allow different expressions in its ranks provided for a new level of ideological pluralism, with negative and positive possibilities. The mass democratic character of the UDF, its broad programme of overt and declared opposition to apartheid, its anti-racist and anti-capitalist posture led to a new phase of militant, sustained and organised opposition to the reform proposals. The perceived anti-capitalist posture reflected the strength of the grassroots in this broad front.

In the first year of its formation the UDF operated as a legal organisation, but the state machinery increasingly sought to find ways to wreck the alliance or to divide it politically. When these efforts failed, including an all-out attempt to foment violent clashes with AZAPO supporters, the state responded by arresting the national leaders of the UDF on charges of treason. The legal battles strengthened the local and international notoriety of the UDF, and responding to the efforts of the regime gave the UDF a dynamic and character of its own. A successful campaign to boycott and expose the sham elections of 22 August 1984 was followed by massive stay-aways in the Vaal triangle. These actions strengthened the collective power of the worker–student alliance and sharpened the links between community organisations, trade unions and cultural groups. Democratic forms of expression in the civic organisations were replacing the community councils, and neither the State of Emergency of 1985 nor the unleashing of death squads could return the apartheid society to the period before the formation of the UDF.

### The UDF and the Grassroots

The question of whether the democracy of the UDF was ideologically sound from the formalist point of view paled as the concrete issues in the communities took precedence in the campaigns. The objective of the popular masses was for the right to democratic participation in all spheres of social existence; the right to decent housing, the right to equality before the law, the right to equal education, the right to work, the right to strike without fear of dismissal, freedom of movement, the right to democratic representation, freedom of association, freedom of expression and ultimately the right to life. In this quest the struggle for democratic rights in South Africa was part of the struggles of oppressed peoples all over the capitalist world.

Capitalism had recognised that the struggle for democratic rights was a struggle for a new social system, hence there was the initial project to hive off the most articulate and energetic professionals in the urban townships. The community

154

councils and the expansion of credit to blacks with collateral were all part of a major strategy to speed the process of class differentiation among blacks. The black local authorities were to speed this process of class formation and were to be a political complement to the work of the National Federation of African Chambers of Commerce.

In the midst of the upheavals and uprisings, the councils of the black local authorities announced rent increases, and increased the electricity and water charges for township residents while voting themselves large salaries, houses, cars, travel allowances and other benefits. To support this new drive to get rich, the local authorities were recruiting another police force to supplement the work of the South African police.

Civic associations developed in a clear response to the state-supported community councils. From the outset the UDF had rejected these councils as part of its opposition to the sham reforms. The campaigns against rent increases were to be major campaigns of the grassroots organs and they strengthened the civic associations in proportion to the strengthening of the UDF. When these civic associations were formed, they were by and large multiclass organisations, but it was the determination of the poor which sustained the rent strikes all across the country. This was demonstrated by the capacity to enforce the stay-aways in the Transvaal in 1984 and in Port Elizabeth in 1985.

Stay-aways involve one of the highest forms of working-class action for they ensure that not only the worker lays down tools but that his whole community is involved in a strike against capital and the state. The successful stay-aways reflected the breadth of the organisational capacity of the community leaders and the links which had been cemented between youths, workers, students and trade unions. The September and November stay-aways in the Vaal triangle in 1984 were militant protests against rent increases and the increase in transportation costs. This strike hit the industrial heartland of the society to the point where the state deployed over 7,000 troops of the SADF. South African soldiers had to be involved in house-to-house searches and were now carrying out police work such as enforcing the hated pass laws. The use of the soldiers was the last call in the arsenal of 'total strategy' for the economic, political and psychological aspects of the war by the state against the popular upsurge challenging apartheid power.

To break the stranglehold of the state in their neighbourhoods, the youths struck at the police, police informers and collaborators of the regime in the townships. Police persons, rent collectors, police informers and town councillors soon found out that the state could not protect them on a twenty-four hour basis. To be effective the grassroots organisers had mobilised to break the cycle of violence in township life which has been so vividly captured by South African novelists. Sports clubs and interclub rivalry, which had in the past been solved through violence, was now defused and sport clubs became important affiliates of the UDF.

The confidence generated by the collective actions of the workers and youth, manifest in the important two-day stay-away in November 1984, carried the popular alliance from one level of awareness to the next. Not even the permanent deployment of troops could save the local system of governance as the civic associations became centres of alternative power. By the time the state declared its ultimate weapon, the State of Emergency in July 1985, many councillors had fled, resigned or lost their lives. Between September and June 1985, 240 black officials and 27 mayors had resigned, seeking protection in special centres established to guard them. Those elements in the communities who favoured dialogue with apartheid were isolated and this was most evident in the areas of the Eastern Cape where the state tried to decimate the leadership of the UDF by launching death squads to decimate the grassroots leadership.

The published reports of the Port Elizabeth Black Civic Organisation (PEBCO) showed that this was a community organisation which was spearheaded by worker elements.[20] Its methods of organising and its frequent mass meetings inspired new awareness and broke the mystique of leadership and respectability which plagued African organisations. PEBCO, as one of the principal affiliates of the UDF, had developed out of links between the community and striking workers in 1980 and had been firm in the struggles around rents, bus boycotts and school boycotts. Popular resistance and popular struggles in the Cape focused international attention on South Africa as the state massacred squatters at Crossroads in February and shot down youths in a funeral procession at Uitenhage on 21 March 1985. This massacre on the 25th anniversary of Sharpeville further exposed the limits of the alternatives for manipulation open to the state. By resorting to mass shootings at Crossroads and Uitenhage, the regime ensured that funerals would also become venues for mobilisation and organisation.

Funerals as venues of mass mobilisation brought the clergy and religious leaders to the fore as the death squads murdered those who were considered the most articulate and effective among the UDF grassroots leadership. This was the case in the assassination of the lawyer Mrs Victoria Mxenge, the assassination of budding trade union leaders and the kidnapping and murder of four community leaders from the Cradock Residents Association — Mathew Goniwe, Sparrow Mkhonto, Fort Catala and Sicelo Mhulawuli.[21] Goniwe was the symbol of a new grassroots leader who had worked in the residents' associations of the rural townships.

Mathew Goniwe had been a political prisoner who had been sentenced to four years in 1977 under the Suppression of Communism Act for teaching youths Marxist doctrines. Self-educated, he obtained his degree while incarcerated and become a teacher in 1982 in Graff Reinet. He returned to Cradock in 1983 to become acting Principal of the Sam Xhalie Secondary School. Efforts by the Department of Education and Training to transfer him and later dismiss him precipitated one of the longest school boycotts of over 15 months, involving over 4,500 students. When the UDF was formed in 1983, Goniwe had helped to organise the Cradock Residents' Association to fight the rent increases introduced by the town council. As a full time UDF organiser in the Eastern Cape, Goniwe was kidnapped and murdered on returning from a UDF meeting in Port Elizabeth. The murder of the four activists followed the disappearance of three others in May 1985.

These murders and disappearances showed that, in spite of the new organisational strength of the popular alliance, there was no military capability to blunt the full onslaught of the death squads of the state. The State of Emergency incarcerated hundreds of grassroots organisers and the death squads killed others. A consumer boycott initiated by PEBCO and supported by the UDF in response to the State of Emergency became the precursor to a national consumer boycott which affected the retail trade. New leaders emerged as known leaders were killed or imprisoned and as the funerals became public manifestations of resistance, religious leaders more and more played leading roles in the UDF.

### The Church and the Popular Alliance

Bishop Desmond Tutu, the Rev Alan Boesak and Dr Beyers Naude are prominent religious leaders who have gained international prominence because of their activities in the popular alliance of the UDF. These church leaders were all part of the mass resistance as they defied the state to officiate in mass funerals. They have been patrons of the UDF ever since its formation.

The Christian Church in South Africa, like its counterpart in Latin America, found that it could not administer the spiritual needs of Christians without paying attention to their social needs. So, in spite of the fact that the organised church, especially the Dutch Reformed Church, had played an important role in justifying apartheid, the churches have been important centres of opposition to the racial separation of the society. In this opposition the multiracial churches have been involved in a debate on the significance and meaning of black theology, with particular reference to issues of liberation theology.[22] Desmond Tutu emerged out of this discussion, and out of the search for the church to be more relevant. Desmond Tutu's elevation to be the Anglican Bishop of Johannesburg and his award of the Nobel Peace Prize in 1984 placed the South African church at the centre of anti-apartheid politics.

The South African Council of Churches has championed the democratic calls of the alliance, but church leaders have been equivocal on the questions of disinvestment and the call for international sanctions against apartheid. This equivocation and uncertainty is even more explicit on the question of violence. Because they were in the main sheltered from the daily violence of the system, they continued to preach non-violence even when they were officiating at mass funerals of youths shot down by the regime. In Latin America, where the philosophy of liberation theology has deep roots, there is no equivocation on the part of church leaders as to the need for insurrectionary violence by the oppressed. Archbishop Romero of El Salvador, who was himself gunned down in San Salvador, said:

> Christians are not afraid to fight. They are capable of fighting but prefer to speak the language of peace. However, when a dictatorship seriously attacks human rights and the commonwealth of nation, when it becomes unbearable and all channels of dialogue, understanding and rationality are closed off; when this happens, the church speaks of the legitimate right to insurrectional violence.[23]

Bishop Tutu in South Africa still has not perceived the right of the mass to military action and his non-violent appeals have been given international publicity far out of proportion to the influence of religious leaders in the popular alliance. It was also in part because of the absence of a united front among the working class, or a clear programme from the liberation movements, that church leaders as patrons of the UDF sought to influence the pace of this mass resistance.

157

**The UDF and the Workers**

From the outset of this alliance there were over 18 trade unions which affiliated with UDF while there were others which felt that the working class should maintain a separate existence. The differences were part of the ongoing differences in the working-class movement regarding the strategies and tactics to be adopted in relation to the popular alliance. The tremendous growth of black trade unions between 1973 and 1983 had imposed a historical task on the working class, and their outstanding problem of legal relations with the state continued to affect the quest by seven of the trade unions to form a federation of black trade union members. But the crisis of capitalism did not await a neat resolution of these differences. Arbitrary dismissals, high unemployment, mass retrenchment, low wages and poor safety conditions precipitated a wave of strikes across the society to the extent that the state statisticians could not keep up with the number of days lost through strikes as they were undecided whether to include the stay-aways in their traditional roster of legal strikes. Employers, accustomed to sacking migrant workers, attempted to sack skilled workers, only to recall them and try to victimise 'ringleaders'. This was graphically exposed in the struggle of SASOL workers after the stay-aways in the Vaal triangle.

Strikes, stay-aways, bus boycotts and consumer boycotts thus became the weapons of the working poor. When the state arrested and kidnapped trade union leaders, just as it had treated community leaders, those differences between unions which sought to affiliate with the UDF and those which felt that the UDF was petty-bourgeois and multiracial faded away. From the outset, the national leadership of the UDF called for greater worker participation in the leadership to define clearly the programme of the UDF. The National Publicity Secretary of the UDF, Mr M. T. Lekota, had in 1984 made an explicit call for workers to give direction to the UDF.[24] Questions over the definition of the UDF and of the links between trade unionism and politics were sharpened by the State of Emergency and even more dramatically in the context of the crisis of capitalism where inexperienced trade union leaders had to cope with the militancy of their members and where the growth of union membership far outstripped the organisational capacities of the union. One such union was the National Union of Mineworkers.

The NUM, which has been in the forefront of militant action, had emerged as one of the most important unions in South Africa — in an industry which historically had opposed unionisation. With the migratory history of mineworkers, the NUM was formed in 1982 and by 1985 had registered more than 200,000 members. The rapid growth of this union reflected the long overdue need for worker representation in an area of the South African economy where health and safety regulations were arbitrarily implemented based on the disposition of employers. In the light of the fact that safety conditions in the mines in South Africa are the worst in the capitalist world, such a union was long overdue if only to try and stop some of the more obvious dangers. Not a day passes when two or three miners are not killed through accidents. Every year, 125 out of every 1,000 gold miners die and the death rate among South African miners is eight times that of British coal miners.

These are the factors which quickened the pace of unionisation among the miners. This process of organisation initially came up against the very conservative

White Mine Workers Union which wanted to maintain job reservation long after the material conditions of the society had undermined this hierarchy in the labour processes.[25] However, once the NUM was registered, it could hardly keep pace with the militancy of the workers. In 1984 and 1985 there were more strikes in the mining sector than in any other sector of the South African economy. These struggles, the sharp bursts of victories and reversals, were acting as the elementary school for a section of the working class which will play a fundamental role in the future development of the working-class movement in South Africa.[26]

One section of capital recognised the limits of the migratory system of labour and the attendant backward technology of the old mines. This fraction of capital, led by the Anglo-American Corporation, has been investing in new technology since the 1970s, and this technology requires higher levels of skills and training than those of the present labour force. Anglo-American would like to see a more stable labour force and thus supports the efforts of the NUM to build a trade union, even though it uses its hundred-year experience to combine with other capitalists to drive down the real return for labour. In the strikes of the past two years, striking miners have been exposed to their own share of violence and arrest of shop stewards and union organisers. The single-handed attempt by the NUM to call a major strike for higher wages in August 1985 in the midst of the State of Emergency showed that, without proper organisation, proper resources and mobilisation, black workers cannot yet mount a protracted strike. For though the working class has crystallised and the trade union movement has grown, these unions do not have the resources to support their workers in long-drawn-out industrial disputes.

Because of this fact, the trade unions are still trying to establish themselves; hence the disagreements between unions on priorities. The dismissal of striking workers in South Africa is still a major area of struggle between the fledgling trade unions and the capitalist class. Thus, in 1985, the NUM retreated from its major strike call to concentrate its efforts in the industrial court for statutory legal rights to protect striking workers. The reversals of this period also revealed to the NUM the necessity for unity. It thus broke from the Council of Unions of South Africa (CUSA) to join the search for unity among the major trade unions. CUSA is still caught up with the question of multiracial unions and remains a part of the Azanian Federation of Trade Unions, a body which objects to unity with multiracial unions. More significantly, CUSA remains firmly under the political influence of the International Confederation of Free Trade Unions (ICFTU).

The real differences between the social conditions of black and white workers and levels of stratification in the working class continue to act as a major obstacle to working-class unity in South Africa. Yet in the past ten years, the organised workers, especially the new trade unions, have made major advances in a period of economic crisis and political repression. Organisational strength, collective action with students and community groups and militant strikes have served to set apart the working people of South Africa in a continent where the state power seeks to either control trade unions or buy off the leadership through bureaucratic and state-run trade union federations. International capital and international labour centres have recognised this alliance and the successes of self-organisation in the past decade; hence the rush to grant scholarships to rank-and-file trade union leaders. It is clear that it is the working class of South Africa which poses a fundamental threat to the future of capitalism in Africa. The social system may be able to make cosmetic changes to apartheid, such as scrapping the sex laws and integrating park benches, or even scrapping the pass laws, but it is impossible for the system in its present form to pay African workers a living wage or concede full democratic rights.

For as long as the workers continue to play an important role in the present popular alliance, then for so long will this alliance confront and challenge the social basis of apartheid. It is for this reason that elements of South African capital seek to form an alliance which excludes the working class and the urban poor. Hence the formation of the National Convention Alliance in the search for a political solution to the crisis with the active support of the rising black capitalists, professionals and collaborators. This project for political control, however, needs a political organisation with some historical legitimacy if it is to succeed.

Capitalism is caught in its own contradictions, for the technological advances of the past 25 years have rendered old political forms outmoded, but the ideas of racial superiority/inferiority hold back social development. While the capitalists search for alternatives in the experience of other neo-colonial solutions, the liberation movements need to study the concrete lessons of recent popular alliances in order to develop a clear programme for the prolonged struggle for human dignity.

### Negative and Positive Lessons of Popular Alliances

Experience elsewhere in the past two decades has shown that only the struggle for real social change, guided by the needs of the most oppressed sections of the community, can end the kind of repression and violence which now dominate South African society. Two different examples of popular alliances in Iran and in El Salvador have pointed to differing possibilities. These alliances evolved in the face of repressive regimes and they have both negative and positive lessons for the South African struggle.

A popular alliance in Iran developed in response to the repressive regime of the Shah and the attempt by the US to turn the society into a policeman for the Gulf. In spite of a massive police/military apparatus and the torture and murder by the SAVAK, the youths, students and workers mobilised themselves to overthrow the Shah. There was no clarity as to the leading ideological/political line and in this political vacuum Iranian nationalism took a religious form. Religious leaders dominated this alliance and emerged as the guiding political force when the mass demonstrations led to the resignation of the Shah. State power and religious fundamentalism fostered new forms of repression as the popular movements and democratic forces were hounded out of the country, driven underground or sentenced to death by the decisive power of the fundamentalist legal code. The repression of women was even more complete in this regime. To deepen this nationalist/religious fervour, the leaders prolonged an unnecessary war with Iraq which was as bloody in sending waves of youth to an early grave as it was in wiping out ordinary fighting soldiers on both sides.

The lesson of this popular alliance was that of a clear defeat for the oppressed masses of Iran.

In El Salvador in Central America, on the other hand, a broad alliance developed in the teeth of the struggle to develop a unified military command to engage the US-supported *junta* in the country. Democratic and revolutionary parties were able to merge in the process of a protracted military struggle. The alliance which formed the military/political front was able to transcend political divisions which historically prevented the full mobilisation of the oppressed. The Democratic Revolutionary Front, FDR, as a front of over 40 labour federations, professional groups, community groups, rural co-operatives and clergy, was formed in 1980 as the broadest coalition ever in the long history of popular struggle in El Salvador.[27] This coalition was the political front of a military alliance which had found the need to unite after years of difficult experience in combat pushed them to pool their collective energies against a *junta* which had murdered 50,000 citizens in four years.[28] The Farabundo Marti National Liberation Front (FMLN) was cemented in 1981 out of a coalition of four guerilla groups which had in the past been divided on political and ideological lines. In the face of the overt attempts by the Reagan administration to crush the FDR/FMLN this political–military front developed a clear programme of prolonged popular war against the *junta*.

Two important lessons can be learnt from the El Salvador experience by the youths of the South African popular alliance:

1) Full freedom of expression for all democratic groups, making allowance for ideological and political pluralism.

2) The prolonged struggles exposed the social-democratic section under Napoleon Duarte which had earlier supported the masses but became the political servants of the military dictatorship.

These lessons are pertinent to South Africa, where the quest for political vanguardism is compounded by the legacies of ethnic consciousness among the toiling masses.

## Conclusion

In the midst of the second major depression of this century when famine, drought, poverty and militarism threaten the very reproduction of life in Africa, the South African masses have stood up for their rights and pointed in the direction of a new popular alliance whose base lies with the toiling masses. The South African black working people continue to make tremendous sacrifices and have, in their recent history, made important gains. One of the more important gains has been the unprecedented level of self-expression and self-organisation which strengthens the resolve of the poor to confront the apartheid war machine. A second gain has been the growth of the organisational strength of the working-class organs, whether in the form of civic organisations, youth and student groups or in trade-union organisation. These achievements have brought to the fore the United Democratic Front, as a popular, multiracial, multi-ethnic, anti-apartheid force.

The UDF, even though clearly influenced by the symbols, songs and ideas of the period of the Congress Alliance and the African National Congress, has developed its own character and dynamism as the front was pushed into the war in the streets of the townships and the leaders arrested or murdered. In the uprisings and the

161

insurrectionary violence which rendered the townships ungovernable, spontaneity was more evident than organisation. Such spontaneity stemmed from the lack of a clear political direction in this multiclass front and the programme was not clearly defined beyond the opposition to constitutional dispensation and the call for equal political rights.

International capital remains equivocal in its response to this surge of mass popular action. The international media gave prominence to the non-violent pronouncements of Bishop Tutu as part of their own search for a solution to the crisis which would be favourable to the recomposition of capitalism. Social-democratic elements in the advanced capitalist countries would like to see the rapid removal of the racial barriers to accumulation to make room for the further deepening of capitalist relations in Southern Africa. A rigid but divided Afrikaans political leadership, constrained by the cumulative results of centuries of internalising the ideology of white superiority, stands in the path of the new thrust for political solutions. Thus, Anglo-American, with its experience of neo-colonial cooperation in Africa, seeks to bring this experience to bear and leads the search for some form of power-sharing; hence the 'Convention Alliance'. Measures to bring the present legal statutes up to the changes in material conditions are being rushed through by the Botha regime in its last effort to remain relevant and to be involved in the share of power.

As the ideas towards power-sharing evolve, capital will require the legitimacy of a section of the national liberation movement to give the concept of power-sharing any credibility before youths, workers, students and the rural poor. The question is whether the political and ideological development within these movements can prevent their cadres and leaders from being consumed by the lure of the social capital of the society. The thrust of the power-sharing strategy, whatever its form or manifestation, is to arrest and direct the energy of the poor into accepting piecemeal reforms. To advance the struggle of the workers for safety and better living conditions requires new organisational forms which build upon the concrete experience of the people.

Capitalism is caught in a fundamental contradiction, for while there is the need to dismantle the racial manifestations of apartheid, it was this very racial form of exploitation which guaranteed super-profits. Capitalism has proven incompatible with democratic forms in Africa, for the concrete conditions of reproduction demonstrated that liberal democratic concepts had no place in societies where force or the threat of force lay at the foundation of the alienation of labour power. Already there are formulations by both Marxists and non-Marxists to justify the present direction of power-sharing, if this includes a section of the liberation movements. These conceptions range from the search for stability and peace, to modernisation, cooperation and development, national reconciliation, development of the productive forces or under the theory of the two phases of the 'revolution', the democratic stage and the revolutionary stage.[29] It is significant that the present African leaders who constitute the OAU do not oppose the social manifestations of apartheid, but only its racial manifestations. But the fact is that racism is embedded in all spheres of production and reproduction. The racial divisions and tribal divisions of the working people include their work environment, their location in the labour process, their communities and their responses to capital at the point of production. In all areas, apartheid was able to enact a striking level of separation between Africans, Europeans, Asians and coloured.

Small areas of racial convergences in the period of the UDF were insufficiently developed to contribute *decisively* to solidarity among the working people of different races and ethnic groups. The important question which arises now is: are the crystallisation of the working class, the development of class forces and class consciousness adequate to develop unity among the working people across the barriers created by legal distinctions, racial exclusiveness and the separate trajectories of several important aspects of culture? The answer to this question can only be grasped in the long quest to humanise the environment and to liberate the society from the constraints imposed by the very organisation of the capitalist system of production. Race as a contradiction among the working people cannot be reduced to easy and simplistic materialist categories; nor can the impact on consciousness and the images of self-worth be dispensed with by laws or declarations of equality.

This is not to say that the short-term objectives of the UDF to dismantle the legal framework of segregation and control will not lead to some changes in the society. But it is to reinforce the fact that only the demands of the working poor for changes in the quality of life and the meaning and purpose of work which can begin to deal with the present contradictions of race or the future politicisation of tribe and region. Imperialism recognises the potential for division even among Africans and hence the tremendous investment in Inkatha.[30]

A social movement and political organisation is now needed which will be able to claim the positive traditions of the Chaka Zulu not as a hero of Inkatha but as a hero of all Africans. Such a movement must be able to inspire racial, ethnic and cultural pluralism in the search for a genuine non-racial society. This must include the harnessing of the rich history and culture of the African past without complexes. Debates on the national question in Africa and the 'national unity' of the independence movement have served to reinforce European languages and culture. African languages are deteriorating as the state cuts off the masses from modern scientific knowledge and new skills. A profound example is in Marxist Mozambique, where the quest for a national language reinforced the limitations of Portuguese language and culture on the society while the negative consequences of ethnic differentiation and consciousness deepened.

Thus a genuine popular alliance which is truly non-racial must have as one of its principal tasks the unearthing and enriching of different cultural heritages, languages and traditions while ensuring racial and ethnic tolerance. Such a task has been difficult even in socialist societies and is ultimately bound up with long-term transformation.

The popular alliance of this period registered a leap forward in the process of self-emancipation, and for this historical achievement to be deepened the movement needs to build on the concrete historical experiences of the working people. This requires a political culture which raises the question of democracy from a standpoint which is not concerned with forms of association with the present state but rather the constitution of a new form of community solidarity. It is a process which ensures that the independent forms of organisation of the people develop their own momentum.[31] A corollary to this is the development of an intellectual culture which breaks the mystique of European intellectual traditions (both socialist and capitalist). It requires the unleashing of an intellectual culture which begins with the 'subjective element'[32] and which illuminates the active history of the toilers and does not treat this history simply as a by-product of the history of the ruling classes. Ideas of liberation, cultural development and social change which are borrowed from other societies and imposed on the people can only lead to other forms of alienation and political reversals.

The social questions of apartheid require a long-term solution and in this process the self-emancipation of the working people must be central. New organisational forms are required and must be built in the process of prolonged popular struggle — not compromise — for social emancipation.

## Notes

1. Barbara Rogers, *Divide and Rule: South Africa's Bantustans* (London: International Defence and Aid, 1980).

2. Bernard Magubane, *The Political Economy of Race and Class in South Africa* (New York: Monthly Review Press, 1979).

3. Robert H. Davies, *Capital, the State and White Labour in South Africa 1900–1960* (Sussex: Harvester Press, 1979).

4. B. Magubane, *Political Economy of Race*, pp. 297–330.

5. *Apartheid, The Facts* (London: International Defence and Aid, 1983) p. 82. Another useful source is the hearings of the United Nations Economic and Social Council, *Activities of Transnational Corporations in Southern Africa and their Collaboration with the Racist Minority Regime in that Area.* (New York: UN, 1980).

6. Report in *Sunday Tribune*, 20 January 1985.

7. One of the most recent exposures was in the papers presented at the Carnegie Inquiry Into Poverty and Development in Southern Africa which was held in Cape Town in April 1984.

8. David Hemson, 'Trade Unionism and the Struggle for Liberation in South Africa', *Capital and Class*, no. 16, 1978, p. 20.

9. Tom Lodge, *Black Politics in South Africa Since 1945* (London: Ravan Press, 1983).

10. Lodge in his book examines the documentation of Soweto uprisings by four or five authors. See also the review of books on the 1976 revolt by Baruch Hirson, *Review of African Political Economy* (ROAPE), January–April 1978. This reviewer made a telling point on the absence of a black intellectual culture in South Africa when he said of the seven books on the revolt,

'All are by Whites, and there has as yet been no news of a book or even an extensive account or personal reminiscences from the pen of an African who took an active part in the revolt. Any such writings will have to come from those who fled into exile — and it is these accounts which are most needed if we are to understand many of the problems that were raised by the revolt. There can be little claims to consciousness, "black" or otherwise, if such analyses do not appear'. p. 107.

11. Archie Mafeje, 'Soweto and its aftermath', ROAPE, no. 11, 1978, p. 18.

12. For one account of the formation and early development of the BCM see Rob Davies, Dan O'Meara, and Sipho Dlamini, *The Struggle for South Africa: A Reference Guide to Movements, Organisations and Institutions*, volumes I and II, (London: Zed Press, 1984) pp. 302–308.

13. *Ibid.* pp. 308–510.

14. Freedom Mkwazaki, 'Education in Crisis: 1976 and Today', *Sechaba*, January 1985, pp. 6–10.

15. Kevin Danaher, *In Whose Interest? A Guide to US–South African Relations* (Washington: Institute for Policy Studies, 1984) p. 21.

16. Davies et al., *The Struggle for South Africa* pp. 325–8.

17. O. R. Tambo, 'Render South Africa Ungovernable' *Sechaba*, March 1985, pp. 3–15.

18. Davies et al., *The Struggle for South Africa*, p. 328.

19. Motsoko Pheko, *Apartheid: The Study of a Dispossessed People* (London: Marram Books, 1984) pp. 185–7.

20. Davies et al., *The Struggle for South Africa*, pp. 359–61.

21. See the Amnesty International release on 'Abduction and Murder', 10 July 1985.

22. John W. de Cruchy, *The Church Struggle in South Africa* (Michigan: Eerdmans, 1978) Ch. 4.

23. Quoted in Mario Mandoy Rodriguez, *Voices from El Salvador* (San Francisco: Solidarity Publications, 1983).

24. Reported in the *Sowetan* 20 December 1984.

25. Ruth First, *Black Gold: The Mozambican Miners, Proletarian and Peasant* (Sussex: Harvester Press, 1983). See especially 'Changes in the Mining Industry in the 1970s'.

26. See the three-part series 'South African Mine Workers: Their Conditions and Rights', *Sechaba*, November 1984–January 1985.

27. Robert Armstrong and Janet Shank, *El Salvador, The Face of the Revolution* (London: Pluto Press, 1982).

28. Rodriguez, *Voices from El Salvador*, p. 3.

29. Ruth First, who was part of this intellectual force of the two stage theory, disavowed this theory in an exchange with Archie Mafeje over his analysis of 'Soweto and its aftermath' in ROAPE, 1978, quoted above. The study *Black Gold* was an important break with the intellectual traditions of dual economy or articulation of modes of production.

30. The cultural traditions of the Zulu people have been studied and re-studied by imperialism in the effort to understand the militant legacy of chief Chaka Zulu. See Lodge, *Black Politics*, for the twists and turns of Buthelezi and Inkatha.

31. Wamba dia Wamba, 'Struggles for Democracy in Africa: The Case of the People's Republic of Congo', *Philosophy and Social Action*, vol. X, nos. 1–2, 1984.

32. A major breakthrough had been made by Walter Rodney in the attempt to recapture the history of an oppressed people as part of the struggle for liberation. See *A History of the Guyanese Working People* (London: Heinemann, 1981).

# Appendix I
## Grassroots Organisations Registered for the National Conference of the UDF, 20 August 1983

**Transvaal**

*Student*
Azanian Students Organization (AZASO)
Turfloop
Wits Black Students Society
Medunsa
Soweto Teachers Training College
Soweto College of Education
Transvaal Regional Committee
Students Tuition Society
National Union of South African Students
  Wits SRC
Congress of South African Students
Soweto
Pretoria
Alexandria

*Youth*
Kagso Youth League
Beneni Youth League
Benoni Student Movement
Alexandria Youth Congress
Lenasia Youth League
Bosmont Youth Organisation
Saulsville/Attridgeville Youth Organization
Lutheran Church Youth League
Soweto Youth Congress
Young Christian Students (YCS), Pretoria
  Branch
YCS, Central Branch
Time to Learn
Reiger Park Youth Movement
SACC Youth Desk

*Worker*
South African Mineworkers Union
Municipal and Central Workers Union
General and Allied Workers Union
South African Allied Workers Union (Tvl)
Orange Vaal and General Workers Union
Johannesburg Scooter Drivers Association
Commercial, Catering and Allied Workers
  Union
Council of Unions of South Africa

*Civic Associations*
Winterveld Action Committee
Mamelodi Action Committee
Federation of Residents' Associations,
  Lenasia

Sendane Civic Association
Reiger Park Tenants and Ratepayers
  Association
Coordinating Rents Action Committee
  (CRAC)
Soweto Committee of Ten
Motllakeng Civic Association
Westbury Residents Action Committee
Naledi Civic Association
Emedini South Civic Association
Mapetta Village Civic Association
East Rand People's Organisation
Tembisa Civic Association
Noordgesig Ratepayers Association
Actionville Rents Action Association
Orlando Civic Association
Extension 9 Residents Association, Lenasia
Soweto Civic Association
Huhundi Civic Association
Soweto Residents Association
Krugersdorp Residents Association
Jabulani Civic Organisation
Ten Morgan Residents Action Committee
Diepkloof Extension Residents Committee
Kincoss Civic Association
Ennedate Civic Association
West Rand Action Committee

*Women*
Federation of South African Women
Women's Group, Transvaal Indian
  Congress
University Women's Group, Turfloop
Womens Group, Glynn Thomas
Pfunanoni Women's Club
Black Sash, Transvaal
Lenasia Women's Group

*Religions*
Ecumenical Visitors Programme
The Grail, Johannesburg

*Political*
Transvaal Indian Congress
Transvaal Anti-PC Committee
Alexandria People's Action Party
Release Mandela Committee (Transvaal)
Anti-Community Council Committee

*Other*
Media Action Group
Detainees Parents Support Committee
Africa Perspective
Community Newspaper Project
SASPU National Newspaper
South African Students Press Union
Community Resource and Information
  Centre
Africa News Association
Khovangano Cultural Group
Labour Resource Centre
SPEAK Newspaper
National Education Union of South Africa
Health Workers Association
Workers Support Committee
Media and Resource Centre
National Medical and Dental Association

**Western Cape**
*Student*
Azanian Students Organisation
University of Cape Town
University of Western Cape
Regional Committee
National Union of South African Students
UCT SRC
Muslim Students Association
Congress of South African Students
18 Branches in Western Cape

*Youth*
Cape Youth Congress
Ocean View Youth
Lavendar Hill Youth
Steenberg Youth
Lotus River/Grassy Park Youth
Wynberg Youth
Landsdowne Youth
Crawford Youth
Hanover Park Youth
Rocklands Youth
Portlands Youth
Westridge Youth
Eastridge Youth
Lentegeur Youth
Tafelberg Youth
Silvertown Youth
Heideveld Youth
Bonteheuvel Youth
Kensington-Facreton Youth
Belhar Youth
Bellville Youth
Elsies River Youth
KTC Youth

Guguletu Section One Youth
Guguletu Section Two Youth
Guguletu Section Three Youth
Guguletu Section Four Youth
New Crossroads Youth
Mau Mau Nyanga Youth
Zwelitsha Youth
Zwelintevanba Youth
Nyanga Youth
New City Youth
Mbekweni Youth
Worcester Youth
Zimele Sege (Paarl) Youth Inter-Church
  Youth
235 Youth Groups throughout Western
  Cape

*Worker*
Media Workers Association
Retail & Allied Workers Union

*Civic*
Cape Areas Housing Action Committee
Lavender Hill Residence Assocation
Steenberg/Retreat Housing Area
  Committee
Hout Bay Action Committee
Kensington and Facreton Ratepayers and
  Tenants Association
Avondale Tenants Association
Ravensmead Residents Action Committee
Lotus River/Grassy Park Residents
  Association
Bellville South Housing Action Committee
Bonteheuvel Residents Association
Hannover Park Residents Association
Kewton Residents Association
Silvertown Residents Association
Schoteshe Kloof Civic Association
Crawford Residents Association
Woodlands Housing Action Committee
Westridge Housing Action Committee
Worcester Housing Action Committee
Valhala Park Civic
Belhar Civic
Manenberg Civic
Rylands Civic
Western Cape Civic Association
Six Township zones

*Women*
United Women's Organization
  Claremont
  Wynberg
  Observatory
  Woodstock

Gradens
Athlone
Paarl
Steelenbosch
Ocean View
Worcester
Guguletu
Langa
Kensington
Mbekweni
Kayamandi
Cloeteville
Zweletlemba
New Crossroads
Nyanga
Women's Front

*Religious*
Ecumenical Action Movement
Young Christian Students
Association of Christian Student
Student Union for Christian Action

*Political*
UDF Regional Committee
Cape Town
Northern Suburbs
Southern Suburbs
Athlone
Mitchells Plain
Townships
Stellenbosch
Paarl
Worcester

*Other*
Detainees Parents Support Committee
Grassroots Newspaper
Western Cape Traders Association

## Natal
*Student*
Azanian Students Organization (AZASO)
University of Durban Westville
University of Natal (Pjietermaritzburg)
University of Natal (Durban)
Durban Medical School
Ngoye
Natal Technikon SRC
Congress of South African Students
(COSAS)
National Union of South African
Students (NUSAS)
Durban SRC
Pietermaritzburg Local Committee

*Youth*
Reservoir Hills Youth Club
Lamontvill Youth
Matinane Youth
Tongat Youth Club
Amoltana Youth Club
Kiva-mashu Youth League
Chesterville Youth Organisation
Umlazi Youth League
Isipingo Youth Organisation
Hel
Progress Youth
Verulam Youth
Massakane Youth
Ashport Youth
Sons of Youth Africa

*Worker*
African Workers Association
South African Tin Workers Union

*Civic*
Durban Housing Action Committee
Asherville Ratepayers Association
Reservoir Hills Ratepayers Association
Reservoir Hills Action Committee
Amoytana
Meerbank Ratepayers
Chatsworth Housing Action Committee
Tongaat Civic Association
Joint Rents Action Committee, Nabanati
Greenwood Park Ratepayers Association
Joint Commuters Committee
Pietermaritzburg Ratepayers
Committee of Concern (Sydenham)
Bombay Heights Ratepayers Association
Umlaer Ratepayers Association
Commuters Association
Committee of Concern (Pietermaritszburg)
Committee of Concern (Wentworth)
Committee of Concern (Verulam)
Phoenix Working Committee
Newlands East Ratepayers Association
Cato Manor Ratepayers Association
St Wendolins Ratepayers Association

*Women*
Kwamashu Women's Group
Durban Women's Group
Natal University Women's Organisation

*Religious*
Young Christian Students
(Pietermaritzburg)
Nazareth Baptist Church

Isilido United Congregational Church
Church of the Nazareth
Diakonia

*Political*
Release Mandela Committee
National Indian Congress
Democratic Lawyers Association
Anti-South African Indian Council
Detainees Support Committee
    Pietermaritzburg
    Durban
UDF Regions
Western Areas
North Coast
Meerbank
Pondoland

*Other*
Social Workers Forum
Pietermaritzburg Child Welfare Society
Claremont Advice Office
Zomani Ladysmith Club
National Medical and Dental Association
    (Durban)
Natal Health Workers Association
Ukusa Newspaper

**Other Regions**
*Students*
COSAS Eastern Cape
COSAS Bloomfontein
NUSAS Local — Rhodes University
Black Students Society — Rhodes

*Youth*
Port Elizabeth Youth Congress
Galvandale Youth
West Coast Youth
Independent Youth Association
    (Bloomfontein)
South Cape Youth
COSMOS
All Saints Youth (Oudtshoorn)
Utinhagen Youth
Westville Youth
Congregational Youth (Oudtshoorn)
St Blaiz Roman Catholic Youth
    (Mosselbay)
Saldanha Youth
Pelikan Ontspannings en Kultuur
    Organisasie
Bloomfontein Youth Congress

*Worker*
Motor Assembly and Components
    Workers Union
General Workers Union of South
    Africa
South African Allied Workers Union

*Civic*
Port Elizabeth Black Civic Organisation
Malabar Ratepayers and Tenants
    Association

*Women*
Port Elizabeth Women's Organisation
West Coast Women's Organisation

*Religious*
West Coast Muslim Association
West Coast Church Organisation
Moravian Church, Genadendal
Catholic Students Association
Transkei University

*Other*
West Coast Traders Association
Border Region Delegation
UDF Interim Committee, E. Cape
South West District Primary Schools
Sports Association
Orange Free State Delegation

# 8 The State and Popular Struggles in Ghana, 1982–86

by Emmanuel Hansen

If I ever wrote the things I have seen and the stories that have passed through my mind they would immediately come to me, asking with unbelief how any son of the land . . . could do such a great disservice to the revolution
Ayi Kwei Armah, *Why are we so Blest?*

In 1980 after a visit to Ghana, Ray Bush, a British student of Ghanaian politics, wrote:

Ghana's need for a social revolution should be apparent to any visitor to the presently strife-ridden West African country. Two preconditions for such an event, however, are missing; these are first, the recognition by the people of the need for structural reform and second, agreement as to the nature of this upheaval.[1]

Really, it was not correct to say that there was no recognition by the people of such a need. On the contrary, the mass of the people expected some kind of fundamental change, but Ray Bush was right in saying that there was no consensus on how this change was to come about. When the coup of 31 December occurred the mass of the urban people, the students and the radical intelligentsia saw it as the fulfillment of these conditions. They saw the coup as the spark which would usher in a revolutionary change and transform the socio-economic and political conditions of the country. Two weeks after the coup I was invited by the new Ghanaian government to act as a consultant on the political situation. My own observations, in an article I wrote shortly afterwards concluded as follows:

It is this class base of the regime and the recognition by the leadership that the contradictions cannot be solved within the structure of the neo-colony, which leads one to think that the present regime provides conditions for a meaningful change in Ghanaian society. To say this is of course not to say that there are no problems or that the changes envisaged will come easily. What is significant about Rawlings' second intervention is that it is a coup with a revolutionary import. It is the unfolding of this process which is now firmly on the agenda.[2]

It is now four years since the coup occurred; and it is now time to examine the extent to which the expected transformation has occurred or is occurring. We need to examine this process, delineate its character, capture its essence, speculate on its future, and bring out the possible lessons which can be gathered from this experience.

170

On New Year's Day 1981 Flight Lieutenant Jerry Rawlings for the second time intervened militarily in the political process of the country, toppling the civilian regime of Dr Hila Limann which had come to power only two years earlier in a free and democratic election. The election was supervised by the Armed Forces Revolutionary Council (AFRC), an earlier military *junta* which Rawlings headed To certain external observers it was therefore something of a surprise that Rawlings who had a couple of years earlier presided over the handing of power to the civilian government would now lead a coup against the same government.

## Crisis in State and Society

The coup occurred against the background of a severe economic and political crisis in the country.[3] At the political level the political system was unable to perform the minimum functions which liberal democratic political theory assigns to the state. Political parties were unable to articulate the interests of the broad masses of the people, nor to act as channels of communication between the mass of the people and their rulers. Neither were they able to socialise individuals into acceptance of the basic political legitimacy of the regime, either in terms of the normative attachment to basic political institutions and processes or rules of political practice or the satisfaction of the basic material needs of the mass of the people. Instead they became instruments for the distribution of spoils, 'essential commodities' as they were called in Ghana, or conduits for the allocation of patronage and political kickbacks. Parliament was not perceived as an important forum of political debate or decision-making affecting the lives of the mass of the people. On the contrary, it showed itself as a scene of unedifying and meaningless political squabbles which seemed to bear little relation, if any, to the problems of the country. The judiciary was totally discredited; it was widely believed, wrongly or rightly, that judicial decisions were not based on the merits of cases presented and tried in the courts but in secret backroom deals which took place in the secret societies to which members of the political establishment overwhelmingly belonged.[4] In the urban areas, violent crimes were rapidly on the increase and Accra's reputation as a city of gaiety and active night social life was becoming a thing of the past. It was widely believed that the forces of law and order were in collusion with the criminals or helpless to deal with the deteriorating situation. Attempts by the government to remedy the situation by recourse to the deployment of extra-legal vigilantes only provoked a strong middle-class backlash. In June 1981 there were repeated clashes between the two ethnic groups in the North, the Konkomba and the Nanumba in the Bimbilla district. It was the worst ethnic conflict in Ghana's post-independence history. Estimates put the figure dead at over a thousand. The forces of law and order appeared helpless. This brought widespread dismay. The government appeared ineffectual. To many people it was not governing.

But it was at the economic level that the effects of the crisis were most acutely felt. By the end of 1981 the balance of payments current account deficit was almost $500 million. By 1981 gold production had fallen from 900,000 fine ounces in 1962 to 333,095; diamond production from a peak of three million carats in the 1960s to under one million forecast for 1982. The figures for other industrial products showed similar decline. Inflation was in three figures and the cost of living showed

171

that Accra and the other urban areas were rapidly becoming some of the most expensive places to live in the whole world.[5] This caused severe hardship to the mass of the people. The whole country showed evidence of social neglect. Public health, education, transport and a network of roads which had been the pride of Ghana in the 1960s now looked like shadows of their former selves. In the urban areas the streets showed pot-holes as big as bomb craters. The crisis affected the legitimacy of the regime. The crisis of accumulation which characterised the regime affected its ability to provide the material base for the reproduction of the class which controlled the state. Hence it was forced to act in a virtual predatory fashion in the use of the state for private accumulation. To the mass of the people the government appeared to be not only unable but even more importantly, *unwilling* to do anything about the situation.

The poor performance of the government tended to undermine its constitutional legitimacy. In Ghana as in many developing countries, the legitimacy of the political order is not a settled issue. Important as constitutional legitimacy is, it is not enough to sustain a government. It needs a material base to breathe life and meaning into it and it was in this that many people saw that the regime had failed.[6] The mass of the people wanted a regime which could meet their minimum material needs, ensure the safety of their families and put some meaning into their lives. Any government, constitutional or otherwise, which appeared to be able to undertake these functions effectively would secure support and legitimacy. Hence when Rawlings came to announce that what had happened was not just the changing of the palace guard, but a revolution, namely something which would transform the social and economic order and consequently their lives, people were prepared to listen, and more importantly to give it their support. For the mass of the people in the urban areas Rawlings had come to symbolise some kind of messianic expectation which had been missing in Ghana since the departure of Nkrumah in 1966.

## Character of the Coup

In order to understand the nature of the unfolding of the transformation process, it is important to grasp the character of the intervention itself. It has been asserted that the elements which effected the coup came from outside the Armed Forces.[7] This is only partly so. The elements which effected the coup came from a number of diverse quarters. Four such groups could be identified. The first was a group of soldiers who were closely associated with Rawlings during the time of the AFRC and who for one reason or the other were either dismissed or retired from the Armed Forces with the coming of civilian rule. Rightly or wrongly, they had came to interpret the action against them as persecution for their support for Rawlings and what he stood for, i.e. 'the common man'. The second group was made up of some of the influential elements in Dr Limann's security network. They were crucial to the success of the coup. The support of this group was critical not only for the purpose of effecting the coup but also for the way in which the coup was perceived, thus determining the response to it. The very visible positions of many northerners in the leadership of the immediate post-coup regime, particularly of Chris Atim and Sergeant Aloga Akata-Pore, did have a sobering and mollifying effect on northern elements in the armed forces and civil society in general. As both of these were presented as having worked together with Rawlings for the overthrow of a northern president and a regime which was perceived as dominated by northerners, it diffused the tendency for the northerners in particular to interpret the action against Dr Limann's government in ethnic terms and to respond to it ethnically.

The third group consisted mostly of civilian activists of the June Fourth Movement and very close friends and associates of Rawlings, each with strong ties to critical social groups and interests which could be summoned in time of need to support the coup and thus provide the civilian backing for it. This group was made up of people like Chris Atim, Amartey Kwei, Captain Kojo Tsikata, P. V. Obeng and B. B. D. Asamoah. There are some who insist on the existence of a fourth group of mostly Ewes who were to assume a predominant position in critical areas of public life, both military and civilian, in the later course of events.

Two things can be noted from this. First, diverse elements effected the coup, some from motives of personal loyalty to Rawlings, some from a sense of grievance and some from a vision of a better future. Each group had its own private conception of what to get from the coup and what society should look like after the coup. This was to become one source of tension. But there was a corresponding source of strength. The close relationship between the coup leaders and the leaders of critical social groups meant that Rawlings was provided with a network of key contacts with organisational links to critical social groups which could be relied upon to provide a civilian base for a future government in the event of the coup being successful, and this was precisely what happened. In this way the coup of 1981 was different from other coups in the country. It had the material base to transform itself into something more fundamental, and this was the initial expectation of the left and the progressive groups which supported it. But this strength in a way was also its weakness. The diverse elements which effected the coup plus the diverse elements in the leadership position (although in the initial stages the progressives commanded a hegemonic position) made it difficult for a coherent policy to emerge. Each group brought to the process a different ideological thrust, and in the initial period there was intense struggle for hegemony not only between the left and right elements but also among different fractions of the left. The specific way in which the process developed depended on how this struggle was to be resolved and which group assumed control over the state. It is to this that we shall now turn our attention.

## The Coup and the Revolution

Fellow citizens of Ghana, as you would have noticed we are not playing the National Anthem. In other words this is not a *coup*. I ask for nothing less than a *revolution. Something that would transform the social and economic order of this country.*

The military is not in to take over. We simply want to be part of the decision-making process in this country. Fellow citizens, it is now left to you to decide how this country is going to go from today . . . I am not here to impose myself on this country, far from it.

We are asking for nothing more than to organise this country in such a way that nothing will be done from the Council, whether by God or Devil, *without the consent and the authority of the people* . . . I am prepared to, at this moment, face a firing squad if what I've tried to do for the second time in my life does not meet the approval of Ghanaians . . .

There is no justice in this society and so long as there is no justice, I would dare say 'let there be no peace'.[8] (Emphasis added)

With these words what was to become known as the '31 December Revolution' was announced to the people of Ghana. There is something odd about announcing a 'people's revolution' to the people but we shall leave this for the moment. In Ghana military coups have been justified on two main grounds: restoration of constitutionality or revolution. Thus when in 1966 the military took power from the government of Kwame Nkrumah, it justified its action on grounds of restoration of the spirit of constitutional rule and democracy which it accused Nkrumah's government of subverting. In 1972 when the military overthrew the government of Dr Busia, the action was justified in the name of revolution. In 1979 when the army again overthrew the military government of General Acheampong and his Supreme Military Council, it was justified in the name of restoration of constitutional rule, and indeed Rawlings who then headed the junta actually presided over the transfer of power to a civilian administration. This time he justified his action in the name of revolution. It is of course naive to think that the mere capture of state power by a military junta would in any meaningful sense of the word constitute a revolution. In this particular instance, the capture of state power was meant to be the beginning of a process which would lead to a fundamental change in the structure of power, class relations, political institutions and processes as well as the basic structure of the production process. In this sense when the supporters of the military junta called the coup of 31 December a 'revolution', they only meant it in aspirational terms. This means the capture of state power would initiate a process of change leading to the unfolding of a revolutionary transformation of Ghanaian society.

Let us first look at the specific character of this revolution and the principles by which it can be evaluated. Going back to the quotation with which we started this section five main ideas stand out. First, there was the stated need for revolution, defined in terms of the transformation of the social and economic order. Among progressive groups and individuals there had for some time existed the idea that Ghana's post-colonial problems were such that only a revolution could change them. What exactly this revolution was to imply has never been precisely articulated. There is, however, a consensus that it involves termination of the control of the local economy by foreign multinational companies, changes in the structure of production and production relations, changes in the class structure of control of the state, creation of political forms which would make the interests of the broad masses of people predominant and realisable and a programme which would initiate a process of improving the material conditions of the mass of the people. Those who broadly shared this position I would identify as belonging to the left. Those who entertained the opposite position that there was nothing basically wrong with the nature of the country's structure of production or production relations or the nature of our economic relations with Western capitalist countries or the structure of power, class relations or the nature of state power, and that only certain aspects of its functioning needed to be reformed, I would identify as the right. I am conscious that in both groups it was possible to find some grey areas, but putting it in such broad terms enables us to situate the argument within a framework which is analytically meaningful. Within each group there were some disagreements as regards the specific policies to be pursued in order to realise the broad objectives. But between the two groups the differences were fundamental. It is important to grasp this. Thus when Rawlings came out with the statement that what was needed was a social revolution necessary to transform the socio-economic structure of Ghanaian society, in a statement which amounted to a political manifesto, he put himself firmly within the camp of the left.

In Ghanaian conditions of the time it is possible to argue that on the whole the mass of the urban workers, the students, and the radical intelligentsia in varying degrees shared the left platform, whereas the professionals, the middle classes, the officer corps of the military, the people of the liberal professions like law and medicine, the petty bourgeoisie located in the distributive sectors of the economy, in academia and in the upper layers of the state bureaucracy as well as the chiefly classes generally shared the right-wing outlook. The peasantry, on the whole usually onlookers in the political divide, inclined towards the position of the chiefly classes. In organisational terms the extra-parliamentary political groups such as the June Fourth Movement (JFM), the New Democratic Movement (NDM), the Kwame Nkrumah Revolutionary Guards (KNRG), the Peoples Revolutionary League of Ghana (PRLG), the African Youth Command (AYC), the Pan-African Youth Movement (PANYMO), broadly shared the left position. The parliamentary parties and the establishment-oriented political organisations such as the Peoples National Party (PNP), the Popular Front Party (PFP), the Action Congress Party (ACP), and the Social Democratic Front (SDF) occupied the right-wing platform. So when Rawlings made his announcement which put him firmly on the platform of the left the various organisations reacted according to their ideological positions.

The second important theme in the transformation process was this: nothing was to be imposed on the people from above, least of all from the *junta*. It was to be a revolution from below, although strangely enough, it started from above. It was the dynamics of the struggle itself which would determine the course of events and in this the mass of the people were to be the main agents of the transformation process. The armed forces were only to be part of the decision-making process, not the decision-making process. The armed forces were to hold the ring and make sure that the dynamics of the revolution reflected the interests of the mass of the people. But this could only be possible if the armed forces shared the same class and ideological interests as the mass of the people. This was one of the problematics of the Ghanaian case. The transformation was to be achieved through the principle of consent. Mass democracy and popular participation were to be important tenets of this transformation.

A third principle of the revolutionary transformation following on the need for mass democracy and popular participation was the concept of the people as constituting the sovereign power in the land. In overthrowing the civilian government the military was only acting on behalf of the people. It was only creating the conditions in which institutions could be created for the people to exercise their true sovereign power which was denied them even under the civilian regime of Dr Limann. A fourth principle of the transformation was the recognition that distributive and popular justice was to be an important and necessary condition for the creation of the new society. The fifth principle was the accountability of the leadership to the led and sanctions for leadership failure. Although a number of contradictions could be pointed out between these principles and the action of the coup, we need not allow these to detain us. It was clear enough as a political manifesto. In fact the speech deserves more attention than has so far been given to it. It is an unequivocal call for revolution defined in terms of the transformation of the socio-economic order achieved through democratic struggle and popular participation by the mass of the people. A cardinal point of this transformation process was accountability and reduction or elimination of inter-group conflict through the promotion of social justice. The military coup was to be a catalyst, a social action which would create the conditions for bringing the transformation process into being.

## The Coup and the Public

Public reaction to the coup was structured along class and ideological lines. Depending on one's conception of what the coup implied, political organisations and social groups reacted with reference to their class interests and ideological predispositions. Thus, the progressive organisation which perceived the coup as a left project, with a potential for opening up avenues for social change which they themselves had been unable to bring about, rallied behind it. Included in this were the mass of the urban working or non-working class and the students as well as the radical intelligentsia. On the other hand, the petty bourgeoisie, located in the distributive sectors of the economy, commerce or industry in academia, in the liberal professions or in the upper layers of the bureaucracy and the Armed Force, generally greeted the coup with dismay and apprehension. Although some of them disdained the corruption and ineptitude of the Limann regime, they were apprehensive of a militarist solution to Ghana's problems. The chiefly classes were also on the whole apprehensive, if not covertly hostile. The peasantry adopted a wait-and-see attitude but on the whole they shared the apprehension and suspicion of the chiefly classes. They had seen so many military coups, liberations, revolutions with a claim to improving their lot but which had not made any changes that they had become cynical.

It is now time to consider how the ideas and principles embodied in Rawlings' first major political statement were put into some programmatic form.

## Government and Administration

The first task after capturing state power was to set up a system of government and administration to run the country and also to translate the ideas of the 'revolution' into practice. A Provisional National Defence Council (PNDC) was formed with Jerry Rawlings as its chairman. It was made up of seven members, four from the military and three from civilian life. Both the military and the civilian members were chosen with the view of enlisting support from critical social groups. Thus the appointment of Brigadier Joseph Nunoo-Mensah was meant to ensure the support of the senior officers of the armed forces, and to present the 'acceptable face' of the revolution. He was widely respected as a good professional soldier and was thought to have good links with the West. Besides, he had a personal stake in the coup. Having been summarily retired by the Limann administration, he entertained some pleasure at seeing the government which had treated him in such a cavalier fashion thrown out. The appointment of Warrant Officer Adjei Boadi, in spite of his being a close personal friend of Rawlings, was to ensure the support of the young officers while that of Sergeant Aloga Akata-Pore was to bind the men of the ranks firmly to the *junta*. The appointment of the civilian members showed the same political considerations. Thus, Armartey Kwei,[9] a militant labour leader, was appointed to the council in order to ensure the backing of the urban working class, while the appointment of Chris Atim Bukari, a former student leader, was to identify the youth and the student movement in a more tangible way with the political process. Father Damuah, an eccentric Catholic priest with a reputation for outspoken frankness, was appointed probably to attract the 'honest and patriotic' sections of the petty bourgeoisie.

The Council was constituted as the highest policy-making body in the country. It combined both executive and legislative functions, although in practice its chairman performed these functions with or without its advice. Law emanated more as decrees from the chairman than as a result of consensus arrived at by members of the Council. At its inception it was expected to form a broad framework of policy to be carried out by another body, the Committee of Secretaries. In practice it turned out to be nothing of the sort. It became a perfunctory body which met infrequently and intermittently on an *ad hoc* basis. Its main function appeared to provide a stamp of legitimacy for decisions taken elsewhere. The diverse elements which made up the membership of the Council gave it the semblance of a national team, although they detracted from its political and ideological coherence.

In view of the way things functioned or rather did not function, certain observers have persisted in asserting the existence of an Ethiopian-style *Dergue* which functioned in a clandestine manner. It is claimed that this was the real political decision-making body. Its composition and *modus operandi* has remained secret. It is clear, however, that if such a body existed its ideological predispositions were different from the left position articulated by the progressive organisations, the urban working classes and the radical intelligentsia.

**The Committee of Secretaries**
The next stage in the establishment of a framework of administration was the formation of the Committee of Secretaries, made up of politico–administrative heads of government ministries and which functioned as some kind of a cabinet. Unlike the Council, it met regularly once a week to discuss day-to-day problems of running the country. It did not, however, share collective responsibility, a fact which hindered its political cohesiveness. Another problem was the need to represent various areas and ethnic groups in the country. This meant that the final body which emerged was even more ideologically diverse and unwieldy than the Council. This affected not only its capacity to develop coherent programmes but

177

the Committee itself often became the scene of intense ideological struggles as different members sought to bring into being programmes which represented their ideological perspectives or that of the group which they represented. An attempt to rectify the situation by bringing out *Policy Guidelines* by which secretaries were to act ended in deadlock and the final document which emerged was a reflection of the ideological incoherence of the leadership. The only thing which could have remedied the situation was the existence of a well-articulated ideological body with a clear programme which would draw the main outlines of policy for the Committee of Secretaries to implement. Indeed, when it was inaugurated, this seemed to have been the expectation. But as no clear ideological line emerged, except from the National Defence Committee which was outside the main structure of government and had in fact no legal basis of power and authority, the Secretaries continued to function according to their ideological predispositions. The result was of course chaos. Neither of these two organisations helped to translate the principles embodied in the quotation into practice.

## Organs of Popular Power

Clearly, if, as we have seen, there were no changes within the existing structure of the state apparatus to accommodate the transformation process, then new machinery would have to be created from outside the formal structures of government. These were what came to be known as the organs of 'popular power' or 'people's power'. They were the main innovations at the institutional level which the coup initiated. For the mass of the urban people and the left in general, they represented the hope of the future and a vision of the new society. It is not surprising that it was this particular innovation which invoked the bitterest opposition from the ranks of the petty bourgeoisie. But it was clear that, if the people were to be the main instruments of the transformation process and the architects of their own destinies, then it was necessary to create certain structures and institutions through which their collective energies could be mobilised and chanelled into social action in accordance with the dynamics of the transformation process. The institutions created were the Workers' Defence Committees (WDCs), the People's Defence Committees (PDCs), the National Defence Committee (NDC), the Citizens' Vetting Committee (CVC), the National Investigation Committee (NIC) and the Public Tribunals. These constituted the counter-institutions of state power of the post-colonial state. Every instrument of the coercive power of the state was countered by one of these organisations. It was not surprising that the right in government and the petty bourgeoisie as a whole, seeing the potential of these organisations for fundamental changes in society, accused the NDC of running a 'parallel government' but this is precisely what a revolution implies: the creation of new and counter institutions which would in the initial stages run parallel to the existing ones until mustering enough material support and strength to replace them altogether. We shall now look at the operations of these institutions and see to what extent they contributed to the unfolding of the dynamics of the transformation process.

### The Defence Committees

If the administrative changes were not spectacular the political changes were, as we

178

have said, the most innovative aspects of the new changes put into force as a result of the coup action and the proclamation of the process of the revolutionary transformation. The Defence Committees were of two types, the Workers' Defence Committees (WDCs) and the People's Defence Committees (PDCs). The formation of these bodies was announced soon after the seizure of power. The WDCs were set up in work-places and the PDCs were set up in neighbourhood areas. The WDCs were to be the main instruments of mobilisation in the structure of production and to some extent in distribution and the PDCs were the main instruments of mobilisation at the level of residence. At the time when the formal leadership of the Trades Union Congress had virtually lost its legitimacy among the rank and file workers due to what was perceived as its compromising position on worker demands, the WDCs became the main centres for the expression of shop-floor militancy and struggle within the labour process, first for the control of the labour movement and secondly for the control of the labour process itself. They were organised and controlled by the workers themselves and displayed worker militancy which had not been seen in the country since the days of the independence struggle. Later the state introduced broad guidelines to exert some control over their actions.[10] The initial phase of their activity was marked by severe conflict within the labour unions against the old leadership and against management in the labour process. A particularly ugly form of this confrontation occurred at Ghana Textile Plant in Tema in November 1982. Initially, the leadership of the PNDC either encouraged or turned a blind eye to these actions as it found it necessary to weaken the labour movement which could be a rival to its claim to the monopoly of power and loyalty of the working class. It was, however, not enthusiastic about the conflict with management. It wanted particular managerial elements to be disciplined whereas the workers wanted the entire concept of the managerial class to be an open question and to use the occasion to review the entire relationship between capital and labour. Initial acts were marked by suspensions, dismissals, indefinite leaves and lockouts of management. The workers were also concerned with participation in decision-making and participation in the planning of the economy at the sectoral level. Also demanded was a more equitable distribution of resources and proceeds. In this the workers became embroiled in a four-cornered conflict with the old leadership of the trade unions, with management, with the petty-bourgeois right wing and with the political leadership of the PNDC.

The most interesting feature of the defence committees, particularly the WDCs, was their relentless struggle for an independent position from the political leadership. Although they supported the general line of the revolutionary process, they were particularly anxious not to subordinate their class interests completely to that of the state. They were particularly pressing on issues of control of the production process, the issue of public corruption, particularly of the managerial classes, equal access to state resources in the form of welfare provisions, equality in the distribution of material goods and services[11] and participation in decision-making at all levels. Their relationship with the PNDC was characterised by conflict and cooperation. The defence committees and other organs of popular power became institutional mechanisms for the expression of class demands, instruments for class struggles and structures for the consolidation of class gains. In this, workers showed a marked maturity compared with workers' actions of previous decades. It was in this context that they rebuffed Jerry Rawlings' exhortation to concentrate on production and leave the realm of politics with the retort, 'production for whom?'. They wanted the question of power to be settled first. The People's Defence Committees similarly took up such questions but here, especially in rural communities, the class lines were not very sharp and their activities were marked by less conflict, although in some cases they also found themselves in conflict against the rural power structure and class privilege. Where this was particularly buttressed by a gerontocracy, the conflict took on the character of generational struggle.

Many political commentators have remarked on the spontaneous origins of the defence committees. Both in terms of their origins and operations they demonstrated the Fanonist concept of the strength and weakness of spontaneity. Their strength lay in the fact that they provided at a very crucial moment and in the absence of formally structured and well-articulated working-class parties, an organisational basis for the conduct of class struggles, the expression and consolidation of class power. Their weakness lay in the mistakes they committed in the process of working out a strategy of struggle: they attacked far too many fractions and centres of power of the petty bourgeoisie simultaneously without waiting to consolidate and then attack the other fractions. They did not pay sufficient attention to the organisation of their rearguard in order to be able to withstand the inevitable backlash once the petty bourgeoisie had recovered from its initial shock. They naively assumed that in their struggle against capital and particularly foreign capital, the state and the political leadership would always come to their aid. But perhaps the most serious weakness was their inability or reluctance to recruit the peasantry and present a worker/peasant front. Some of their members did show certain features of infantile leftism in behavioural rather than doctrinal terms but later charges of 'ultra leftism' as the reason for their suppression could not be sufficiently substantiated. It was an excuse for opportunists and the rightist elements in the PNDC to suppress them as they did not fit into the new scheme of things being planned.

It would appear that the concept of the PDCs and WDCs had existed in the JFM where they were called *Revolutionary Committees* before the onset of the coup of 31 December. It was regarded as an important organisational nexus of the JFM. The idea seems to have originated after the visit of Jerry Rawlings and some of his very close associates to Libya in the summer of 1980. It is even claimed by certain JFM supporters that in certain areas they had existed in embryo form prior to the coup. So when, soon after the coup, Rawlings made his announcement about the defence committees, he was in fact appealing for the implementation of a programme which was already in existence. The fact that it was embraced by practically the whole nation, and not just the JFM, was an indication of the existence of revolutionary ferment at that time. This explains its spontaneous character. The first issue of the *Workers' Banner*, organ of the JFM, contained the following:

Only the revolutionary institutions of the (civil and uniformed) workers, poor people — *Revolutionary Committees* of Workers, Soldiers, Policemen, Farmers,

Peoples Congresses etc. – can enable all of us to take active part in government, to have a voice in the utilisation of our wealth, to demand which fishing nets or cutlasses should be imported . . . These committees of the ordinary people, will hold mass meetings such as durbars of the other ranks in the barracks or peoples congresses in the towns and villages, on the farms, in the factories, mines, shop floors everywhere, to debate national issues and to take decisions affecting the lives of the ordinary people. That is why the *peoples committees* represent the highest form of democracy. The budget proposals will be debated by the farmers in their villages, the workers in the factories, mines and on the shop floors, the soldiers and police in their barracks and their collective decisions will become the law of the day.[12]

This is the clearest expression of the ideas and the concept of the Defence Committees. In the way they were envisaged the Defence Committees were to be engaged in a number of activities. They were to be the main instruments of participatory democracy and the expression of the power of the people. They were to be the mechanisms by which the people were to protect the 'gains' of the revolution. In certain areas they formed food and agricultural brigades and did useful, if contentious, work in the rural areas. In the urban areas they engaged in the mundane task of refuse collection which had practically broken down as the state did not have the vehicles nor the materials in the form of disinfectants to cope with the mounting refuse piled sky-high in many areas of Accra and the urban areas. They also appointed themselves price control inspectors and patrolled the markets — some with troops — to bring down prices to their 'realistic' level. In certain areas they started to assume judicial powers and to settle local disputes in the way that the political parties had done in their early and formative years.[13] They exercised powers of arrest although unlike their counterparts in other countries they never had powers of meting out sanctions[14], and there was no legal basis for any of the functions they performed. Throughout the period, the state refused to give them legal backing.

One particular area where the support of the committees was very crucial in consolidating the regime was in the area of intelligence and security. At the time when it appeared that the security network had practically broken down and the regime had not had time to build a new one, these organisations played a vital role in monitoring the movement of 'suspicious' people. They regarded the regime as theirs and were prepared to defend it with their lives if possible and some indeed did. On 19 June 1983 when the regime faced its most severe danger in the form of a near-successful coup attempt, it was the PDCs and WDCs which mounted road blocks and rallied unreservedly to the support of the regime.

If the defence committees did useful work, there were certain aspects of their activities which attracted criticism even from the leadership of the PNDC. Jerry Rawlings, in his most generous tribute so far to the defence committees, before the move to the right, declared in a major policy statement in July 1982:

We would not be exaggerating if we said that since the introduction of the People's Defence Committees and Workers' Defence Committees, notable contributions have been made to our national progress. In the first place these institutions have provided for the first time a mechanism by which the man in the street can take a meaningful part in the political process . . . The introduction of these institutions has arrested the cynical apathy which had gripped this nation.[15]

But he also went on to say:

Let us have the courage to state that in certain cases, these organisations have not always acted in ways which we can be proud of. In certain areas they have reportedly assumed police powers, made rash allegations against management personnel, and have had problems with local trade unions. Some have been infiltrated by agent-provocateurs and counter-revolutionaries and in certain areas they have constituted themselves as political witch-hunting committees.[16]

The assessment of the defence committees were mixed and depended largely on normative attitudes towards them. Those who saw them as instruments of class struggle and expressions of working-class power applauded their political role, whereas those who saw them as labour brigades deprecated their political roles and made unfavourable judgements about them. In the initial stages they offended potential allies by a show of unnecessary belligerence and a stridently anti-Western and anti-establishment position which in the frustrating circumstances of Ghana at the time was understandable, and did provide some entertainment and political therapy for the masses but was not necessarily appropriate, nor did it help their long-term cause; they were to adopt a needlessly anti-clerical posture which brought them into premature confrontation with the establishment churches. They did not wait to consolidate class power before moving on to the next stage. This also was understandable in the face of the refusal of the leadership even to discuss the question of the programme of the 'revolution'. They were perhaps over-zealous in enforcing legislation against the petty bourgeoisie in a situation which some perceived could easily provoke a backlash which they were too weak to contain. Here too their position must be understood. Their legitimacy depended on continuing support from the mass of the workers which in turn depended on their ability to resolve the question of power as quickly as possible. They have been accused of not forming alliances with other classes but considering the many times that the workers had been sold down the river by progressives and 'progressive juntas', preaching working class salvation, it was not surprising that they adopted a purist, almost exclusivist and politically puritanical outlook. Any association with any of the discredited leaders or social groups would have undermined their legitimacy in the eyes of the mass of the workers.

**National Defence Committee**
In its original form, the National Defence Committee (NDC) was called the Interim National Co-ordinating Committee (INCC). In July 1982 its name was changed to the NDC and its composition enlarged. This was an attempt to remedy some of its problems. It was set up to co-ordinate the activities of the defence committees. It would appear that there was some disagreement in the leadership over its establishment.[17] It provided some kind of secretariat for directing and supervising the activities of the defence committees. It was made up of the representatives of the progressive organisations in the country selected more on an individual than an

organisational basis. Early statements by Jerry Rawlings, certain leaders of the government as well as the progressive organisations, gave the impression that the NDC was to provide the nucleus of the organisation of a political movement but nothing came out of it.

The NDC organised the defence committees on the basis of zones and districts and was responsible for political education and training of cadres, two activities which were also to be the source of considerable friction and conflict with the government. It appointed political commissars to the police and the armed forces. It published its own newspaper the *Nsamankaw* in order to propagate the ideas of the 'revolution'. It saw itself as being in the forefront of the revolution. Its inability to function very smoothly was as much an effect of the hostility and lack of support from the PNDC as its own sectarianism, which the various representatives of the main progressive organisations indulged in freely. Like the defence committees it came in for a lot of criticism from the political leadership and from Rawlings in particular from the middle of July 1982 till it was abolished towards the end of the year. It was reconstituted the following year, only to be abolished again in December 1984.

The NDC became the organisational focus around which leftist groups and individuals coalesced and functioned. It was, however, not an organisation of leftist political organisations. Although membership was drawn predominantly from the left groups, personnel were selected more on the basis of individual merits than their organisational links. But care was taken to ensure, though unequally, the representation of all leftist groups. The NDC was composed predominantly of students and its ideological frame reflected the stridency of student leftism. Its behavioural tendency also reflected this tradition. Its preference for the politics of conspiracy and its tendency towards sectarianism and factionalism undermined its effectiveness as a vehicle for coalescing all leftist forces and a mechanism for building a left political movement out of the various groups. In its initial phase it tended to be suspicious of the older generation of the left associated with Nkrumah and sought to keep it at arm's length. As essentially a student group it was not surprising that its approach to politics was governed by the intellectualism of campus politics. It did not seem to differentiate between the exercise of state power and the capture of a junior common room political machine. Another problem was also the intense rivalry and mutual suspicion between the two main groups — the NDM and the JFM.

**The Public Tribunals**
The public tribunals were bodies set up to promulgate and institute the ideas of popular justice. They were to respond to three main problems in the system of the administration of justice in the country: its slowness and extremely cumbersome procedures, its inflexibility and intimidating character particularly to people of the lower classes, its alienating circumstances in class terms, its class character and widespread corruption. Rightly or wrongly, it was widely believed by the mass of the people that for ordinary persons the courts were not centres for the administration of justice and dispensation of fairness but mechanisms for enforcing class privilege and instruments by which the ruling class held on to power and intimidated its

opponents. Over the years the judicial system had been open to the most blatant political interference with the administration of justice. It was a known fact that any military adventurer who had in the past captured political power could secure pliant justices to do his bidding. It had not been particularly different under civilian regimes. There were two particular aspects of the judicial system which were oppressive to the mass of the people: its class character and the politically partisan nature of its functioning. The purpose of the public tribunals was to rectify these and to provide the mass of the people with a judicial system which could dispense popular justice and fairness.

It should be emphasised that this was not the first time that special tribunals have been set up in the country. Right from the time of the First Republic special tribunals have been very much a feature of the judicial system, but this was the first time that special tribunals had been set up in response to the demands of class justice: a symptom of the intense nature of the class consciousness in the country. The operating procedures of the tribunals were different from the ordinary courts. First there was no appeal and secondly rules of evidence and criminal procedure were different. A tribunal could even try accused persons *in absentia*. Its composition was to reflect the class character of the country. Only its presiding judge had to be a person with some professional knowledge of the law. Unlike the special courts set up in the past, the extent of its jurisdiction was unlimited. It could sit on any case and there was no body to supervise it or review its decisions except the head of state who had the power to reduce and not increase sentences. It could and often did pass the death sentence. Initially there was no appeal, a provision which aroused considerable opposition from the incumbent Chief Justice as well as members of the Bar, the establishment churches and certain civic groups. This feature was later changed to allow retrials and appeals.

Initially the operations of the courts aroused considerable public interest. The early proceedings where high public officials, those often regarded as the high and mighty and therefore immune from legal action, were accused of political corruption or misuse of public office drew approval from the public. To see these people being openly rebuked for crimes they were alleged to have committed or confessing to a catalogue of crimes before a board made up of ordinary people like themselves restored the confidence of the lower classes in the judicial system and provided some kind of psychological satisfaction. But the severe punishments it meted out brought mixed reactions. For the mass of the people, however, it was a good system which demonstrated the legal equality which for a long time had merely existed in the books. There was provision for legal representation, but the Bar Association boycotted the tribunals; it claimed that they violated fundamental principles of human rights and it opposed the concept of popular or people's justice which it regarded as nothing more than kangaroo courts. Thus the high and mighty did not have the benefit of using their wealth to engage the most brilliant legal minds to assist their defence.[18] Later on as the tribunals began to devote more and more attention to 'political crimes' against the state, public interest began to wane as it was also perceived that they were being used by the regime to keep itself in power. Secondly, the fact that it took so long to try military personnel who were accused of crimes against civilians undermined the legitimacy of the courts.

What really led to the waning of public interest in the tribunals was the move by the state itself as part of its general disengagement from populism to de-emphasise the class nature of the tribunals. It began to show anxiety about the tendency of the mass of the people to see the tribunals as instruments in their hands to protect themselves against judicial encroachments from the petty bourgeoisie right. Now the tribunals have lost their initial popular appeal and are regarded as instruments with which the government seeks easy conviction against its defined political opponents. They are now looked upon in the same light as the 'traditional' courts, not as instruments for the dispensation of popular justice or mechanisms for removing the traditional injustices and weaknesses of the judicial system. Now the public tribunals are even being accused of corruption.

**The National Investigation Commission (NIC)**
The NIC was a body set up to investigate all cases of corruption both actual and potential. It was empowered to investigate the finances and bank accounts of anyone it deemed worthy or anyone whose bank deposits amounted to 50,000 cedis or more. Anyone unable to give a satisfactory explanation of such monies was liable to face forfeiture. Its stated purpose was to discourage corruption and *kalabule* and mop up excess liquidity in the system. Although the Commission did some useful work in the initial phase of the coup by unearthing many cases of corruption, its net effect was to undermine public confidence in the banking system. Its other ambition of nipping out crimes of corruption before their commission was not very successful and in course of time it was subjected to the same kinds of accusations by the mass of the people as the public tribunals. It was accused of allowing people of influence and wealth to escape scrutiny.

**The Citizens' Vetting Committee (CVC)**
This body was set up to investigate and punish cases of corruption. Unlike the NIC which confined itself to purely investigatory activities and did not mete out punishment, the CVC sessions were public affairs of a more or less judicial nature. It had wide powers of investigation and was mandated to investigate the lifestyle of any person or persons whose personal and social life did not seem to accord with what was presumed to be his or her known income. It was particularly active in chasing tax-evaders, and cases of bureaucratic corruption such as the granting of import licences, cases of over-invoicing and under-invoicing, irregular bank loans, customs violations and infringement of price control as well as currency regulations. Since most of those who appeared before it were members of the petty bourgeoisie it was seen by some as an instrument against this particular class.

The political significance of these bodies has declined considerably in recent years with the movement away from 'populist nonsense' to 'pragmatism'. Some of the organisations like the NDC have been abolished. Others have been allowed to operate but their political character has been de-emphasised and their technical functions stressed; specifically their class appeal has been suppressed. For instance the NIC and the CVC have been merged together into a single body called the Commission for Revenue Collection run by petty-bourgeois members of the bureaucracy. Their political character as an instrument of transformation has been shorn and the new body has become just like any other bureaucratic organisation.

The organs of popular power were set up in response to the pressure of the forces released by the coup of December 1981 and subsequent events; and they were moved by the momentum of these forces. They did not belong to the formal structure of the bureaucratic apparatus of the state and the existing state organisations did not have any direct supervisory control over them or their actions. They were subject in the last analysis only to the control of Jerry Rawlings as head of state, chairman of the Provisional National Defence Council and chairman of the National Defence Committee. In this way they enjoyed a considerable autonomy and it could not be otherwise for they could not be subject to the control of the very organisations and state structures they were supposed to transform.

## Progressive Organisations and the Coup

In addition to the organs of popular power there were also political organisations and groups which provided varying degrees of support for the regime and for the process of political transformation. These were the six progressive organisations. They were the June Fourth Movement, the New Democratic Movement (NDM), the Kwame Nkrumah Revolutionary Guards, the African Youth Command, the People's Revolutionary League of Ghana and the Pan-African Youth Movement. Of these the most important politically were the June Fourth Movement and the National Democratic Movement and I shall concentrate on these two.

### The June Fourth Movement

This owes its origin to the incidents of 4 June 1979 when Rawlings first seized power. It took its name from the political incidents of that day and the significance of that episode in the history of the struggles of the mass of the people in the country for emancipation. In August 1979 when it became clear that in spite of appeals from some of the militant students, Rawlings and the AFRC were determined to proceed with plans for demilitarisation and to hand over power to a civilian administration, they began to plan for the formation of a movement which would act as a political watchdog and protect the 'gains' of the June Fourth Revolution. The initiative came from a small group of militant student leaders who had visited Cuba in the summer of 1978 in connection with the World Festival of Youth. Cuba provided both the ideological inspiration and the political model in the form of the July 26 Movement.

After the hand-over of power this small group of students formed the June Fourth Movement and approached Rawlings to be the Chairman. Overcoming his initial suspicion of political organisations, he was quick to recognise what an enormous advantage it would be to have at his disposal such a group which he could use as a platform in his conflict with the PNP administration which had then embarked on a policy of persecution against him and his close associate Captain Kojo Tsikata. He therefore agreed to become Chairman of the JFM while Kojo Tsikata became a member of the central committee. Chris Atim was the General Secretary. Thus began the uneasy love affair between Rawlings and the JFM. The

186

movement organised huge rallies at each anniversary of 4 June and presented Rawlings as its prize speaker. The leaders relied on the charismatic personality of Rawlings to capture the imagination of the Ghanaian public. He on his part used the movement as a platform to defend the AFRC and its record in office and to personally vindicate himself.[19] JFM leaders were ecstatic and began to talk of how Rawlings had 'matured' from his idealistic position of preoccupation with the 'moral revolution' of the 1979 period to a much clearer appreciation of the 'objective forces' of history.

This was the humble beginning of the JFM. After the coup it became the bandwagon of individuals with all kinds of radical causes. Ideologically it spanned a wide spectrum. The dominant ideological position was the neo-Marxist dependency/underdevelopment school in various forms. The intellectual influences came from Fanon, Cabral, Walter Rodney, Nkrumah, Paul Baran and André Gunder Frank. Whatever attention was paid to the Marxist classics was devoted, understandably, to Lenin but also to the version of Marxism from Progress Publishers of Moscow rather than to the works of Marx and Engels. The political vision of the membership spread across a wide spectrum of the left and sometimes not so left. Thus, some people favoured a Ghana modelled on Cuba, while others in the JFM looked to a Scandinavian welfare state model. What did bind many of the supporters together was the sense of outrage at the performance of the political leadership under Dr Limann, a deep sense of youthful idealism and the belief that with 'activism' and committed leadership Ghana could be pulled out of the rut. The JFM prided itself on activism. Its political and ideological mouthpiece was the *Workers Banner*. After the coup, taking advantage of resources of the state, it became the ideological mouth of the left too.

**The New Democratic Movement**
The NDM seems to have started in 1980. The moving spirits appear to have come from the Law Faculty at the University of Ghana where a mixture of Mandel's Marxism and dependency/underdevelopment theory was being propagated. It was seen, wrongly or rightly, as more of an academically oriented political discussion group than a serious political organisation contending for power. It prided itself on its ideological and intellectual purity. Its activities were very much confined to students. It was reputed by its critics to have spurned political activity, claiming prematurity of 'objective political conditions'. Its intellectual and ideological mouthpiece was the *Direction* which pre-dated the movement itself. At the time of the coup of December 1981 it had practically ceased production. After the coup it came out infrequently only to cease publication soon after.

**The Progressive Organisations, the Coup and the Revolutionary Process**
As we indicated earlier the JFM was ecstatic about the coup. It embraced it as if it had been organisationally part and parcel of the planning process; it behaved as if the coup was its own. In a way it sought to appropriate it and articulate its political programme. It moved to constitute itself as the political wing of the revolutionary process using the NDC and the defence committees as its main instrument and to

187

define the terms under which other political organisations were to play a part. If possible it was not going to allow any other group to dislodge it from the position of hegemony which it carved for itself. What was even more significant, it did not perceive itself as organisationally distinct from the PNDC government. It brought to the coup much-needed student and popular support; some of the early supporters had been student leaders. Prominent among these was Chris Atim who, as we have seen, had become General Secretary of the JFM before the coup, and was later to become a member of the PNDC.

The NDM's initial reaction to the coup was the opposite of that of the JFM. It showed initial scepticism and caution, which its supporters attributed to political maturity although JFM cadres impatiently dismiss it as a piece of political opportunism. The NDM initially argued for organisational affiliation to the NDC and the military junta. Although this in itself could not guarantee success, as the experience of Ethiopia shows, it was the correct position. It did not, however, make it a condition for collaboration and before long it was vying with other organisations for positions on the NDC and in government. It sought to find a foothold among certain sections of the labour force, particularly among the workers at the Ghana Textile Factory in Tema. It claimed that its relationship with the junta was based on 'critical support' although the record of its collaboration showed more evidence of support than critical appraisal.

These political groups formed the organisational basis of the transformation process. In addition there were clusters of unorganised left positions which also claimed support for the transformation process. Some of these were old Nkrumahists. At the class level the urban working or non-working class on the whole supported what it saw as the revolutionary thrust and so did the lower stratum of the petty bourgeoisie. Tema, the industrial capital of Ghana, was particularly noted for worker militancy. The political slogan and mobilising battle cry was 'power to the people' and the ideological platform was the National Democratic Revolution. This was the slogan and platform around which the regime sought to unite various sections of the left as well as a certain fraction of the petty bourgeoisie to its politics of transformation.

It would seem that here we have a military group which in many respects does not accord with the general character of a coup as we have seen it on the continent. It was what one might call a 'leftist *junta*' with active participation from the ranks of progressive groups and individuals, both civilian and military.[20]

## Dynamics of the Transformation Process

The first six months of 1982 witnessed the most fervent expression of revolutionary activism the country has seen since the days of nationalist ferment in the mid-1950s. There were rallies, demonstrations for one cause or another and discussion groups everywhere. Politics became supreme and everything became subject to the most detailed political discussion. There was a resurgence of working- and non-working-class political activity which has not been seen in the country since the early days of Nkrumah. Defence committees sprang up everywhere and there was considerable turmoil in the sphere of production as workers sought to use their newly acquired power to wrest control both from the official rung of the trade union leadership and also from management. In April 1982 rank-and-file militancy led to the removal of the official leadership of the TUC and its affiliated unions and the installation of an interim leadership called the Association of Local Unions. It would appear that during this time the radical intelligentsia, the lower fraction of the petty bourgeoisie in the bureaucracy and the working class as well as a fraction of the petty bourgeoisie in the armed forces (designated as the 'left' soldiers) held hegemony of power in the state and in the political process as it unfolded. But this coalition was still not sufficiently strong to impose its vision of the political community on society at this time, nor to institutionalise its new definition of politics. This was to be determined by the process of the class struggle and the unfolding of further events. Nevertheless, the influence of this class was sufficiently strong to be expressed in certain policies.

First, the government directed that all workers at Ghana Industrial Holding Corporation (GIHOC) who had been dismissed in June 1980 as a result of demonstrations should be reinstated immediately. This precedent of the expression of worker power was used to extract concessions from management. Not only that, it gave notice to management that in future such arbitrary dismissals would not be tolerated. Secondly all soldiers who had been dismissed from the armed forces from the time of the hand over of power by the AFRC in September 1979 to the time of the coup in December 1981, were declared reinstated. There was a sense of euphoria in the ranks, a feeling that justice, popular justice, had at last been done. Furthermore, there were a number of specific directives which clearly reflected the interest and influence of the urban working class. There were directives freezing all rent increases for an indefinite period. In certain areas, particularly the Eastern Region, there were even stipulated rents depending on size and quality of accommodation available. With three-digit inflation over a period of time, the cost of living had reached such a point that housing, transport and food more than consumed the monthly take-home pay of the average worker. It is therefore not surprising that these were some of the areas in which the new power and influence of the working class made itself felt. Furthermore, there was a directive that no tenant should be evicted so long as he continued to pay rent, and landlords were put under severe restrictions as regards the disposal of their property and estates. In some cases workers went to seize what they regarded as 'vacant' properties for occupation. Groups of workers and soldiers from the defence committees also started to implement the recommendations of the Disposal of the Confiscated Assets Committee. This was a public committee which had recommended the seizure and disposal of the properties of certain individuals in 1979 under the AFRC, but the succeeding PNP administration had not implemented it. As the properties were those of the petty bourgeoisie it was not surprising that there was some kind of understanding among the parliamentary parties not to implement it. The implementation of the recommendations of this committee implied in some cases the seizure of urban properties, particularly housing, and their allocation to other urban residents.

In a mood reminiscent of the Bolshevik revolution previous owners of houses confiscated by the state were invited to have first preference in choosing which parts of the house they would like to occupy before the rest was allocated to others. It was such incidents which struck the greatest fear into the property-owning members of the petty-bourgeois establishment. Price control legislation was very strictly enforced and workers, through the defence committees and later the trades unions, took an active part in the distribution of 'essential commodities'. In certain areas workers ransacked lodges to reveal their sordid secrets and demanded the abolition of the state judiciary. The organs of popular power provided an institutional basis for the expression of this mood if the whole thing was not to degenerate into anarchy. It has to be noted, however, that most of these initiatives were achieved through executive directive or entirely on the initiative of the workers and not by decree. Hence in the ensuing conflict it was easier for the right to argue that there was no legal basis for the actions.

But it was at the level of production that some of the most intense class and political struggles took place. In some cases workers dismissed or suspended their management or asked them to take 'indefinite leave'. Interim management committees on which workers were adequately represented were set up to run state corporations and industries. The system of interim management committees enabled some kind of control to be exercised on the intense struggle which was going on between labour and management at this time. This system of management committees was introduced into all state corporations and statutory bodies. Not even the universities were exempt. Future university councils were to have on their boards both students and workers. The period saw an intense struggle between labour and capital. At the level of production this was expressed in the form of a conflict between labour and management. This was a classic case of *class action* in the sense that the actions taken against management were not limited to particular members of the managerial class but to the class as a whole. Where in the past individuals notorious for bad relations towards labour were singled out for punishment, in this case individuals noted for exemplary good labour relations were singled out for exemption from the general action taken against the management. Similarly, workers' initiatives taken with respect to housing were no longer taken against particular landlords regarded as notorious but against *landlordism* as a political and social phenomenon. This constituted a marked change in the consciousness of the workers from previous periods. The second significant point about these initiatives was that they were policed by the workers themselves. Taking advantage of the fluidity of the situation, workers sought alliances with soldiers and policemen who broadly shared their view of politics. Hence they operated under the umbrella and protection of these units. In certain areas there was a strong solidarity between such soldiers and the workers.

The mass media reflected this changed mood. Strident attacks on capitalism, imperialism, neo-colonialism and the Western powers reminiscent of the *Evening News* during the time of the anti-colonial agitation, became noticeable. The *Daily Graphic* became the *People's Daily Graphic* and gave increasing coverage to political discussions from a class point of view. With the appointment of members of the radical intelligentsia to the top posts in the national radio and television services, radical opinions gained prominence in news coverage, and international news coverage was tinged with a distinctly anti-Western flavour. In February 1982 in a controversy over an alleged invasion of Ghana supported by the US, the

*People's Daily Graphic*, hitherto not known for intemperate language, editorialised as follows:

Has the U.S. not told lies before? Did America not invade the Dominican Republic in 1965? Why did the U.S. displace a democracy with a totalitarian regime in Guatemala in 1954? Has democracy not been subverted in Brazil and Chile? Why were the huge (sic) massacres in the name of 'freedom' in Indonesia in 1965–1966? Vietnam is too sordid to mention.

We wish our readers to know that America's attitude toward 'freedom' in the Third World countries is quite contrary to whatever they propagate. The working principle in the Third World countries is ECONOMIC FREEDOM, which means nothing more than freedom for U.S. business to invest, sell and repatriate profits. They force Third World countries to provide a certain kind of INVESTMENT CLIMATE (you remember) and then a specific form of stability.

To achieve all these, they request for certain kind of machinery (military intelligence, very useful) to crack down on rabble-rousers, unruly students, workers organisations and true democratic processes. Readers who are in doubt can throw their minds back over the past two years in Ghana.[21]

It is a mark of the change of the times and an ironic twist of history that by 1985 such sentiments could no longer be expressed and the regime had provided just such an 'investment climate' for finance capital. In the political debates of the time the more specifically political papers such as the *Workers Banner* and *Nsamankaw* took leading positions. The political battle cry 'power to the people' was sufficiently evocative to serve as a mobilising slogan and the ideological platform of the National Democratic Revolution was sufficiently vague to accommodate various sections of the left and the not-so-left — more so as the specific modalities of its expression and implementation were never articulated. Although this made it possible to present some kind of a united front in a situation both of intense sectarianism which prevailed on the left and of general fluidity in the system, it enabled all kinds of contradictions to be contained and all kinds of contradictory causes to be espoused in the name of the revolution.

Although the power and influence of the working people was at its height at this time, their political strength was demonstrated more by preventing state initiatives they deemed detrimental to their class interests than in producing gains or institutionalising the gains they had made. It indicates both their strength and weakness.

It is important to note that none of the policy outcomes at this time reflected the interests of the peasantry. There was no attempt to mobilise them although there were important local issues and grievances around which they could be mobilised in support of the regime and their own independent class interests. This was particularly the case in areas where peasant displacements had occurred as the result of multinational involvement in agriculture or the activities of the petty bourgeoisie in large-scale agriculture. This was one of the most serious organisational weaknesses of the entire political process. Admittedly, there was no serious land question in Ghana comparable to the cases of Kenya, Algeria, Ethiopia or Zimbabwe, although in certain areas it was important enough to manifest itself in class conflict. Here the young militants threw away the advice of Fanon and Cabral and set on a course which counted the most numerous class out of the political process. The peasants became onlookers as the political process unfolded. In some cases they became apprehensive and hostile as some of them were subjected to rough handling by soldiers who had gone to urge them to bring their commodities to the markets for sale at controlled prices. There were rumours of soldiers and activists going round seizing commodities for forced sales. To make this situation worse some of the market women in the distributive sectors of the economy who had fled to the rural areas for safety at the outset of the severe enforcement of price control legislation, spread stories of soldiers, police and political activists assaulting traders. This naturally frightened the peasants even more. The women persuaded the peasants not to take their commodities to the markets for fear that they might be seized by soldiers. The consequence of this lack of peasant mobilisation was a severe brake on the revolutionary process. Later the regime came out with specific measures to ensure peasant support but it was too late and the bureaucratic manner in which it was implemented did not win friends from the peasant community for the government.

### Economic and Social Measures

We have already outlined the crisis of economy and society in Ghana on the eve of the coup of 31 December. Six months after the coup the situation became worse. As the government attempted to control prices in the face of rampant three-figure inflation by trying to enforce price control legislation, traders and merchants responded with the age-old trick. They withdrew their wares from the market, which of course aggravated the situation. In addition the harvest was bad and was to be worse the following year. The government was unable to meet the wages and salaries of the personnel in public corporations; nearly all of them relied on government subvention. The situation was so bad that a recourse to deficit financing seemed difficult. To put it bluntly, there was no money even to print money! What was the response of the regime to this situation? Up till now the regime had only responded with 'ad hoc' and punitive measures. But it was clear to all that something more than this was needed to deal with the desperate situation, something which would stimulate growth and development. At this point the regime came under severe pressure from both the workers and its militant left as well as from the petty-bourgeoisie organisations and the right-wing members in its own ranks to define its sense of direction. Each side lobbied and pressed for policies which accorded with its ideological predispositions and class interests. The right argued that what was needed in such a desperate situation was a short-term practical measure. It contended that it was not the time for any ideological experiments whose success could not be guaranteed. It saw the solution in terms of the infusion of massive foreign assistance and investment and a restoration of the full neo-colony. The left, on the other hand, argued that it was precisely such a desperate situation which dictated sweeping changes. It saw the solution in terms of fundamental changes in the structure of the economy with the mobilised mass of the people providing the main dynamo.

Neither side was strong enough to impose its conception of developmental paradigm on the society. The regime, however, was inclined to the position of the right. One prominent member of the right who was virtually the economic adviser to the government succeeded in getting Standard Bank to advance substantial credits to the government, apparently with a promise for more if it behaved sensibly, i.e. did not make any drastic changes in economy and society. This put subtle pressure on the left to match the right's capacity to attract foreign finance. The left was manoeuvred into a position in which its contribution to the transformation process was measured in terms of its ability to attract financial assistance. Once this became the defined political parameter, the question of the transformation was effectively put on the shelf and the way to the continuation and strengthening of the neo-colonial economy was now firmly on the agenda. This was to prove extremely damaging to the left and its prospects and the transformation process as a whole.

In response to this pressure from the right, in April 1982 a delegation set off for Eastern Europe and Cuba to solicit economic and financial support. It was received warmly but no cash offerings were promised. The Soviet Union was wary of 'leftist *juntas*'. It adopted a policy of 'wait and see'. Certain promises of technical assistance were, however, made. The Soviet Union and Eastern Europe were prepared to resume work on the technical projects they were forced to abandon in the wake of the overthrow of Nkrumah in 1966. Cuba moved in to provide training for security officers. But as the regime had come to define its developmental options and needs in terms of cash offerings, the assistance from Eastern Europe and Cuba could not help. In view of the way in which it had defined its developmental needs, it saw negotiations with finance capital in the form of the IMF and the World Bank as the only viable option. From this it is clear that those who maintain that the regime abandoned its early progressive thrust because of the 'ultra leftism' of the JFM or the pressure of US destabilisation measures are either ignorant of the facts or plainly dishonest.

But in order to come to terms with finance capital certain preconditions had to be fulfilled. This implied jettisoning the revolution, accepting a different paradigm of development in which foreign capital played a crucial role, demobilising the masses, undermining working class organisations, stopping class conflict, realignment with the right or a fraction of it, a massive devaluation of the local currency, liberalisation of the economy, removal of government subsidies, and cutting down of government expenditure and support, particularly for public enterprises. This meant a restoration of the market economy and a roll-back from the limited welfare measures for which Ghana had been renowned since the time of independence. Once developmental needs were defined in this narrow way, political legitimacy for Rawlings and some of the petty-bourgeois right which cohered around him depended on the ability to attract foreign finance and satisfy the consumerism of the petty bourgeoisie as a whole, and this was to become the main programme of the PNDC. This put the left at a decided disadvantage.

This brings us to the main problematic of the post-colonial state: the crisis of accumulation. This issue has been confused with a debate on the merits of socialism and capitalism. The question is that given the fact that the accumulation crisis is the main problematic of the post-colonial state what developmental option offers the best chance of responding to it? It is now accepted even by the ardent devotees of modernisation theory that the development model of the West cannot be replicated in today's developing countries due to historical and structural differences. When we consider this against the background of the current crisis of capitalism, it becomes obvious that the only viable alternative is a self-reliant autonomous development relying on the mass of the people as the main dynamo of development.

Since Rawlings was inclined towards the rightist option, a condition for such development was an agreement with the IMF and the World Bank. To achieve this he had to create a conducive domestic political climate. This implied a strategy to abort the revolutionary process, jettison the left, and remove left influence from important areas of decision-making and undermine the emerging autonomy of the working-class organisations. This was the task he was to perform on behalf of finance capital in the coming months. The second half of the year saw a period of intense political struggle in the country. Although fundamentally it was a conflict between imperialism and its local support base on the one hand and the broad masses of the people on the other, within the country its expression took many forms and there were many secondary contradictions. The major conflict was of course between the right and the left, but there was also a conflict between the right and the regime. The period also saw a conflict between the left and the regime as well as within the left itself. Here we shall concentrate on the basic issues of the conflict between the right and the left and that between each of them and the regime.

### Conflict and Contradiction

The 31 December coup did not start off conflict and political struggles in Ghana. It simply intensified them and gave them sharper focus. For the progressive forces the coup appeared initially to provide a congenial framework in which to conduct these struggles. The main contradiction was of course between imperialism and the broad mass of the people. At this time it was expressed in the form of an intense conflict between on the one hand the petty bourgeoisie located in the top hierarchy of the military, the liberal professions of law, medicine and academia, the distributive sectors of the economy, the top echelons of the bureaucracy, industry and commerce and local representation of transnational corporations, the real compradorial elements, and on the other hand the progressive forces made up of the urban working class, the radical intelligentsia and the lower ranks of the bureaucracy. Although there were some contradictions among various fractions of the right, particularly between the internal and external wings, it is far too insignificant to dwell upon. Sometimes, in the perception of the participants the secondary contradictions were to assume a position of utmost importance. The period between June 1982 and December 1983 were the most intense moments of the conflict. The basic issues of the conflict revolved around five questions; the conduct and character of politics; the objectives of the political process; the pattern and sources of recruitment to political office; political ideology; and organs of popular power. We shall deal with each of these in turn.

The rightists charged that public policy was idiosyncratic, chaotic, spasmodic and without any consistent plan. They also decried the authoritarian populism of the regime and denounced arrests, detentions, political violence and the human rights record of the regime. One particular incident which was to raise general opprobrium was the notorious murder of three High Court judges and a retired army officer in circumstances which looked like political murder. Accusing fingers were pointed at the government and the attempt was made to use this issue to mobilise mass support against the government.

It was also claimed that the regime had developed a wrong conception of Ghana's developmental problems. In the typical fashion of Africa's petty-bourgeois right wing, it was argued that the problems of the country were exclusively economic and not political. They were problems of production. What had to be done was to devise strategies to increase the production of exportable commodities. This should be the main objective of public policy. It had nothing to do with imperialism or ideology or socialism with all its attendant problems which the regime was trying to force on Ghanaians (although the regime had never espoused socialism as an official ideology). It was argued that socialism was alien to the character of the Ghanaian. The economic problems of Tanzania and Guinea were pointed out with satisfaction as examples of the unworkability of socialism. The 'success stories' of Ivory Coast and Kenya were cited as the models of economic success which Ghana should emulate. What was needed was good policies and not romantic experiments of an ideological nature. It was a strong liberal argument but an argument which appealed principally to one class.

Another complaint was that government was associated with people who were far too young, inexperienced, untried and of low educational quality. The rightists were particularly alarmed at the appointment of Amartey Kwei, Chris Atim and Sergeant Aloga Akata-Pore to the PNDC. What they were really complaining of was that these people did not belong to the establishment from which Ghana's political leadership had been traditionally recruited and that their style did not reflect the social behaviour of that establishment.

Another issue which the right was to seize upon was the ideological question. This has always been a controversial point in Ghanaian politics. It argued that what Ghana needed were men and women with practical bent of mind to respond to the problems of the country and not people whose only competence lay in their ability to formulate abstract ideologies which were of foreign origin and had no relevance to the development of the country and were even at variance with the culture, traditions and norms of the people.

The right reserved its severest attack for the organs of popular power, particularly the defence committees and the public tribunals. It argued once again that Ghana's problems did not necessitate the creation of new structures to solve them. The country already had an excellent constitution. What was needed was the will to work it. To the defence committees its attitude was initially hostile, claiming that workers could never lead the country and that the defence committees were nothing more than vigilante groups who were only anxious to appropriate and share what others had worked hard to accumulate. It contemptuously characterised their membership as those who had 'achieved nothing in life' and asked when hard work and success became crimes. Later it was to adopt a more subtle tactic. It conceded that due to the rampant corruption in the country there was need for some reform. The concept of the defence committees was one way to achieve this but it decried its class and political character. It should confine itself principally to problems of production and not politics and it should embrace the entire population.

The left countered all these arguments. It conceded that public policy was characterised by indecision and lack of consistency. But this was due not to any inherent weakness of left political behaviour but to the regime's policy of trying to balance the interests of the petty-bourgeoisie right and those of the mass of the people. What was needed was a clear direction of policy in conformity with the tenets of the transformation process and in the interests of the broad masses of the people. On the question of class conflict and political violence it accused the right of being hypocritical and asserted that political violence had always been part of the political process of the country. In the past when the mass of the people had been the victims, the right had not complained. The record of the right's period in office did not show that it was faithful to the liberal ideal or even to parliamentary democracy. The left argued that it did not create class conflict. It was rooted in the material conditions of inegalitarian societies, and quoted with relish Rawlings' statements: 'So long as there is no justice, I would dare say that "Let there be no peace"', or 'To say that there are only two tribes in this country, one rich and the other poor, is not to invoke tension but to state a fact. If we do not want this situation to break into conflict we shall have to narrow the gap between the rich and the poor.'[22] It countered the charge that militants appointed to high political office were young and inexperienced by saying that in a country where the majority of the population was young, principles of democracy demanded their adequate representation in all areas of the decision-making process. The real reason for the right's opposition to the militants was their class and ideological position. They pointed to the sordid political record of the right when it controlled the state.

On the question of ideology it was argued that, far from the right's position that Ghana's political problems were not ideological, they were primarily so and what was needed was a clear ideological frame in which to situate policies. It was the failure of past regimes to do this which had brought the problem. In pursuing an ideological course it was doing nothing more than trying to rectify this. In its view the organs of popular power were crucial to the whole process of the new definition of politics. Since the wealth of the country was produced by the mass of the people it stood to reason that they should have the power to decide how it was to be produced and how it was to be distributed. The organs of popular power were an instrumental mechanism in this process and saw the problem of production as organically linked to the question of power. Each side showed a clear ideological position. If anything was to demonstrate the ideological nature of Ghanaian politics it was this political debate between the right and the progressive organisations.

The right used its occupational organisations such as the Bar Association, the Association of Recognised Professional Bodies, and the establishment churches as instruments in its struggle against the left and the regime. Its ideological mouthpieces were the *Echo*, *The Business Weekly* and *The Free Press* which were used to propagate its position. The *Standard*, the outspoken mouthpiece of the Catholic establishment, usually reflected the broad ideological line of the right, but managed to avoid the insensate stridency of the right and devoted more attention to the human rights question.

We have already stated that the left was in conflict not only with the right but also with the regime and within its own ranks. In its conflict with the regime it was to raise similar issues and argue for the adoption of policy in line with its own ideological predispositions. It dwelt on the issue of the conduct and character of politics, the objectives of the political process, organs of popular power, the need for a clear ideological position, and sources and patterns of recruitment to high political office.

Considering the contradictory elements which cohered uneasily in the regime, it was not surprising that the left's advocacy of the causes outlined above and its pressure on the regime to adopt them was to lead to tension and eventually open rupture. The issue which aroused most conflict and controversy was the question of 'direction', i.e. the main strategy for the revolutionary process. It crystallised around the debate over economic policy. The way in which the conflict was manifested appeared as if the issue was a narrow debate over devaluation.[23] That was how the regime presented it. We have already recounted how the ideological platform of the New Democratic Revolution had allowed all sorts of contradictory policies to be pursued in the name of the revolutionary process. The left was dismayed that the regime had, as early as March 1982, started talking to the representatives of finance capital in the name of the IMF and the World Bank with a view to arriving at some common understanding. It feared that the government was about to make a deal behind its back. It was particularly outraged that the regime did not allow free debate on the issue. Matters came to a head at the first ever joint meeting of the NDC and PNDC secretaries in August 1982. There, the government unfurled its plan for seeking credits from the IMF and the World Bank and for a substantial devaluation of the local currency as a policy response to the monetary and fiscal crisis. The progressive organisations had been critical of Dr Limann's attempt to reach some kind of accommodation with the same bodies. In fact the KNRG had disengaged from the PNP on precisely this point, and both the JFM and the NDM had been critical of the PNP's economic policies on this very point.[24] For them to endorse the same position from a 'people's government' did not only appear the hallmark of political opportunism but also political suicide, quite apart from whatever merits the case might have. It argued that Ghana had seen many devaluations but that had not solved the country's problems. What proof was there that what was being recommended would solve the problem? Delegates maintained that devaluation by itself could not solve the crisis of the Ghanaian economy, and that if applied at all, it should be situated within a socio-economic framework which would allow for the fundamental problems of underdevelopment to be tackled. To respond merely to the fiscal and monetary aspects of the problem was to attack the symptoms and not the cause. These were the political positions expressed at the meeting and the government's position was rejected with near unanimity.

The meeting included leading members of the progressive organisations who used the occasion to raise the whole question of 'direction', i.e. developmental strategy. The strength of feeling was so strong that a committee was appointed under the joint secretaryship of Mahama Bawa of the JFM and Yao Graham of the NDM to work out a more comprehensive developmental strategy than the mere

197

response to the monetary and fiscal problems. A government delegation on its way to Washington for talks with the IMF was consequently advised to conduct only 'exploratory talks'. This was one of the few occasions in which the two rival organisations worked amicably for the revolutionary process and the result was very encouraging. The report which came out managed to fit the devaluation into a developmental framework which recommended autonomous and self-reliant development based on mass mobilisation.[25] This report was, however, not implemented. Instead a new plan, the Economic Rehabilitation Plan (ERP) under the direction of the Secretary for Finance and Economic Planning, was prepared.[26] The left, particularly the JFM, felt betrayed. The *Workers Banner* made virulent attacks on the government and in particular two officials it felt were responsible. This obviously worsened the relationship between the left and the PNDC. Jerry Rawlings in particular was irritated by the position of the left. It is clear that later reports that the left was suppressed because it was unable to present an alternative programme cannot be substantiated.

Between October and November a number of incidents occurred which brought the tense relations between the left and the regime to the point of rupture. On 28 October there was a confrontation between troops loyal to Sergeant Aloga Akata-Pore and those loyal to Jerry Rawlings, but open conflict was avoided. The following day at an open air meeting in Gondar Barracks, then seat of government, heated exchanges took place between Jerry Rawlings and a group of officers who expressed dissatisfaction with the progress of the revolution and voiced criticisms of Kojo Tsikata, the security boss, in particular. Later that morning Accra was thrown into confusion when it was rumoured that the government had been overthrown. It transpired that at a zonal meeting of the Accra Defence Committees a leader of the People's Revolutionary League of Ghana, one of the six progressive organisations, had announced that Chris Atim and Sergeant Aloga Akata-Pore had taken control of the government and Rawlings and Captain Kojo Tsikata had fled the country. Who authorised the announcement is still a mystery. Whatever might have been the motive behind this, Rawlings interpreted it as an attempt by the left and in particular the JFM to overthrow him. From then on relations between the JFM and the regime deteriorated irreparably.

On 23 November there was an unsuccessful attempt to overthrow the government. Those arrested were from the right. The government, however, insisted on seeing the two events as linked and consequently proceeded to suppress the left both in the military and in civil society. Many militants, particularly from the JFM, were arrested and detained. Sergeant Aloga Akata-Pore and the troops closely associated with him were also arrested on charges of incitement to mutiny. Chris Atim, co-ordinator of the NDC, resigned, charging 'betrayal and derailment of the revolutionary process' and making damaging accusations against Jerry Rawlings and Kojo Tsikata.[27] He later fled the country. Other cadres also resigned, disengaged or fled the country. The JFM was confused and demoralised by these events. By December 1983 the movement had been effectively suppressed and the entire left was on the defensive. The NDC was dissolved, to be reconstituted later. The regime then began to woo the NDM which now came out in support of the ERP. It hoped to gain from the misfortune of its rivals and looked forward to capturing the places on the NDC vacated by the JFM. The honeymoon, however, did not last long.

By December 1982 the regime had created the political conditions to enable it to launch the ERP and by April the following year it was in a position to present the first budget based on the ERP and the understanding it had reached with the IMF. Together the two documents showed all the essential ingredients of the IMF/World Bank strategy for coping with economic crisis: devaluation of the currency, liberalisation of the economy, retrenchment or redeployment (as it was called) of labour, dismantling of the public corporations, cuts in public spending, and reduction in welfare. Strangely enough, to these were added nationalisation of foreign trade and mobilisation. This enabled the PNDC to argue that it was following its own internal development plan which only happened to coincide in certain essentials with the IMF/World Bank stabilisation policy. It was clear, however, that the last two items were meant for the consumption of what remained of the domestic left and never intended for implementation. In addition, other political initiatives were taken as a way of creating the social and political basis for the implementation of the programme: the development of a 'strong' (meaning authoritarian) government with a centralised centre of decision-making. This means that while the PNDC talked of the need to decentralise administrative structures it moved to centralise political decision-making and initiated moves to undermine the limited autonomy of the defence committees and organs of popular power. 'Populist nonsense' now gave way to 'pragmatism'. The left was dismayed by such a turn of events. The NDM, however, continued its policy of 'critical support' hoping to gain political hegemony with the departure of the JFM. In the long run it was the left as a group which lost.

**The Turn to the Right**

The state now began to incline decisively towards the positions advocated by the right. On all the major issues of the conflict between the right and the government, the PNDC now intervened in the political process on behalf of the right and capital while at the same time taking punitive measures against *individual and particular* members of the petty bourgeoisie against whom it had particular grievance. This gave the impression that it was still on the 'left' course. One thing, however, became clear from this time onwards: public policy no longer reflected the interests of the workers or the mass of the people. They were now to bear the burden of the new development strategy.

From the beginning of 1983 the leadership mounted an attack on the urban workers, the defence committees and the organs of popular power as a way of undermining their limited autonomy and preparing the way for strengthening the dominance of finance capital. This was important if the ERP was to be implemented successfully. This is one of the serious dangers of populism. It could unify the working class with the rhetoric and slogans of popular participation and deliver them to the dominance of capital. The implementation of the ERP imposed severe hardships on the working people. The devaluation of the local currency by over 1,000 per cent by the middle of the year put local prices effectively beyond the reach of most people. The cedi which was exchanging at the bank rate of 2.75 to the dollar now officially exchanged at 90 cedis to the dollar. At the parallel market which is the real exchange rate at which goods and services are exchanged it was almost three times as high. In 1986 the cedi was worth only three per cent of its value in 1981 when Rawlings seized power. Even as far back as 1984 the Secretary for Finance and Economic Planning conceded that workers' real income had declined by 80 per cent in real terms.[28] A large number of workers have lost their jobs in the wake of the 'redeployment' exercise. The removal of subsidies on transportation and agricultural inputs have hiked domestic prices. The drastic cut in government spending and the attempt to roll back the limited welfare state of the Nkrumah period has meant that the cost of all services including health and education has gone up to such levels that only the very high and mighty can afford them. There has even been the unprecedented move to institute tuition charges for university education. The increase in the producer price of cocoa does not match the corresponding increases in the costs of consumer items. A statement attributed to a retired civil servant sums up the feelings of the mass of Ghanaians.

> When Jerry Rawlings came to power in 1981, he criticised our hospitals as graveyards of the working people. Now four years and several hundred million dollars worth of loans later, the hospitals are still graveyards and the labourer's daily wage will not even buy a loaf of bread[29]

Workers demands for higher wages to cope with the situation have been dismissed as 'populist nonsense'. Early in 1985 the government sought to impose further financial constraints on the working people by abolishing allowances. Only a threatened general strike led to a change of heart.

In addition to the above, certain changes at variance with the earlier progressive anti-imperialist thrust of the transformation process have been instituted. The defence committees have been replaced with committees for the defence of the revolution (CDR) and shorn of their class, political and ideological character. They are now virtually labour brigades. They have also been placed under the control of the district administration. The NDC has been dissolved for the second time and replaced with the Secretariat for the CDR. Production and not politics is now the watchword. It is clear that these former organs of popular power are no longer seen to be the agencies of radical social change. The Interim Management Committees have also been abolished and replaced with Joint Consultative Councils in which workers have only advisory roles, just as in the past. And PNDC secretaries have been urging management to reassert itself. As we have seen, the investigatory tribunals in the form of the CVC and the NIC have been replaced. In addition to these measures, the government has set up Regional Consultative Councils which constitute formal structures for right-wing input into the decision-making process. Well-known luminaries of the right function prominently in these bodies. Furthermore many of the right-wing politicians who fled the country during the time of the AFRC and who were tried and sentenced *in absentia* have been amnestied on condition that they clear themselves. In the mass media the strident anti-imperialism which had characterised the earlier phase of the transformation process has disappeared[30] and members of the radical intelligensia who had controlled the news media have been purged. Jerry Rawlings has made direct overtures to the petty-bourgeois right, and in particular the chiefly class. And the Asantehene is today reportedly one of his closest advisers. Prominent members of the right have been appointed to high public positions of which the most notable is the appointment of Justice D. F. Annan, a former Appeal Court judge, to membership of the PNDC and chairmanship of the National Commission for Democracy responsible for working out new institutional structures of democratic rule. We have already noted how the public tribunals have also lost their political character and become merely mechanisms for securing easy convictions. The old evils which Rawlings had previously railed against — like bribery, corruption and embezzlement — have resurfaced.

Within the military, with the suppression of the 'left' soldiers, the regime has moved to reinstate the authority of the senior officers and based its rule on the armed forces with the service commanders collectively forming some kind of a directorate similar to what General Acheampong established when he instituted the Supreme Military Council. Retired military officers, some with questionable political records in past regimes, are now surfacing in increasing numbers in the government.

External funding agencies and finance capital have been ecstatic about these changes and have praised the government for its courage, boldness, sense of realism and pragmatism. Government leaders have started to boast about the economy picking up, and impressive figures about new growth rates are being bandied about. Foreign visitors to Ghana are now impressed with the availability of consumer goods. The reaction of the majority of Ghanaians, however, is different. Although the right has been supportive of the measures taken against the left and the working class, its reaction to the economic measures has been mixed. The petty bourgeoisie in commerce and industry find it difficult to meet the cedi equivalent of the import prices of their products which have jumped up as a result of the devaluations. Some also have been complaining of difficulties in meeting wages. The contradictory relationship between labour and capital reveals itself clearly in this. And the IMF though anxious to add Ghana to its list of 'success stories' in Africa is getting worried about the onset of 'adjustment fatigue'.[31]

The PNDC has conceded on practically all the points raised by the petty-bourgeois right in its conflict with the government and it is now in a position to affect policy outcomes in its class and ideological interest, but it is still suspicious of Jerry Rawlings. It regards him as temperamentally erratic and unstable and therefore unpredictable in policy terms; he could turn to the left again at any time. The petty bourgeoisie is also worried about the persistent reports of the violation of human rights, arrests and torture of detainees and the rumours of secret executions. Attacks on the Catholic establishment started with the reported public vituperation against the Catholic Archbishop of Kumasi, Rev Akwasi Sarpong, by no less a person than the chairman of the PNDC himself and continued with the banning of the *Standard*, the mouthpiece of the Catholic establishment and an advocate of the petty-bourgeois liberal position, presumably for its outspoken criticism of the government. Neither attack has reassured the right. Besides, for the petty bourgeoisie the only political arrangement which will satisfy it is one which will guarantee it unconditional hegemony, amounting to a virtual surrender of the

Rawlings faction. For this and other reasons it is still suspicious of Jerry Rawlings and will back moves to replace the regime. It has recently renewed its call for demilitarisation and a return to constitutional rule.

The left has been dismayed by these trends. With the suppression of the JFM and the abolishing of the NDC nearly all left political groups have disengaged from the regime. In January 1985 the NDM associated itself with a trenchant public criticism of the government, attacking its economic record.[32] Although this tended to look like its final disengagement from the government, its leaders were quick to point out that it was in line with its policy of 'critical support'. The KNRG has also openly repudiated the regime and called for demilitarisation. At a recent annual congress of the National Union of Ghana Students (NUGS) a resolution was passed calling on the government to give a timetable for return to representative government.[33] On the labour front there has been some restlessness and resurgence of militancy. In recent times the TUC has been very critical of the government's economic policy. With the suppression of the defence committees as instruments for articulating and fighting for class demands, worker militancy has returned in the labour unions. In January 1986 Accra District Council of Labour passed a resolution accusing the government of lack of workable policies in housing, education and finance and linked the four-year rule of the PNDC with that of General Acheampong as a political failure.[34] We have already referred to how early in 1985 only the prompt restoration of workers' allowances, which had been abolished under further austerity measures, averted a national strike. Workers' demonstrations have occurred in Accra, Tema and Legon. Now the workers are not merely asking for economic changes to cushion them from the effects of the devaluations as they did in 1983. They are beginning to question the very basis of the government. If one were to remember that the areas where the demonstrations have occurred, namely Accra, Tema and Legon, at one time did represent solid support for the regime, it is now clear that the mass base of support for the regime has gone.

Interestingly enough the government has responded to its legitimacy crisis and the dilemma of military rule in the same way that General Acheampong and his SMC did: intimidation, political repression and attempts to work out new political structures.[35] Thus, there have been arrests and detention of labour leaders, journalists and leaders of the progressive organisations. In April 1986 four leading members of the left, Kwesi Pratt (KNRG), Akoto Ampaw (NDM) Kweku Barko, formerly of MONAS and Ralph Kugbe of the Accra District Secretariat of the CDRs were arrested and detained.[36] With regard to creating new structures the government has been trying to resuscitate what is left of the JFM and use it as a political base. It has also quietly initiated a process of consultation with the right wing of the PNP and certain influential individuals in the establishment with a view to forming a non-party corporate state *à la* Union Government which would allow it to maintain hegemony. This it hopes will enable it to solve the dilemma of military disengagement. Needless to say these efforts have so far not been successful. On the contrary, they have aroused negative reaction from the petty-bourgeois political organisations as well as the left.[37]

## Conclusion

It is clear from what we have been saying so far that the PNDC has now lost its mass base and the progressive thrust of the earlier days has disappeared. It is difficult to see how the revolutionary principles contained in Jerry Rawlings' first declaration after the coup of 31 December can be attained in the present structure. Two questions arise from this. First, what accounts for the abortion of the revolutionary process when it started from what by all accounts would appear as fairly auspicious circumstances? What impact has this experience had on left struggles and what should be the relationship between the left and 'leftist juntas'? What lessons can one learn from the Ghanaian experience?

Before we embark on this a few remarks on the nature and political significance of military regimes are in order. There is nothing unique about a military regime. It is nothing more than the political expression of state power at a certain conjuncture of history. Whether it inclines to a progressive or reactionary position will depend on the class forces behind it and the political position of the leadership. Nevertheless, there is something specific about the military which affects the style and conduct of politics but not its substance: it affects the specific form in which decisions are taken more than the content of the decisions. One is the hierarchical structure of military establishments. For any successful revolutionary initiatives to be taken this must be broken but military men are so welded to this as part of their mental make-up that it becomes very difficult to shake. The second is consciousness of the military establishment and its behavioural norms. Military initiatives are secret operations. In military operations the element of surprise and secrecy is crucial for the success of any operation. When the military has come to power by the process of a coup which itself depends on the successful application of these behavioural norms, it becomes very difficult for it to open up channels of decision-making completely to its civilian support base. But this is precisely what any transformation process based on the mass of the people demands and this is one of the most difficult aspects of the process of transformation initiated by the military. But the military has to overcome this difficulty if it is to be successful in its efforts at launching the process of transformation. So to be successful the military has to shed these two important military behavioural norms. In effect it has to demilitarise itself. This is the source of the problem. It is important to keep this in mind in the discussions which follow.

Taking this as a starting point, what should be the position of the left towards the military, especially 'leftist' military juntas of the type we have been discussing? This is a problem which has bedevilled the left in Africa for some time and will continue to persist given the crisis of state and society in Africa and the tendency of the incidence of 'leftist juntas' to increase. It would be wrong and presumptuous to designate a blueprint for all left organisations in Africa but the class position we have taken allows us to establish the parameters in which a specific strategy dictated by praxis should be situated. There is a tendency in certain sections of the left to be dismissive of all military juntas as objectively reactionary. There is also another position on the left which tends to embrace all military juntas so long as the necessary populist posturings are made. Both positions are fraught with dangers. The military is not a class; it is an institution and as such it has organisational features and behavioural norms which help it to maintain coherence and act with a certain degree of uniformity. But it is a multi-class group and under certain conditions of social and political stress, such as obtain in periods of crisis in state and society, not least in Africa, the organisational features which give it coherence and uniformity are weakened and its multi-class nature comes to the fore pulling in a different direction. In this way it is possible, as Judith Marshall has pointed out,[38] for the military to incline downwards or upwards depending on its internal structure and objective social conditions. Depending on this analysis the left could cooperate if its analysis of the situation shows that there are reasonable grounds for thinking that such cooperation will open up possibilities for deepening the class and ideological consciousness of the mass of the people and strengthening and solidifying left organisations and advancing the class struggle as a whole. Such cooperation should only be at the level of *organisations* and not individuals and should be based on certain specific conditions.[39] Even if these conditions are fulfilled it does not mean that success will come, as the case of Ethiopia clearly demonstrates, but failure to do so will only spell disaster to the left. In Ghana it would appear that the 31 December coup did appear to offer the prospect of meeting these conditions but the left made many serious strategic mistakes in working out the modalities of its co-operation with the junta. Today it is perhaps fair to say that the left has suffered more in organisation and ideological terms under this regime than any other.

The second question we need to answer is why the revolutionary process was so easily aborted. Four main answers have been given to this question. We shall confine ourselves to positions on the left.[40] The JFM has on the whole attributed it to the 'revolution betrayed' thesis.[41] It has accused Jerry Rawlings of using the left to consolidate himself only to discard it at a convenient opportunity. It is a left reformulation of the conspiracy theory of politics. The NDM in its public posture has tended to blame imperialism although privately the leaders have also blamed Jerry Rawlings for not being 'clear' politically. They see the problem as his 'inability' to see the class question, his erratic temperament and tempestuous nature. The NDM has also attributed the failure to the 'ultra-leftism' of the JFM.[42] There are also certain people on the left, particularly the foreign observers, who see the problem in terms of 'historical inevitability'. 'What is the alternative?', they frequently ask when confronted with an explanation for the policy changes.

Quite frankly, I find these explanations inadequate and unpersuasive. Although in a politically fluid situation such as existed in Ghana from January 1982 to October 1983 the type of leadership is extremely important in giving a sense of direction, and providing inspiration and helping to solidify nascent institutions, this is not enough to explain the situation. Even if Jerry Rawlings sought to subvert the revolutionary process, wilfully and cunningly, as claimed by the JFM, or unwittingly through political ignorance or lack of ideological clarity as claimed by the NDM, certain material conditions made it possible for him to succeed. To use consciousness or personality as explanation for social phenomena is idealistic.

I also find the second explanation which hitches everything on imperialism and CIA destabilisation unhelpful. It may make good local propaganda but it is bad social science. As to the argument that imperialism forced the regime to change course, it flies in the face of the facts of the situation. It was clear quite early on that although the leadership of the PNDC did appear unsure of its direction, it was quite certain of which direction it did not want: the revolutionary mobilising option. Secondly, although it would be wrong to underestimate the determination of imperialism to negate Third World revolutions, Ghana is not Angola, Mozambique, Zaire or Egypt. Imperialism's strategic interest in Ghana is not crucial. It is true that Ghana is regarded as some kind of a pacesetter in Africa and its success could trigger other countries to follow its example, but imperialism's global strategy for Africa does not stand or fall with the success of the Ghana revolution. Besides, imperialism will always be there. If one were to use imperialism as an alibi in this way then one should not expect any revolution to succeed in the Third World. An external force can compel a revolution to make compromises on strategies but not on the fundamental question of the principles of the revolution. The Cuban revolution succeeded in spite of imperialism and the CIA and so did the Vietnamese revolution. It is true that imperialism has learnt a lot since then but so has or should the left. Besides, as many of those who invoke the spectre of imperialism and CIA destabilisation have supported and continue to support the ERP, it is inexplicable how they can on the one hand support the ERP and on the other hand blame imperialism for the failure of the revolutionary process. For the only theoretical basis on which the ERP can be supported is an acceptance of the position that (1) capitalist accumulation is possible under the conditions of the neo-colony; (2) that imperialism can develop an underdeveloped country like Ghana; and (3) capitalist accumulation is not incompatible with the demands of popular democracy.

As for the talk that the regime had to come to terms with imperialism because there was no option, it does not even deserve a response. This position of the market Marxists of the Warrenite school effectively rules out the possibility of any revolutionary thrust or autonomous development in the Third World. At another level, we could ask: 'if there is no option, then what justification is there in making the coup against a democratically elected government?' One would be naive to think that in an issue of this sort the role of imperialism is unimportant but there are crucial internal conditions which should be examined. These are the state of the left political organisations, their organisational and structural coherence, their political ability and leadership effectiveness, their relationship with the regime as well as with other left organisations, their strategic alliances with other classes, their relationship particularly with the peasantry, their ideological posture and capacity to make a serious study of the objective conditions from a position of praxis. On many of these issues the left was wanting. So long as the left puts emphasis on idealist conditions such as the personality of Jerry Rawlings or external factors, it prevents itself from making a study of the objective conditions and engaging in the kind of auto-criticism which is crucial if the lessons of this experience are to be learnt and future disasters avoided.

## Notes

1. Ray Bush, 'What Future for Ghana?', *Review of African Political Economy*, September–December 1980, p. 86.

2. See 'The Military and Revolution in Ghana', *Journal of African Marxists*, no. 2, 1982, p. 21.

3. For information on the crisis of the Ghanaian economy see: Tetteh A. Kofi and Emmanuel Hansen, 'Ghana — A History of Endless Recession' in Jerker Carlsson (ed.), *Recession in Africa*, (Uppsala: Scandinavian Institute of African Studies, 1983); John R. Campbell, 'Class and State in the Political Economy of Ghana', *Mawazo*, vol. V, no. 2, 1984; John Struthers, 'Inflation in Ghana (1966–78): Perspective on Monetarist v Structuralist Debate', *Development and Change*, vol. XII, no. 2, April 1981; World Bank, *Ghana: Policies and Program for Adjustment*, (Washington, DC: World Bank, 1984); some account of the deterioration of the Ghanaian economy also appears in Naomi Chazan, *An Anatomy of Ghanaian Politics: Managing Political Recession, 1966–1982* (Boulder, Colorado: Westview Press, 1983) and Mike Oquaye, *Politics in Ghana, 1972–1979* (Accra: Tornado Publications, 1980). For a more encouraging picture of the recent Ghanaian economy see: Margaret A. Novicki, 'The Economics of the Rawlings Revolution', *Africa Report*, September–October 1984, pp. 42–7; 'Ghana', *Financial Times* 20 May, 1986; 'Ghana: Three Years of Economic Recovery,' *West Africa*, 13 January 1986.

4. Ghana has been notorious for these secret societies whose history goes back well into the colonial period. The well-known ones are the Oddfellows and the Freemasons.

5. See *Financial Times*, 5 February 1982.

6. Disappointment was particularly felt due to a sense of euphoria associated with the Armed Forces Revolutionary Council (AFRC) and a heightened sense of public expectation which accompanied the handing over of power to the civilian administration in September 1979.

7. Kwame Ninson, 'Ghana: The Failure of a Petty-Bourgeois Experiment', *Africa Development*, vol. VII, no. 3, 1982, p. 37.

8. First broadcast speech to the nation by Flt. Lt. Jerry Rawlings, Chairman of the PNDC, 31 December 1981.

9. He was to meet a tragic and inglorious end at the stake, executed after his indictment by a public commission and subsequent conviction by a court for being implicated in the notorious murder of three High Court judges and a retired army officer. Two other high-ranking members of the government, Sgt. Aloga Akata-Pore and Capt. Kojo Tsikata, the current security boss, were also indicted by the same public commission but the Attorney-General decided that there was insufficient evidence to bring them to trial. See *SIB Report*, Accra, 1983.

10. NDC, *Guidelines For the Formation and Functioning of the People's Defence Committees*, Accra, undated.

11. At the University of Ghana hospital at Legon, senior members, that is members of the teaching and senior administrative staff, received medical attention before workers and other university personnel irrespective of time of arrival at the OPD, the nature of illness or the gravity of the medical problem. The Legon WDC demanded that in future attention should be on first come, first served basis.

12. *Workers Banner*, vol. I, no. 1, 20–27 October 1981.

13. There were complaints that the defence committees had assumed judicial

powers. But in Ghana it was not unusual for new authority structures, even if their formal powers did not include it, to assume some judicial functions. Thomas Hodgkin, *African Political Parties* (Harmondsworth/: Penguin, 1961), relates similar experiences in the formative years of the CPP.

14. It would appear that in Ethiopia during the time of the 'Red Terror', they exercised the power of meting out sanctions. See Rene Lefort, *Ethiopia: An Heretical Revolution?* (London: Zed Press, 1983).

15. Speech to the nation delivered on radio and television on 29 July 1982.

16. *Ibid*.

17. Zaya Yebo, 'Ghana: Defence Committees and the Class Struggle', *Review of African Political Economy*, no. 32, April, 1985, pp. 67–8.

18. For the mass of the people, advocacy means nothing more than the ability to detect 'loopholes' in the law in order to free 'guilty' defendants. Hence the tendency to regard the entire legal profession as morally reprehensible. For many ordinary Ghanaians their direct experience with the legal system is that of an instrument of class oppression. It is therefore not surprising that a combination of these two factors has created in the mind of many a strong suspicion and hostility towards the legal profession as a whole.

19. See statement by Jerry Rawlings, *Daily Graphic*, 9 June 1980, p. 4.

20. For an excellent essay on leftist juntas see Befekadu Zegeye, 'On the Nature of "Leftist Juntas"', *Monthly Review*, vol. XXXI, no. 3, 1979. See also Henry Bienen, 'Populist Military Regimes in West Africa', *Armed Forces and Society*, vol. XI, no. 3, 1985.

21. *People's Daily Graphic*, 2 February 1982.

22. Speech to the nation delivered on radio and television on 29 July, 1982.

23. Yao Graham tends to present the issue in this way. See 'Politics of Crisis in Ghana: Class Struggles and Organisation, 1981–84', *Review of African Political Economy*, no. 34, December 1985.

24. See *Direction*, vol. I, nos. 4 & 5, 1980. Rawlings' own initial position reflected this mood. As late as 5 January, 1982 in a radio and television broadcast, he was to declare: 'We believe that instead of putting our stake in the Investment Code's fundamental faith in foreign investment we must put our trust in our own industrialists who are capable of building for us a strong industrial base.'

25. Existing political literature on the contemporary situation has been surprisingly silent about this report. This is so even of writers on the left. See Adotey Bing, 'Popular Participation Versus People's Power: Notes on Politics and Struggles in Ghana', *Review of African Political Economy*, no. 31, December 1984; Victoria Brittain, 'Ghana's Precarious Revolution', *New Left Review*, no. 140, July–August 1983. Even Yao Graham, who was one of the joint secretaries of the report and was the person who presented it, manages to avoid mentioning it in his two contributions on the subject. See his 'Ghana — The Politics of Crisis: Class Struggle and Organisation 1976–1983', paper presented at the Conference of the Review of African Political Economy, University of Keele, 29 September 1984; 'The Politics of Crisis in Ghana: Class Struggle and Organisation 1981–1984'? The only exception to this is Zaya Yebo's 'How the IMF Tamed a "Leftist" Apostle', *Africa Events*, January 1985.

26. *The Report of the Committee of the National Defence Committee and Secretaries on the Economy* is a general framework of development strategy based on autonomous development, self-reliance and national mobilisation which accommodates fiscal and monetarist policies into its framework. The ERP on the

other hand is a monetarist programme of adjustment and sectoral growth based on exogenous strategy of development to which has been tagged a programme of nationalisation and mobilisation. The last two items do not fit into its framework nor can they be subsumed under its theoretical underpinnings. It is therefore not surprising that they were not implemented. The two programmes are very different and one cannot support both without ending up in a contradiction.

27. See letter of resignation 3 December 1982.

28. *West Africa*, 26 March 1984, p. 655.

29. Quoted in *Financial Times*, 20 May 1986, p. 15.

30. In spite of this, popular expressions of anti-Americanism, when permitted, can still be vented. A particularly violent one was the 1986 demonstration against the US and Britain following the American invasion of Libya. In the ensuing melée one policeman was shot dead.

31. *Financial Times*, 20 May 1986.

32. 'Statement on the Political and Economic Situation', signed by Fui Tsikata and Kwame Karikari on behalf of the NDM.

33. NUGS has also called on the government to release four well-known members of the left recently arrested.

34. See *Talking Drums*, 24 February 1986 for a reproduction of the complete statement.

35. For the literature on the dilemma of military disengagement from politics in Ghana see: Emmanuel Hansen and Paul Collins, 'The Army, the State and the "Rawlings Revolution" in Ghana', *African Affairs*, vol. 79, no. 314, 1980; 'Politics of Demilitarisation: The Case of Ghana, 1966–1983', paper presented to the 10th General Conference of the International Peace Research Association, Gyor, Hungary, 29 August–2 September 1983; 'Politics of Military Disengagement: The Case of Ghana', paper presented to the Conference on the Transition to Democratic Rule, Buenos Aires, 27–29 August 1985.

36. *West Africa*, 5 May 1986.

37. At a recent symposium held in Accra on the theme 'Ghana: 20 years since Nkrumah', Mr H. T. Provencal, a former leading member of the CPP and now chairman of the KNRG, reportedly questioned the government whether the JFM was being reorganised as a political party. The report read: He [Provencal] said he had learnt during the past few weeks that the JFM was being organised to become the vanguard for the revolution . . . He said the government might . . . be opening itself to confrontation, and that "we cannot have another Acheampong era"', *West Africa*, 7 April 1986, p. 725.

38. Judith Marshall, 'The State of Ambivalence: Right and Left Options in Ghana', *Review of African Political Economy*, no. 5, January–April 1976.

39. It has to be noted, however, that the decision of the left to cooperate and seek to advance its cause under the umbrella of a junta is a sign of weakness and not strength.

40. For the right the question is irrelevant.

41. *Revolutionary Banner*, vol. I, no. 1, May 1985; see especially the article captioned 'The Big Betrayal'.

42. Yao Graham in his 'Politics of Crisis in Ghana: Class Struggle and Organisation, 1981–84', comes very close to this position.

# 9 Popular Alliances and the State in Liberia, 1980–85

by Peter Anyang' Nyong'o

I proceed from the assumption that different possibilities of development exist in almost every political system and situation. The triumph of one of these possibilities depends not only on objective factors and conditions, but also on many subjective ones, and some of these factors are clearly accidental.

Roy Medvedev[1]

We did not come to power to follow the footsteps of those we overthrew. We came to rebuild our country along progressive lines; power is not for us, *it is for the people* because, if they fail to support us, there will be no revolution.

Brigadier-General Thomas Quiwonkpa, then Commanding General of the Liberian Armed Forces[2]

In an earlier version of this chapter[3] my main aim was to show how the Liberian army, under the leadership of Master-Sergeant Samuel Kanyon Doe, had 'stolen the revolution' from the Liberation popular masses and begun a steady, deliberate process of restoring the *ancien régime* of the true Whig rulers. My main thesis was that the revolution had come too soon; the Movement for Justice in Africa (MOJA), which has worked consistently to put together a popular alliance of the Liberian people, had not even had time to transform itself into a political party and to prepare itself for the capture of state power. Instead, the mercurial adventurism of the Progressive People's Party led by Gabriel Baccus Mathews, towards the end of 1979 and in early 1980, forced the William Tolbert government to take drastic measures that highly antagonised the broadest section of Liberian society, and created the stage for the military to intervene in politics 'to save the people' from a whole host of government sins — committed by both commission and omission — which were not then difficult to come by.

General Doe — at that point in time a mere Master-Sergeant — and his group of seventeen NCO co-plotters had not been involved in the long and arduous task of doing political battle with the True Whig regime. If anything, as soldiers, they had been quietly on the payroll, however miserly this was, of this regime. Yet when the regime seemed thoroughly discredited and there seemed to be a possibility that the organised masses could usher in a new social order, the army quickly stepped in and started dictating the terms of social change. Soon it became clear that the men in uniform were not acting in the spirit of Brigadier-General Quiwonkpa's words above; in fact they were not really interested in a drastic departure with the past but with its restoration with them in the political driving seat. Why was this the case?

One hypothesis that I advanced in 1982 and which I still stand by is that, for an army to take over political power easily and successfully through a coup, it must look for a conjuncture when that act can generate sufficient support from the populace so as to get an immediate source of legitimacy. Usually, a successful army coup will come when those who wield political power have virtually lost the social base of their rule, or narrowed this base to the extent that knocking it off becomes an easy surgical operation. As the Chinese say, such an easy coup occurs when the rulers 'have lost the mandate of heaven'. A coup that is carried out without the previous rulers substantially losing their social base usually establishes itself by sheer armed might, purges and a reign of terror; such was the case with Pinochet's coup in Chile in 1973. In the Chilean case, as the Popular Unity Government under Salvador Allende was advancing a popular revolution through the democratic process, defenders of the old order — US imperialism and their Chilean allies — brought about a counter-revolution through a military coup. In the case of Liberia, as the True Whig social base seemed to have been thoroughly eroded, and it looked more and more likely that progressive forces were gathering strength in the political sphere, the military intervened to stop these forces from coming to political power in their own right. There is sufficient evidence to show that US imperialism was sympathetic to a military *dénouement* without necessarily determining to the last letter who would be president after the coup.

The second hypothesis then advanced was that, when the military steals the political initiative from progressive forces in this manner, it always seeks to adorn the political garbs of the revolutionaries and to speak their progressive language. But the army, especially the ones prevalent in neo-colonial Africa, cannot become revolutionary overnight. If anything, such radical language is quite often used in a very opportunistic manner, with a lot of form and very little content. As some writers have argued:

> Military radicalism does not constitute a distinct political genre. The military caste has chameleonic traits. When it ventures on the political arena, it adopts a protective political colouring. Such ventures occur invariably during times of crisis, when the balance of social forces begins to shift. The choice of pigmentation — which element within the caste takes the initiative, and what political attitude it adopts — depends mainly upon and reflects the dominant characteristics of the social confrontation. It may adopt a conservative line if the threatened *status quo* has staying power; or, it may turn 'revolutionary' if the underdogs appear irresistible. In either case, the goal is power and the advantages it can secure for the caste. When that goal is contested by other groups, the colouring fades quickly, revealing the animal beneath.[4]

This, of course, has been true almost to the letter with regard to the military regime in Liberia over the last five years.

Let us, however, add a caveat to this hypothesis. There may be cases where the military personnel have themselves been involved in the political process of making a revolution, like the poor soldiers were in the Bolshevik revolution. In this regard, when the revolutionaries finally take over state power, the soldiers do not come into the political scene *qua* soldiers, but as part of the revolutionary forces; they do not seek to monopolise the armed might of the state, but to arm all the popular forces in defence of the revolution. It may also be possible that, within an established bourgeois army, a group of soldiers may join the popular forces secretly and plan, over a long period of time, for a revolutionary transformation of society: this was the case in Portugal under the fascist dictators Salazar and Caetano. The revolution may simply involve the dismantling of a dictatorship and the setting up of a truly democratic society in which all popular forces can thrive. Such soldiers may finally take over state power through a coup and create a social climate in which the popular forces can organise themselves democratically. In this case, the soldiers may go a long way in abolishing the repressive organs of the old society and creating democratic institutions after the coup. Again it is the long involvement of the military in the political process on the side of the popular masses that explains their post-coup behaviour. Unless the popular forces striving for a revolution are aware of these historical facts, they have no business joining hands with soldiers who make coups and instantly brew themselves like cups of soluble coffee into revolutionaries.

The case of Liberia over the last five years is important to us in many respects. For one thing, there is the acute awareness of many progressive forces in Africa today that the most immediate and urgent item on the agenda for the struggle of the popular masses is the democratic one. For those societies which have been formally independent since the sixties, there has been the establishment of varieties of non-democratic regimes which call themselves one-party states, military states, people's democracies, popular republics etc., etc., but where the general rule is that the popular masses have little or no voice in politics. Yet it is the masses that bear the burden of reproducing both the mammoth state machinery and the capitalist society it superintends. When, therefore, crises hit these societies, those who wield political power have very little notion about what to do since they are, for all intents and purposes, alienated from those they rule. Or, if they make any prescriptions, the factors they take into consideration are hardly those that can really deal with the plight of the popular masses.

For those societies where independence was recently won through armed struggle like Angola, Mozambique, Guinea-Bissau, Cabo Verde and Zimbabwe, there is the dilemma regarding how far the established states can tolerate further popular participation in politics and the thorough democratisation of social and economic life. These societies are faced with both internal and external problems which the political leadership need to solve in truly revolutionary and democratic ways.

There is finally the case of South Africa where the struggle of the popular masses for a democratic society has been going on for over eighty years and has just reached a decisive phase. Here the major question is posed in its most naked and dramatic form: what type of society will the impending revolution usher in and to what extent will the presently mobilised popular masses continue to play a decisive role in managing their own affairs in the new society?

The case of Liberia is important because, in many ways, it is a laboratory where all these problems have been posed and where the masses, for the moment, have lost the battle for gaining a democratic society. Yet Liberia is the oldest of the African republics. Never formally colonised, it has had, nonetheless, all the trappings of a colony. Having been established as 'a colony of free people' it did, nonetheless, experience an apartheid society for about 130 years. Having attempted to dismantle apartheid in 1980, it nonetheless saw the restoration of this society through the backdoor under a democratic facade. It is this latter phase where the counter-revolutionary role of the army becomes important and where again the Liberian experience becomes an indispensable lesson for the popular masses struggling for a democratic society elsewhere in Africa.

But to what extent are we justified in arguing that the *democratic question is the most urgent item on the agenda for the popular masses in Africa*? In the case of South Africa this is self-evident: the principle of one man one vote has never been even formally granted to the Africans who are the majority in the population, nor does the apartheid regime recognise the African as entitled to equal citizenship with the white man. At its simplest, democracy recognises equality of all human beings. This equality is then extended to the political arena to bestow citizenship to all members of modern republics. This means further that, in the formation of governments, processes and institutions must be devised whereby the individual has the unfettered freedom to choose, control and change those who govern him and the policies that determine what happens in the public sphere. That is why there is so much emphasis on individual rights and freedoms in democratic philosophies and traditions: rights to assemble, associate and discuss; rights to speak, organise and dissent; in short, the freedom to put one in a position to determine how the organised might of state power is going to affect one's life.

Democratic thought did not develop in a vacuum; it developed in a context whereby class society, like that in South Africa, was organised in such a way that political power was used by a minority to deny such rights to the majority so that the minority could enjoy certain material advantages and privileges at the expense of the majority. While the majority laboured every day to determine their existence, the minority simply appropriated the products of their labour by political fiat. The minority, organised as a ruling class, used ideological, military, political, legal, and religious institutions and systems of control to live off the surplus labour of the majority, the latter being deliberately denied any form of organisation to defend themselves from oppression and exploitation. This is what was typical of feudal society in Europe when democratic thought sprang up there in the 18th and 19th Centuries. The thought did not spring up all of a sudden, it sprang up as a result of tensions and crises that spanned generations in feudal society and always threatened the reproduction of that society. From time to time peasants rebelled against their landlords and killed tax collectors; at other times the king would feel that certain landlords were not surrendering what was due to him as head of the realm; at other times men who went to trade overseas in the name of 'his or her majesty', not being of lordly origin, found that they came back with wealth but had no right to decide how it was used. Finally there arrived the long process of capital accumulation which produced the new town burghers, men of wealth but not of royal blood, new creatures in society who could control vast means of production but had no political power to turn land into capital; these burghers felt feudalism was a fetter to their class interests and the form of state that defended it had to go. Individual freedoms were to be fought for not for their own sake but for the sake of being able to advance concrete material interest in society.

If we look at the writings of John Locke,[5] we find that there is a great deal of emphasis on property as the only legitimate criterion for acquiring citizenship rights or bestowing such rights on the individual. Locke has rightly been described as the 'bourgeois ideologue'; people, he argues, only come to associate in politically organised societies in order to safeguard their properties, either in themselves (as saleable commodities, i.e. wage labour) or in their movable assets or profit-bearing assets. The extent to which one owns property will determine the degree of one's citizenship: the principle of universal equality in citizenship is not granted by Locke. Those who have more property have more at stake in civil society, they must therefore control how this property is produced and disposed of: they must control political power.

We now know from history that, based on such Lockean ideas, the bourgeoisie waged struggles against the aristocracies of those days to make tremendous advances in the political sphere in establishing their class rule in society. They obviously allied with the other non-capitalist classes other than the feudalists in their class war; at other times the feudal classes fought back by mobilising the non-capitalist classes against them. Thus we see the battles, in England for example, over the Corn Laws and factory legislation where landowners and the new bourgeoisie fought against each other, arguing in defence of the interests of the working class only because they wanted to advance their own class interest. In the case of the Corn Laws, the factory owners opposed protection of the domestic corn production so as to allow workers to live off the low wages they received from their employers: the bourgeoisie had reasons to fight on the side of the workers. In the case of the factory legislation, workers wanted better conditions of work, shorter working hours and better wages; the landowners supported the workers mainly to hit back at the factory owners remembering how they — the landowners — had been 'done in' over the Corn Law legislation. When it came to battling for the right to vote, to form trade unions and organise political parties of their own, the working class found they were very much by themselves; but decades of unrelenting struggle finally forced the bourgeoisie to give concessions to the workers and popular masses in creating the modern bourgeois democratic republic in Britain.

A confusion has always arisen as to why Karl Marx, who was so concerned about emancipation from all forms of oppression and exploitation, should have been such an enthusiastic supporter of the democratic republic. Marx, in actual fact, bitterly denounced the class character of the democratic republic but supported its coming into being. His reasoning was simple: the democratic republic he viewed as the most advanced type of political regime in bourgeois society and wished to see it prevail over more backward and 'feudal' political systems. But it remained to him a system of class rule, indeed a system in which the bourgeoisie rules most directly.[6] But as the bourgeoisie does this, it necessarily creates a society in which certain contradictions emerge which will, in the final analysis, spell the doom of bourgeois rule.[7] Every now and again the bourgeoisie will even try to negate the very nature of bourgeois society if it sees its interests threatened by such contradictions, but it cannot do so and survive at the same time. The flowering of a bourgeois democratic republic therefore creates the objective conditions in which the oppressed classes can organise and prepare, over a long-term perspective, for their emancipation from the rule of capital. That, indeed, will be the day when classes in bourgeois society will have been abolished and a completely new society, a communist one, will have been born. But that is in the future; as of now, the popular masses must struggle under concrete historical circumstances to create conditions for the realisation of that distant future, and that means making the best out of the bourgeois democratic republic.

We saw, of course, that in South Africa such a republic does not, as yet, exist: it must be created. But we also saw that where it exists elsewhere in Africa, the form is much more important than the content: the bourgeoisie is continually locked in contradictions whose resolution — from their own perspective — must involve the curtailing of the full maturing of their own republic. We also noted that, in almost every independent African republic, the struggle by the popular masses for their democratic rights takes many forms, and meets with varieties of responses — in terms of the existing regimes — by the bourgeoisie. Nowhere is this more dramatised today than in Liberia where all aspects of the democratic struggle by the popular masses have been condensed into five tense years since 1980. By tracing the history of Liberia, understanding how the crisis of 1979–80 came about and analysing how the programme of the popular masses was hijacked by the military, we shall seek to see how the interests of both the domestic and the international bourgeoisie interact and conflict in keeping back the advancement of the bourgeois republic in Africa so as to deny the creation of objective conditions in which the interests of the popular masses would be better served. In this regard, what the Doe regime has done in Liberia is to stage a counter-revolution.

## The Making of an Apartheid Society

When slavery became an obsolete method of recruiting labour in capitalist North America, abolitionists clamoured for its disbandment so that slaves could be let loose into the open labour market.[8] This was in the middle of the 19th Century. The abolitionists, such as the American Colonisation Society, also advocated the 'going back to Africa' of the surplus labour, hence the foundation of the Maryland State Colonisation Society which became responsible for the foundation of Liberia as 'a colony of returned negroes'.[9]

For quite some time therefore, 'the returned negroes' treated Liberia as 'their colony' and the native Liberians — obviously the majority — as 'the aborigines' in the same way in which the whites of South of Africa were to treat native Azanians. The Constitution of the Republic of Liberia founded by these negro settlers in 1847 stated very clearly that 'the purpose of the state is to provide a home for the dispersed and oppressed children of Africa, and to regenerate and enlighten the benighted continent'. Thus, in this mission of 'regeneration' and 'enlightenment', 'none but Negroes or persons of Negro descent should be admitted to citizenship'.[10] Further, 'that none but citizens should be entitled to hold property; and that only property-holders should be entitled to vote or hold executive office'.

Thus these 'oppressed children of Africa', returning to the continent to 'enlighten and regenerate' it, came with a mixed bag of feudal, Lockean and zionist/apartheid ideas to oppress and exploit those they found in the continent in the interests of their benighted class privileges. The republic they founded was truly a republic of the ruling class in the platonic sense; 130 years were to pass before a semblance of a modern bourgeois republic was born. In the meantime, as the years passed, 23 wars were fought against the Dei, Gola, Vai, Grebo, Kissi, Loma, Bassa, Kpelle, Sapo, Krahn, Mano, Gio and Krio peoples who defended their land, culture, and sovereignty. Of course the returned negroes were only able to impose the so-called republic on the indigenous peoples through the concerted efforts of western imperialism: US, British and French. In fact, after the First World War, the British were so sceptical of Liberian independence that they even suggested that the US should formally proclaim her colonisation of Liberia.

It should be remembered, however, that the 'returned negroes', or the Americo–Liberians, did not always rule Liberia as a united and homogeneous group. Depending on their place in the social process of production and their relationships with external capital, they always tended to form various 'groupings' or alliances *vis-à-vis* the control of political power. The early struggles over which section of the oligarchy would rule Liberia was finally decided in 1878 when the True Whig Party ascended to prominence and kept that position until a century later. The TWP had been founded in 1869 by dark-skinned Liberians in opposition to the then ruling Republican Party which was largely controlled by Liberian mulattos. The TWP then organised itself in such a way that, in spite of the succession of one president by another in a very executive system of government, continuity would always be preserved. There were even times when the TWP, respecting the fact that the constitution allowed for other parties to exist, sponsored the formation of rival parties to 'make believe' this constitutional proviso. Such parties would only help them identify the 'deviants' and class enemies. In order to preserve their rule, they were never shy to make a complete mockery of the electoral process open only to members of the caste, as happened in the 1920s.[11]

Under the de facto one-party TWP rule, it was traditional for the outgoing president, who was also the 'standard-bearer' or titular head of the party, to name his own successor and then force the nominee upon the party chiefs for official endorsement and nomination prior to submission to the electorate. Hence, it was not the people's (the enfranchised negroes) trust, but the winning of the outgoing president's trust, that was crucial in getting 'elected' to the powerful executive office.[12] Thus the TWP not only exercised 'caste power' within society, but, within this caste, it made sure a distinct class project was carried down the century through the personal rules of the various presidents who 'succeeded' each other. It was this over-reliance on a strong executive power, wielded very much by a personalised presidential regime, that finally became the undoing of the TWP domination of Liberian society. It is important to try and understand why the Americo–Liberians could only defend their class interests under such a state in which they were both dependent and vulnerable.

## Imperialism, the Domestic Ruling Class and the People

From the rise of the True Whig power to about 1930, there was really not much capital investment in Liberia. A quasi-slavery society existed with the Americo–Liberians living off the sweat of the indigenous peoples. Towards the end of the

1920s, however, a new factor entered into Liberian history. This was North American capital. And this capital, strongly supported by the State Department, fused an alliance with the TWP ruling oligarchy to lay the solid foundation for the kind of political economy over which both William Tubman and William Tolbert were to preside in the post World War II period.

Although Liberia had been traditionally close to the US for historical and economic reasons, the US did not get very deeply involved in domestic Liberian politics until the 1920s. In 1922, the Harding and Coolidge administrations went out of their way to encourage private American investment in Liberia. Thus, in his search for an independent source of rubber for American manufacturing, Harvey S. Firestone received a substantial concession from the Liberian government for the development of rubber in 1926. The Liberian government had actually acquiesced to Firestone's own proposal to take a 90-year lease on approximately 100,000 acres paying a negligible one-cent-per-acre annual tax. To add a sugar coating to the otherwise unpalatable agreement, the Finance Corporation of America, a Firestone subsidiary, extended a loan of $5 million to the Liberian Government which was duly accepted. Behind all these transactions was the State Department, always twisting the hands of the Liberian Government to concede to terms favourable to Firestone. Decades were to follow, as we shall subsequently see, during which the Liberian economy was systematically underdeveloped and the domestic ruling class grew less and less capable of rationalising the oppressive and exploitative social order to the awakened popular masses.

The first crisis came in 1930 when the League of Nations discovered that Liberia still practised slavery in the heyday of the free enterprise system, and that Firestone, in cahoots with the TWP ruling class, was the direct beneficiary. Embarrassed by the discovery, Firestone was ready to accede to the League's proposals of turning Liberia into a Trusteeship Territory under the League until internal conditions changed, i.e. until the apartheid state was abandoned for a bourgeois republic. The TWP ruling caste, however, could not afford voluntarily to lose their privileges to suit the niceties of an enlightened world, with or without Firestone. They therefore agreed to some reform proposals by the League's Commission of Inquiry but strongly resisted a Trusteeship status. Firestone, in the meantime, quietly stood by their side while the State Department did the footwork to cool things in the diplomatic circles. In 1934, Great Britain even proposed the expulsion of Liberia from the League of Nations; it was the US which came to the salvation of the True Whig state. The US then followed her political and diplomatic successes by pumping more capital investment into Liberia to help create a truly market economy and conditions for the development of free labour. But the going proved difficult, especially in the agricultural sector.

The Americo–Liberians, although coming back to Africa as 'settlers', never actually engaged themselves as agricultural entrepreneurs in the manner in which the Boers did in South Africa or the *wazungu*[13] did in Kenya. If anything, after escaping agricultural work as slaves in the US, they could not stomach messing their hands up with soil again. Instead, they looked for prestigious forms of earning a living in a country in which capitalism had not yet developed to the extent of creating, within its pores, such jobs as accounting, conveyancing, insurance, real

216

estate speculation, bank managers and so on. Thus the negroes wanted to be lawyers in a land where there were few capitalist conflicting relations of production to be regulated and reduced to law. The relations between Firestone rubber plantation and its workers were, by fiat, fixed by the state as that between the slave and his owner. They wanted to be business brokers in a land where such business was yet to be created, depending on whether the capital infused by the Americans in the thirties was successfully valorised. The majority of the negroes therefore resorted to *compradorial* activities, living off both the indigenous population and international capital as traders and conmen. So as to force the natives to acquire tastes for imported commodities, they got the state to levy 'hut tax' on every native — payable only in cash, i.e. the dollar. This also made it possible for Firestone, after the League of Nations incident, to get people ready to offer themselves as free labour if only so that they could get the money required for tax payment.

By 1940, Firestone plantation employed 25,000 workers — obviously the biggest employer. In 1943, the US decided to build a port for Monrovia with 'lend-lease' funds estimated at $22 million; more opportunities were created for wage labour for native Liberians. These projects also brought more white-collar jobs for the Americo–Liberians who, obviously, saw their fortunes more and more tied to the development of US capital in Liberia.

Between 1944 and 1946, a number of missions from the US dealing with public health and economic, educational, geological and agricultural conditions visited Liberia and studied her requirements.[14] The American Foundation for Tropical Medicine initiated, in Monrovia, an Institute of Medicine which received the support of liberal grants from the Firestone Company. In 1948, after further modifications, the Monrovia port was opened as a 'free port'. In subsequent history, the free port became a substantial earner of foreign exchange. It was as a result of this free port that expansion in iron production, for example, occurred. And with the development and export of Liberia's primary natural resource — iron ore — the US government initiated a massive foreign aid programme in conjunction with the UNO with the purpose of creating a much more expansive capitalist market in Liberia. In 1950, a General Agreement for Technical Assistance and Co-operation was concluded between the US and Liberia. In 1953, the Liberia Mining Company or the Christie Concession (in which the American Republic Steel Company had an interest) completed the first stage of the development of the iron ore deposits on Bomi Hills. A year later, annual exports to the US stood at one million tons of high grade iron ore.[15] More American investment entered into the cocoa (E. R. Stettinius) and timber (Letourneaus group) exports. From the very beginning the US was the leading foreign investor in Liberia and Liberia's single most important 'trade partner'. As the US foreign investment grew both in the plantation and mining sectors, so did the compradorial and functionary class of the Americo–Liberians also expand. From these 'returned negroes', there was an insignificant development of an indigenous class of capital: they remained a comprador and bureaucratic bourgeoisie *par excellence*.

In the 1960s, European capital joined the Americans in Liberia. The Liberia American–Swedish Minerals Company brought its rich Nimba iron ore mine into production in 1963. LAMCO went further by constructing Africa's first pelletising

217

plant at Buchanan, building a new port at Buchanan and a railway running for 170 miles (274 km) from the port to the Nimba mines.[16] Thus, to this very day, of the 493 kilometres of railway communication in Liberia, Lamco alone owns over 50 per cent.

In the Bong Range mines, another company — Delimco (German Liberian Mining Company) — started iron ore extraction in the early 1960s. Thus, by 1962 total foreign investment in Liberia amounted to approximately $445 million with about 75 per cent of this contributed by the mining and rubber concessions both of which were further dominated by American capital.

But by the very nature of these investments, both the mining and the plantation sectors grew as 'enclave economies' in Liberia: they created very little dynamic effect in the domestic economy. Instead, as a result of bribing, they made away with huge non-taxed profits which simply led to the further underdevelopment of Liberia.[17] But the underdevelopment was a two-party affair: on the one hand were the owners of foreign concessions who made profits at the expense of Liberia; on the other were members of the domestic ruling class who received financial and other logistical support from these foreign capitalists so as to make their political dominance possible. This comprador and bureaucratic bourgeoisie served as advisers and lawyers to, and minor shareholders in, foreign companies. By the 1970s, less than one per cent of Liberians received more than half the nation's income. It is interesting to note that, when the coup took place in April 1980, the 13 members of Tolbert's cabinet — plus Tolbert himself — were accused by the soldiers mainly of having accumulated too many houses and fat bank accounts locally and externally.[18]

## Economic Growth and the Gradual Erosion of TWP Hegemony

Analysing economic data on Liberia up to the 1950s, Robert Clower et al.[19] concluded that the Liberian economy experienced *growth without development* from the 1930s onwards. They observed that foreign investment in the primary sector of the economy comprised the engine that fuelled the double-digit economic growth rates of the 1950s. However, very few Liberians benefited from such growth: it was mainly the bureaucratic and comprador bourgeoisie that were the associate partners in this growth.

William Tubman of Maryland became Liberia's president in 1944. He presided over most of the investment expansion and, through an iron fist, made sure that the majority of the Liberians who were not beneficiaries did not rock the boat. The True Whig oligarchy was organised in such a way that the church, cultural institutions and education bound members of the class/caste tightly together. Organised into a kind of *broederbond* outside the state, the TWP oligarchy boasted one of the largest Masonic Lodges on the African continent. Under Tubman and Tolbert, the size and glamour of the Freemasons' headquarters competed only with that of the Executive Mansion.

Tuan Wreh has argued that the birth of the Tubman era saw political bossism at its zenith.[20] Tubman packed the Legislature with his servants, cronies and favourites, many of them illiterate. One had functioned as his social secretary, another as his official chauffeur and another as his valet, another was his ward, a fifth was his business agent, and a sixth served as his press secretary. Chiefs elected on the basis of Tubman's selection were largely illiterate, and to follow debates in the legislature had to use interpreters to translate from English, the official language, into their own dialects. In any case Tubman himself had no more than a highschool education, and one is right to wonder why, among an oligarchy which boasted of lawyers and doctors with American degrees, such mediocrity was suffered in the executive and legislative branches of government. The explanation is to be found, perhaps, in the fact that both the comprador and the bureaucratic bourgeoisie — the real bourgeoisie of the Americo–Liberians — depended on the state to maintain their class positions, and the Bonaparte at the top found it easy to manipulate them to do his own bidding while serving their interests.

Most institutions in civil society, especially those which in any way represented — or could represent — popular forces, were cowed, suppressed or somehow made inoperative by Tubmanism. The University of Liberia, founded in 1951, the press, the trade unions, professional organisations and even the churches were cowed into chanting only one chorus: that from the Gospel according to St William. Bourgeois professions, by their very nature, tend to produce self-styled liberal democrats. Such were to be found in the law profession, the churches, journalism and the university. Yet their attempts to criticise the apartheid system and the oligarchical rule of True Whiggism met with severe and prompt repression. International capital, which survived by the stable superintendence over their properties by True Whiggism, did little to defend 'the rights of man' in Liberia. No careful employer would take someone once jailed or detained for opposing Tubman without first securing clearance from the chief executive, and then only as a vassal not a free man.[21]

Albert Porte, one of Liberia's veteran liberal critics of True Whig rule, wrote to Tubman in August 1951 criticising the President's squandering of a poor country's resources by buying a luxurious personal yacht at $150,000 from public funds. Porte further reminded Tubman that Liberians never felt free to speak on such issues, that there was a tendency for those in power to behave as if the people did not mean anything.[22] 'The Love of Liberty that Brought Us Here'[23] seemed to apply only to the True Whig oligarchy; perhaps once this liberty to exploit the masses wantonly was finally lost, 'the love of money will finally take them back to the United States of America'. It is in this spirit, actually, in which Tubman replied to Porte. He reminded Porte that the likes of him had no right asking what happened to public funds since the amount of tax they pay was nothing compared to that the president himself, the big companies and the foreign-owned monopolies paid.[24] The root of Tubman's authoritarian power was not the Liberian people but the power of imperialism and domestic comprador/bureaucratic capital in a society in which other social classes were underdeveloped and politically unorganised.

Tubman's 'open door policy' to foreign capital and businessmen — Syrians and Lebanese — hardly considered or protected the interests of the Liberian people, let alone indigenous businessmen: this led to the beginnings of an expanding *constituency of discontent*. Foreign entrepreneurs and merchants, doing close deals with the President's small circle of protégés and family, took over the country's economy and had first claim to the scarce currency for internal circulation.

Liberians were squeezed out of comprador business as the Tubman inner circle and their foreign allies sought more for themselves. Many shopkeepers were affected, and it became very clear to the Liberian business community, who had been part of the True Whig coterie, that the 'standard-bearer' was getting a little out of hand, and more checks and balances were needed even within the politics dominated by the caste. The Liberian Business Association, together with the churches, started humming for some liberalism through the press. They found their most forthright spokespeople at the University of Liberia which systematically started emerging as 'the conscience of the nation'. Such public figures as Albert Porte and Tuan Wreh also became indispensable to this crusade for greater liberalism in society.

Financial institutions became reluctant to advance liberal, long-term loans to Liberian businesspeople but would readily do so to foreigners as these were stable and could not be affected by 'presidential take-overs'. At the same time, such fractions of foreign capital grew more arrogant; there was little effort made by them to Liberianise their personnel even at very low positions of employment. No proper accounting systems were kept by these foreign concerns and, as Liberian businessmen became 'a losing class', so did the Liberian economy also become 'a losing economy'.

Togba-Nah Tipoteh points out that, by the end of the 1970s, Firestone alone had made some $500 million in profits, over three-quarters of which were exported and in some cases, formed part of the company's retained earnings. The profitability of Firestone was such that it financed some of the other subsidiaries of the Firestone Rubber and Tyre Co. In the midst of such profitability, it is useful to note that after half a century of Firestone's operations in Liberia, the company's oldest employee, a rubber tapper, with 50 years' service, had a monthly pay of $50. During the 1970s the real wages of Firestone's rubber tappers declined by approximately 50 per cent.[25] Yet we know that a capitalist economy can only develop if more and more people are coming into the market-place with more and more wages to spend on commodities produced by capitalist enterprises in both agriculture and industry. But here was the case that these two sectors of the economy were basically *extroverted*, to use Samir Amin's phraseology[26], and such extroversion could only produce a retrogressive economy marked by certain high sectoral growths with very little spread effects in the domestic economy and ever more alarming social indicators of unemployment, malnutrition, disease, ignorance and poverty.

With the expansion of missionary education after the Second World War, and the establishment of the University of Liberia in 1951, both primary and secondary education started to produce employable literates. It was mainly the children of the 'country people' who attended the U of L. Most children of the oligarchy went abroad, mainly to the US, and came back to serve automatically in government and the foreign-owned private sector. Education was already creating a class division within the new middle class. Some children of the country people also found their way abroad after college, and there a new world was open to them, a world so different from their native land that they started to think seriously about the lack of middle-class values at home and what to do about it. This new petty bourgeoisie, far from desiring to revolutionise all society for the broad masses and oppressed peoples, thought much more in terms of changing the social conditions by means of which existing society would be made as tolerable and as comfortable as possible for them. For example, during the Tolbert era, from 1973 to the coup of 1980, the rapid expansion of educational facilities at the primary and secondary levels led to 20 per cent unemployment among school leavers alone in the capital city of Monrovia. Most of these depended on their 'educated relatives' for their livelihood; in other words, the dependency ratio in the urban areas went up by leaps and bounds. The new middle class had reasons to be restless. They demanded more rational allocation of public resources, more equitable distribution of income, more say by the people in the affairs of government.

As popular pressure was beginning to simmer, William Tubman did not realise that, in the final analysis, he would always depend on the repressive apparatus of the state to keep him in power. Yet the armed forces remained neglected and poorly paid. The Barclay Training Centre, an army camp that housed the 'defenders of the nation' in slum barracks with dusty alleys and open drainage, had the misfortune of overlooking the luxurious Executive Mansion in which the 'standard-bearer' presided over the opulence of the TWP oligarchs and the misery of the men in arms. Contradictions were maturing on every front.

In the rural areas, the snakes of sickness continued to swallow the Liberian children, and ignorance, like a stubborn elephant, went on knocking the people down to pray to their gods for salvation since they did not know what else they could do in such a cruel environment. Sons and daughters of the Liberian peasants who had heard of the neon lights of Monrovia escaped to that equally god-forsaken city, looking for their last port of solace. Here they joined the ranks of the unemployed, and listened to voices which could tell them where Jerusalem could possibly be found. As sons and daughters of the Liberian peasantry voted with their feet from the countryside, fewer hands were left there to produce the country's staple food, *rice*. Peasants, too, discouraged by poor market mechanisms, produced mainly for their immediate subsistence. This rice scarcity provided an opportunity for the comprador bourgeoisie to play commerce with the basic needs of the people. Tubman and his cronies, Tolbert and his family, started to import rice and to charge ever-increasing prices. A nation that can produce its own rice therefore ended up spending 8 million dollars a year importing this commodity under Tubman, the main importing agents being, of course, the president, his relatives and his protégés. And this was a 'tradition' that William Tolbert inherited and carried to its most absurd conclusion.

## The Birth of Popular Organisations and the 'End' of TWP Rule

The two most important popular organisations that were finally responsible for bringing down the TWP were the Movement for Justice in Africa (MOJA) and the Progressive People's Party (PPP). PPP was urban-based; MOJA was both rural and urban in its programmes and support. The PPP, led by the mercurial Baccus Mathews, depended much more on the exploitation and articulation of popular grievances at particular conjunctures; MOJA was much more concerned with building a popular movement from below which could educate people, make them much more economically self-reliant and give them a vision of the future in which they could take the making of their own history into their own hands. As such, we

221

shall be more concerned with MOJA as a popular movement rather than with the PPP as a political party of the urban crowd led by an intelligentsia which, like most nationalist parties of the pre-independence era, was much more target-oriented: getting into the governor's mansion on the crest of the mobilised people's power.

Initially formed to share information 'on the very bad conditions of the people of South Africa and other African countries', MOJA soon focused its attention on the Liberian political scene and become the most outspoken and active political organisation of the country. But MOJA was not formally organised as a political party as such: it operated as a people's 'self-help' movement and eschewed any transformation into a political party until such time that the people were conscious and well-organised enough to demand such a transformation.

The activities of MOJA were directed at changing the lives of ordinary Liberians for the better through such projects as improving communal rice growing among peasants and arranging better terms of sale for them; organising unions among urban workers and providing them with legal aid; helping student unions with problems of organisation and diffusion of information among the people. MOJA, in doing all this, became a powerful social force in a society where class organisation had been known only at the very top where the True Whig oligarchs organised themselves outside the state apparatus as Freemasons and inside the state apparatus as a political party and state functionaries.

As a people's organisation, MOJA took up certain causes that affected members of the popular classes in their confrontation with the state. When the Liberian legislature decided to legalise gambling in 1974, MOJA campaigned against it and succeeded in persuading President Tolbert to veto the bill. When Albert Porte, the veteran pamphleteer, was sued for libel by Tolbert's influential brother for accusing him of illegally 'gobbling business', MOJA launched a massive campaign to defend Porte. The libel suit was later withdrawn. MOJA followers involved themselves in a variety of constructive projects like adult education, helping the dock and mine workers, and even trying its hand at integrated rural development in Grand Gedeh County through its corporate affiliate SUSUKUU. Such local efforts were systematically interpreted into an international context which related the problems of the Liberian poor with those of the victims of imperialism elsewhere in the world. Development projects went hand in hand with discussions of liberation movements elsewhere in Africa. The system, of course, got wind of this and many MOJA militants were victimised. Its president, Togba-Nah Tipoteh, lost his job as an economics professor at the university on account of his activism in the political world. Some were subjected to indignities; some were even arrested and imprisoned. But determination, resolve and a sense of political purpose kept the MOJA militants going.[27] Progressive members of the Church, like Dr Nya Kwaiawon Taryor, formed some of MOJA's militants. Voluntary — but anonymous — contributions came from the liberal wings of TWP and some business circles who were growing weary of the backwardness of their own regime.

In 1979, therefore, MOJA decided to challenge the monopoly of the TWP by putting up a candidate in the mayoral elections of Monrovia. The candidate was the unassuming University of Liberia political science professor, Amos Sawyer, another MOJA militant. The election campaign was, for MOJA, a trial balloon:

222

how committed was the TWP to the republican constitution of Liberia which allowed for pluralism in the political process? To what extent were the internal contradictions within the TWP oligarchy — between reformists and conservatives — serious and deep enough to allow another party to challenge the TWP without necessarily inviting outright repression? In other words, was there room for qualitative change in the system through the democratic process? Could class struggle for change in state power be successfully waged on the democratic terrain? If Sawyer succeeded, could MOJA then go ahead and form a political party of the popular masses — the majority — to challenge the minority rule of the TWP? Though supported by MOJA, Amos Sawyer stood on an independent ticket.

Francis 'Chu Chu' Horton, Sawyer's opponent put up by the TWP, was a veritable child of the establishment, but an establishment gradually being disowned by some enlightened Americo–Liberians. Sawyer, a graduate of North-western University, could not, by Liberia's True Whig laws, be a voter in Monrovia because he was disqualified by the property clauses of the constitution. There were members of the Americo–Liberian intelligentsia who found this a repugnant clause that abused the basic intelligence of modern civilised beings. As the Sawyer For Mayor Committee argued: 'the law says that only those who own property can vote, and we know that Liberia belongs to all people, not only a few property owners'.[28] The TWP could not defend this Lockean principle even in their midst. The campaign demanded, among other things, that the True Whiggers declare their assets: a full list of property owners was needed, showing what type of property, just to know whether or not there were some fraudulent voters among the TWP who could not qualify even by their own standards of who a qualified voter was. The TWP backtracked by postponing the elections and declaring that the property clauses were outdated in modern Liberia and needed to be changed. But the political point had been made by MOJA and the stage was now set for a class battle with the TWP directly on the political terrain.

In the meantime, Tolbert did not attend to the much more urgent problem of feeding the nation. The rice issue was becoming more serious every day. Shortages were growing rampant. There was a need to improve the domestic production of rice so as to supply the domestic market adequately. Tolbert's approach was a typical World Bank recipe: increase the price of rice and the domestic producers will respond by growing more. What he did not understand was that, once the price was up — payable in dollars even domestically — importers would bring more from outside, flood the market, manipulate the distribution mechanism, and siphon their quickly-earned profits to overseas accounts. And this is what happened, the President himself giving the lead.

In November 1978, Dr Patrick Sayon of the University of Liberia had written a paper entitled 'The Politics and Economics of Rice Production in Liberia'.[29] In this paper, Sayon warned the government that given the conditions of life in Liberia, to raise the price of rice was politically suicidal. Mr Tolbert and his finance minister, the Honourable James T. Philips Junior, were the most important rice producers commercially; they also engaged in rice imports when their domestic supply was short. The peasants produced mainly for household consumption and confined rural markets. The urban markets were supplied by the big *commerçants* with close

223

connections with the ruling oligarchy.

The University of Liberia, MOJA and PPP united on the rice issue; more pressure was brought on the government to do something. Few workers, it was pointed out, with such low wages in the plantations and the urban sectors, could afford to buy rice at $23 per bag. The True Whig Party ignored the growing public discontent and the political mileage the 'alliance' was getting out of the issue. Instead, Tolbert and his party stalwarts concentrated on building an expensive conference complex to house the OAU summit in 1979 and decided not to give Liberia 'a bad image abroad' by publicising the rice issue. On 14 April 1979, however, there was a downing of tools by urban workers, street demonstrations and strikes by students in both the university and the high schools that took even MOJA by surprise. The whole thing was by and large spontaneous; but once it started, MOJA and PPP stepped in to give it direction. PPP members were the most vocal in the frontline of the urban crowd.

Tolbert reacted in panic. Leaders of student unions and the PPP and certain popular figures were picked up and detained. And instead of relying on his own armed forces to restore 'law and order', Tolbert invited troops from the Republic of Guinea under the 'mutual defence treaty' he had signed with Sekou Touré in January 1979. It was quite clear to the Liberian armed forces that their Commander-in-Chief did not have much confidence in them. The 'rice riots' have been described by one Liberian social scientist as 'the straw that broke the camel's back'.[30]

MOJA reacted to Tolbert's draconian measures by writing to him and requesting a National Commission of Inquiry to look into the reasons that led to the rice riots. MOJA further requested that the commission be given subpoena powers and immunity. Tolbert agreed to set up the commission but stripped it of all meaningful powers. Further, he packed the commission with his own protégés to the extent that, out of the 31 members, only 5 could be counted on to represent any dissenting voice from the Tolbert crowd. The commission was further directed to submit its report within 30 days. Despite the short time, and notwithstanding the pro-regime membership of the commission, its report was reasonably forthright and highly analytical with regard to the *causes* of the riots.

> It stated, for example, that the riots were a manifestation of serious social, economic and political problems with deep root causes in our national society. These problems of justice, liberty and equity are neither exclusively the outcome of the national policies of the incumbent administration; nor yet can we convincingly characterise them as conspiratorial designs externally motivated. They are in a real sense a culmination of more than 100 years of national leadership that appears to have eroded its constituents' participation in a meaningful way . . . Despite the fact that the constitution guarantees to all the enjoyment of fundamental human rights including the right to a decent standard of living, there are serious ills which plague our society.[31]

One wonders whether a man like Doe could have had the courage and sense of decency to set up an inquiry into the doings of his own regime, like the military invasion of the University of Liberia that he was subsequently to order when the university students and dons protested his detaining Amos Sawyer in August, 1984.

Tolbert, however, had that soft side to him: the decency of a bourgeois democrat in spite of the limitations of his own regime. In fact, it can be argued that as these contradictions mounted, the liberal wing of the TWP seemed to have been successfully arguing for some reform and more enlightened government; they were prepared grudgingly to concede full citizenship to the popular masses of Liberia.

The Commission, further, made specific recommendations on the programme of action that the regime needed to adopt:

(a) the university, having been closed after the riots, was to be opened unconditionally;

(b) amnesty to be given unconditionally to those detained as having instigated the riots: this included Baccus Mathews and Boima Fahnbulleh;

(c) the President was to dismiss members of his cabinet who were directly or indirectly accountable for precipitating, or poorly reacting to, events of April 14: these included Burleigh Holder, the President's son-in-law; King, the Minister for Defence and the Chief of Immigration;

(d) the President was to dismiss members of his family who were in high government posts since this constituted a conflict of interest and often led to nepotism. These included his daughter, who was an Assistant Minister for Education and his son-in-law who was an Assistant Minister for Public Works;

(e) there was to be an open market for rice imports rather than the giving of import rights to just a few select companies known personally to the President.

Tolbert reacted by freeing the detained, but agreed to open the university only under very stiff conditions and only after the OAU Summit was over. Meanwhile, Tolbert stationed soldiers on the Monrovian campus to keep a strict watch over the students. Elsewhere, the Guinean troops were visible enough to keep both the Liberian army and the civilian population in check. Already these were signs that it was the right to command through physical might that determined, in the final analysis, who ruled. The Liberian army obviously got a hint from this. Feeling beleaguered from many directions, Tolbert started an extended tour of the various counties and territories, making liberal speeches and promising impending reforms in the body politic. But as Boima Fahnbulleh pointed out then, the society was already in a state of ferment 'because the developing consciousness of the people has outstripped the institutions which were designed to cater for the consciousness of a different historical era'.[32] In other words, the social basis of True Whig rule had been significantly eroded by the growing political awareness, mainly as a result of MOJA's work, among the people.

## The Progressive People's Party and the Precipitation of the Crisis

Between April and November 1979, the PPP felt an urgent need to take the political initiative in forcing a showdown with the Tolbert government. Following the release of Baccus Mathews and his associates from detention after the 'rice riots', the urban crowd in Monrovia felt victory was on their side. The fiery speeches of Mathews, their leader, only helped to fuel a sense of crisis and some impending change. In November that year, the PPP decided to call a 'mass strike' and a demonstration as a sign that the TWP, in spite of its promises during its own party convention that October, had not done anything concrete to improve the conditions of the Liberian people. MOJA opposed plans for the mass strike; their argument was that neither the PPP nor MOJA had the capacity to control or direct such a strike. Moreover, it was not really called for: the TWP seemed prepared to tolerate a liberal atmosphere in which both PPP and MOJA could benefit by concentrating on educating the masses and organising them for a longer-term and more certain assault on state power. A mass strike, MOJA argued, would be adventurist: it would unnecessarily heighten tensions and disrupt the small gains the Progressive Alliance of Liberia — the co-ordinating body of the two groups, the students and the unions — had achieved. Baccus Mathews, however, went ahead with his plans, calling for a midnight 'march on government house' by the masses of Monrovia. The outcome was to be expected: not much was achieved except for some amount of 'heroism' on the part of Mathews and Queya, together with other PPP colleagues, who were duly thrown into detention and charged with treason. Their trial was set for April 1980, to coincide with the anniversary of the rice riots.

There was an immediate mass reaction against these draconian measures, but Tolbert also held to his guns arguing that his duty was to govern, and he had gone on record as allowing those who want to govern to follow the democratic process and get elected in the 1983 elections. To be fair to Tolbert, his regime had not proscribed PPP before the 'mass strike' nor had the regime done anything to prevent MOJA from forming a party and preparing for the elections. It was mainly for the latter reason that MOJA suddenly found more and more anonymous contributions filling its coffers. Somehow the general feeling must have been spreading among the liberal wings of the TWP, the churches and even some of the business community that Tolbert had, indeed, 'lost the mandate of heaven', and MOJA seemed a genuine movement full of dedicated individuals who could provide sound leadership for Liberia and restore the confidence of the people in their government. But, at the same time, some people thought otherwise: they prepared for a military solution to stop any possibility of MOJA coming to power.

The question worth asking is whether the army intervened to pre-empt a much more substantive change under the hegemony of MOJA or whether, led by strong feelings of patriotism, the army merely wanted to accelerate the process of ending the TWP rule by undertaking the necessary surgical operation. If the soldiers acted to pre-empt a revolution led by MOJA, with whom or on whose behalf were they acting? Whose class project was the military coup?

## Soldiers and Counter-Revolution

It is now part of history that the principal objective of the military takeover in Liberia was to destabilize the work of MOJA and *abort the struggle* of the Liberian people for democracy in Liberia. Non-military efforts directed at putting an end to the work of MOJA failed miserably; thus the resort to military means.

Togba-Nah Tipoteh[33]

Some people think that because the military is in power we are going to change the face of our country. This, I've told them, we are not going to do.'

Samuel Kanyon Doe, Head of State and Commander in Chief of the Armed Forces[34]

226

Since the Second World War, many progressive social science researchers have observed that the US and her Western allies have striven to prop up unpopular and repressive regimes in the Third World. When such regimes are threatened by their own people through popular movements that struggle for fundamental changes in society so as to bring about progress, the US and her allies have always sought to defend such regimes against their own people for the sake of preserving the free enterprise system under the superintendence of 'the devil they know'. But when 'the devil they know' becomes absolutely indefensible, and when popular forces gather so much strength and credibility that their coming to power — if left to be determined by the people and the democratic process — is a foregone conclusion, imperialism has always been ready to support, financially, logistically and through other forms of manoeuvre, the military *coup* as a pre-emptive strike. Such a coup, becomes a counter-revolution. Properly speaking, writes Ralph Miliband:

> a counter-revolution may be said to have occurred when a regime of the left, Communist or not, has been overthrown (or for that matter replaced by legal means) and where the successor regime pushes through a series of economic, social and political measures designed to assure or restore the power, property and privileges of landlords, capitalists and other segments of the ruling class who have been threatened with dispossession or who have actually been dispossessed by the regime which the counter-revolution replaced. This involves the return to landlords and capitalists of their land and factories and banks, and of property in general, where it has been taken from them. It also involves the reaffirmation of their power and preponderance *by the suppression* of the defence organisations of the subordinate classes — parties, trade unions, cooperatives, clubs and associations. It further involves *the suppression or drastic curtailment of civil rights*; the physical suppression of opposition leaders, of agitators, subversives and enemies of the state; and the political restructuring of the state in authoritarian directions. . . . *It is not essential for a revolution actually to have occurred for a counter-revolution to be mounted: the apparent illogicality is purely in the semantics, not in the reality.*[35]

A counter-revolution may be initiated to *abort* an impending revolution.

In Liberia, MOJA actually had a programme of undertaking a truly bourgeois–democratic revolution from the grassroots to the top. Its leaders had credibility in society; they had very few class linkages with imperialism. If anything, their nationalism, rooted in a sincere commitment to social reform, justice and a curtailment of the privileges of the imperialist and the domestic (comprador and bureaucratic) bourgeoisies threatened both these classes. Added to this was the *strategic importance of Liberia* to American imperialism in Africa, the Middle East and the Asian continent. State Department hawks could not afford to lose Liberia politically at a time when they had just lost both Iran and Afghanistan. The global perspective of imperialism obviously has a great deal of bearing on the successes or failures of a people's movement meant to establish democratic forms of government even in some of the tiniest republics in the world today. Such popular movements must be led by people who are acutely conscious of the global politics of particular conjunctures so as not to fall prey to imperialist machinations. To gain a democratic society, albeit imperialist powers themselves mouth the defence of democracy everywhere, is not necessarily the same as undertaking a project that,

227

*ipso facto*, will be supported by all imperialist democracies; it all depends on the conjuncture, the polarisation of global interests, their strategic calculations and, quite often, their knack for opportunism. Given their strategic and capitalist interests in Liberia, the US could not have stood by and watched events unfold there without seeking to initiate, direct and even determine the outcome of every major action. But before we analyse how the US has been supportive of the counter-revolution, let us lay bare US interests and imperialist control of Liberia in its political, military and strategic aspects.

### Imperialism and Counter-Revolution

We noted earlier that the US is the largest foreign investor in Liberia.[36] That does not need to be laboured once again. But the US has other strategic investments in Liberia of military, logistic and ideological types. First there is the Voice of America transmitter station that broadcasts news and ideological propaganda to Africa, the Middle East and parts of the Soviet Union from Liberian soil. Second, there is the telecommunications relay station transmitting diplomatic traffic between Washington and more than 40 US embassies in Africa. Third, there is the navigational station, OMEGA, which enables ships and aircraft to calculate their positions continually.[37] This is important because, fourth, the US can use Robertsfield international airport outside Monrovia to land large military and transport planes that may be necessary for counter-insurgency operations in the continent. Fifth, Liberia boasts of the largest CIA establishment in Africa: this number of CIA personnel is stationed there not to spy on the less than three million Liberians but to be occupied with continental operations from what the State Department must regard as a safe haven.

It would be wrong, however, to argue that the US knew, to the last detail, when Tolbert would be assassinated and who would emerge as the military ruler; this would be an extremely naive way of reading back into the events. What can be said, from the evidence already available from public sources, is that the US embassy in Monrovia had a military alternative option to the beleaguered True Whig regime, an option that was meant to keep MOJA from gaining political ascendancy. One option was to rely on the officer corps to initiate the coup: Major Jerbo, described as a western-educated, well trained professional soldier with a great deal of popularity among the ranks, would have been a suitable candidate for the Americans. A Jerbo-led coup would also bring in civilian politicians, perhaps under the premiership of Baccus Mathews in a cabinet subordinate to the Jerbo-led Military Council. There would be no problem bringing in more moderate and liberal True Whig stalwarts such as Ellen Johnson-Sirleaf and others to provide continuity with the old order. Gabriel Baccus Mathews has been described as 'a good friend of the Americans'.[38] While he was Doe's Foreign Minister in the first post-coup cabinet, he even called for resumption of diplomatic relations with the Zionist state of Israel. Given his rather amorphous mass following among the urban crowd and some sections of the rural peasantry, and his undeniable ability on the platform, he would have been the typical mediator between imperialism and the people who would keep the latter satisfied with rhetoric while the imperialists continued very much as before.

That Jerbo was killed by Doe's men while trying to escape across the Mano river into Sierra Leone after the coup is a good enough evidence to show that the NCOs who undertook the coup were afraid of him. Moreover, from the evidence given by Thomas Quiwonkpa, the original 'strong man' of the military regime, it is clear that the NCOs knew of an officers' plot to stage a coup; and they were obviously aware that the officers had the backing of the Americans.[39] Again it is quite obvious that the immediate move by the NCOs was to form a National Redemption Council (NRC) in which the officers were not in the least represented. The number of officers who suffered executions and disappearances is yet to be determined, although Quiwonkpa indicated that he knew them and blamed the 'panic elimination' on General Doe himself. Further, the kind of civilian alliance that the coup-makers moved first to make obviously pre-empted any American-led attempt to discredit them with the people: they brought into the civilian cabinent MOJA, PPP and TWP representatives, let alone members of the military itself. *West Africa* was led to comment:

> This cabinent is one of reconciliation and is also full of high talents — it contains three former members of Tolbert's Cabinet, leaders of the PPP (including Baccus Mathews as Foreign Minister), of MOJA (Fahnbulleh and Tipoteh, as Minister for Education and Economic Planning respectively) and some military representatives.[40]

Yet Idi Amin had also formed such a cabinet when he overthrew the Obote government in January, 1971; his was one flowing with university professors thrown in to head ministries within their own academic specialisations; permanent secretaries who became political heads of ministries they had all along run as technocrats; army officers whose credibility as professional men was hard to question; a Commissioner of Police whose record in the civil service was exemplary. Yet Amin soon went to commission all these men into the military and bring them directly under his command of mediocrity. Just about a decade later, Samuel Kanyon Doe did exactly the same with the Liberian cabinet so exalted by *West Africa*. Like Amin, he used these men as show-pieces to win immediate credibility and legitimacy and soon started discarding them in preference for those he could manipulate and control, if not keep in total fear of his system to the extent that the Cabinent came to mean nothing. But Doe did not travel as fast as Amin did; the reason being that the US embassy was not sitting idle: they soon adopted a strategy of winning the new regime to their side and keeping it away from the influence of the likes of Tipoteh, the Socialist bloc of countries and other anti-imperialist forces. This they did through lavish aid that in one year outstripped more than ten times what they had given Liberia since 1911.

Thomas Quiwonkpa said, in the interview referred to above, that the coup could not have succeeded without the physical elimination of Tolbert. He personally 'led the boys' to the eighth floor of the Executive Mansion where Tolbert slept and one of them, the late Nelson Toe, pulled the trigger that killed Tolbert. Doe, in the meantime, was hiding in the 'flower bush' around the Mansion compound 'keeping watch'. Yet it is this man who kept watch, not Quiwonkpa nor Weh Syen, who was named by them — at the urging of Quiwonkpa himself — to be Head of State. The reasoning was perhaps quite simple: Doe, being a Krahn by nationality, came from a minority group, and could perhaps be a more acceptable candidate across the board. But both Quiwonkpa and Weh Syen could have individually calculated that Doe would be a mere 'passing cloud'; once things settled, the real strong man — Quiwonkpa — could take over. But this is not a very plausible strategy. The only other credible strategy is that Quiwonkpa was himself very much in the know of the American-arranged coup, and he saw himself as rising within the army hierarchy if he supported the NCO coup which could eventually return Liberia to the kind of civilian rule acceptable to the Americans. Given Quiwonkpa's stature, ideological inclination, support in the army and the antipathy that soon developed between him and Doe, it is quite reasonable to accept this last hypothesis as the most plausible. Moreover, he was the man that the Americans seemed to have relied on most for contact within the PRC, and Doe was right to suspect that 'someone else was being groomed for power to take his place'. It did not take Doe long to eliminate Quiwonkpa — much to the displeasure of the Americans. Again *West Africa* commented:

> Quiwonkpa is a highly professional soldier who enjoys enormous respect within the rank and file of the Liberian armed forces. Doe's recruitment of him after the overthrow of Tolbert in 1980 was not as much due to the role he played in the actual coup operation but rather because of the respect and following he commands in the army. Brigadier-General Quiwonkpa's greatest achievement was to instil discipline and training in the largely illiterate and reckless Liberian military forces, especially after the 1980 coup. To this end, he has remained loyal to the revolution.[41]

Then later *West Africa* added: 'Quiwonkpa was said to advocate a quick return to civilian rule and was better regarded by the Americans . . . perhaps that is why he was so much of a threat to Doe.[42]

It is understandable that Doe, once he became head of state and wanted to remain so, must have forced the Americans and the True Whig stalwarts to accept him as *the* President. The execution of the 13 members of Tolbert's cabinet and the assassination of Tolbert himself, followed later by that of his son, A. B. Tolbert, served a strong enough warning to the civilians that the army was not to be opposed. At that point in time, Doe's overtures to the popular masses, his speaking of their revolutionary language — 'in the cause of the people, the revolution continues' — obviously gave his regime more legitimacy and justified his draconian measures against what were regarded as the real corrupt elements of True Whig rule. But Doe became acutely aware of the 'staying power of the old order', and its determination, with American backing, to get rid of him if he flirted too much with the progressive forces. At the same time, the interest of the army was not really to change the old order, but to make the old order accept within its midst those previously kept out. Doe's strategy was therefore two-pronged: on the one hand, extend an olive branch to members of the old order by bringing them back into the government while distancing himself from the representatives of the popular forces, particularly MOJA — this would please the Americans and win them over to him; on the other hand, eliminating all opposition to his rule, especially those within the military and the PRC who might be regarded by the Americans as the more 'acceptable forces' of military rule — this would displease the Americans but there is little they would do short of assassinating him. Anything was possible, but Doe stubbornly followed both strategies, even finally forcing his candidature for the civilian presidency — much to the displeasure of both the Americans and the restored TWP now firmly in government without necessarily controlling directly the executive branch. The reasons why the 'mediocre' Doe was able to stage the counter-revolution must be sought first in the interpretation of events as they have unfolded, and secondly by drawing some parallel from the past history of European society so as elaborate on a common phenomenon.

In the *Eighteenth Brumaire of Louis Bonaparte*, Karl Marx tried to explain how and why Louis Napoleon, a mediocre military leader, arose to be the unchallenged head of the French Republic during the period 1848–1852. This was the time when the French bourgeoisie, so disorganised as a class, attempted to perfect their rule through parliamentary democracy but failed, delivering themselves on a silver platter to be ruled and terrorised by 'the chief of the Society of December 10 . . . and the head of the lumpenproletariat'.[43] The sequence of events was as follows.

There was first of all the overthrow of Louis Philippe and the formation of the *provisional government* from 24 February to 4 May 1848. All social strata were pleased about Louis Philippe's downfall: the urban and revolutionary proletariat because it would give them the opportunity finally to organise for a *democratic socialist republic* aided by the radical intelligentsia; the bourgeoisie because finally there was a chance for a *parliamentary democracy*; the army were elated in that they had time for activity, 'keeping law and order' in a society which was almost 'gone mad' with joy, some of the lumpen in the army took the occasion to loot and get away with stolen property; the peasants saw the birth of the republic as yet another chance of getting private property in land and doing away with any remaining shackles of landlordism. The government that was formed was provisional in all respects: nobody wanted to take any permanent decision and everybody wanted his particular type of republic to be born as the new and permanent reality on the French soil. As Marx notes:

> Nothing and nobody ventured to lay claim to the right of existence and of real action. All the elements that had prepared or determined the revolution: the dynastic opposition, the republican bourgeoisie, the democratic–republican petty bourgeoisie, and the social–democratic workers, *provisionally* found their place in the February 'government'.[44]

In the meantime, the kinds of discussions that were going on within this provisional government started to worry some of its members. The bourgeoisie, in particular, were worried about 'the socialism' of the social–democratic workers: how could they use democracy to abolish private property? After all, as far as the bourgeoisie was concerned, it was to enter the kingdom of unfettered acquisition of private property that they had overthrown Louis Philippe! If this was what parliamentary democracy meant, then it needed to be limited, it needed to be guided, it should enjoy less freedom of speech, there should be some preconditions regarding who was 'really qualified' to be a member of the parliamentary bourgeois republic. 'The

French bourgeoisie balked at the domination of the working proletariat . . . It destroyed the revolutionary press; its own press was destroyed. It placed popular meetings under police supervision; its salons are under the supervision of the police.'[45]

Part of the outcome of trying to limit democracy was to make the *executive branch* of government stronger. Yet this executive branch, led by someone regarded as a 'provisional head', had been there for a long time and had seeped deeply into the crevices of society. This executive branch, with its bureaucracy and its armed institutions, is what Bonaparte headed as the 'provisional president'. It had within it men who were neither bourgeois nor of the bourgeoisie; these were men of bureaucratic careers, paid hirelings of the state who might be content to serve any power provided their livelihood was assured. These were the sons of peasants who had escaped the dreary life of the countryside for the glamorous life of bearing arms and wearing polished shoes; they were now under the command of Bonaparte and told to keep 'law and order' by the class they regarded as *cultivé*, but a class that now really needed them to keep the anarchists and socialists from running away with state power. By balking at strengthening parliamentary democracy, the bourgeoisie only gave the opportunity for the executive branch to grow strong in government, and quite soon the logic of this government meant the bourgeoisie, too, were to lose their bourgeois freedoms. Writes Marx:

> The bourgeoisie confesses that its own interests dictate that it should be delivered from the danger of its *own rule*; that in order to restore tranquillity in the country its bourgeois Parliament must, first of all, be given quietus; that in order to preserve its social power intact its political power must be broken; that *the individual bourgeois* can continue to exploit the other classes and to enjoy undisturbed property, family, religion, and order only on condition that his class be condemned along with other classes to like political nullity; that in order to save its purse it must forfeit the crown, and the sword that is to safeguard it must at the same time be hung over its own head as a sword of Damocles.[46]

The second step was when the revolutionary proletariat, realising that parliamentary democracy was becoming nothing other than the most direct rule by the bourgeoisie, and that every day the freedoms it thought it had won were being whittled away, decided to revolt and take to armed struggle. Along with it came some of the revolutionary peasantry, those who had been awoken from the slumbers of rural life. The bourgeoisie appealed even more directly for Bonaparte to mobilise the army and restore order. There was now no time for discussion, no time for the niceties of secret ballots and voting: Bonaparte argued it was time for government and order, and both the bourgeoisie and the conservative peasantry agreed; so did those who, in their millions, served the state as its servants. The revolutionary proletariat was crushed, and all other classes came under the rule of Bonaparte as his subjects. 'The struggle seems to be settled in such a way that *all classes*, equally impotent and equally mute, fall on their knees before the rifle butt.'[47]

What is finally significant about the rise of this Bonapartist state, the state where the executive power becomes so powerful and so independent of the bourgeoisie while defending capitalist society, is that it had a particular *class content and class base*. The bourgeoisie as a class was not yet organised well enough to rule: it was a weak bourgeoisie, divided up into so many fractions and factions, with so many parties and clubs to represent its interests, and without any organised community of interest. Moreover, this bourgeoisie was threatened by the upsurge of a revolutionary proletariat whose weakness lay in its lack of organisation but whose strength was derived from its rhetoric and clamour for change. While the revolutionaries discussed ideas of change and of getting to socialism, the bourgeoisie conspired about how they could at least defend the regime of private property. The peasantry, in the countryside, lived under a mode of production that was a hindrance to their being organised politically. Yet, being the majority and steeped in tradition, they remembered their past and dreamed of the glorious future which folk heroes could bring. Here, among the peasantry, were to be found true Frenchmen, to be counted upon to defend the nation if need be. The central factor uniting all these classes was not only their nationality, but the fact that they were governed by a state which, over a long period of time, had taken over many responsibilities 'on behalf of everybody' in civil society. Parliamentary democracy was aimed at bringing the power of civil society into taming this state machine and making it act 'according to the will of the people'. But as a result of the class divisions and class paralyses described above, the executive power overthrew parliamentary power and then Napoleon himself became the executive power. Bonapartism came along with a peasant society, a bourgeoisie that had lost the power to rule politically, a working class repressed and disorganised and a strong state bureaucracy, civil and military, which could be mobilised to govern a capitalist society.

Miliband has taken Nicos Poulantzas to task for suggesting that Marx designated Bonapartism as the 'religion of the bourgeoisie', and that Poulantzas erroneously takes Marx to mean that Bonapartism was 'characteristic of *all* forms of the capitalist state'.[48] On the contrary, what Marx did say was that Bonapartism in France 'was the only form of government *possible* at the time when the bourgeoisie had already lost, and the working class had not yet acquired, the faculty of ruling the nation'.[49] We have attempted to sketch in the above résumé of the arguments in the *Eighteenth Brumaire* how this happened historically.

But this phenomenon did not begin and end with France of the mid-19th Century; the concept of Bonapartism becomes important in the analysis of political processes because history keeps repeating itself. Here is the case of Liberia where, with the disintegration of the oligarchic True Whig rule, the Liberian bourgeoisie had lost the power to rule politically but the working class and the awakened peasantry, under the leadership of MOJA and PPP, had not yet acquired the power to rule. The strongest part of the state bureaucracy — the armed forces — forced a coup 'to save the nation', made all classes which had been clamouring for change hope for heaven; but this army coup, once it came firmly into the hands of Samuel Doe, delivered only the earth to these excited classes. Without ruling politically, the bourgeoisie was at least happy that their private property, their investments, were in safe hands. But this time we are not talking simply about the small Liberian bourgeoisie, we must also take into account the imperialist governments which, in neo-colonial countries, since they cannot directly rule politically, set the objective conditions for nurturing contemporary Bonapartes.

It goes without saying that the influence of the US in Liberia, in both her economy and internal politics, is enormous. If the US wanted to, it would almost be able to choose a president for Liberia, but somehow this cannot happen so directly. The principle of sovereignty limits the extent to which a foreign power can interfere directly in the internal politics of a small nation. A foreign power can finance or mastermind a coup, as indeed the US did in Chile in 1973 and as South Africa did in Lesotho in early 1986. But even after such a coup is successful, the 'interfering foreign power' cannot really determine how politics is run on a day-to-day basis. It is quite possible, therefore, that a client regime can go against the wishes of such a foreign power in certain of its policies under the shelter of sovereignty, and such policies could easily unleash conflicts quite unintended by, and unwelcome to, the foreign power.

Hence the US has always had a double attitude regarding her role in Liberia's internal politics: on the one hand it wants to make sure that those who run Liberia's political affairs are staunchly within the US camp; on the other, it does not want to be too directly and openly associated with the processes of policy-making for fear of accusations of imperialism and discredit when such policies fail. Hence, even with regard to such a directly dependent client state, US political protégés manage to run internal politics with some amount of autonomy.

It is in an attempt to limit this autonomy that US imperialism tends to prefer Bonapartist regimes in such places as Liberia to democratically-elected and people-controlled regimes. A regime that does not have a strong authoritarian centre and which has multiple centres of political power where the voices of the people matter is much more difficult to control. When, therefore, the US seems to champion 'free-and-fair elections' as the hallmark and the litmus test for democracy in Africa, it is *not* with the aim of seeing popular power through, but of seeing limited bourgeois reforms — including Bonapartist ones — given credibility and grounds for legitimacy.

## The Doe Regime and Counter-Revolution: or 'Sliding Back to the Old Ways'

The coup took place in April 1980. In May, the *Quarterly Economic Review* observed: 'The real difficulty facing the new government is how to reward both those who engineered the coup and those who openly welcomed it.'[50] To the former, Doe gave membership in the PRC; 3,000 more army recruits (friends, relatives, tribesmen etc.) were made; and there were promises of better living conditions and higher salaries. To the latter Doe gave promises of a better future. The only group forgotten by the *Quarterly Economic Review* were those who had worked hard to change society not through a coup but through a social revolution in the interest of the popular masses. On these, Doe, American imperialism and the local bourgeoisie rapidly turned their backs: they were dismissed from the government, detained, forced into exile and finally banned from the political process altogether.

Economically, the situation was difficult right from the very beginning: there was recession in the markets of Liberia's two export commodities — iron ore and rubber — the previous regime had spent lavishly on the OAU summit, adding to Liberia's foreign debt at a time when she could hardly pay for needed imports; the real GNP per capita had been falling for the previous four years; corruption was rife in state bureaucracies, hence one of the reasons for the coup; coffee, cocoa and timber could be encouraged as foreign exchange earners but they had to be grown first, yet foreign capital was reluctant to enter a still unstable Liberia; private capital, in panic soon after the coup, started to flow out — a total of $25 million was disinvested within the first month of the coup. Technocrats within state bureaucracies and the academics and professions in the new cabinet advised the regime that something quick had to be done to 'restore confidence in the economy' and to refuel the engine of growth. By November 1980 the majority of the foreign investors who controlled over 90 per cent of the economy made it known that they had suspended business activities pending the publication of the new government's economic programme. Some investors even pulled out altogether; more than $40 million, a third of the total deposits in the commercial banking system, had been withdrawn and taken out of the country as of November 1980. The government moved first to publish its budget and make its economic philosophy known.[51] It fully embraced the old order and reassured all investors that their properties were safe in Liberia. More than that it welcomed, and was prepared to implement, the IMF austerity measures.

To begin with, it passed anti-strike legislation and froze the wages in the private sector. The minimum wage for civil servants was fixed at $200 per month, that of the soldiers at $250: an improvement over the Tolbert era. But, in that same breath of improving wages, all wage-earners were then expected to engage in a compulsory saving scheme whereby all people earning more than $750 per month had to buy national savings bonds by May 1981, worth two months' salary, while those earning less were to use one month's salary. The government promised that this would act as a saving, to be eventually paid to them with interest. The secret behind it was that the state had to realise some revenue to pay for its debts as a condition for receiving deficit financing from the US, West Germany and the IMF.

By January 1981, the US had promised $20 million in foreign aid, plus foreign military sales. At the same time, through the support of the US, the IMF initiated a two-year stabilisation programme giving Liberia access to $85 million. The World Bank, too, offered $3.2 million.[52] 'The aid gesture, the biggest ever, was recommended by US Assistant Secretary of State for African Affairs, Chester Crocker, after it was felt that the new PRC government in Liberia would come under the influence of Libya if the Americans were not there with cash first'.[53] What this commentator forgot to add was that the Americans blamed the 'Libyan connection' on the 'socialists' in Doe's government like Togba-Nah Tipoteh, Boima Fahnbulleh and other MOJA sympathisers. In his attempts to consolidate himself in power, Doe now decided to use this Libyan and communist red herring to hound out of government and influential positions all those he felt would challenge him or would limit his authority. As long as he eliminated them on charges of being socialists, the old guard clapped and cheered, and the US was only too ready to come to his side with more help. Without this steadfast US support and help, the Doe regime would not have stabilised. As the old guard gave him support, they were rewarded with positions in government from which they were removed, reshuffled and even disgraced at Doe's will. Doe became stronger by the day.

The first 'maker of the revolution' to go because Doe feared him as a potential rival was Thomas Weh-Syen. In August 1981, as Vice Head of State, he was accused, along with five other members of the PRC, of plotting to overthrow Doe's government. A brief secret trial followed, and Weh-Syen and his comrades were summarily executed. In 1982, following accusations by the student body that Doe's regime was 'sliding back into the old ways and betraying the revolution', five students were accused of treason and condemned to death. A last-minute reprieve by the head of state saved their necks. A coup attempt was reported in November 1983 and some thirteen army officers were executed secretly at the orders of Doe. Early in 1984, the Commander-General of the Army, Thomas Quiwonkpa, was accused by Doe of plotting to overthrow him. Quiwonkpa escaped secretly and avoided execution. By mid-year, Doe turned on a group of civilians and some members of the armed forces for plotting to overthrow him: this was the biggest group to be accused of treason by Doe. In August 1984, Doe detained them. The list included: Isaac Nyeplu, former Minister of Justice; Amos Sawyer, who had announced that he was Chairman of the Liberian People's Party, formed as part of the process to return the country to civilian rule; Dusty Wolokolie, the interim Secretary-General of the LPP; George Kieh, lecturer in politics at the University of Liberia; Major-General Nicholas Podier, Speaker of the Interim National Assembly set up in July that year and previously second in command of the state as Co-Chairman (with Doe) of the then dissolved PRC; two colonels, Larry Borteh and Jerry Friday, members of the INA. In 1985 Doe charged, and then released, several members of the now defunct TWP who were forming rival parties in preparation for the elections leading to civilian rule; these included, among many, Ellen Johnson-Sirleaf, the intellectual and financial technocrat who had close allies in the higher echelons of the financial bourgeoisie of the US. Also detained and then released were Tuan Wreh and Harry Greaves Senior, executive members of the Liberian Action Party (LAP) as was Sirleaf; Baccus Mathews, leader of the United People's Party (UPP); and Edward Kesselley, leader of the Unity Party (UP).

As Doe took all these steps, and as the liberal press, the radical intellectuals and 'public opinion' condemned him, he seems to have continued marching on, with international capital keeping on pumping money into Liberia and modernising his army. The old guards, in spite of their verbal protestations, also accepted every post he offered their members, to the extent that, by 1983, the full list of public officials read like TWP government stage two.[54]

The crowning experience of the consolidation of Doe's regime and the final act of the counter-revolution was the process of the 'return to civilian rule'. The coup was undertaken, according to the first pronouncements of the coup-makers, to clean society of the old government and prepare society for a new government and a new society; in this regard, the coup-makers, as Quiwonkpa was quoted earlier, wanted a revolution. Given Liberia's conditions and history, this revolution would be nothing short of a bourgeois–democratic one: universal adult suffrage, civil liberties, equitable share of social wealth, a government chosen by and accountable to the people, etc. etc. As such, Doe's government was to be *provisional*.

But while everybody believed in this provisionality, including even Commanding-Generals like Quiwonkpa and Vice-Chairmen like Nicholas Podier who were wont to remind Doe of his temporary power whenever they could, Doe and his lumpen army thought otherwise. While the MOJA and PPP militants prepared for the transition back to civilian government and the Americans provided the resources to create a climate in which 'this would be possible', Doe and his cronies built his army with the resources Uncle Sam gave him. While the TWP old guard sought amongst themselves who could best represent them in a civilian government, Doe was already giving many of their members key positions in the state, and promising them that if they behaved as good boys, such positions — and even better ones — were for keeps when his kingdom would finally come; such TWP old guards included men like Emmett Harmon, Chairman of the Special Elections Commission, described as a 'septuagenarian throw-back to the Tubman years'.[55] Doe used this commission successfully to put everybody out of gear while his own party marched on to 'victory' in the October elections of 1985.

Because the bourgeois–democratic elements wanted a democratic return to civilian rule via the parliamentary road, Doe gave them the responsibility of framing the new constitution. The onerous task of chairing the constitutional commission Doe bestowed on Dr Amos Sawyer, professor of political science and a MOJA militant. The constitution that was finally produced, in May 1983, was a replica of the US one, true to Liberia's heritage of dependency. The government was to be divided into three branches: the Executive, Legislature and Judiciary. The executive, headed by a president elected by universal adult suffrage to serve for a period of four years — renewable only once by the same process — was also to comprise a cabinet appointed by the president with congressional confirmation. The legislature was to consist of two houses: The House of Representatives and the Senate; representatives in the former would serve four-year terms. Anybody of a sound civil record and over 25 years of age could be a legislator, and legislators plus presidential candidates had to be sponsored by their political parties in a pluralist process of political competition for the people's votes. Voters, in their turn, had only to be 18 years and more, bona fide residents of their constituencies and registered as such to vote. The election of a party to form a government, as well as that of president and legislators, was by simple majority.

Nonetheless, by the time the Provisional Constitution was approved by the PRC, and before the latter was abolished by Doe and its members converted into the Interim National Assembly (INA) for purposes of interim legislation before elections were held, Article 83 of the constitution, and Decree 88A of the PRC passed just before its dissolution became a fetter to those who wanted to form parties at the displeasure of Doe and his backers. The victims were to be those who had forged the 'popular alliance' before the coup, the likely winners of a democratic election. If the people were to vote, they were not to be allowed to elect their real representatives. Article 83 read:

> Parties or organisations which, by reasons of their *aims* or the behaviour of their adherents, seek to *impair* or *abolish* the free democratic society of Liberia or to endanger the existence of the Republic shall be denied registration; others who may have been registered but have during campaign displayed physical force or coercion in promoting any political objective, shall have their registration revoked.[56]

Decree 88A passed by the PRC shortly before its dissolution in July, 1984, stated that anybody convicted of spreading malicious rumours about public figures could be imprisoned for ten years. Further, the Special Election Commission (SECOM), required that, for any party to be registered, it had to pay $150,000 in cash or securities and be sponsored by at least 750 signatories from at least six counties. Provisions were made for any members of the public to challenge such signatories; such challenges could be settled by SECOM or appealed through the courts.

In August 1984, at least 10 parties announced they would seek registration and prepare for elections. The first was Baccus Mathews for the United People's Party (UPP). Then came General Doe's announcement that he was forming his own party, the National Democratic Party of Liberia (NDPL). Amos Sawyer and his MOJA lieutenants announced the intention to form the Liberia People's Party (LPP). Of the remaining seven, all of which were different groupings of former True Whiggers as well as liberal members of the old order, only Edward Kesselley's Unity Party (UP), the Liberian Action Party (LAP) of Counsellor Tuan Wreh and Liberian Unification Party (LUP) of the old school teacher Gabriel Kpolleh, remained on the scene. The others fused into the two major True Whig formations: LAP and LUP.

It was well and good forming political parties: the next most difficult task was to operate as one. And this task Doe made impossible. First, Doe rallied the sympathies and quiet approval of the old order by using SECOM to refuse outright, on some flimsy legal grounds, under both Article 83 of the Constitution and Decree 88A, registration to both UPP and LPP. In any case the constant harassment of the officials of these parties, including detention under Decree 88A, made it almost impossible for them to organise in any way. Being parties 'of the left', the right did not really mind their being eliminated from the race. But, if we say, 'on the one hand this . . .' the sentence can only be complete if we proceed to say 'on the other hand that . . .'. In Liberia, political language was not like that; the right thought only of one hand; and even this one hand Doe proceeded politically to malnourish almost to death.

Elections were due in October 1985. By the beginning of 1985, only Doe's party, supported by a whole array of public officials, businessmen, traditional chiefs, the army of lumpen and an assortment of peasants from this or that county had been registered. LUP, LAP and UP were still battling for registration. It was not until a few months before the elections, in the August/September period to be precise, that these three right-of-centre parties were finally registered, perhaps only to give credence to Doe's 'free and fair' elections — something the Americans were really yearning for to give credibility to the regime in Congressional circles back in Washington. Yet this 'free and fair' argument was only valid as far as the right-of-centre parties were concerned. The US never really felt it necessary that she should put her foot down and force Doe to register both LPP and UPP before any election could be regarded as 'free and fair'. Doe did not lose the significance of this double-standard behaviour on the part of the US. If the democratic process could be manipulated to keep out of power those the US did not like, it could also be manipulated to keep out of power Doe's rivals, LUP and LAP. The US was subsequently to be forced to accept this reality and live with Doe, no longer a

Bonaparte but a presidential despot.

In practical terms, Liberian objective conditions did not favour a free and fair election, notwithstanding the very narrow alternatives the voters had with LPP and UPP out of the race. Liberia has not had a published census since 1960. Second, the constituencies set up originally by the Constitutional Commission, or proposed by them, were 're-delineated' after 1984 to suit the prospects of Doe's party. Third, the public was not given a fair chance to check the voters' list. Fourth, any candidates belonging to the parties opposed to Doe faced intimidation and could not freely campaign. Fifth, even after holding the elections, the results could not be announced until after 15 days, and then only by SECOM. This gave SECOM (packed by True Whiggers, Doe's tribesmen and his close cronies hand-picked by him) enough time to doctor the results and announce the expected winner — Doe. The same SECOM refused these other parties the right to have representatives at the polling booths and at the counting of votes.

Given all this, and the fact that Doe, while a candidate for the presidency, was still the actual president of an 'interim' government, one is reminded very much of what Napoleon Bonaparte did with his provisional government while all other classes contending for power were busy doing just that: contending for power and not consolidating the power because they lacked it. Doe had the power, and the True Whig bourgeoisie which had lost the power to rule, individually in the defence of their property, and nationally in the defence of their investments, were finally to be forced, through the barrel of the gun, to settle down and contend with he who was to govern: Doe. As Alex Haig once said, 'someone must be in charge here'. In the case of Liberia, even the State Department which had clandestinely masterminded a coup against Doe following the unpopular elections, was finally forced to accept the Haig ultimatum once Doe had forced himself back into power.

### The Elections of October 1985

On 15 October 1985 the General and Presidential Elections were held. The four contending parties, the United Democratic Party of Liberia (UDPL), the Liberia Action Party (LAP), Liberia Unification Party (LUP) and the Unity Party (UP) fielded candidates in almost all constituencies for the 26 senate seats and 64 House of Representatives seats. On the face of it, voting seems to have gone smoothly, but, once the casting of the ballots was over, irregularities were revealed which made a sham of the whole process.[57]

First, soon after voting ended, SECOM announced that it would take two weeks to count the ballots, enough time to rig the results in favour of Doe and his party. Second, instead of relying on the counting process at each polling station by election officials as stipulated in the constitution, SECOM chairman Hermon further announced that he would appoint a 50-member committee which would centrally count the ballots. Among the 50 hand-picked members of the Ballot Counting Committee were two Doe senior aides, 19 Krahns like Doe and several avowed supporters of the NDPL.

Thirdly, it was found that during the voting itself certain polling stations and centres had been opened up which were not in the statute books. For example, the Barclay Training Centre was not meant to be a polling station, but soldiers did

239

actually vote there, to the surprising approval of SECOM officials. What is worse, NDPL officials are reported to have illegally handled ballot boxes during polling day. A telex sent to General Doe by one John Beh and reproduced in *West Africa*[58] revealed quite clearly that the NDPL was involved unashamedly in this practice. In opposition strongholds, genuine ballot boxes were diverted to strange destinations on their way to Monrovia. Some were destroyed or deliberately burnt. The *International Herald Tribune* reported from Monrovia that a large mound of voting slips had been found burning on 21 October in Margibi County: the *Tribune* reported a 'senior member of the government' as saying that the ballots were from a county that had voted 95 per cent against General Doe. On 18 October, several ballot boxes were removed 'in an illegal manner' from the back entrance of the SECOM offices in Monrovia and taken to an unknown destination while replacements, obviously stuffed with pro-Doe votes, took their place. On the night of 18 October, a lorry packed at the national police headquarters containing ballot boxes from Nimba county disappeared — never to be seen again.[59]

### The Election Results

The chairman of SECOM, H. Hermon, announced on 29 October 1985, that General Doe was the winner of the presidential elections having received 50.9 per cent of the vote. Doe's runner-up was Jackson Doe of LAP with 26.4 per cent, while Gabriel Kpolleh of the Liberia Unification Party came third with 11.5 per cent. Last on the list was Edward Kesselley, presidential candidate for the Unity Party with 11.1 per cent. Except for Doe's NDPL, which took 21 of the 26 senate seats and 51 of the 64 seats in the House of Representatives, all the other parties disputed all results and called the election a big fraud. The Liberia Unification Party called for the cancellation of all the election results and the other two parties joined in to call for fresh elections under an independent supervisory team.

According to independent estimates that *West Africa* quoted approvingly,[60] Samuel K. Doe could not have possibly won the elections. Jackson Doe, the LAP candidate, is estimated to have received approximately 60 per cent of the vote, followed by Edward Kesselley with Kpolleh and the General running neck-and-neck for the third spot. Doe did not seem to have been endorsed by any of the counties; even in his own native Grand Gedeh county he was overwhelmingly rejected by the popular vote. But what was really to be expected?

### Fabricating Popular Support

Vote-rigging and electoral fraud on a large scale has occurred elsewhere in Africa. The popular masses are made fun of almost every year from one African republic to another. Presidents get elected 'unopposed', or get returned to power with '99.99 per cent of the vote' when the people have neither voiced their overwhelming consent nor did they vote in their millions to record such astronomically high percentages of voter turn-out. Yet African regimes feel they must from time to time submit themselves to the popular will without having the slightest intention of making such a will real, or respecting its genuine verdict. Why is this phenomenon so prevalent in Africa?

There are many reasons that we can advance but here we will stick to the Liberian experience which illustrates quite vividly what goes on in the rest of the continent.

First, when the Doe regime started the process of restoring civilian authority, it did not do so out of its own volition; it did so as a response to the pressure put upon it by the popular masses. As Togba-Nah Tipoteh observed,

> History recalls that within a few days following the 1980 *coup d'état*, workers and students' groups under the leadership of MOJA members demonstrated in their thousands calling the Doe government to return Liberia to civilian rule. *Within a few weeks after these demonstrations, the MOJA leadership, through Dr. Amos Sawyer, advanced to the Liberian government details on initiating the process of returning to civilian rule by first establishing the National Constitution Commission* with the responsibility for drafting a new Constitution. It was under this *mass pressure* that the NCC was established with Dr. Amos Sawyer as its Chairman. Thus, the Commission was set up, not because of the Doe regime's interest in the return to civilian rule, but on account of the massive demonstration of the demands from a wide cross-section of the Liberian people.[61]

Second, once Doe submitted to this pressure and set in motion the work of the NCC, he sought systematically to demobilise MOJA and to frustrate the work of the NCC. In August 1981, Doe implicated Togba-Nah Tipoteh in an alleged coup in which the Vice Head of State, Weh Syen was imputed to be the ring leader. Tipoteh fortunately was out of the country, and following the execution of Syen and four other members of the PRC, resigned from the government and did not return to Liberia. MOJA's president was thus forced to operate politically from exile, a state of affairs with obvious disadvantages to the popular movement. While the NCC was doing its work and was just about to come out with a draft constitution, Doe announced that the government had no funds to pay for the rest of the remaining process of the return to civilian rule. The NCC Chairman reacted by opening a bank account to which citizens could voluntarily deposit contributions to finance the process of returning the country to civilian authority. As contributions started flowing in, Doe changed his mind and made funds available to the NCC.

Third, when it was, of course, obvious that there was an overwhelming popular support for the new constitution and the restoration of civilian authority, General Doe not only went ahead to join the process by forming a party of his own, but he intensified the practice of terrorising the popular masses and their leaders and 'mongering fear' in society as a whole. There were frequent announcements of planned coups and attempted coups. In August 1984, Amos Sawyer, now declared leader of the MOJA-backed Liberian People's Party, was detained for allegedly plotting a coup against the regime. Popular protest led to the invasion of the University of Liberia by Doe's troops, the mass murder and arrests of students and the urban crowd, and the subsequent elimination of both the LPP and the UPP from the electoral process.

Fourth, when only four parties were left in the electoral process — i.e. Doe's NDPL, representing the military regime; the LUP, a Doe proxy; and the LAP and UP representing various factions from the old order — the popular masses were hardly left with any choice. In essence, they were now to choose between the military regime 'organised within the state as political party', and the old order 'organised outside the state as various political parties claiming to have been reformed in different degrees'.

LAP's presidential candidate, Jackson Doe, had been first Vice-Chairman of the TWP. His running mate was a former judge in the True Whig regime. The executive of the party comprised some leading True Whig figures and government officials of the Tubman and Tolbert regimes. LAP, in the final analysis, was the TWP restored with facial plastic surgery in the sense that its chairman, Tuan Wreh, was a known public critic of the Tubman/Tolbert regimes from a liberal perspective. Tuan Wreh was meant to give LAP the necessary liberal respectability and a public image of reform orientation. The substantial class project of LAP was to continue True Whiggism without its former apartheid politics.

LUP's presidential candidate, Gabriel Kpolleh, was a former teacher and President of Monrovia Consolidated Schools System Teachers' Association. Doe frequently declared at campaign rallies that Mr Kpolleh operated under his 'wings and patronage', contentions Mr Kpolleh was obliged to deny with neither much vigour nor conviction. Obviously Doe did not harass Mr Kpolleh as much as he did other presidential candidates, a clear indication that he was prepared to offer a proxy in the electoral process to give the latter outward credibility while, in reality, there would be no real party competition. When, in April 1985, leaders of the other rival parties were arrested and detained following the 'Flanzamaton affair',[62] Gabriel Kpolleh was noticeably absent among Doe's culprits.

The Unity Party's presidential candidate, Edward Kesselley, had held various ministerial offices in the Tolbert government; he was also Chairman of the Constitutional Advisory Assembly which revised the draft constitution for General Doe's approval. Like LAP, the UP's executive comprised several members of the old TWP hierarchy.

It was telling that, when SECOM announced the official results of the presidential elections, it was the much less popular Gabriel Kpolleh who came third behind LAP's candidate Jackson Doe, relegating Edward Kesselley to the last spot. Doe, obviously, while he found it difficult to crush LAP completely, attempted to divide the TWP ranks by raising his proxy to third position. The unofficial count, as observed earlier, rated both Jackson Doe and Edward Kesselley way above the other two. Within the limited choice that the voting public had, the restored True Whig parties had the upper hand over the two other parties representing the military regime. But, even here, Doe was compelled to perform an 'electoral coup' against the True Whiggers to maintain himself in power. Doe refused to respect the verdict of the popular will, but claimed the electoral coup as the legitimate verdict of the people. But did the people really have a choice? Even if the elections had been 'free and fair' within these narrow confines, would the people have had a party that truly represented them?

When the democratic question is posed as a mere choice among competing political parties in a formally and legally 'free and fair' election, it greatly limits what the *content* of democracy is about. Democracy, at least in its liberal form, is regarded essentially as the ability of the people to govern themselves, and to institute and control processes of government whereby public policies are made (a) by those who truly represent the people, (b) in the interest of the people and (c) in defence of the sovereignty of the people as an independent nation. The democratic process ensures not only that the people can autonomously organise themselves politically independently of the state, but that, in the process of political organisation, political formations are allowed to flourish which represent different interests among the people. It is from this process that the governors are elected and it is within this process that the governors are kept accountable to the people.

It is therefore clear that, once the LPP and the UPP were eliminated from the electoral process, no election in Liberia, however 'free and fair', could be taken as having offered the popular masses a chance to truly choose their representatives. In this particular situation where it is very evident that the most popular political formations were the LPP and the UPP, the October 1985 election was really an election imposed on a semi-sovereign people.

The US government, which has all along apparently been concerned about restoring democracy to Liberia, never raised much objection when the LPP and the UPP were eliminated from the electoral process. Indeed, from the point of view of the US, as long as the Liberians had a 'choice' of more than one political party to vote for, democracy was guaranteed. Even if this 'choice' did not take into account the most popular parties, it was still regarded as democratic, and the State Department went ahead to pronounce what happened in October as an exercise in democracy with a 'respectable ally'. But Congress thought otherwise; the manner in which Doe cheated his rivals invited congressional disapproval, but too late. Congress, too, should have put its foot down much earlier, when Doe started interfering with the electoral process at the parties' registration stage. At that time, however, the undemocratic practices that Doe unleashed against the 'left parties' did not so much concern the Americans. When such practices were finally unleashed against the right parties that the Americans favoured, Doe had scored such a significant mileage against all his foes that even the Americans could not redress without actually overthrowing Doe through a military coup.

### Quiwonkpa Strikes Back

On 12 November 1985, Thomas Quiwonkpa, the former Commanding General of the Liberian Armed Forces, attempted to overthrow General Doe's government through a military coup. Following the rigged elections, Quiwonkpa knew there was a wide constituency of discontent against the Doe regime in Liberia. Coming from Nimba County from which Jackson Doe also hailed, Quiwonkpa knew he had a primary constituency to count on for support. The popularity of the coup was evidenced by the short-lived mass rejoicing that followed in Monrovia during the brief period Quiwonkpa was in power.[63]

It is difficult to say why the coup attempt failed. Much more important, however, is the way in which the US State Department reacted and the political advantage Doe got out of the coup attempt. While the coup was in progress, the State Department reported approvingly about it. When it failed, the State Department was wont to warn Doe about respecting human rights and redressing the political iniquities that led to the attempt. Doe, of course, reacted by blaming foreign interference (Sierra Leone and Cuba) and unpatriotic Liberians (Quiwonkpa and company) for having recruited mercenaries to destablise his regime. In the

243

meantime, he banned all public discourse on the political situation in the post-coup period, purged the army, detained political rivals and set himself up as the only guide for political reconciliation and future stability.

There was nothing that Doe would have appreciated more than an atmosphere in which repression appeared justified, or where repression could be justified on the basis of restoring stability and keeping law and order. The aftermath of the attempted coup gave Doe just such an atmosphere; and the extent to which he has consolidated his unpopular regime through the use of 'justified repression' has not only been to his advantage, but also the advantage of those who, in future, will find it easier to argue that the repression was necessary since there was no other 'practical alternative'. Thus the time for the popular masses to be mobilised independently of the state and to have a regime based on the genuine support of a popular democratic alliance in Liberia may yet be a long way away. That seems to be the major outcome of Doe's counter-revolution.

## Notes

1. Roy Medvedev, *Let History Judge: The Origins and Consequences of Stalinism* (London: Macmillan, 1972) p. 359.

2. *Africa*, no. 116, April 1981, p. 23.

3. A. Nyong'o, 'Soldiers and Counter-revolution in Liberia', *Journal of African Marxists*, no. 3, 1982.

4. John Markakis and Nega Ayele, 'Class and Revolution in Ethiopia', *Review of African Political Economy*, no. 8, p. 108.

5. John Locke, *Of Civil Government* (London: J. M. Dent 1926).

6. See, for example, K. Marx and F. Engels, 'Address of the Central Committee of the Communist Party', 1850.

7. See K. Marx and F. Engels, *The Manifesto of the Communist Party*.

8. Eric Williams, *Capitalism and Slavery* (New York: Capricorn Books, 1966).

9. E. Eastman, *A History of the State of Maryland in Liberia* (Monrovia: Department of State, 1956).

10. See, for example, Lord Hailey, *An African Survey* (London: Oxford University Press, 1957), p. 238.

11. See Amos Sawyer's address before the Special Election Commission in submitting papers for the registration of his own party, the Liberia People's Party (LPP) when he recalled:

> Mr Chairman, in 1927, a body of men which was constituted as the Elections Commission of the Republic of Liberia brought much disgrace to our country by presiding over the most extensively rigged elections in our history. The lack of integrity of those men leaves us today stained with the disgrace of being recorded in the reputable Guinness Book of Records as having elections which were the most rigged elections ever recorded in history.
>
> History recalls that during those elections, the opposition candidate, Mr T. J. R. Faulkner, polled 9,000 votes out of an electorate of 15,000 eligible voters. The incumbent, President King, polled 243,000 votes — 15 times more than the total electorate of 15,000. It may occur to some that it is possible to cheat without providing so glaring a discrepancy; for it did seem clear that the chairman and members of the Elections Commission of 1927 did get slightly carried away in their dishonesty and dishonourable deeds. But such shameful occurrences usually have smaller beginnings because in 1923, Mr King had won by 45,000 votes when the qualified voters were less than 7,000. It is from such unchallenged beginnings that dishonest men mobilise the courage to move on to larger levels of dishonesty.
>
> Mr Chairman, members of the Commission, it was the low level of literacy, the low level of political awareness and the poor technology which made communication primitive in 1923 and 1927 that spared the members of the Elections Commission and their posterity the shame which [their dishonesty] so justly accrued to them. But things are different now. You are undertaking your assignment at a time when [the] political awareness of our people is highest.

12. Tuan Wreh, *The Love of Liberty* (Monrovia: Wreh News Agency, 1978), p. 1.

13. Mzungu is the Swahili word meaning white man. Wazungu here is the plural form meaning white men or white settlers.

14. Lenin, for example, argued in his *Imperialism: The Highest Stage of Capitalism*, that such missions and survey teams should not be looked at in terms of the philanthropy of imperialists; they are a very conscious act by imperialists when they seek to prepare the ground for the future exploitation of a territory.

15. Hailey, *An African Survey*, p. 237.

16. In terms of infrastructural development, foreign capital was here playing the classical progressive role that Marx and Engels had identified in the *Manifesto of the Communist Party*. The tragedy is, however, that in the case of Liberia, this infrastructural development broke few Chinese walls. If anything, the countryside was siphoned of its strength and left to slumber under the yoke of underdevelopment while surplus value was extracted and accumulated abroad.

17. In a single five-year period, 1956–60, the two trail-blazers, Firestone and the Liberian Mining Company, together garnered pre-tax profits of over $160 million, an average of $32 million a year in a country whose total population was just under one million (see, for example, R. Clower et al., *Growth Without Development* (Evanston: Northwestern University Press, 1966) p. 133.

18. See, for example, *West Africa*, 21 April 1980.

19. Clower et al., *Growth*.

20. Wreh, *Love of Liberty*.

21. *Ibid.*, p. 5. Tuan Wreh further adds that 'If there was any persistent opposition or criticism of his policies, William Tubman had such men not only jailed and removed from their employment, but even deprived of their citizenship or literally hacked to death.'

22. Albert Porte, *Thinking About Unthinkable Things The Democratic Way* (Monrovia 1967).

23. This is the motto of those who founded the Liberian Republic. It proved as hollow as the post-1980 'revolutionary' slogan, 'In the cause of the people, the struggle continues', was to prove.

24. Wreh, *Love of Liberty*, pp. 20–21.

25. See Togba-Nah Tipoteh, 'The Need For Real Growth', *West Africa*, 15 April 1985.

26. Samir Amin, *Neo-Colonialism in West Africa* (New York: Monthly Review Press, 1973).

27. For a more detailed account of MOJA activities in Liberia, See Nya Kwaiawon Taryor (ed.) *Justice, Justice: A Cry of My People* (Chicago: Community Press, 1984). See also the review of this book by J. Pal Chaudhuri, 'Rice and Rights', *West Africa*, 15 April 1985, pp. 736–7.

28. *The Broom* (organ of the 'Sawyer For Mayor' Committee), October 1979.

29. *Mimeo*, University of Liberia.

30. This quotation is from Patrick Sayon in a private conversation with the author in 1980. Although the government's official version of what happened underplayed the havoc and destruction caused by both the police and the demonstrators, it is reliably known that police opened fire on the demonstrators and killed at least 100 people (as opposed to 49 in the official version); 600 people were wounded (as opposed to 'some' in the official version); more than $50 million worth of property was destroyed (as opposed to $36 million in the official version). See also 'Liberia's April 14 Indictment', *West Africa*, 14 April 1980.

31. *West Africa*, 17 June 1985.

32. *West Africa*, 21 April 1985.

33. In Taryor, (ed.) *Justice, Justice*.

34. *Africa*, no. 116, April 1981, p. 25.

35. Ralph Miliband, *Class Power and State Power* (London: Verso, 1983) pp. 236–7.

36. According to the most recent figures, total US private foreign investment is about $5 billion. Most of this is accounted for by investments from Firestone, the Uniroyal rubber plantations, LAMCO (in which Bethlehem Steel has 25 per cent interest) and local banks and affiliates of Chase Manhattan Bank and Citibank. Since 1980, official US aid has increased ten-fold, thus Liberia has the *highest* US aid per capita in Africa, approximately $70–80 million per annum. Most of this aid goes to the military, in terms of equipment, training and accommodation. William Lucy Swing, the US Ambassador to Liberia, gave the following details in 1984: 'The four-year military programme totalling some $43.5 million is the *most* ambitious security assistance project the US has ever undertaken since bilateral military aid to Liberia began in 1911'. See 'Liberia–US Relations', *West Africa*, 21 May 1984. The US Congress Sub-Committee on Foreign Affairs, in its 1985 hearings on 'US Aid For Africa during Fiscal 1986', devoted $1,300 million for the whole continent but gave 'particular focus on aid to Sudan and Liberia'. 'The Sub-committee's focus on Sudan and Liberia', it was argued, 'rises out of Congressional concern over the political instability of the regimes in these two countries widely viewed as key American allies in Africa'. A quick calculation shows that 50 per cent of the aid for fiscal 1986 will go to Sudan, Liberia, Somalia, Kenya and Zaire. The place of the popular masses in these countries' 'democracies' leaves a lot to be desired. See *West Africa*, 8 April 1985.

37. 'Liberia–US Relations', *West Africa*, 21 May 1984.

38. *West Africa*, 16 August 1985.

39. 'Quiwonkpa Breaks His Silence', *West Africa*, 17 June 1985. See also 'Liberian Revolution Founders', *West Africa*, 9 June 1980. It is reported here that 'Liberia's new Minister of Defence, Major Samuel Pearson . . . and officers had discussed overthrowing the old regime but had never been sure which of their fellow officers they could trust. He suggests that Doe picked members of his own tribe to stage the coup because there was already a bond of loyalty between them.'

40. *West Africa*, 21 April 1980.

41. *West Africa*, 7 November 1983.

42. *West Africa*, 16 January 1984.

43. K. Marx and F. Engels, *Basic Writings on Politics and Philosophy*, L. S. Feuer, (New York: Anchor Books, 1959), p. 334.

44. *Ibid.*, p. 326.

45. *Ibid.*, p. 334.

46. *Ibid.*, p. 333.

47. *Ibid.*, p. 336.

48. Miliband, *Class Power.*, p. 33. See also Nicos Poulantzas, *Political Power and Social Classes* (London: NLB, 1973).

49. *Ibid.* But see also K. Marx, 'The Civil War in France', in *Basic Writings*, pp. 349–391.

50. Economic Intelligence Unit, *Quarterly Economic Review* (Ghana, Sierra Leone, Gambia, Liberia) May 1980.

51. *Quarterly Economic Review*, November 1980.

52. *Africa*, no. 113, January 1981, p. 19.

53. *Africa*, no. 121, May 1981, p. 30.

54. See, in particular, *West Africa*, 2 May 1983.

55. See *West Africa*, 26 August 1985.

56. See *West Africa*, 2 May 1983.

57. In Washington the State Department described Liberia's elections as being 'remarkable' for their 'orderliness' and 'participation'. Bernard Kalb, a State Department spokesperson, described irregularities as 'exceptions to the general rule'. *West Africa*, 28 October 1985.

58. *West Africa*, 4 November 1985 p. 2297.

59. All this information was provided to the public and the press by the Liberia Action Party in the weeks following the 'elections'. Neither Doe's government nor SECOM denied their validity. Instead, SECOM chairman Hermon used a legal technicality in claiming 'proper procedures' would be used to determine whether or not such claims were true.

60. See 'Liberia: A Dream Deferred', *West Africa*, 4 November 1985.

61. Togba-Nah Tipoteh, President MOJA, 19 October 1984, statement on the 'Situation in Liberia on the Eve of the Elections', reported in *Review of African Political Economy*, no. 32, April 1985, pp. 89–92.

62. Lt. Col. Moses Flanzamaton was accused, in April 1985, of having attempted to assassinate Doe at the Executive Mansion. The attempt, in which Doe miraculously escaped unhurt, was bizarre in the way it was conceived, executed and reported, leading most people to believe it was pre-arranged by Doe to achieve certain political ends. It was no wonder, then, that in the wake of the attempt, Doe detained Tuan Wreh and Harry Greaves Sr. (LAP leaders), Edward Kesselley (Unity Party presidential candidate) and Baccus Mathews because they were 'involved' in the assassination attempt.

63. See 'Doe Foils A Coup Attempt', *West Africa*, 18 November 1985.

# 10  The State and Labour in Kenya

by Michael Chege

The most urgent issue in contemporary Africa is obviously its economic and social crisis. Hunger, declining economic productivity and *per capita* income, inflation, rising debt burden and balance of payments deficit represent some of its more widely-publicised manifestations.

The most urgent problem for Africa in the long term, however, still remains the need to transcend underdevelopment and mass poverty; to transform backward, predominantly agrarian economies into modern industrial ones. As is by now well established, the causes of and prescriptions for Africa's underdevelopment are issues which have occasioned considerable academic and political debate. The neo-classical economists of the 'development economics' mould placed emphasis alternately on capital, entrepreneurship, 'cultural change', balanced growth, unbalanced growth, human investment, development planning, etc., before they became engrossed in their own paradigmatic crisis and a yawning credibility gap between promise and performance.[1] In the meantime, Paul Baran's argument that capitalism in the periphery tended to take a degenerate and corrosive form, found belated but widespread acceptance especially in the Third World. In Africa, this is clearly evidenced in the enduring popularity of Walter Rodney's *How Europe Underdeveloped Africa*[2] and subsequent country studies premised on the role of imperialism in the 'underdevelopment' of Africa and the latter's 'dependency' on the capitalist 'centre'.[3] Here again emphasis has been placed alternately on 'unequal exchange', 'articulation of different modes of production', the weakness of the African bourgeoisie, 'blocked industrialisation', etc., leading to what David Booth has characterised as a theoretical impasse.[4] Warren's critique of dependency and its associated theoretical positions, as Booth remarks, is at once useful and faulted. It is faulted because it tends to shortshrift some of the colossal set-backs which the internationalisation of capital has suffered in specific states or regions of the Third World, as for instance in most states of contemporary Africa.

If one omits the neo-classical approach to African development for a moment, one is confronted by one general expectation which pervades the Marxian and neo-Marxian explanations. This is the belief, seldom explicitly spelt out, that if African underdevelopment is broached from the standpoint of the analytical category which is considered paramount, other problems will prove easier to overcome. 'Genuine' development would occur and this might heighten the prospects of socialism in Africa, or at the very least a more humane society. Thus

248

'delinking' would eliminate national exploitation inherent in unequal exchange, raising the national surplus, enhancing national accumulation, and perhaps helping the development of a planned socialist economy. Similarly, the notion that internationalisation of capital is taking place in Africa places hope in the concurrent emergence of a capitalist class which will preside over industrialisation and hopefully its revolutionary byproduct: a Third World working class. For the most part the initial impulse is seen as arising from social classes at the top.

On the whole, then, one is struck by the paucity of studies which seek to explore what is happening to social classes at or near the bottom of African societies. It is probably unfair to assume that the peasants, urban poor, or the working class will automatically take a certain political position once certain economic measures are implemented from the top, in an almost mechanical fashion.

Because the response of the Western working class to capitalism, and even imperialism, has been at odds with certain interpretations of Marxism, discussion on economic and political predispositions of 'labouring men' has a long tradition in western social science. Indeed this discussion is part and parcel of the debate on strategies for achieving socialism in the West. In contrast, research on the African working class (and on the peasantry) has barely picked up.[5]

This chapter aims at exploring the social and economic characteristics of the working class in Kenya after independence, and at understanding its paramount socio-political concerns. It is of necessity a preliminary essay in a wide area which calls for more detailed investigation. Before describing the objective conditions of labour in post-colonial Kenya, it might be useful to begin with a brief review of received conceptualisations of the working class in African society.

## The Working Class in Africa: A Conceptual Overview

Over the years, a catalogue of attributes which supposedly distinguish the African working class from other working classes has found its way into the social science literature on the subject. But only recently have some of the conventional theoretical positions been subjected to rigorous criticism. To anticipate the conclusion to be arrived at in this section, the fundamental socio-political characteristics of the working class in Africa may not be radically different from those observed in working classes elsewhere in similar stages of capitalist development. Yet there are also basic differences which arise from the specific forms which industrial development and urbanisation in Africa have taken.

For a start it has long been asserted from both left and right that the African working class was historically averse to revolutionary political action in general and unconcerned about fundamental social transformation of African societies. Thus, Peter Gutkind asserts that 'the political history of the African worker . . . indicates a locally-based reactive political consciousness rather than a broadly-based class consciousness'. He concludes: 'At no period during colonialism have African workers revealed such a high degree of political will and organisational skill as to pose a major threat to colonial rule'.[6] But it was Frantz Fanon who was most uncompromising in depicting the African proletariat as a 'privileged', 'pampered' and reactionary class in league with the new African bourgeoisie.[7] From the right, Elliot J. Berg and Jeffrey Butler argued that African trade unions were primarily

249

concerned with economic grievances of the workers. Except in Kenya and Guinea where union *leaders* were also party leaders, trade unions were largely devoid of nationalist politics and programmes.[8]

All this is probably not saying too much. Lenin recognised the fact that, left on their own, workers were only capable of acquiring a 'trade union consciousness'; an articulation of their economic disadvantage as opposed to revolutionary consciousness consistent with their 'imputed' rationality as the vanguard and beneficiaries of socialism.[9] The political articulation of the latter therefore fell on militant intellectuals. Case studies on the historical evolution of the European working class do not challenge this proposition substantially.[10]

Secondly, the African working class is depicted as a 'labour aristocracy';[11] a skilled economically privileged social stratum in comparison with the peasantry and the urban unemployed. Fanon's position is of course consistent with this idea, so forcefully defended by H. A. Turner.[12] In turn, Giovanni Arrighi and John Saul, in a supposedly Marxian analytical framework, were to identify skilled labour in multinational corporations and the salariat in the public sector as the aristocracy of labour whose political position was antithetical to that of the peasantry, the working poor and wholesome national development in general.[13]

As M. P. Cowen and Kabiru Kinyanjui have shown, the notion of a privileged labour aristocracy and the conclusions drawn from it are untenable on both factual and theoretical grounds.[14] In their estimation, the higher income brackets of labour have suffered secular erosion of real incomes, 'a devaluation of labour power'. What is more, the position of a labour aristocracy is difficult to support from logical deduction of the Marxian law of value in general and of exploitation in particular, as Geoffrey Kay demonstrates.[15] In fact, as Arthur Hazlewood cryptically remarks with regard to the working class in Kenya, any proposition that labourers, even skilled ones, are comparatively well-off would have to be believed by 'someone without experience of the way they live or with his nose firmly buried in the figures'.[16] It should come as no surprise that the most militant sections of the Kenyan working class are to be found in the ranks of the so-called labour aristocracy. Once again there is hardly any novelty in that finding for anyone familiar with the social history of labour outside Africa.[17]

Finally, much issue has been made of the fact that the African working class is not a proletariat in the generic sense of the term: most labourers maintain a foothold in the countryside.[18] The existence of labour totally alienated from land ownership is yet to happen. This reality serves to distinguish the historical pattern of proletarianisation in Africa. At the outset, therefore, it is necessary to inquire whether it represents a transitory phenomenon. In the meantime one needs to take note of the sociological development of working-class consciousness in Africa. More specifically, one most note the objective and subjective parameters of ethnicity, which is a social factor associated with attachment to a worker's area and community of origin.

While on this subject it may be worth noting the high premium which workers generally attach to decent and humane treatment by their employers. Students of labour who are wont to stress workers' response to economic factors alone are likely to go astray. As we shall have occasion to demonstrate, it is not only the working-class perception of ethnicity which calls for study, rather employer–employee relations where *race* is an essential difference. As has been observed elsewhere in industrial relations, labour unrest is more likely to arise in conditions where workers feel they are being exposed to humiliating social circumstances at work;[19] where their contribution is not reciprocated by material and *non-material* rewards.

## Growth and Change of the Kenyan Working Class

Both proportionately and in absolute terms, Kenya has one of the largest labour forces in Africa. Accurate and up-to-date statistics for comparative purposes are as usual difficult to locate. Table 10.1 provides employment and population statistics for a selected number of African states, and may help to underscore the general point being made here.

**Table 10.1**
**Employment and Population Statistics for Selected African Countries**

| Country | Number in Employment | Population in 1982 (millions) |
|---|---|---|
| Kenya | 1,038,100 (1982) | 18.1 |
| Zimbabwe | 1,042,600 (1982) | 7.5 |
| Cameroun | 381,430 (1981) | 9.3 |
| Tanzania | 607,730 (1980) | 19.8 |
| Malawi | 323,000 (1981) | 6.5 |
| Burundi | 49,100 (1982) | 4.3 |
| Liberia | 126,000 (1979) | 2.0 |

*Source:* Employment figures from ILO, *Yearbook of Labour Statistics 1983*; Population statistics from World Bank, *World Development Report*, 1984.

The size of Kenya's labour force in wage employment doubled between 1963, the year of independence, and 1983. The trends at five-year intervals are illustrated in Table 10.2

**Table 10.2**
**Growth of Wage Employment at Five-Year Intervals**

| Year | Wage Labourers (thousands) | Growth over previous 5 Years |
|---|---|---|
| 1963 | 539.2 | −8% |
| 1968 | 606.4 | 12.5% |
| 1973 | 761.4 | 25.5% |
| 1978 | 911.6 | 19.7% |
| 1983 | 1093.3 | 19.9% |

*Source:* Kenya, *Statistical Abstract (Annual)*, various issues.

It is habitual in many developing countries for additional employment to be created by a progressive expansion of the public bureaucracy. Where this happens, rising numbers in wage employment may not represent the growth of a labouring class induced by expanding productive capacity, and it may mislead to speak of industrial relations in such a context. So it might be necessary to gauge which economic sectors in Kenya had been responsible for the expansion in wage employment over the two decades of Kenya's independence.

Table 10.3 displays the percentage distribution of wage employment by sector at five-year intervals between 1968 and 1983.

**Table 10.3**
**Distribution of Wage Employment by Sector Percentage**

| Sector | 1968 | 1973 | 1978 | 1983 |
|---|---|---|---|---|
| Agriculture | 31.4 | 34.9 | 26.6 | 21.1 |
| Mining | 0.5 | 0.4 | 0.3 | 0.3 |
| Manufacturing | 11.6 | 12.4 | 14.3 | 13.6 |
| Construction | 5.3 | 5.3 | 6.1 | 5.5 |
| Electricity/Water | 0.9 | 0.7 | 1.0 | 1.6 |
| Commerce | 7.0 | 6.1 | 6.9 | 7.3 |
| Transport | 8.5 | 5.8 | 5.6 | 5.0 |
| Services | 34.8 | 34.3 | 39.2 | 45.6 |
| Total | 100.0 | 100.0 | 100.0 | 100.0 |

It should be clear that between 1968 and 1978 no dramatic change occurred in the sectoral distribution of wage employment despite a 50 per cent increase in the number of employees. Manufacturing and services (including government services) expanded their shares of labour absorption marginally, mainly at the expense of agriculture. Changes which occurred between 1978 and 1983 reflect mostly an increase in the share of the services sector. This is accounted for primarily by the heavy recruitment into central government employment. This has happened at a time when employment in agriculture has either remained fairly steady or declined marginally, thus resulting in a diminishing share of the latter in total wage employment. On the whole, government-owned enterprises and the government proper have expanded their share of hired labour from 40 per cent in 1970 to 48 per cent in 1983; in effect this leaves most wage labourers under the private sector.

As in the industrial distribution of Kenya's labour force, the geographical distribution of wage workers has retained essentially the same proportions over the last twenty years. In 1964, 26 per cent of Kenya's employees were to be found in Nairobi. In 1983 the figure was 28 per cent, though as already mentioned, it was 28 per cent of double the 1964 labour force. Rift Valley Province was the next largest labour catchment area with 29 per cent of the national employees in 1964 and 22 per cent in 1983. In 1983 Central Province came third with 14 per cent as was the case in 1964, while the share of the Coast (including Mombasa) remained at around 13 per cent. Nyanza and Eastern Provinces had 8 per cent of the country's labour force each.

With regard to job category, it hardly needs to be remarked that most of the workers are in the unskilled and low-income category. In 1983, 48 per cent of the enumerated labourers were earning under 1,000 Kenya Shillings per month. This works out to a 12,000 shillings income per year. As in everything else, however, the amount of material deprivation is always relative. In 1983, the *per capita* income in Kenya was estimated at 3,520 shillings, which is barely a third of the income of a labourer at the higher income end of the scale. A more accurate index of worker deprivation is the share of wages in the total industrial product, about which we shall have something to say later.

In concluding this overview of the morphology of the working class in Kenya, it is necessary to look at the degree of unionisation prevailing. Trade unions are the vehicle of political expression for labour; they are also the institutions through which collective bargaining with employers is done. The degree of political organisation of labour is reflected in the strength of its trade unions. A strong labour movement is a unionised labour movement.

Trade unions in Kenya operated under highly restrictive colonial labour laws right up to the time of independence. In the early colonial period unionisation arose first among Asian workers. Asian construction workers under the leadership of the late Markhan Singh were already unionised by the time of the 1937 strike, the first of its kind in the colony. Unionisation by African workers followed. By 1950, African trade unions at the Mombasa port and in the interior were strong enough to have caused a number of strikes. In the political tumult which preceded the Mau Mau rebellion, a highly effective general strike was called in 1950 by the East African Trade Union Federation, led by Fred Kubai and Markhan Singh.[20] After the 1950 strike and with the onset of the Mau Mau rebellion, the colonial government was reconciled to the existence of 'responsible' African trade unions. A limited degree of unionisation was allowed. The Attlee Labour government in Britain seconded experts to Kenya to help in the process.

Nevertheless, unionisation occurred slowly and with a highly varying effectiveness from one industry to another. There are several reasons for this. Among them is the high turnover rate of union leaders since, as Sandbrook demonstrates, trade union office-holders have habitually used their positions as a springboard into higher political positions.[21] Equally important is the highly constrained political and legal framework within which unions have been forced to operate in the post-independence period, a factor we shall dwell upon shortly.

In the circumstances, membership in the trade unions fluctuates. At least until the 'check-off' system of subscription to the unions was legislated in 1965, membership dues fell into arrears, weakening the union financial and personnel base. The 'check-off' system permitted compulsory deduction of union dues from wages, and vastly improved the situation over the previous period.

Still, by 1969 Sandbrook found that only one-third of the labour force in formal wage employment was unionised.[22] It is probably still the case today. The best organised unions are to be found in manufacturing, trade, marketed services and in the government-owned enterprises like the harbours, railways and tele-communications. The least organised labourers are those in agriculture, forestry and kindred areas. Not surprisingly, workers in agriculture are also the least paid. Some of the reasons for this may be found in the manner in which the state has reacted to the development of the labour movement since 1963.

## State Policy Towards Labour

As Berg and Butler remark, the Kenya Federation of Labour (KFL) under the leadership of Tom J. Mboya became a rare case of a trade union federation involved in the nationalist politics of colonial Kenya. Actually, Mboya was anxious that individual unions confine themselves to routine industrial relations matters leaving 'political' issues to the trade union federation.[23] In the 'coalition government' which preceded the granting of independence to Kenya by Britain, Mboya became the first African minister of labour. From that period on, in or out of the labour office, Mboya was to lay the foundations of industrial relations policy for Kenya which was to prevail almost intact over the next two decades.

The *first* pillar of this policy was the creation of a single trade union federation subservient to what Mboya, and the capitalist-minded wing of the ruling Kenya African National Union (KANU), saw as the appropriate developmental path; essentially a free-enterprise economy. This explains why the contests in the labour movement from 1963 to 1965 pitted Mboya and his protégés at the KFL against the Kenya African Workers Congress (KAWC) led by Dennis Akumu and Ochola Ogaye Mak 'Anyengo, both of whom were within the socialist wing of the party. There was a wide schism between, on the one hand, Mboya's (and Kenyatta's) policy favouring rapid economic growth within a market framework and with a labour movement causing minimum disruption, and on the other, their opponents who sought immediate tangible gains for labour and greater state ownership of productive enterprises.[24] A war of words between the two factions prevailed.

In August 1965, three workers were killed and over 100 injured in a feud at a union meeting in Mombasa. Almost immediately, the government appointed a ministerial committee to look into the reorganisation of the labour movement. Mboya was easily its most knowledgeable member on the issues at stake. In a month, the committee's report was out. It recommended the dissolution of both KFL and KAWC and their replacement by a Central Organisation of Trade Unions (COTU). COTU would have exclusive rights to represent industry-wide unions. All officers of registered unions would vote for the COTU executive, but the President of the Republic was given the right to appoint the three top COTU executives from the list of the poll winners. In other words, the COTU executive was to serve on sufferance of the head of state. The 1965 reforms also introduced the 'check-off' system and disallowed trade union affiliation with international labour unions.

In the first COTU elections of 1966, Clement Lubembe, a Mboya supporter, won the election for the secretary-generalship. Although fights and schisms within the movement were to continue, the system has remained largely intact to the present. As a matter of fact, Dennis Akumu, Lubembe's erstwhile opponent, was to win the secretary-generalship in 1969 and to begin an illustrious term of office which distinguished him as the most accomplished COTU secretary general so far.

The *second* aspect of state control over labour activities consisted of a series of 'tripartite agreements' between labour, government and the Federation of Kenya Employers. Essentially, the employers would pledge to hire an additional 10 per cent of their labour force if the unions would refrain from industrial action and additional wage demands for the next twelve months. The first of these, another Mboya brainchild, went into effect in 1964, the second in 1970 and the third in December 1978.

We are as yet to see a detailed analysis of the workings of the tripartite agreements. One thing however is certain: the unions have decried the policies of the employers and have consistently accused the latter of bad faith.[25] Their argument is that the agreements favour employers, who enjoy greater profits while real wages fall.

The *third* and perhaps the most important aspect of the Kenyan government's industrial relations policy concerns the machinery for resolving industrial disputes. Although the 1964 Tripartite Agreement involved a 'no strike' clause, unions nevertheless went on strike throughout 1964 and 1965 in a number of industries. In 1965, therefore, the government found it necessary to adopt legal measures restricting the scope of work stoppages by the unions.

This took the form of the 1965 Trade Disputes Act. Like the colonial labour laws of yore, the Act prohibited strikes in 'essential services' which were defined rather broadly. 'Sympathy strikes' were also outlawed. If a union in the 'essential services' category had industrial grievances, it should first report a dispute to the Minister of Labour. If the minister failed to intervene directly in 21 days, he could refer the dispute to the Industrial Court. The court's decisions, like all court decisions, were binding on both parties. This left unions in 'essential services' in an unenviable position: they could only call a strike with the consent of the industrial court, a highly unlikely event.

In the non-essential services sector, the Minister of Labour is empowered to appoint a 'Board of Inquiry' to investigate the reasons for industrial disputes, and to recommend disputes to the Industrial Court for reconciliation. The minister has powers to declare strikes and threatened work stoppages illegal until the full arbitration mechanism is exhausted.

The novelty of the Industrial Court in Kenya deserves mention if only because a number of African states have found it worth studying and copying. At its inception in 1965 and ever since, the court has been presided over by a magistrate (later, judge) appointed from the ranks of the Kenyan judiciary. In hearing cases, he sits with two appointees from the labour movement appointed by COTU, and two appointees nominated by the Federation of Kenya Employers. In 1971, however, the Act was amended giving the Minister of Labour full rights to nominate two appointees, one each from the labour movement and the employers.

The wage increments which the court awards are strictly limited. From time to time, the Ministry of Finance and Planning provides 'wage guidelines' to the Industrial Court to guide it in matters of arbitration. These guidelines provide a 'floor' for minimum wage increments, and recommend maximum increments by wage category. In general, the guidelines recommend higher rates of increment for the low income workers as opposed to the middle and higher income earners.

Although the effect of the guidelines is disputed, evidence seems to favour the view that they have accelerated the decline in real wages at the higher level of the labour force. Apologists for the court argue that its awards are invariably in line with wage agreements negotiated voluntarily out of court. Hence court awards more or less reflect the market price of labour. Critics of the wage guidelines, among them successive COTU leaders, argue that stipulated increments have lagged behind the annual rates of inflation, causing the workers to suffer a loss in real income. Finally, to revisit the 'labour aristocracy' thesis, Cowen and Kinyanjui argue that 'it is the wage of skilled workers, as revealed by the wage awards by the industrial court and particularly since the application of wage guidelines, which have shown the slowest rate of increase'. After taking stock of consumer price increases, they concluded: 'It is most likely that the real wages of skilled workers have fallen sharply, more so than for unskilled workers and as much as for semi-skilled workers'.[26]

Because the Trade Disputes Act still leaves chances, however slim, of strikes and because, as we shall see shortly, work stoppages nevertheless occur without reference to it, the state has occasionally used political and administrative fiat under any pretext to ban strikes altogether. This happened in August 1974 in the wake of a number of strikes at the harbour, railways, banks and the airport. In June 1981 the unions agreed with the government to opt out of any industrial disputes.

It would be wrong to give the impression that the mechanism described above is sufficient to ward off repressive state intervention. The latter is always a last resort. Drastic steps have been taken periodically. In 1980 the state deregistered the Civil Servants Union and the University Staff Union. As early as 1969, the government had ordered the teachers' and civil servants' union to disaffiliate from COTU. Union leaders have been arrested for calling strikes without recourse to the established arbitration machinery.

## The Labour Movement's Response
### Collective Bargaining

On account of the fact that most industrial disputes have continued to be resolved by employer–employee bargaining, it is probable that the Trade Disputes Act has had the effect of restraining unions from adopting too militant a stand in industrial relations. The price to be paid for striking is a high one, not least for the union leaders themselves.[27]

The overall effect of collective bargaining on wages is not easy to discern. It would be necessary to calculate trends in real wages per sector countrywide which is not easy. A very rough indication of the trends could be obtained by calculating the *per capita* real earnings for the manufacturing sector in Nairobi over the period 1974 to 1983 when inflation was particularly high. Using the Nairobi middle income consumer price index as the deflator, we obtained the figures in Table 10.4.

As we have already seen, manufacturing labour is relatively well organised. Yet the statistics tell the story of a 12.7 per cent decline in real wages over the last decade. This is not a particularly dramatic fall in real income.[28] It is probable that the situation elsewhere is worse, but this calls for more detailed investigation.

### Strikes

On account of the foregoing, one might expect some positive correlation between the decline in real wages and the occurrence of strikes. In other words, one might expect strikes to take place most in periods when the rate of inflation is highest, and

**Table 10.4**
**Real Per Capita Earnings in Manufacturing in Nairobi**

| Year | Money Wages £ | Constant Wage (1974 Prices) |
|------|---------------|------------------------------|
| 1974 | 548.9 | 548.9 |
| 1975 | 632.0 | 545.0 |
| 1976 | 679.0 | 543.0 |
| 1977 | 766.1 | 603.0 |
| 1978 | 841.1 | 553.0 |
| 1979 | 901.8 | 533.0 |
| 1980 | 976.3 | 519.0 |
| 1981 | 1121.5 | 479.0 |
| 1982 | 1202.4 | 432.0 |
| 1983 | 1318.4 | 478.0 |

*Source:* Kenya, *Statistical Abstract*, various issues.

the erosion of purchasing power fastest. There may be something to this highly economistic interpretation but our reading of the evidence in contemporary Kenya suggests that the recourse of the working people to strikes is motivated by more than the dissatisfaction caused by the purchasing power of wages.[29]

We examined the annual rates of inflation as measured by the middle income wage-earners' consumer price index for Nairobi and enquired whether it bears any relationship to the number of days lost in work stoppages between 1974 and 1983. Table 10.5 summarises that information.

**Table 10.5**
**Price Increases and Days Lost through Strikes**

| Year | Consumer Price Rise (%) | Strikes/ Days |
|------|--------------------------|----------------|
| 1974 | 23 | 127,951 |
| 1975 | 5 | 8,755 |
| 1976 | 8 | 26,248 |
| 1977 | 14 | 9,227 |
| 1978 | 10 | 39,337 |
| 1979 | 15 | 33,083 |
| 1980 | 17 | 32,479 |
| 1981 | 41 | 40,257 |
| 1982 | 39 | 27,659 |
| 1983 | 27 | 18,448 |

*Source:* Kenya, *Statistical Abstract*, and Ministry of Labour.

At first glance there appears to be a positive correlation between the rise in consumer prices and the number of days lost in strikes. It is clear that working days taken by strikes rose, especially after 1978, concurrently with a new inflationary spiral peaking in 1981, which also saw the highest annual price rise in the decade, 41 per cent. Even the record number of 127,951 days lost to industry in 1974 coincided with an inflationary bout that year, associated with the first oil crisis.

Trade union leaders themselves often underscore the damaging effect of price increases overleaping wage rises. After the government announced a 28 per cent increase in the minimum wage in August 1973, Dennis Akumu, as COTU Secretary General, retorted that 'a 28 per cent rise is nothing compared to a 100 per cent price increase'.[30] In the heat of the railways strike in 1974, J. Mollo of the Railway Workers' Union bemoaned the fact that consumer prices had risen by 33 per cent between 1971 and 1973 and wages had not kept pace.[31] Each year, COTU publicly puts up the case for a pay increase citing inflation as the major reason.

There is no denying the fact that most workers are terribly concerned about the purchasing power of their wages and the benefits they derive from employment. The difficult conditions under which most of them live would make a denial of that fact objectively untenable. Indeed, as already asserted in an earlier section of this paper, the concern for day-to-day material problems is the stuff ordinary working-class life is made of. But it is one thing to assert that workers may have genuine grievances and misgivings about their wages and working conditions and quite another to maintain that declining real wages will cause them to strike. And thus, although the statistical data and the political statements of union leaders presented above may be read to mean that strikes arise from falling real wages, a careful reading of the situation suggests that other factors may be more important.

To begin with, careless reading of the statistics could lead one astray. A prolonged strike in a few industries could yield the same statistic in days lost as an economy-wide general strike lasting a short period. Yet both would represent totally different social and political circumstances: the former being symptomatic of a crisis within a single firm or industry, while the latter represents a grievance felt nationwide by the working class. For anyone interested in understanding the working-class socio–political disposition, it would be fatal to ignore such differences.

A detailed reading of the industrial distribution of labour–time lost due to work stoppages suggests that strikes tend to be confined to a few industries in a given year and that this concentration tends to shift to different economic sectors over time. Thus, of the total labour time lost to strikes in the private sector in the record year 1974, 50 per cent were accounted for by the bank workers. Strikes in manufacturing industry alone accounted for 72 per cent of the days of work stoppage in 1978 and in 1981 strikes in the agricultural sector amounted to 61 per cent of the national labour time taken up by work boycotts.

What is more, it would appear that strike incidence is generally higher in those areas of the economy where wages are comparatively higher, again casting doubts on the 'quiescent labour aristocracy' hypothesis. This is almost certainly the case with the multinational-dominated manufacturing sector in Kenya, the sector with the highest frequency of strikes since 1965.

In the circumstances, the sources of industrial unrest must be sought within *specific industries* or economic sectors. But once again this is a virgin territory which social science research in Kenya has barely began to explore. At the moment we might be content to point out two directions in which we surmise the answer may lie. *Firstly*, and pursuant to our comments on the Marxian understanding of the exploitation of labour, it could be argued that workers who observe (and *understand*) the rising ratio of surplus value to variable capital, i.e. the learned and the skilled, are most prone to strike. There are indeed indications of a decreasing wage share in national output. But since, as we shall observe shortly, this issue is seldom if ever a contentious one in industrial disputes, one might conclude that issues like inhuman treatment, racialism and dismissals are merely the ideological veneer which this 'objective' discontent assumes. For a number of reasons, difficult to detail here, I find this line of enquiry deficient in the same manner as Mannheim's position on the social basis of knowledge. Despite my pessimism it is still a line worth pursuing.

The second approach to an understanding of the basis of working class unrest in Kenya lies in the hypothesis briefly outlined earlier, in which working-class behaviour is predicated on the maintenance of a delicate social contract between themselves and their employers. As long as labourers feel that their contribution to industry is being reciprocated within reasonable limits, materially and otherwise, the chances are that they will concentrate their politics on the 'trade union' grievances which concerned and irritated Lenin and dozens of revolutionaries since Marx. The limit to this balance is reached when capitalist employers assume policy positions which are injurious to the human dignity of labour or, more importantly, to *job security*.

Thus, of the 765 trade disputes studied by Sandbrook in Kenya between 1969 and 1972, '68 per cent related to dismissals while only 11 per cent were concerned with terms of service'.[32] This evidence is sufficient to warrant a prolonged inquiry into why labour in Kenya (and we believe elsewhere) is prone to take a militant line over breach of decent human relations at firm level and over job security than for most other reasons. In concluding this part of our inquiry we propose to examine two case studies of industrial unrest in Kenya, which may shed a little light into the issue.

### Humane Industrial Relations and Workers' Militancy: Two Case Studies

Our first case study concerns a prolonged strike in an agro–industrial firm — Chemelil Sugar Factory — in the late 1960s and early 1970s. To the extent that African employees in this firm were primarily in the unskilled job category, they represent the sector of agricultural labour which is the worst paid section of the labour force. This case also represents a rare instance of industrial unrest in a rural setting.

Our second case study represents union militancy at the opposite end of the spectrum: bank employees in the capital city, Nairobi. On average, wages in the financial sector are the highest of any industry. Bank workers were until recently largely employees of multinational corporations and can thus be classified as a labour aristocracy if such a category actually exists.

The Chemelil Sugar Company was the forerunner of a number of sugar industries established in Western Kenya by the government in the period between 1969 and 1980 with a view to making the country self-sufficient in sugar. With West German technical support and finance from Germany and Kenya, the factory commenced operations in June 1968, after a considerable delay in construction. Sugar-cane, the basic input into the factory, was to be obtained from the company's estate and from smallholder co-operatives in the adjoining area. As the company's operations commenced, industrial relations problems set in, and these were to plague its productive capacity for a good part of the initial six years.

At an early stage when the factory and plantation network was being put in place — November 1967 — workers threatened a strike because, as the secretary-general of Kenya Union of Sugar Plantation Workers (KUSPW) put it, of slow Africanisation, poor wages and arbitrary dismissal of plantation workers.[33] But as if to show which one of these reasons concerned the workers most, a strike was called in August 1968. It was so effective that the newspapers wrote of the factory and plantation being 'paralysed'.[34] The reason for this highly effective work stoppage was a simple one which was to recur in subsequent years: arbitrary dismissal of labourers, which the company workforce saw as racially motivated. Indeed 'racialism' was to be a recurrent explanation at union level on why industrial unrest persisted at Chemelil. In this, the union leadership saw itself in conformity with the government's policy of 'Africanisation' and with the stridency of the nationalism of a new state. And so strong were these feelings that 3,000 individuals stayed out of work despite a declaration by the Minister of Labour that the strike was illegal. When work resumed after a few weeks, the company insisted on not reinstating some 287 workers. In doing so, it sowed the seeds of the next strike, whose effect was even greater.

The government must have realised that something was amiss with the expatriate management, even though it was slow to act. A Board of Inquiry, set up by the Ministry of Labour under the Trade Disputes Act, came out in favour of the reinstatement of the 287 dismissed workers, but the company baulked and dithered. In 1969 it came out with a statement that the 287 workers were required to apply afresh. In the same year, the government renegotiated a new management contract with Booker International, the well-known British conglomerate in the sugar industry. Nevertheless, grievances against racialist attitudes of expatriate management continued and the union persisted in seeking the reinstatement of the workers dismissed in 1968, but without much effect. In December 1970, Dennis Akumu, on behalf of the Sugar Plantation Workers' Union, threatened to call a strike over the issue of reinstatement but nothing was to happen until over two years later when once again dismissals were made and the workers rose as one.

In April 1973, Chemelil Sugar Company dismissed Mr Onyango Midika, its personnel and training manager, and its only African employee in management, together with twelve others. It was a fatal error. Almost immediately the entire labour force downed their tools and the strike was judged 100 per cent effective.[35] As usual in these matters some violence was used by the strikers against reluctant compatriots and expatriate management. The latter in fact were forced to barricade themselves in their houses. An attempt by the Ministry of Labour to declare the strike illegal failed to change the situation.

Mr Midika was overwhelmingly popular with the workers and this was vindicated by his election to Parliament in 1974, in the constituency where the factory is located.[36] He had stood with them against European management on some very basic human demands. In one of the few instances where an ordinary workman, as opposed to the educated union leaders, explained the reasons behind the strike, a shop steward said that expatriate managers had 'abused' Africans, and that workers had been denied 'uniforms and boots'.[37] Midika's own explanation was that he had lost his job because he objected to racialist recruitment of management staff and stood firm in favour of Africanisation. The Industrial Court found the Company in breach of contract and ordered it to pay Mr Midika a full year's salary. Reorganisation of management was undertaken and the situation settled, if somewhat uneasily. By 1976, Midika, then a member of Parliament, could be heard calling for Africanisation of the last major expatriate-held post: General Manager.[38] At least on one front the battle had been largely won.

The case of the bank workers represents over a decade of confrontation between bank employees and the Kenya Bankers Association, the employers' association. Once again questions of racialism have often been raised and the bank workers have shown considerable aptitude to close ranks across formal company lines.

The background and sequence of the 1976 bank strike are spelt out by Cowen and Kinyanjui.[39] The Kenya Bankers Association resisted both the unionisation of bank 'supervisory staff' and wage increments in the years preceding 1974. Towards the end of 1974, after arbitration by the Industrial Court on unionisable ranks, the bank shop stewards called a strike over wage increments. It is significant that the union which bank workers nominally belong to, Kenya Union of Commercial, Food and Allied Workers, denounced the 1974 strike and called for a return to work. It is therefore hardly surprising that bank workers have been seeking to form a union of their own, the Kenya Union of Bank Employees, against resistance from the government.

The 1974 crisis was the forerunner of a long struggle in which the bank workers sought improved wages and terms of employment. But just as important, bank workers have voiced loud complaints against what they considered racialist and insolent attitudes of their employers in general and the Kenya Bankers Association in particular. The justification for these complaints is to be found, for example, in the comments of Mr P. E. D. Wilson to the Industrial Court in 1980 when he remarked that African bank cashiers pilfered or lost three million shillings belonging to the banks each year.[40] At this juncture the presiding judge had to admonish him against making racialist remarks.

In early 1982, workers at the Bank of Baroda went on strike, charging the Indian-owned bank with racial discrimination and circumventing government policies on Africanisation and exchange control. The important point here is the similarity of these charges — but workers had less luck on their side. It was subsequently revealed that three senior government officials had received loans from the bank.

The next major confrontation arose in 1984 and this time the arena was Barclays Bank. The issue was wages and allowances as usual. Barclays' workers requested other bank workers to join them. Sympathy strikes in other banks ensued and for a day or so chaos reigned in the banking industry. At this juncture the racial and arrogant attitudes of the employers' association had become a major issue and the employees were seeking the ouster of the chief executive of the Kenya Bankers

Association, an expatriate.

Two major themes arise from the foregoing narrative. Firstly, the concern with 'trade union' type of grievances above all else and *secondly*, the tendency for strikes to be triggered by poor industrial relations on the part of management. Invariably the latter are the *immediate* cause of the strike and the former the *long-term* causes.

## Conclusion

The chapter began with a discussion of the paradigmatic conception of the role of the working class in Africa. This, as we saw, is a highly contested terrain. What our study on the structure and development of the working class in Kenya appears to indicate is that, despite a phenomenal growth in labour force, the social and political dimensions assumed by the country's putative proletariat are those of a gradualist and reformist character. This is consistent with what most writers on the problem in and out of Africa have found. Richard Jeffries in his remarkable study of the Sekondi railwaymen found them 'liberal reformist' in orientation.[41] At the height of the sugar workers' strike, Dennis Akumu, who was never apolitical, was to profess that he would be 'the last man to hurt the Kenya economy' and that he was essentially against lack of Africanisation at Chemelil.[42] And Mr I. Kubai of the bank workers (who was to be briefly imprisoned) remarked that he 'did not want chaos in the banking industry', but harmonious working conditions.[43]

There is scant evidence that, as Sandbrook thought, 'unionised workers constitute one of the few social forces championing the ideal of social equality'.[44] Yet they have real grievances and a distinct feeling of disadvantage. The restrictions placed on the labour movement by the state are real enough as already pointed out. But since the historical role of the political mobilisation of labour has lain with social classes outside it, the beginning of real change must be sought from there.

## Notes

1. See for instance Hirschman's magisterial survey, 'The Rise and Decline of Development Economics' in A. O. Hirschman (ed.) *Essays in Trespassing: Economics to Politics and Beyond* (Cambridge: Cambridge University Press, 1981).

2. Walter Rodney, *How Europe Underdeveloped Africa* (Dar es Salaam: Tanzania Publishing House, 1972).

3. See for instance Colin Leys, *Underdevelopment in Kenya* (London: Heinemann, 1975); Richard Harris (ed.) *The Political Economy of Africa* (London: Schenkamn, 1975) contains essays on Ghana, Nigeria, Kenya, Tanzania, Zambia and South Africa; Rhoda Howard, *Colonialism and Underdevelopment in Ghana* (London: Croom Helm, 1978); Peter C. W. Gutkind and Immanuel Wallerstein, *The Political Economy of Contemporary Africa* (Beverly Hills: Sage, 1976).

4. David Booth 'Marxism and Development Sociology: Interpreting the Impasse', *World Development*, vol. XIII, no. 7, 1985.

5. However, see the essays in Richard Sandbrook and R. Cohen, (eds) *The Development of an African Working Class* (London: Longman, 1977); Robin Cohen, *Labour and Politics in Nigeria* (London: Heinemann, 1974); R. D. Grillo, *African Railwaymen* (Cambridge University Press, 1973); Richard Jeffries, *Class Power and Ideology in Ghana; The Railwaymen of Sekondi* (Cambridge: Cambridge University

Press, 1978) is an excellent treatment of the issues raised in this paper. See also Richard Sandbrook, *Proletarians and African Capitalism* (Cambridge: Cambridge University Press, 1975).

6. Cited in Richard Sandbrook, *The Politics of Basic Needs* (London: Heinemann, 1982) pp. 138–9.

7. Frantz Fanon, *The Wretched of the Earth* (Harmondsworth: Penguin Books, 1967) p. 86.

8. Elliot J. Berg and Jeffrey Butler, 'Trade Unions' in James S. Coleman and Carl G. Rosberg (ed.) *Political Parties and National Integration in Tropical Africa* (Berkeley: University of California Press, 1964).

9. V. I. Lenin, *What Is To Be Done?* (Moscow: Progress 1972).

10. See for instance E. P. Thompson, *The Making of the English Working Class* (London: Victor Gollancz, 1965) for England; and Barrington Moore Jr., *Injustice: the Social Basis of Obedience and Revolt* (London and New York: Macmillan, 1979) pp. 126–353 on the German working class from 1848 to 1919.

11. David Rosenberg, 'The Labour Aristocracy in the Interpretation of the Working Class in Africa', Nairobi Institute for Development Studies Working Paper no. 315, 1977, reviews the discussion on this issue at length.

12. H. A. Turner, *Wage Trends, Wage Politics and Collective Bargaining* (Cambridge: Cambridge University Press, 1966) esp. p. 13.

13. G. Arrighi and J. Saul, *Essays on the Political Economy of Africa* (New York: Monthly Review, 1973).

14. M. P. Cowen and K. Kinyanjui, *Some Problems of Capital and Class in Kenya* (Nairobi: Institute for Development Studies, 1977) pp. 32–55.

15. Geoffrey Kay, *Development and Underdevelopment: A Marxian Analysis* (London: MacMillan, 1975) p. 54.

16. See for example Barrington Moore, *Injustice*, pp. 160–1.

17. Rosenberg, 'The Labour Aristocracy'.

18. See Sandbrook, *Politics of Basic Needs*, p. 127, for a brief review of the issue and a lengthy bibliographical note.

19. For the history of the labour movement in Kenya see Anthony Clayton and Donald Savage, *Government and Labour in Kenya, 1896–1963.* (London: Frank Cass, 1973).

20. Alice H. Amsden, *International Firms and Labour in Kenya 1945–1970* (London: Frank Cass, 1971); Markhan Singh, *History of the Trade Union Movement in Kenya to 1952* (Nairobi: East African Publishing House, 1969); Richard Sandbrook, *Proletarians and African Capitalism* (Cambridge: Cambridge University Press, 1975).

21. Sandbook, *Proletarians and African Capitalism*, p. 52.

22. *Ibid.* pp. 14–15.

23. Tom Mboya, *Freedom and After* (London: Andre Deutsch, 1963) pp. 195–6.

24. There were also policy differences on the international affiliation of Kenya's labour movement.

25. One easy way out for employers was to reclassify temporary employees as permanent employees up to the required number. That way a firm would pay a declining real wage without burdening itself with an additional 10 per cent of employees.

26. Cowen and Kinyanjui, *Some Problems of Capital*, p. 37.

27. Some union leaders and shop stewards have suffered arrest for calling strikes.

28. In a separate study the author observed a 28 per cent fall in academic real

263

wages at the University of Nairobi between 1979 and 1983.

29. See the discussion on this in the first pages of this chapter especially with regard to comparable historical experiences elsewhere.

30. *African Contemporary Record 1973–74*, p. B178. Actually the rate of inflation in 1973 was a mere 2 per cent over 1972. Between 1967 and 1973 prices had risen barely 20 per cent.

31. *African Contemporary Record 1974–75*, p. B206.

32. Sandbrook, *Proletarians and African Capitalism*, p. 169.

33. *East African Standard*, 30 March 1968. Akumu had become leader of the sugar workers after his ouster from the Dockworkers Union in 1965 and an interval in detention.

34. *East African Standard*, 23 August 1968.

35. *East African Standard*, 26 April 1973.

36. He had in fact become the leader of KUSPW in the interim.

37. James O. Otindi testifying to a Board of Inquiry set up by the Ministry of Labour. See *East African Standard*, 1 November 1973.

38. *East African Standard*, 4 September 1976.

39. Cowen and Kinyanjui, *Some Problems of Capital*, pp. 50–53.

40. *East African Standard*, 18 April 1980.

41. Jeffries, *Class Power*, p. 201.

42. *East African Standard*, 26 April 1973.

43. *East African Standard*, 25 May 1981.

44. Standbrook, *Proletarians and African Capitalism*, p. 29.

# 11 Popular Alliances and the State in Swaziland

## by Joshua Mugyenyi

This chapter seeks to examine the nature of the state in Swaziland and its role in suppressing and subverting popular participation in the political process as it seeks to maintain and sustain the interests of the dominant classes. The chapter further examines the possibilities of the emergence of popular alliances that may seek to change the *status quo* and what the project of such an alliance would be. The present state in Africa is a logical extension of the colonial state which primarily served the interest of foreign capital and its local allies. In the process of serving these interests, the state became militarised and highly repressive as far as the indigenous people were concerned. This feature of the state has not changed substantially with independence. More resources are still spent on consolidating the material base of the dominant classes — domestic and foreign — rather than on the socio–economic welfare of the popular masses. When the latter realise that their contribution to the creation of the social wealth is hardly matched by public policy in favour of their own welfare, they are likely to withdraw their services and resist state commands. In various part of Africa there has been peasant resistance to commodity production on which the state relies for foreign exchange. Under such circumstances, the state may resort to various measures of 'extortion' to sustain its fiscal base. Such measures simply demonstrate one important phenomenon: the reduced capacity and capability of the state to govern authoritatively and legitimately.

It has been argued that when the state experiences a deficit in authority and legitimacy, conditions may arise for the dominated and exploited social classes to challenge the existing power structure and institute popular power. For such a popular movement to emerge and succeed in altering the power relations, it must be organised well enough to take full advantage of the favourable conditions. This chapter contends that, in the case of Swaziland, the state has systematically sought, through various economic and political projects that will be examined below, to pre-empt any organisation by the popular classes. Whenever the state has felt sufficiently threatened by internal popular movements, it has never hesitated to call for external help, particularly from the Republic of South Africa. This 'external element', both imperial and sub-imperial, keeps most African neo-colonial regimes buoyant in spite of having lost substantial legitimacy among the popular masses.

In comparison to many other African countries, it may seem that talk of popular alliances in Swaziland is too futuristic. This is a country that attracts attention by its tiny size, the monarchical non-party political system, and its very warm — even

265

enthusiastic — political and economic relationship with the Republic of South Africa. There is, however, more to the country than that: Swaziland, in the 1960s and 1970s, had competing political parties some of which made it their business to represent and organise labour all the way to a general strike. The same period was characterised by organised trade unions which won several concessions from the owners of capital. There was even a Swazi liberation movement which briefly operated from Mozambique and aimed at overthrowing the state by revolutionary means. All these attempts were in time crushed by the state. What was behind this upsurge of apparent class consciousness and its current dominance will become clear in subsequent analysis.

## Power, Land and Labour in Colonial Swaziland

The contemporary Swazi neo-colonial state and the present power relations are a culmination of a complex historical process that started in the middle of the 19th Century. The discovery of gold in South Africa in the 1880s, and other industrial activities that resulted, created an urgent need for a cheap and dependable labour force. The Boers from the Transvaal wanted large grazing areas as well as access to the Indian Ocean — which meant part of Swaziland. The British wanted to invest in large commercial agricultural enterprises. There was also a chance that Swaziland was sitting on large reserves of a variety of minerals. The South Africans and the British were therefore keenly interested in the Swazis' land and cheap labour, and this would obviously entail political control to facilitate land alienation and the exploitation of labour. Through trickery, arm-twisting and negotiation, Swaziland was landed with a settler–estate class comparable to the one in Kenya. By the turn of the century, Swaziland had been thoroughly penetrated by settler and international capital. The emergent colonial state was structured to preserve and reproduce conditions under which capital accumulation took place.

In order to secure conditions for capital accumulation, the colonial state performed two related functions: expropriation of land and creation of a large pool of cheap labour. Land alienation altered the agrarian structure very significantly. The Swazi population was pushed into poor and overcrowded settlements (reserves). As a result, migration to mines and foreign-owned commercial farms was set in motion. Production at the homestead level, as a consequence of the loss of labour, was organised mainly for subsistence and to feed any remaining reserve army of labour at virtually no cost to the state.

As in other settler colonies, Swazi peasant farmers were not encouraged to produce commodities that would compete with settler commercial farms. Extra-economic mechanisms were used to ensure this. Foreign and settler capital deliberately conserved the 'traditional' rulers as junior partners so as to use them in the control of labour and peasant commodity producers. The colonial state grudgingly relinquished mineral rights to the king and guaranteed his control over all Swazi land not used for white settlement. The king in turn, using his traditional authority, ascertained how land was to be used by his subjects. Protected from above by imperial power, and supported from below by the wealth generated in a feudal economy, the king was well placed to be the most dominant political force in 'independent' Swaziland.

Control and use of land had been very central to politics in Swaziland even before the colonial state was firmly established. The Dlamini's rule over the kingdom, after their military and political subordination of several rivals, revolved around their control and use of grazing and arable land. By the time colonial expansion made contact with the Swazi society, the latter was organised as a hierarchy in which the king and chiefs extracted tributes and free labour from their subjects. As Booth suggests, pre-colonial administration was 'more closely an army of occupation camped in hostile territory than a settled administration'. It would also appear that the Swazi population lived as mobile pasturalists until they were forced to live in scattered military towns for protection. The generally held view that the Swazi society was originally organised around a homestead as a basic unit of production and consumption may be misleading. On the other hand, it appears that the notion of a homestead was a response to the colonial state's alienation of land and its desire to establish 'order' and extract labour power on a more predictable and regular basis. It may be inaccurate, therefore, to argue that the pre-capitalist mode of production was organised around a homestead. Rather, it is more tenable to look at a homestead as an economic and organisational consequence of capitalist penetration in Swaziland.

What is certain is that a degree of exploitation did exist in the pre-colonial Swazi society. Considerable economic surplus was generated, and significant inequalities resulted. Compared to the colonial period, however, this process was on a very small scale. Land was more or less freely available until South African and British capitalist interests embarked on a massive exercise of expropriation. Historically Swaziland alienation goes back to the days of the so-called Great Trek. Afrikaners in the Cape and the British colonial administration disagreed over agrarian issues, among others. The British administration seemed to obstruct the Afrikaners from acquiring massive pieces of land for themselves and their descendants. Between 1835 and the early 1840s, about 13,000 Afrikaners decided to move north-eastwards in search of more land. This movement thrived at the expense of Xhosas and Zulus, whose land was alienated. The trek aimed as far as the north of the Limpopo, and Swaziland was an immediate victim. Out of fear and a sense of self-preservation, Swazi king Mswati ceded a large piece of territory to the expanding Boers in 1845.[1]

The impact of the discovery of gold in South Africa created new-found wealth and desire for further economic expansion. Grazing and capital investment opportunities and mineral prospecting brought British and Boer adventurers pouring into Swaziland in search for land concessions. By 1893, scores of companies worth £2 million were floated in Britain on the strength of the concession acquired. It was under the Mbandzeni rule that concessionaires benefited most. Although Swazi kings did appear to benefit materially from mineral rent paid by the colonial state, the rate at which land was being alienated sparked off strong protests and deputations to the Colonial Office in London. The colonial state acted pretty fast: Swaziland Partition Act of 1907 awarded two-thirds of the total land in Swaziland to concessionaires. This expropriated land included all the known and potential mineral locations as well as water resources necessary for mining and irrigation. The Swazi population was pushed into the remaining poor one-third in scattered and fragmented blocks (reserves) that could at best sustain elementary subsistence farming.

In 1909 the colonial state designated Swazis still holding out on concession land as squatters who had no rights whatsoever. The 1913 Proclamation No. 24 authorised the white settler farmers to evict the squatters after a period of five years.[2] To ensure a minimum of resistance, the colonial state granted large and relatively fertile pieces of land to the king and the chiefs. As Crush observes, following major land alienation the new agrarian structure confirmed settlers in exclusive ownership of land surface to facilitate capital accumulation; provided Swazis with significant land control to reproduce their short-term subsistence needs; preserved the essential political structures of the pre-capitalist state, and hence reproduced the power of the Swazi ruling class over its subjects; and minimised the likelihood of violent protest against the state.[3] Indeed the alliance of foreign and settler capital and the 'traditional' ruling group in Swaziland was the basic concern of the colonial state through which economic and political domination of the country was realised.

The other essential condition for capital accumulation was the creation of a large pool of cheap labour. Giant gold mines and a whole host of other economic activities had sprung up in South Africa. Large settler capitalist agricultural farms and the need to produce food for nearby emergent industrialised centres required cheap labour to minimise costs and maximise profits. Heavy taxation by the colonial state and the monarchy created an involuntary migration of workers to South African mines and the local cash economy.[4] The expropriation of land had, in any case, created conditions that ensured a nation of migrants. By 1920, it is reckoned that between 25 per cent and 40 per cent of the Swazi male working population was in the Transvaal. Cheap labour within Swaziland was conceived as a major inducement for a huge inflow of foreign capital. Thus Swazi cheap labour was financing the colonial state, settler and international capital and the monarchy.

After the Second World War, capital penetration in Swaziland intensified. Multinational corporations, encouraged by the colonial state's open door investment policies, started to control all the commanding heights of the economy. To date, sugar production is controlled by the Commonwealth Development Corporation (CDC — formerly called the Colonial Development Corporation) and Lonrho; timber production is controlled by Anglo-American Corporation, Courtlands and CDC; wood pulp by Courtlands and CDC; minerals by Anglo-American; pineapple plantations by Libbys; meat production and processing by Anglo-American and Imperial Chemical Storage; tourism by Rennies and Southern Sun; finance by Barclays and Standard Banks; and retail trade by O. K. Bazaars.[5] The settler capital controls smaller estates producing sugar, citrus, cattle, cotton, tobacco, vegetables and maize. Commercial activities in main urban centres are also controlled by the settler bourgeoisie and outlets for South African companies. Where foreign capital is not involved, the settler bourgeoisie has established a monopoly in production and distribution, largely at the expense of the local petty bourgeoisie.

Several other mechanisms have been employed to integrate Swaziland further into the South African economy, which serves as a major submetropole for Western capital in the region: Swaziland belongs to the South African Customs Union and the Rand Monetary Authority, both of which are firmly controlled by South Africa. The Customs Union revenue is very important for the running of the state but it also serves South Africa in monitoring and shaping economic policies of the Swazi state. Membership of the Rand Monetary Authority simply means that Swaziland does not have fiscal and monetary policies and instruments of its own, which in turn means that the state has less than a residual control over economic policy, planning and development. These close policy and monetary associations between Swaziland and South Africa make absolute nonsense of the former being a member of the Southern African Development Coordinating Conference (SADCC), whose major objective is to disengage from South Africa's economic, political and industrial domination in the region.

All in all, Swaziland has now established a historical role as supplier of cheap labour to foreign capital (particularly to South African industry) and consumer of its products, importer of manufactured goods — South Africa supplies 95 per cent of Swaziland's total imports,[6] and exporter of primary commodities that are mainly produced on large settler commercial farms. Foreign and settler capital is also a major source of wage employment. The colonial state presided over the establishment of a state–capital alliance that has produced a weak, dependent neo-colonial economy.

## Labour versus Capital

Political and labour union action against capital and the colonial state hardly took place among the peasantry because of the tight political grip the monarchy, through the chiefs, had over the allocation and use of land. The main challenge to capital and the colonial state was a somewhat fragile alliance between the working class and a section of the petty bourgeoisie that was hitherto largely excluded from any organ of state control.

The boom years in the 1940s and 1950s saw settler, British and South African capital expansion in an environment of increasing labour shortage. Nonetheless, in the 1960s the following factors turned a labour shortage into a surplus.

1) Farm mechanisation, a result of further capital accumulation, displaced substantial wage employment opportunities.

2) Gold mine employment and related industrial activities which were levelling off led to less demand for labour in these sectors.

3) The expanded education system was producing more school leavers than could get jobs.

4) Swaziland was experiencing a very high rate of population growth, due, no doubt, to improved standards of living and medical facilities.

In response to this excess supply of labour, local industries froze wages and reduced or even abolished incentives which had been institutionalised in the 1940s and 1950s. This created a recipe for industrial unrest and the organisation of workers into labour unions. To add to the basic complaints of low wages and extremely poor working conditions, the workers objected to the 'Nduna' system in which the Swazi National Council (the king's main advisory body) appointed

269

individuals to handle disputes between workers and employers.[7] This was a deliberate attempt by the colonial state, the monarchy and the employers to subvert and pre-empt workers' organisations, and therefore to control the labour process. The workers found a ready ally in the Ngwane National Liberation Congress (NNLC) — which had broken away from the Swaziland Progressive Party.

The NNLC was led by elements of Swazi petty bourgeoisie which had been excluded entirely from the traditional political structures. It also attracted educated Swazis who were to eager to challenge the monopoly of the settler class interest. The NNLC's main policy position advocated localisation, transfer of mineral and land rights to a representative and elected system of government and labour unionisation. The party's stance, which appeared to challenge the alliance between the monarchy and European capital and espoused vaguely defined socialist goals (Nkrumah was its main hero), appealed to the working class. NNLC leadership and working-class following — the nearest to a popular alliance Swaziland has ever had — resulted in the relentless labour strikes and rapid unionisation that characterised the 1960s and 1970s. A few examples are appropriate.

In 1962, Usuthu Pulp workers put down their tools in protest against the introduction of the infamous 'Nduna system', unacceptable wage structure and unfair dismissal of fellow workers. Wage increase convinced workers to go back to work. During this dispute the Usuthu Pulp workers, encouraged by their collective action, formed the first registered trade union in Swaziland — the Pulp and Timber Workers Union. Complaints similar to those at Usuthu Pulp precipitated another strike at Ubombo Ranches — a large foreign-owned estate that deals with cattle ranching, sugar and rice production. As a deterrent measure a mobile force of Swaziland police was posted to the area in further anticipation of more labour unrest.

In 1963 strikes spread to Peak Timbers, Havelock Mines, Ubombo Ranches again, and Swaziland Plantations at Piggs Peak. By the end of the year, Dumisa Dlamini, an NNLC official, managed to organise a general strike that shook the monarchy and the whole edifice of international/settler capital. The colonial state had to invite British troops stationed in Kenya to bring the situation back to normal. These troops stayed until just before independence.

It is necessary to appraise the general impact of the labour strikes in a wider framework. Did they constitute a 'primitive rebellion' that collapsed under the alliance of international capital and the internal elements? Were they aiming at restructuring power relations and the state? Was this an attempt at a revolt by Third World masses at the national level referred to by Mansour[8]? Was this the kind of movement enjoying popular support without organising popular power that Mamdani[9] refers to?

Although the NNLC and sections of the working class were viewed by the settler and foreign interests as a threat, the former really did not aim beyond the establishment of a bourgeois social democracy. They did not question the basic principles of the existing structures and the dominant interests were not fundamentally challenged. The NNLC was basically fighting the colonial state's familiar obstruction to the growth of a powerful domestic bourgeoisie and its tendency towards allegiance with aristocratic elements to consolidate monopolistic practices, a case that reinforces Beckman's[10] theorisation of the colonial state in Nigeria.

Besides, the base of the revolt was very narrow. The feudal relationship that gave chiefs political leverage through control and distribution of land resulted in a submissive peasantry. As we shall note later, this weapon has been used most effectively in the neo-colonial state to ensure a docile and politically inert rural population. As a result, the working class did not have political support from the peasantry to sustain the revolt. One may say that the objective conditions obtaining at the time could not sustain a revolt. And once the working class lost the initiative and opportunity of establishing a strong popular alliance with the peasantry, the place they were to occupy in the independence coalition was not surprisingly subordinate.

## Preparation for 'Independence': The Bourgeois–Peasant Alliance

The period shortly before Swaziland became independent was characterised by the emergence of a number of political parties, each with specific economic and political interests. Characteristically the British wanted to hand down the Westminster model of government as they did in other colonies. Through constitutional and electoral manipulation, the colonial state cemented and strengthened the alliance between international/settler capital and the traditional leaders at the expense of the small petty bourgeoisie, peasants and workers who were not coherent and organised enough to constitute a challenging force.[11] What were the interests at stake? The settler community, scared of possible nationalisation, socialist rhetoric and numerical inferiority, wanted to entrench itself in power, preferably on an equal power-sharing basis with forces representing the Swazi traditional rulers. Settler interests crystallised in a political party, the United Swaziland Association (USA). The monarchy was interested in consolidating the mineral and land rights that it had acquired under colonial rule. Forced to operate within a Westminster model, the monarchy formed its political party, Imbokodvo National Movement (INM) to organise its drive for control of state power. The petty bourgeoisie wanted to challenge the dominance of the monarchy, particularly the control over mineral rights and a share in a representative government. The most significant of these opposition parties was the NNLC.

Events leading to Swaziland's independence in 1968 were essentially a conspiracy between the foreign/settler capital and the traditional rulers against the bourgeois opposition parties and organised labour. The king's INM and the settler pro-South Africa USA were given an electoral advantage by the colonial state. Constituencies were carved out in such a way that urban areas, where NNLC was very strong, were absorbed in rural areas to the advantage of INM. The white settlers were given more representation than their numbers deserved. Thus although NNLC gained 12 per cent of the total votes in 1964, it did not get a single seat in the Legislative Assembly. The INM/USA Alliance 'swept' the polls.[12] During the 1967 independence constitutional talks, the NNLC was excluded completely. Only INM and USA negotiated with the colonial government. Elections were held in the same year and NNLC obtained 20 per cent of the total votes but again gained no seats in the assembly. Intricate gerrymandering saw to this.

Although INM changed its position and advocated universal suffrage, a position against USA interests, the latter easily came to terms with the king's party. The reasons were quite obvious: INM was popular among the majority of the Swazis and its conservatism and traditionalism offered a stable environment for capital accumulation. The king's negative attitude towards labour unrest and strikes impressed foreign and settler capitalist interests; the radical rhetoric from the opposition parties made INM a more predictable ally with capital. Having ensured that capitalist interests were secure, USA simply vanished and some of its members surfaced in INM. The king was granted mineral rights and a right to appoint one-fifth of the Legislative Assembly and half of the Senate.

At independence, the traditional rulers, using the INM bandwagon, easily captured state power. The opposition disintegrated further and most of their members quietly joined the king's side. It should be noted that the INM takeover at independence was primarily determined by the political and economic interests of the dominant capitalist classes which, functioning in alliance with traditional pre-capitalist social classes in society, further dominated the ideological universe of the peasantry to give the INM a majority in an election which, by bourgeois–democratic standards, was free and fair.

## The Neo-colonial Challenges

The neo-colonial state that emerged at independence was structurally linked to and penetrated by settler and multinational capital and overwhelmingly dependent on South Africa. However, as Beckman[13] points out, dependency analysis, useful as it is, has 'a tendency of reducing contradictions in a neo-colonial society to the nation dimension, paying little attention to the dynamics of class formation'. The argument is thus sustained that capitalist penetration creates domestic forces with their own dynamic. This critique may help in the analysis of the indigenous social forces that have emerged as a result of social differentiation since independence, and have hence established fairly strong and discernible relations with the state in the process of capitalist development in Swaziland. For purposes of analysis, therefore, we shall distinguish between the external and internal neo-colonial relationships that together constitute the challenge to the Swazi state.

### External relationships

The state–capital alliance, and almost total subordination of the economy to settler and international capital (particularly South African and British multinationals), have thrived in the neo-colonial period. More than that, Swaziland is a pawn in the so-called 'total national strategy' of the South African regime. Historically, the countries neighbouring South Africa have been subordinated to serve the needs of capital accumulation in the sub-metropole by producing cheap labour and as markets for South-African-produced commodities. Another important cornerstone of the apartheid regime has been that of creating 'buffer' states as a protective barrier for South Africa itself.[14] With the liberation of Angola, Mozambique and Zimbabwe this strategy collapsed. South Africa's so-called outward-looking policy of luring allies within the members of the Organisation of African Unity did not succeed beyond Malawi, the only country that established an embassy in Pretoria.

Feeling more isolated and open to ANC infiltration, the Pretoria regime embarked on direct military occupation (of Angola), cross-border raids against ANC bases and cadres (in Mozambique, Lesotha, and Botswana), acts of economic sabotage (in Angola), arming and training anti-government guerrillas in the region (MNR, UNITA and ILA), the killing and kidnapping of ANC officials, and even the attempt to overthrow governments considered unfriendly (Seychelles).

As part of this 'total strategy' Pretoria has embarked on creating 'anti-Marxist' neighbouring states and giving them economic carrots with a hope of reducing ANC training operations and denying the USSR a toe-hold in the region. As a result South Africa has encouraged closer economic ties with these countries. Swaziland, a principal participant in this scheme, has been 'rewarded' for 'good behaviour'. For example, South Africa has helped Swaziland build a railway link to Richards Bay, which compounds the latter's dependency, and a supplementary R50 million payment under the Customs Union agreement.[15] Negotiations for the transfer of Kangwane Bantustan to Swaziland are still going on. In return the Swazi State has clamped down on ANC cadres, returning some to the Republic, and opened its economy even wider for South African products to be sold, ironically enough, in practically all the SADDC member countries. South Africa has also used Swaziland to make use of the advantages given to the latter by the Lomé Convention.

These measures have involved Swaziland in the armed struggle in South Africa, but on the wrong side. They have also weakened her commitment to the SADCC's primary objective of de-linking from South African capitalist domination. Internally, these policies have split the ruling class into two factions that have evidently disagreed on the land deal and the role of South Africa in Swazi politics.

**Internal forces and their challenges**
Internal forces that have put in motion the process of social differentiation in Swaziland are ultimately linked to the external relationships that have created a neo-colonial dependent enclave. However, the Swazi state has initiated certain policies which have created a fairly independent dynamic of their own and which cannot be fully understood by simply sticking to the dependency analysis. The specific forms of state intervention probably account for the differences between Kenya and Tanzania on the one hand, or Swaziland and Uganda on the other, when all of them were exposed to the same expansionist capitalist mode of production.

The two most significant internal causes of social differentiation are: First, the state's encouragement of the formation of a local petty bourgeoisie and the dramatic widening and consolidation of the material base for the 'middle class' in general and the traditional ruling clique in particular. Second, the Rural Development Programmes, ostensibly introduced to benefit the rural poor, which have differentiated the peasantry and facilitated the formation of 'kulaks' who have easier access to agricultural inputs, finance and extension services.

**Emergence of a petty bourgeoisie and widening of material base**
We may recall that the colonial state deliberately discouraged the emergence of a petty bourgeoisie basically to protect the monopoly of settler capital. Potential

local traders and small-scale producers were starved of finance, knowledge and technology; land tenure on Swazi Nation Land was not conducive to significant accumulation; and at independence large sections of the middle class were excluded from state power. With increased education and the memories of the effective labour strikes that were organised by the disgruntled emerging petty bourgeoisie, the traditional rulers realised the importance of a stable, mainly urban, middle class.

The 1971 Land Speculation Bill which restricted the sale of land to foreigners, unless it was deemed to be in the national interest, and the 1974 Land Tax Order which was essentially meant to punish absentee landlords whose land was not being fully utilised, were measures that facilitated accumulation by the Swazi middle class.

Further, purchases from title deed to Swazi Nation Land gave yet another opportunity to certain well-placed Swazis to purchase land, something which was practically impossible during the colonial days. The Small Enterprises Development Corporation (SEDCO) was established by the state to give technical advice and financial assistance to local businessmen — an attempt to create an indigenous capitalist class. Ownership of property and business enabled more Swazis to secure loans from banks and building societies. With this newly acquired economic power, the mainstream of the middle class has been trying to gain access to state power and patronage. The palace coups that have occurred in the country since the death of King Sobhuza II were largely a result of fierce disagreements between sections of the middle class. The traditional rulers who control the state machinery are now extremely worried about their capacity to contain this new group which, from time to time, has been able to ally with foreign/settler capital in a bid to shape and control state policies.

The Swazi traditional rulers have also used state machinery to build a solid material base for themselves. It should be remembered that in the case of Swaziland, the state is not involved in the extraction of surplus value through directly productive activities.[16] It relies on taxation revenue from the private, foreign-controlled sector, foreign aid and Customs Union. Until recently, therefore, the Swazi rulers had a weak economic base. However, the state apparatus has enabled them to accumulate, largely in cooperation with foreign capital. The main vehicle for capital accumulation by the Swazi rulers is an institution called Tibiyo Taka Ngwane. When the king won the battle for control of mineral rights, he created Tibiyo as a depository for the revenue from mineral royalties. The company then acquired interests in foreign-owned enterprises in asbestos, iron ore, coal, agribusiness, tourism, banking, insurance monopoly, newspaper industry and the national airline. Tibiyo has also purchased land that is now under sugar cultivation. A survey carried out by Sonko[17] shows that Tibiyo executives do not themselves agree whether their organisation is a public enterprise. However, it is known that Tibiyo is not subject to public accountability. It is outside the control of Parliament and the Treasury. Although it benefits from the commanding heights of the economy, Tibiyo's operations are not part of the National Development Plan, and its revenue is not subject to government taxation. It is only accountable to the king and its board of trustees who are appointed by the king. Tibiyo probably has more income than the government, but this is not easy to establish because of lack of public accountability.

It is evident that Tibiyo has secured a material base for the continuity of the Swazi rulers, particularly the monarchy, and the reproduction of foreign capital. It has also diverted funds necessary to carry out economic policies in the direction of a self-reliant development process. This has contributed to a facet of the state crisis articulated well by Bernstein:

> Inability to ensure the distribution of minimally adequate supplies of food staples on terms obtainable by most people who have to secure food from outside their own production (and especially those in cities), exacerbates the perennial 'legitimation crisis' of most African regimes, hence accentuating the spectre of political instability.[18]

### The impact of Rural Development Programmes

Rural Development Area Programmes (RDAPs) started in earnest in 1970. They included a package of agricultural inputs, extension service, land use planning and tractor-hire pools. The programmes, according to the government, were meant to serve three fundamental objectives:

1) to increase production of crops and livestock;
2) to improve the living standards of the rural people;
3) to protect natural resources.

Swaziland Development and Savings Bank, wholly owned by the state, was established apparently to meet the credit requirements of small-scale farmers. The state secured funding from the UK, World Bank, African Development Bank, US Agency for International Development, and the Swaziland Government. From 1977 to 1982, RDAPs had a total planned cost of $60.35 million.

All RDAPs are on the Swazi Nation Land (SNL) — which is the core of the reserves that were created by 1907 proclamation — where the vast majority of Swazis live. On SNL, land is allocated by the chief and cannot be bought or sold. From figures available, RDAPs cover roughly 60 per cent of SNL and they are of two types: first, the minimum-input RDAPs; and second, the maximum-input RDAPs which over and above a minimum common to all RDAPs were supposed to be recipients of land development, farm inputs, social infrastructure (schools, clinics etc.), technical assistance, management training, monitoring and evaluation and exposure to consultancy facilities.

Even before RDAPs are evaluated on their achievements, their very existence is a recipe for rural differentiation. Rural Swaziland has been divided into Rural Development Areas (RDAs) and non-RDAs. The RDAs themselves are divided into minimum and maximum input areas. Large rural areas and populations have therefore been denied access to important agricultural production inputs. The Ministry of Agriculture and Co-operatives (MOAC) chose areas to be covered by RDAPs 'on the basis of good development potential, good communication, the interest of the people in rural development, ecological homogeneity, coherent physical configuration and population density'. Clearly these criteria have an in-built bias against the marginalised rural poor who, ordinarily, should have been the target of rural development projects.

Another important dimension of the RDAPs is the differential access to loans. Swaziland's commercial banks do not give loans to individuals without security. As we have noted land on SNL is not a commodity to be bought and sold and therefore the rural population cannot use it as collateral to secure bank loans. So the major beneficiaries of the banking system are the so-called 'progressive farmers' who use their cattle and other assets to secure loans. Even the Swaziland Development and Savings Bank, which was established primarily to serve the small-scale farmers, gives most of its loans to established businessmen and estate developers. The loans that are secured for agricultural production normally go to large commercial agricultural farms, mechanisation and cattle fattening — i.e. to urban petty bourgeoisie and a cluster of emerging 'kulaks' in the rural areas. So most of the poor peasants either do not bother to apply for loans, or when they do they are usually turned down.

The agrarian structure inherited from the colonial administration, mismanagement, the rising costs of agricultural inputs (controlled by South African companies) have led to substantial failure on the part of RDAPs. Maize yields have at best remained stagnant, resulting in maize imports, and milk production has fallen dramatically as table 11.1 shows.

**Table 11.1**
**Milk Production and Imports (litres)**

| Year | Swaziland Production | Percentage of total milk consumed | Imported milk from South Africa |
|------|------|------|------|
| 1975 | 528,944 | 29.8 | 1,159,147 |
| 1976 | 914,264 | 28.3 | 1,537,720 |
| 1977 | 442,693 | 12.9 | 2,162,741 |
| 1978 | 291,844 | 6.6 | 2,739,997 |
| 1979 | 340,851 | 6.6 | 2,747,839 |

*Source:* G. Magagula, 'Land Tenure and Agricultural Production in Swaziland', University of Swaziland, mimeo, 1983.

RDAPs have failed in most of their objectives. However, they have benefited international capital, government officials and other go-betweens. 'Rural development' is now big business. It offers contracts and employment to construction firms, international experts, bankers, fertiliser, seed and chemical manufacturers and distributors, government officials and extension workers. RDAPs and the consolidation of the economic base by the Swazi rulers and the rest of the petty bourgeoisie have contributed to social differentiation and class formation with an autonomous dynamic.

**The crisis facing the Swazi State**
Through 'rural development' programmes and building the material base for the Swazi rulers and the petty bourgeoisie, the state has initiated and facilitated rapid solid differentiation which has in turn led to a steady process of class formation amongst the indigenous Swazis. National resources have been diverted to the

promotion of the aspiring 'middle class' and the ruling clique at the expense of achieving basic needs for the majority of Swazis. Vicious quarrels amongst different factions of the bourgeoisie have weakened the state's ability to relate to economic and social development. All these internal processes and contradictions, however, still operate within the dependent neo-colonial framework that has been established by external/settler capital.

The Swazi state is subject to export instability that is currently shifting to a monoculture (sugar); it is overwhelmingly import-dependent on South Africa. Recession and inflation have meant stagnant wages and lowering of living standards. Production on the homestead has been declining because of cost of inputs, scarcity and inappropriate use of land, low returns to labour and the consequent migration from rural to urban areas. As a result Swaziland imports over 50,000 tons of maize, the staple food, from South Africa every year. The stagnating economy has prompted an unacceptable level of unemployment. It is estimated that 8,000 school leavers join the job market every year and there are no openings for a quarter of them.

Unemployment affects teachers, university graduates and labourers. Obviously desperate about the levels of unemployment, the Minister of Labour was quoted as having 'called for a national prayer to solve the job crisis. He said prayer would help the nation to find a solution for the current unemployment perpetuated by the economic recession'. A new term 'sidlani' has had to be coined to describe unemployed youth gangs — the lumpens — which are now notorious for house break-ins and hold-ups in urban areas. The level of crime has dramatically increased causing social instability and decay.

These crises have heightened contradiction and confrontation between capital and labour. Sporadic labour strikes still continue to occur. The foreign/settler capital and state alliance is interested in low wages and therefore cheap labour for accumulation. Low wages also have a tendency to force the wage earners to retain social and economic ties with rural homesteads in the production of agricultural output, which means that the chiefs and the traditional system still have room to manipulate wage labour. These are the conditions that have led to workers' opposition, industrial action and political activity.

One of the most dramatic labour strikes was staged by school teachers in 1977. Citing low wages and poor conditions of service, the teachers, through their national association, boycotted classes. The state swiftly designated the Teachers Association as a political party and promptly banned it. An attempt was made to force the teachers back to class. Immediately, though, students rallied behind their teachers on a countrywide basis and paralysed the entire educational system. The rioting students attacked government property and even stoned cabinet ministers. Since then the Teachers Association has bounced back to life but is constantly harassed. Only this year the Association's chief spokesman was transferred, sacked, then reinstated and promoted to the headquarters and finally retired — all in a space of two months, in order to demobilise and disorganise the Association.

In 1982, hundreds of workers on Ezulwinin Electric dam downed their tools because of low wages, harsh conditions of service and the racist attitudes of management. In 1984, sensing that the state was interfering unduly in the university administration and using some students to spy on others, University of Swaziland students (supported by fellow students from teacher training colleges and the College of Technology) organised a successful class boycott. The state responded by closing the university, dismissing all the student leaders, firing and deporting the Dean of the Faculty of Social Science, dismissing the Assistant Registrar for Student Affairs — who, ironically, is a traditional chief — and finally sending the police to occupy the campus for three months to ensure tight control of the daily affairs of the university.

Corruption in high places has also weakened the capacity of the state to formulate economic policies and halt conditions of underdevelopment. In 1984 the then Minister of Finance alleged that high-ranking government officials had been involved in a massive fraud of public funds amounting to E13 million* and threatened to establish an enquiry into the matter. He was promptly arrested and detained under the emergency provisions which were established when the Independence Constitution was overthrown in 1973. He is still languishing in jail.

All these tensions have distracted attention from development issues and caused atrophy and social decay. The primary and secondary contradictions have threatened individuals and groups who control state machinery and the conditions under which accumulation has been taking place. The South African state, besieged internally by the contradictions it created, and externally by threats of economic sanctions and political isolation, is slowly going down with the Swazi economy.

## Forms of State Repression

We have indicated that the state and the economy are both facing severe crises. The legitimacy of those controlling the state is dwindling. Instead the state has become an arena of intense factional fighting for access, control and patronage. In order to retain state power, control labour and reproduce conditions for continued accumulation, the state has become militarised and oppressive. The following are some of the ways employed by the state to frustrate participation and the development of democratic processes.

### The Land Tenure System as a Mechanism for Political and Social Control

The biggest single weapon that keeps the peasantry subdued is the control by the chiefs over the allocation of land. With a population growth rate approaching 4 per cent per year, land is becoming very scarce in the SNL. The average holding per homestead is 2.75 hectares and is dwindling by the year. Table 11.2 indicates that land shortage is the biggest constraint the peasants face in their production cycle. The notion that once land is allocated, an individual has a considerable degree of security of tenure, including the right to pass the land on to his children, is becoming untenable. Thousands of peasants have been removed forcibly, banished, resettled or simply dumped in the middle of nowhere, clearly reminding one of the South African removal techniques. A casual perusal of the local press gives one a frightening picture.

---

* E = Emalangeni: Swazi currency pegged 1:1 with the Rand.

278

**Table 11.2**
**Constraints on Peasant Production**

| Peasant's reasons for not growing cotton/tobacco | (percentages) |
|---|---|
| Not enough land | 22.6 |
| Not enough labour | 18.9 |
| Does not know how to grow these crops | 10.3 |
| Not enough money/capital | 12.5 |
| Climate not right | 9.1 |
| Bad soil | 3.1 |
| No specific reason | 7.5 |
| Other | 14.3 |

*Source:* De Vletter, *The Swazi Rural Homestead*, SSRU, 1983.

At least 400 people, caught in a feud between their community leaders, have been ordered to move out of their area at Ekupheleni near Ngwenya. The villagers, who are made up of 40 families, have been given until the end of the month to get off the land or face forceful eviction. (*The Swazi News*, 5 May 1984)

Villagers at Esidwala area looked in stunned shock as two old women and twenty children were frog-marched out of their homes at gunpoint by paramilitary force. The women were held with their arms on their heads as bulldozers demolished their homes with their belongings. Two families were then loaded into police vans, driven to a lonely stretch of the road and dumped. (*The Times of Swaziland*, 28 May 1984)

Three hundred families, involving 1,000 people, were ordered to move their homes out of a government farm. The order was issued by the Minister of Agriculture. (*The Times of Swaziland*, 27 September 1984)

Five families were given a deadline to leave their land by the Minister of Interior . . . the local leaders said the families were generally disrespectful and defiant to the authorities. (*The Times of Swaziland*, 9 October 1984)

More than 15 families from Kamkhweli have been kicked out of their area and dumped into wild veld. They were kicked out because they refused to pay allegiance to Chief Manpini Ndzimandze whom they rejected saying he arrived in the area later than them. (*Swazi Observer*, 22 October 1984)

Twenty people have been forced to sleep in the open after their homes were crushed by a bulldozer near Oshoek. (*The Times of Swaziland*, 29 November 1984).

Simunye Sugar Company, belonging to a British multinational company, displaced 550 families with approximately 5,000 people involved. The above examples cover a very short period of time but give an idea how the state and capital have been pushing peasants off the land and how chiefs use their power of land allocation as an instrument of social and political control. Other peasants, hearing of these forced removals and evictions, tend to remain docile and subservient. This partly explains why the peasantry did not come to the support of the working-class strikes in the 1960s and thereafter. However, the attitudes of some of the displaced peasants indicate their defiance of traditional authority and their continued readiness to fight for their rights. This may necessitate new state repressive measures to match increasing urbanisation which has somewhat undermined land allocation as a principal instrument of state control and repression.

### Traditional Courts

Taking advantage of a 1951 legal instrument by which the colonial government allowed the establishment of Swazi courts, the traditional rulers have institutionalised a system of Swazi National Courts to run parallel to the 'modern' legal court system.

The Swazi courts are presided over by appointees of the monarch and do not allow legal representation. Land, marital and other civil cases are normally settled in these courts. Since the rules of procedure are not written, the chiefs and other traditional functionaries use the system to consolidate their power and induce compliance and political control.

### Attempts to Control Labour

The state's main strategy to control the process has been to create institutions that would weaken organised labour and prevent emergence of a coherent trade union movement. As an attempt to contain the contradictions between capital and labour that were already evident during the colonial period, the state provided for the setting up of Works Councils which were democratically elected by workers in each production unit. The workers and management were equally represented but the latter provided the chairman. There was no machinery, however, for work councils in a whole industry or between several industries to cooperate in joint industrial action. This arrangement prevented the emergence of national labour organisations.

The most controversial method of labour control was the provision for the appointment of Ndabazabantu — king's representatives in large industrial concerns. These appointees were supposed to cooperate with work councils and were paid by the respective companies. The functions of Ndabazabantu included the following:

> He will encourage the workers and build a sound sense of responsibility, respect and discipline — inspire the workers with a feeling of regarding the industry in terms of a partnership — teach the workers to realise that any realisation of profits will result in better wages and better social conditions in their villages.

The role of Ndabazabantu was almost universally resented. Almost all the labour strikes had a major grievance with the king's representative and his manipulative role in the control of labour. The state, however, set up a national wage board to determine the minimum wages and averted a major labour revolt.

Although trade unions were not disbanded by a specific legal instrument, their operation was made impossible. Police permission was needed for meetings, and relentless victimisation of trade union leaders caused many labour organisations to fold up. At the moment there is one trade union — for bank employees — that is reckoned to be harmless and dominated by petty bourgeois interests. Thus avenues for labour organisation have been systematically eroded by the state.

**Abolition of Representative Institutions and Introduction of Repressive Measures**
As we noted earlier, the popularity of the NNLC was growing in every successive election. In the 1972 elections Dr Zwane's section of the NNLC won three seats in the Assembly; the rest went to the INM. This limited success of the NNLC, which concentrated around sugar factory workers, was not taken lightly by the Swazi rulers. In 1973, the king announced the following drastic measures:

1) The Independence Constitution was abrogated and the king assumed full powers.

2) Political parties, including the king's INM, were dissolved. This move was aimed specifically at NNLC.

3) Parliament was dissolved.

4) A state of emergency, which is still running, was declared. No meetings or processions of a political nature were allowed without express police permission.

5) Provision for detention without trial was established. (It is ironic that some of the then influential individuals who subscribed to this provision and helped in its formulation have since been detained.)

6) As a clear sign of growing militarisation of the state, the Swazi rulers established a national army of 650 men to enhance their coercive capability. As would be expected the new army was trained and supplied by South Africa.

**Establishment of Tinkundla System**
In place of the Westminster model of parliamentary supremacy, in 1977 the king announced the Tinkundla system of administration which was grafted onto the traditional chiefly system. This strengthened the hold of the Swazi rulers beyond their pre-capitalist stronghold. It is around this administrative system that elections, rather selections, take place. Parliament, the cabinet and other remnants of the Westminster model essentially rubber-stamp decisions taken by traditional political structures whose procedures remain secret, unwritten and highly personalised. This is an important variant of the de-participation process in the kingdom.

**The Electoral System**
To recover some of the legitimacy that was lost by the introduction of the draconian measures of 1973, and to appease Western allies, Swazi rulers decided, in 1978, to re-establish parliament and elections. The King's order-in-council No. 23 established this authority. Elections are conducted in the open; there is no register of voters, no ballot papers and boxes, no political rallies and campaigns.

Four individuals are selected in each one of the 40 tinkundlas, and on the voting day (equivalent to general elections), anybody who appears to be 18 years and above files past their preferred candidate while an official counts the heads. The two candidates with the highest number of votes join their counterparts to form an 80-member electoral college. The state presents a list of candidates to the members of the Electoral College who then choose 40 out of the given names. These become

Members of Parliament. The King nominates another 10 to make a House of Assembly of 50 MPs. The House and the King each nominate 10 individuals who constitute the Senate. Among the MPs, the King nominates the Prime Minister and the Cabinet.

The 'open' elections have a tendency to intimidate voters to toe the official line. In any case the state ensures that it nominates its trusted functionaries at all stages of the 'electoral' process. The system also undermines the role of political parties and other democratic processes. These elections do not offer any serious system by which personnel running the state can be controlled and changed by Swazi citizens. It simply endorses the status quo. However, it must be admitted that this 'endorsement' is achieved at very little material and human cost when you consider elections in other countries such as Uganda.

**Feudal Rituals and Ceremonies**
Certain rituals and traditional ceremonies have been deliberately preserved to legitimise the monarchy and dampen the spirit of critical political inquiry and possible political action. Incwala annual ceremony is supposed to renew the king's medicinal and rain-making powers as well as powers to protect his own people. The idea is to mystify and legitimise the king as superhuman. Umhlanga (Reed Dance) is another annual event where thousands of supposedly virgin maids converge at the queen mother's residence. The king is supposed to select one of these maids for a wife. This is another exercise at enhancing the 'symbolic capability' of the king which is part of the legitimising process.

Then there is the unwritten and mysterious but apparently omnipresent Swazi Law and Custom. This is supposed to be the spirit and framework handed down by ancestors that guide the behaviour of the Swazis at individual, group and state level. No single ordinary Swazi appears to know exactly what Swazi Law and Custom means — and what is the function it is supposed to serve. On a number of occasions the state has had to refer to this framework to justify its behaviour and rationalise inconsistencies and irregularities that would otherwise be challenged in normal courts of law. In 1983, the Law Department at the University of Swaziland secured project funds to try and write down Swazi Law and Custom so that it could have legal definitions and meaning. The state, however, blocked the project. Demystification would have undermined an important source of legitimacy for the monarchy.

**The Use of the *Government Gazette***
Major political changes have been effected through announcements, by rival political factions, in the *Government Gazette*. Normally such announcements have procedurally ignored institutions such as Parliament. Major dismissals such as that of the Queen Regent, the Authorized Person (who used to be principal official in the State Supreme Council, Liqoqo), cabinet ministers and other important officials have all been effected by the *Gazette*. Most political observers in Swaziland seem to have agreed that 'Politics of the *Gazette*' clearly undermine due processes by which important appointments and dismissals should have been made. Contradictions in the use of the *Gazette*, however, abound. The political factions that first successfully

used the *Gazette* to effect dismissals have in turn been stripped of their official positions through the same organ.

## Conclusion

The embryonic alliance between the working class and part of the middle class that appeared to be taking off in the 1960s and 1970s appears to have collapsed under the weight of foreign and settler capital in collaboration with Swazi rulers. The accumulation process has, however, resulted in rapid expansion of the working class and the emergence of an indigenous Swazi middle class. The latter has arrived with its own economic interests and agenda that have complicated power sharing at the national level. The external and internal factors, as we have noted, have compounded Swaziland into a neo-colonial dependent political economy.

The state's contribution towards the weakening of potential popular alliances does not necessarily suggest that the former has become stronger. On the contrary, there are signs that the state is being weakened. Increasing unemployment, overcrowding on Swazi Nation Land, factional infighting and rapid turnover of state managers have all tended to weaken the state.

Land allocation, a major mechanism for control of the peasantry, together with the grip the chiefs have over their subjects, is slowly being eroded by increased levels of education and political awareness and by the process of urbanisation. It is important to note that some peasants were thrown off their land because they were regarded by local leaders as disrespectful and defiant to authority. Some peasants simply refused to pay allegiance to their chiefs and rejected them altogether. These are ominous signs that the traditional mechanisms for social control hitherto used in Swaziland may be increasingly challenged and defied by the populace. The monarchy is likely to lose its relatively strong following as its capacity to control the state, and in particular the emergent middle class, begins to be doubted and challenged. The case in which one political faction overthrew the Queen Regent and promptly sent leading princes into political wilderness clearly indicated the weakening posture of the monarchy in Swazi politics.

The political and monetary crises in South Africa have also further weakened Swaziland's import capacity and foreign reserves. Although South African business may, in the short run, rush its capital to Swaziland as political instability gains momentum in South Africa, this trend cannot survive for long.

Is there a positive relationship between a weak (and weakening) state and the emergence of a popular alliance? Is a weak state a necessary precondition for major restructuring of the same? Informed opinion and past experience in Africa are quite divided on this matter. There is a view that a weak state offers a golden opportunity for the collapse of authoritarian regimes and emergence of popular movements and alliances. This optimistic view may be supported by the Cuban experience where, by the time of the revolution, the state had reached such an advanced state of atrophy that prostitution counted as one of the strongest sectors of the economy. However, in many African countries, weak states have resulted in more repressive regimes where cliques have taken advantage of the situation and terrorised the rest of the population into submission. Uganda is a case in point where the state institutions have so completely broken down that several armed factions and warlords operate outside the jurisdiction and control of the government of the day. The resultant situation has not gravitated towards the emergence of popular alliances as yet.

In Swaziland the weakened state has responded to pressure by clamping down on rival political structures. For the moment it would appear that the bases of popular alliances are not yet organised enough to translate their popularity into popular power. As the state gets weaker and its traditional methods of control and repression are challenged, new and more sophisticated control mechanisms are likely to be introduced to curb opposition. As in many other African countries, this latter phase is likely to be characterised by more state-inspired violence.

The mass resistance in South Africa and the possibility of substantial political changes will have a profound impact on political affairs in Swaziland. Just as the present regime in the kingdom relies on Pretoria's tacit political, economic and military support, so will the potential popular alliances when qualitative political and economic changes take place in South Africa. Alliances across borders are likely to be decisive in the future. Although organisationally the emergence in Swaziland of popular alliances and popular democracy seems to be too futuristic, the material conditions for profound social change exist in abundance.

## Notes

1. A. Booth, 'The Development of Swazi Labour Market, 1900–1968', *South African Labour Bulletin*, vol. VII, no. 6, 1982.

2. M. Fransman, 'Labour, Capital and the State in Swaziland', *South African Labour Bulletin*, vol. VII, no. 6, 1982.

3. J. Crush, 'Diffuse Development: Botswana, Lesotho and Swaziland since Independence', *Current Bibliography on African Affairs*, vol. XIII, no. 4, 1980.

4. J. Daniel, 'The Political Economy of Colonial and Post-Colonial Swaziland', *South African Labour Bulletin*, vol. VII, no. 6, 1982.

5. I. Winter, *Rural Development in Tropical Africa*. (New York: St. Martins Press, 1981).

6. Daniel, 'Political Economy of Swaziland'.

7. N. Simelane, 'The State and the Working Class: The Case of Swaziland', *Southern African Studies: Retrospective and Prospect* (Edinburgh: University of Edinburgh, 1983).

8. F. Mansour, 'Third World Revolt and Self-reliant Auto-centred Strategy of Development', (Dakar: IDEP, 1977).

9. M. Mamdani, 'The Break up of the East African Community: Some Lessons', AAPS Conference, Dakar, 1983 (unpublished paper).

10. B. Beckman, 'Neo-Colonialism and the State in Nigeria' in M. H. Bernstein and B. Campbell (eds.) *Contradictions of Accumulation in Africa* (Beverly Hills: Sage, 1985).

11. Winter, *Rural Development*.

12. J. Halpern, 'Swaziland', *South of the Sahara*. (London: Europa Publications, 1984).

13. Beckman, 'Neo-Colonialism'.

14. R. Davies and D. O'Meara, 'South Africa's Strategy in Southern African Region: A Preliminary Analysis', Institute of Southern Afrian Studies, National University of Lesotho, 1983 (unpublished manuscript).

15. *Ibid.*

16. Winter, *Rural Development.*

17. K. Sonko, 'Tibiyo Taka Ngwane: A Private or Public Enterprise', mimeo, University of Swaziland, 1985.

18. Bernstein and Campbell, *Contradictions of Accumulation.*

# Index

286